In...

Wel... ...to ...11! Here begins Hikaru, Umi and Fuu... ...gical realm of Cephiro. This new adventure sta... ...t it does help if you know a bit about the first series before you begin. For those of you who are new to Rayearth, or if you just need a little refresher course, here's what happened in the first series...

Hikaru, Umi and Fuu were three Tokyo schoolgirls with nothing in common, that is until they were magically summoned to the land of Cephiro. An ancient wizard (with a childlike body) named Guru Clef told the girls that they were the Magic Knights, the legendary heroes from another world who were prophesized to save Cephiro from Zagato, a sinister man who held the land's ruler captive. After receiving some magical armor, called "guards," the girls began their quest.

Along the way they befriended Presea, the blacksmith, Ferio, a wandering swordsman, and Mokona, a bizarre white puffball who became their guide. In order to become true Magic Knights, the girls first had to unlock the Mashin (or Rune Gods, as they're called in the anime). These ancient spirits function like "mecha" in combat, as well as providing guidance to the girls from within their own souls.

Armed with new powerful weapons and even more powerful Mashin, the girls journeyed to Zagato's fortress to rescue Princess Emeraude. Much to their surprise, the Magic Knights discovered that Emeraude wanted the Magic Knights to slay her. Zagato was bent on destroying the knights only to protect Emeraude, the woman he loved. The tragic nature of Cephiro's existence is based on the leader, or "Pillar," devoting herself 100% to her country. When Emeraude fell in love with Zagato, she could not be with him because of her duty, and so she chose to die rather than live in sorrow. The Magic Knights defeated Emeraude, but it left the three girls scarred for life and sent them back to earth in tears.

Now we rejoin the girls one year later, more mature for their experiences, holding many regrets for what they were forced to do. Perhaps the future holds happier times for these young ladies from another world who are so pure of heart.

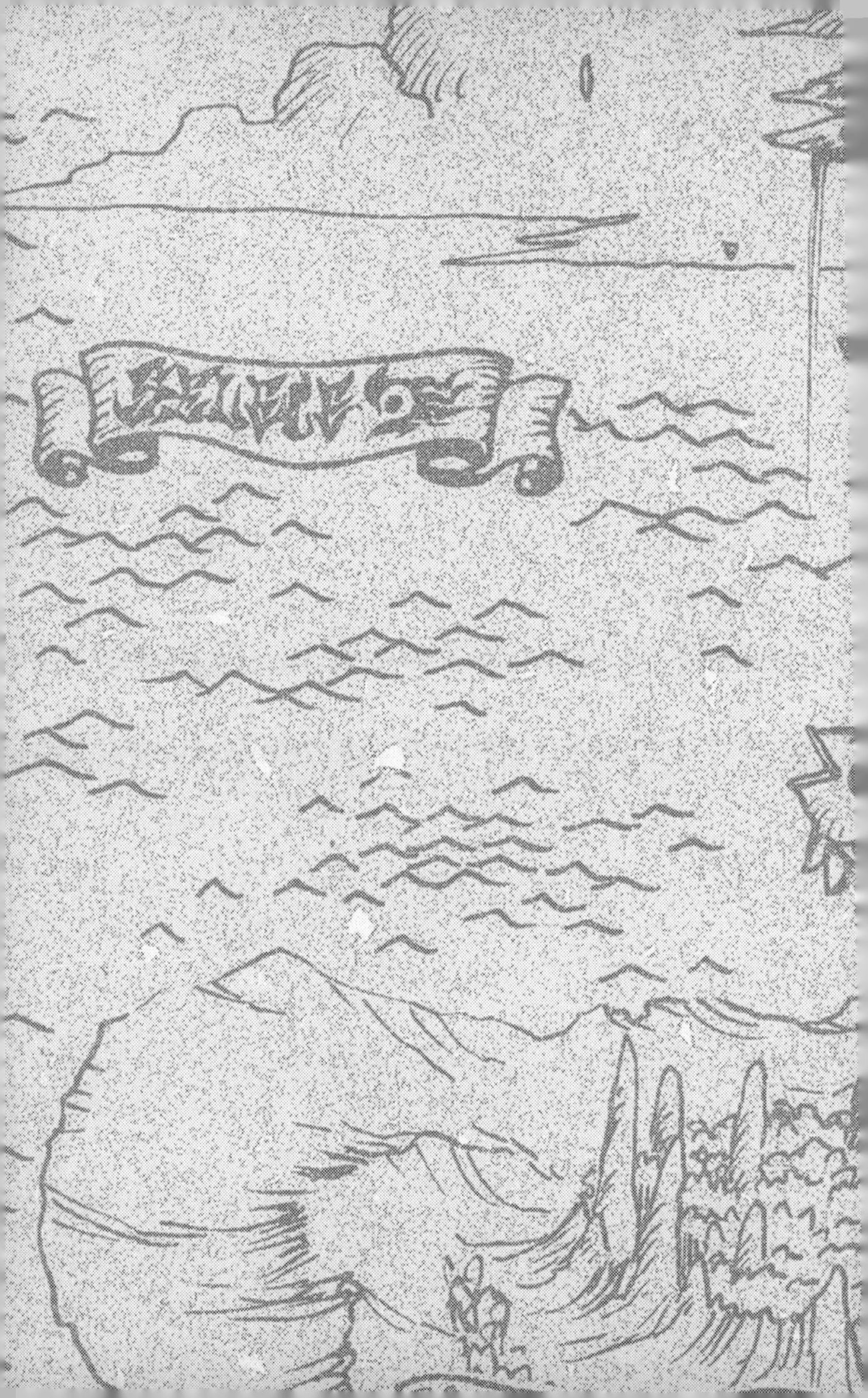

ALSO AVAILABLE FROM TOKYOPOP

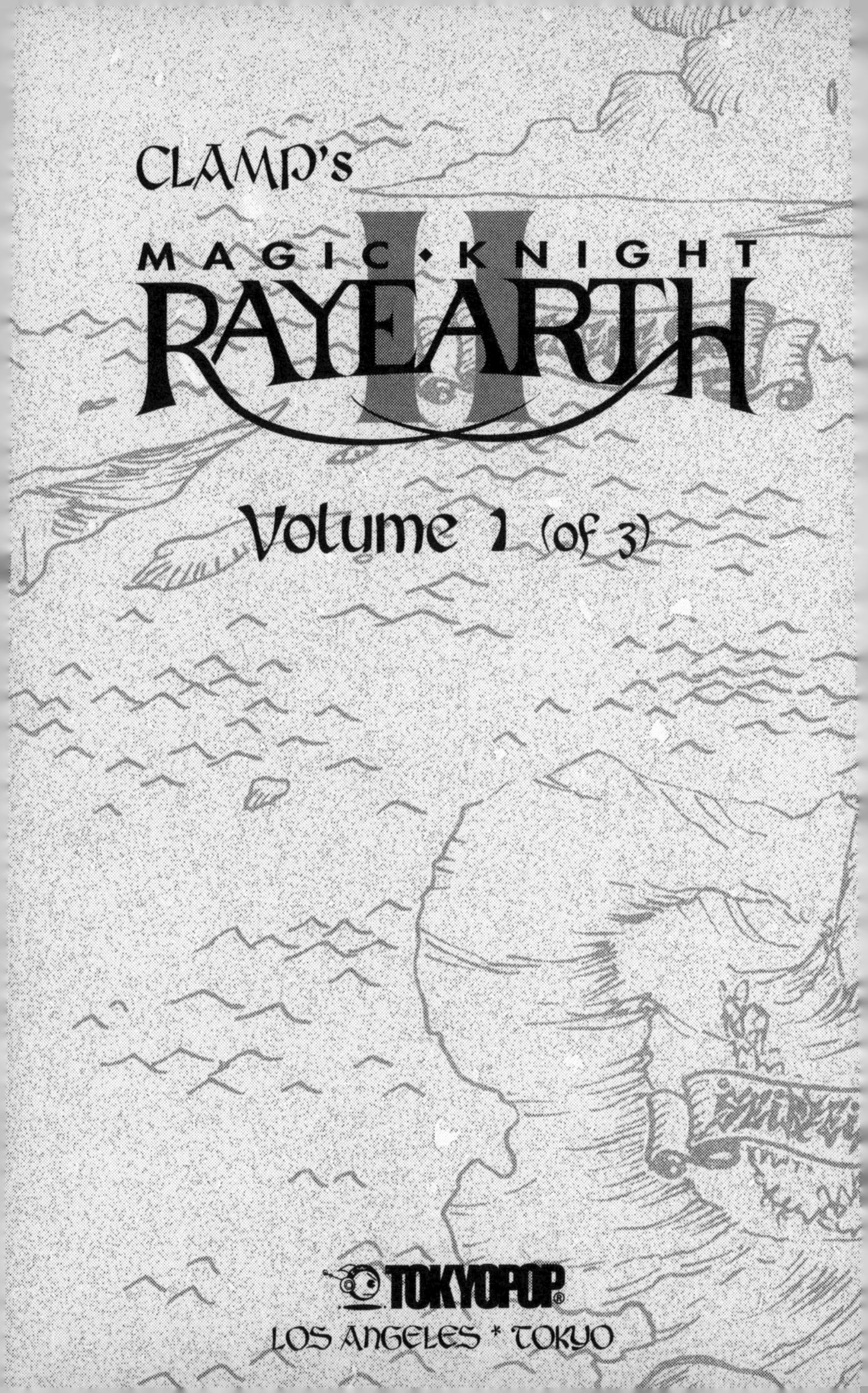

CLAMP's

MAGIC • KNIGHT RAYEARTH II

Volume 1 (of 3)

TOKYOPOP®

LOS ANGELES * TOKYO

Translator - Anita Sengupta
English Adaption - Jamie S. Rich
Copy Editors - Bryce Coleman, Carol Fox
Retouch - Paul Morrissey
Lettering - Monalisa de Asis
Cover Layout - Patrick Hook

Editor - Jake Forbes
Managing Editor - Jill Freshney
Production Coordinator - Antonio DePietro
Production Manager - Jennifer Miller
Art Director - Matthew Alford
Director of Editorial - Jeremy Ross
VP of Production & Manufacturing - Ron Klamert
President & C.O.O. - John Parker
Publisher & C.E.O. - Stuart Levy

Email: editor@TOKYOPOP.com
Come visit us online at www.TOKYOPOP.com

A **TOKYOPOP** Manga

TOKYOPOP® is an imprint of Mixx Entertainment, Inc.
5900 Wilshire Blvd. Suite 2000, Los Angeles, CA 90036

Magic Knight Rayearth II Vol. 1 ©1995 CLAMP.
First published in 1995 by Kodansha Ltd., Tokyo.
English publication rights arranged through Kodansha Ltd.

English text © 2003 by Mixx Entertainment, Inc.
TOKYOPOP is a registered trademark of Mixx Entertainment, Inc.

ISBN: 1-59182-266-1

First TOKYOPOP® printing: April 2003

10 9 8 7 6 5 4 3 2 1

Printed in Canada

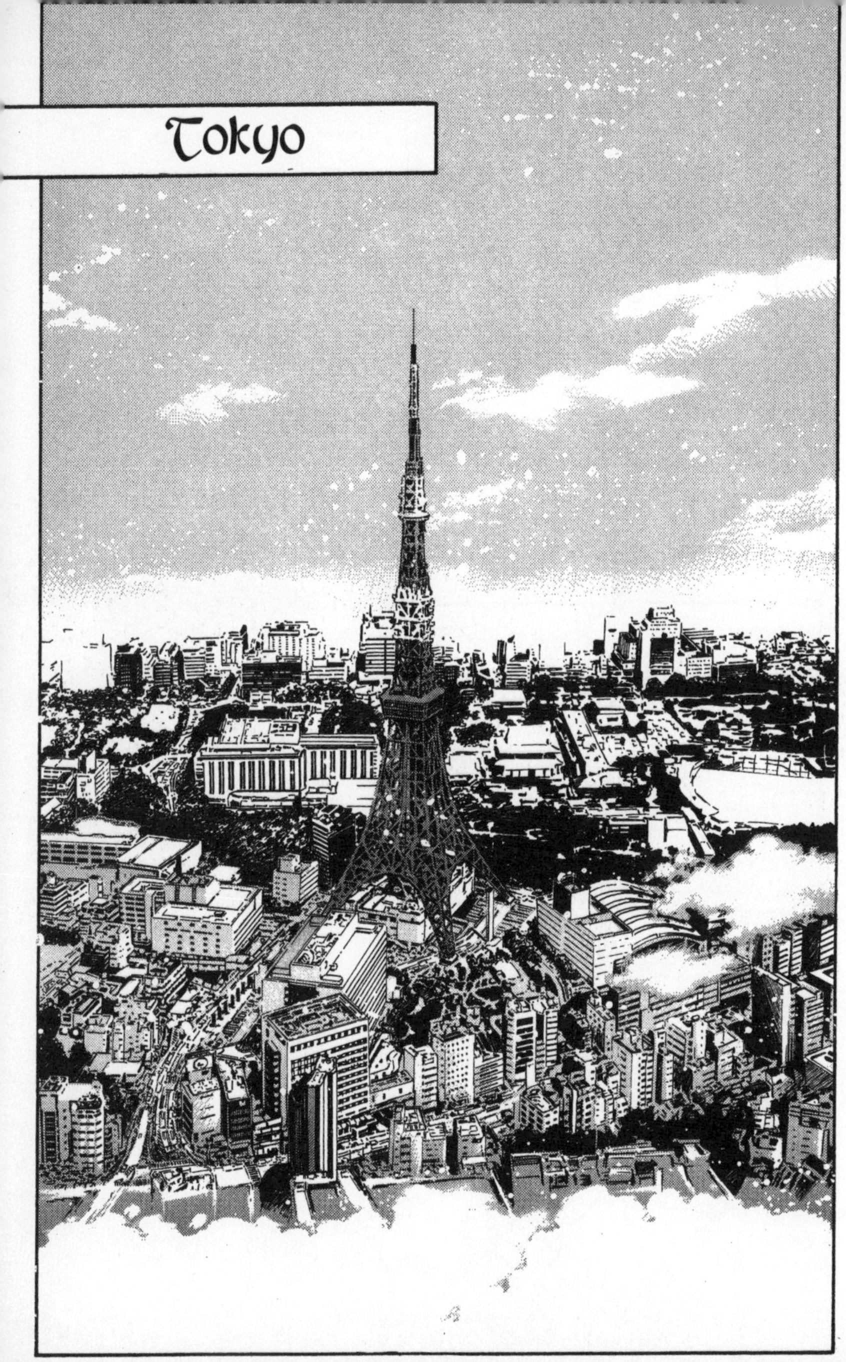
Tokyo

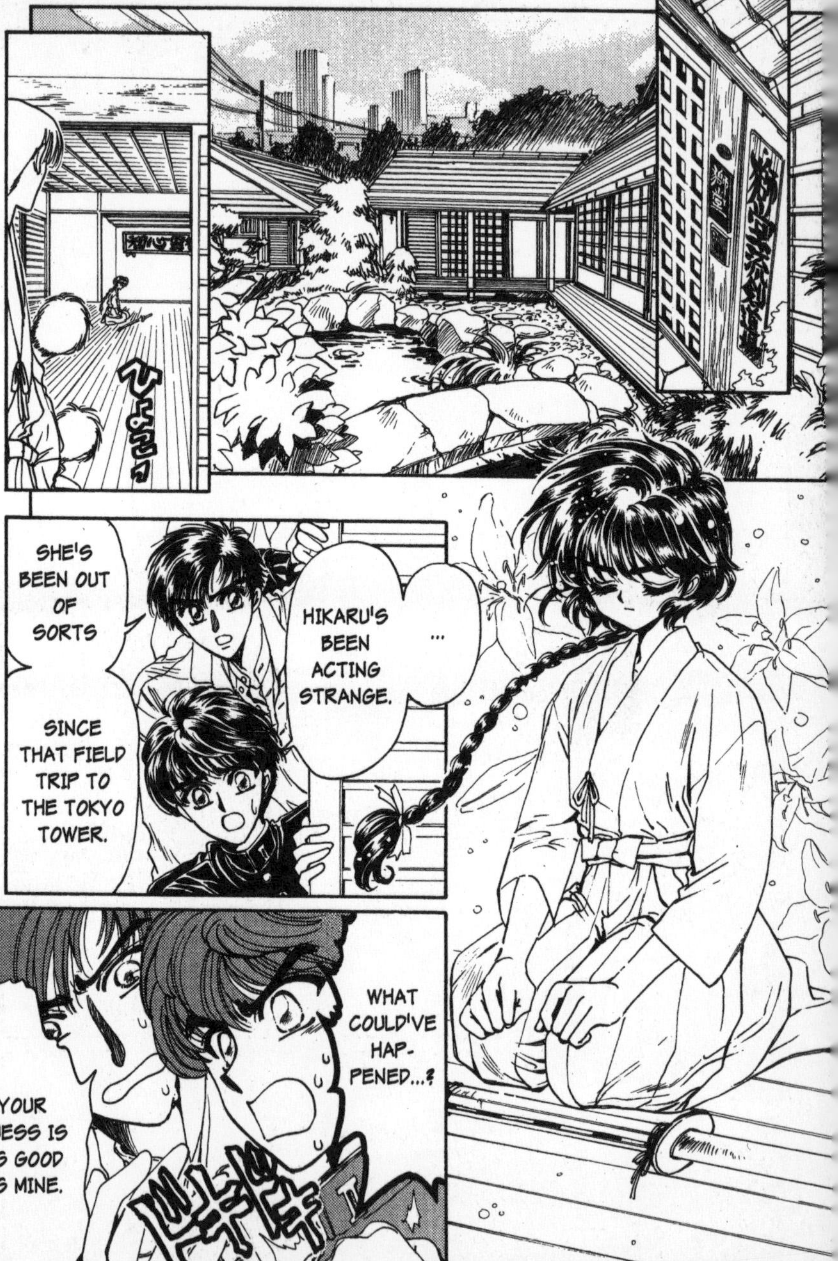
...
HIKARU'S BEEN ACTING STRANGE.
SHE'S BEEN OUT OF SORTS
SINCE THAT FIELD TRIP TO THE TOKYO TOWER.
WHAT COULD'VE HAP-PENED...?
YOUR GUESS IS AS GOOD AS MINE.

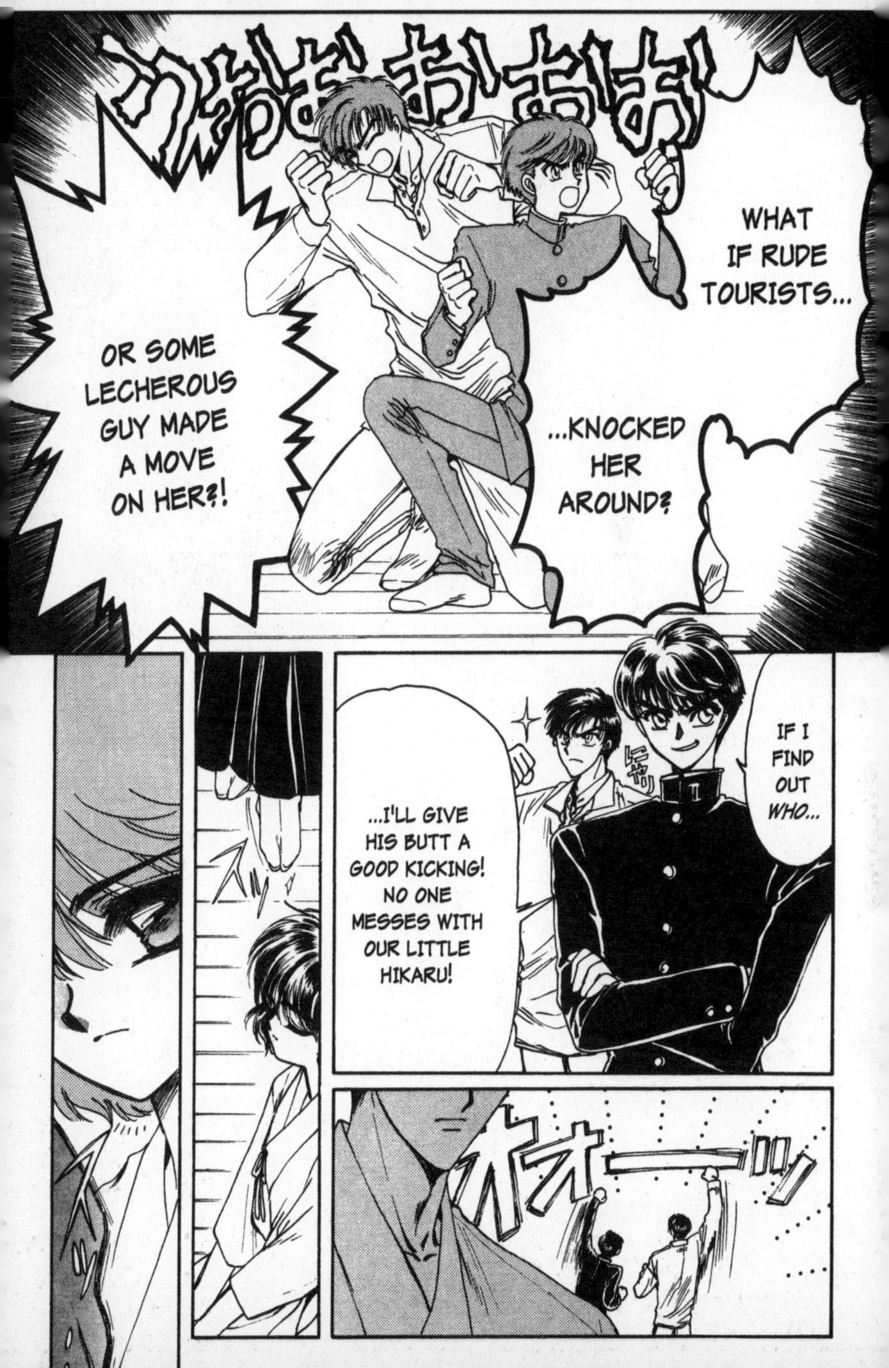
WHAT IF RUDE TOURISTS...
...KNOCKED HER AROUND?
OR SOME LECHEROUS GUY MADE A MOVE ON HER?!
IF I FIND OUT *WHO*...
ニヤリ
...I'LL GIVE HIS BUTT A GOOD KICKING! NO ONE MESSES WITH OUR LITTLE HIKARU!
オオーーッ

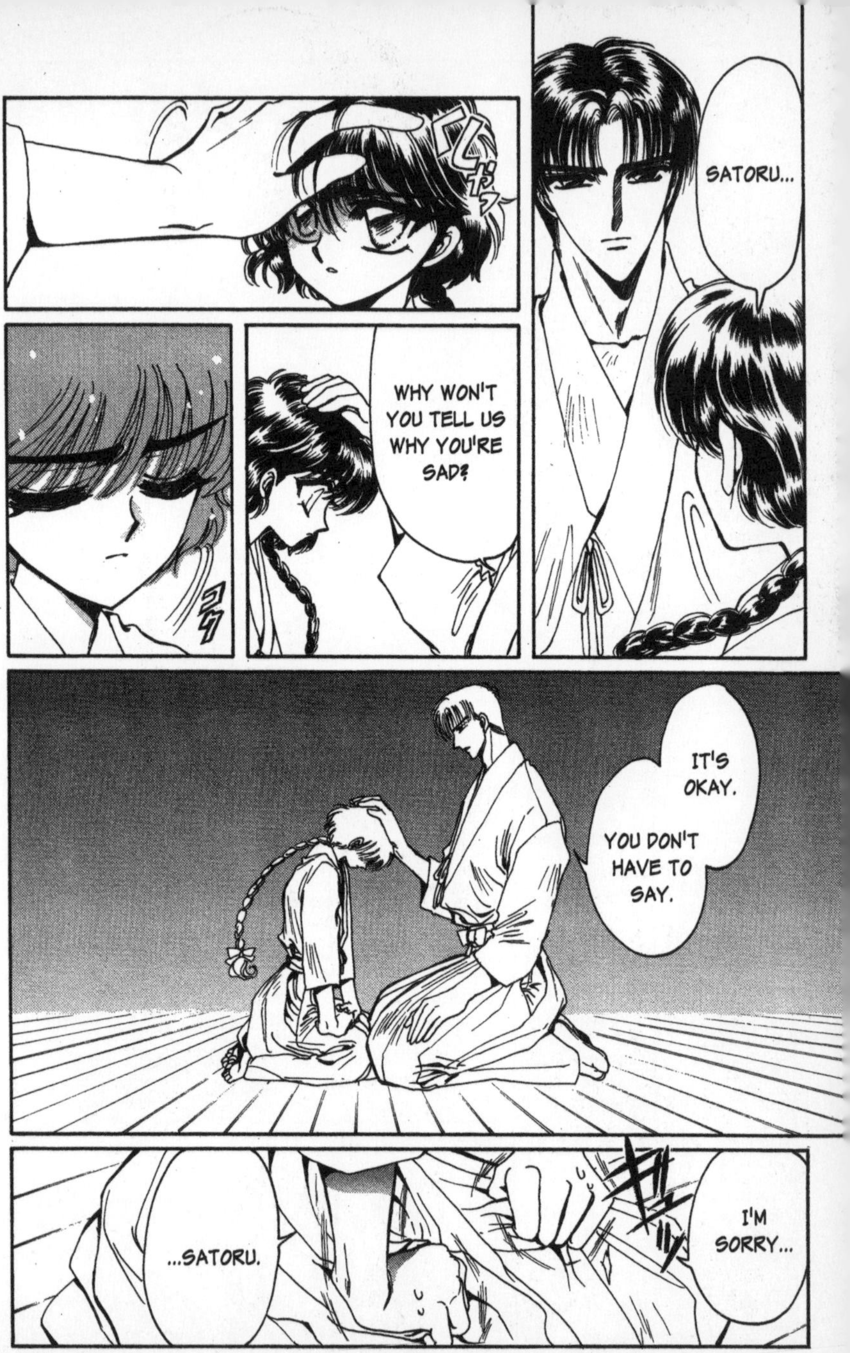
SATORU...
WHY WON'T YOU TELL US WHY YOU'RE SAD?
IT'S OKAY.
YOU DON'T HAVE TO SAY.
I'M SORRY...
...SATORU.

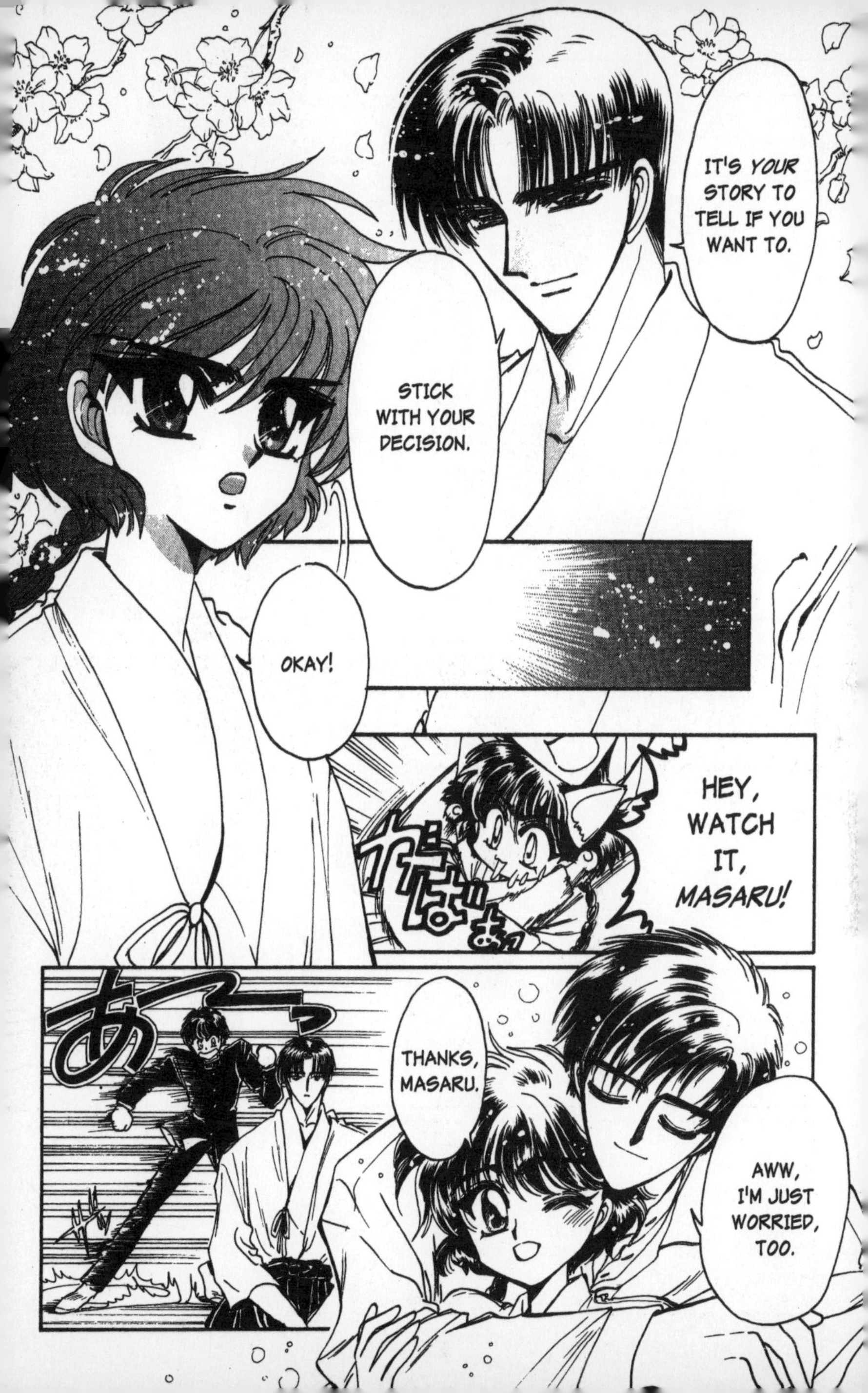
IT'S *YOUR* STORY TO TELL IF YOU WANT TO.
STICK WITH YOUR DECISION.
OKAY!
HEY, WATCH IT, *MASARU!*
THANKS, MASARU.
AWW, I'M JUST WORRIED, TOO.

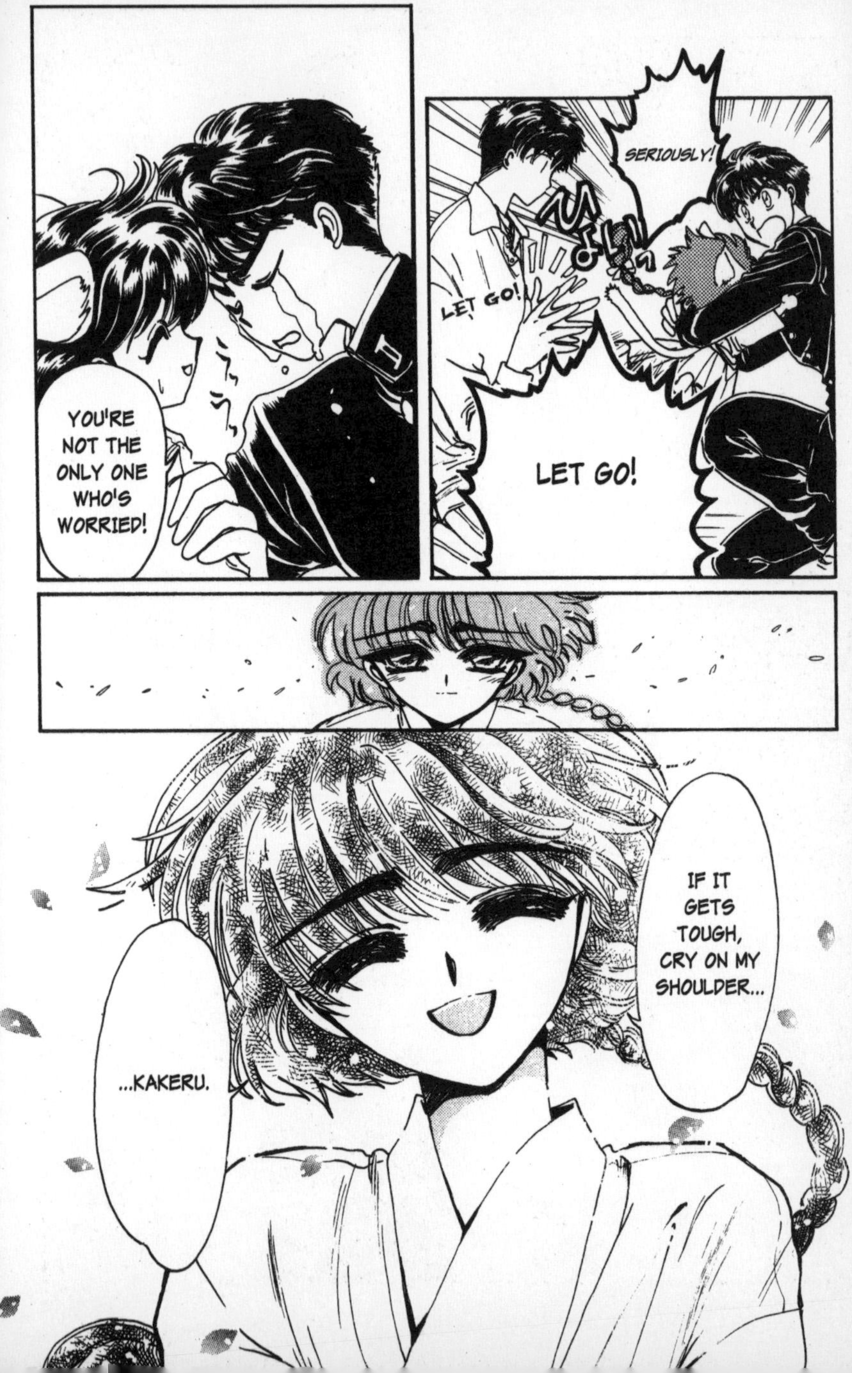
SERIOUSLY!
LET GO!
LET GO!
YOU'RE NOT THE ONLY ONE WHO'S WORRIED!
IF IT GETS TOUGH, CRY ON MY SHOULDER...
...KAKERU.

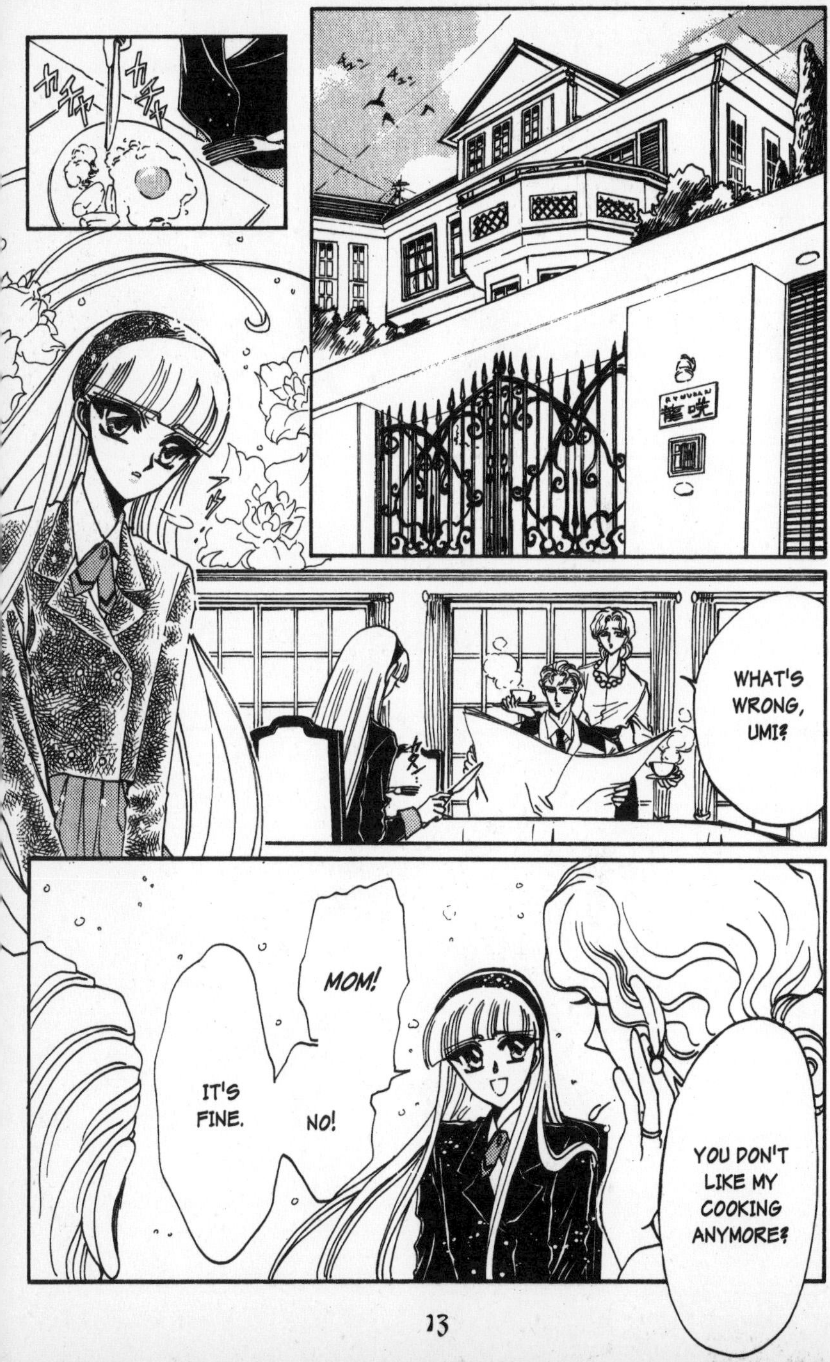
龍咲
カチャ
カチャ
WHAT'S WRONG, UMI?
YOU DON'T LIKE MY COOKING ANYMORE?
MOM!
NO!
IT'S FINE.

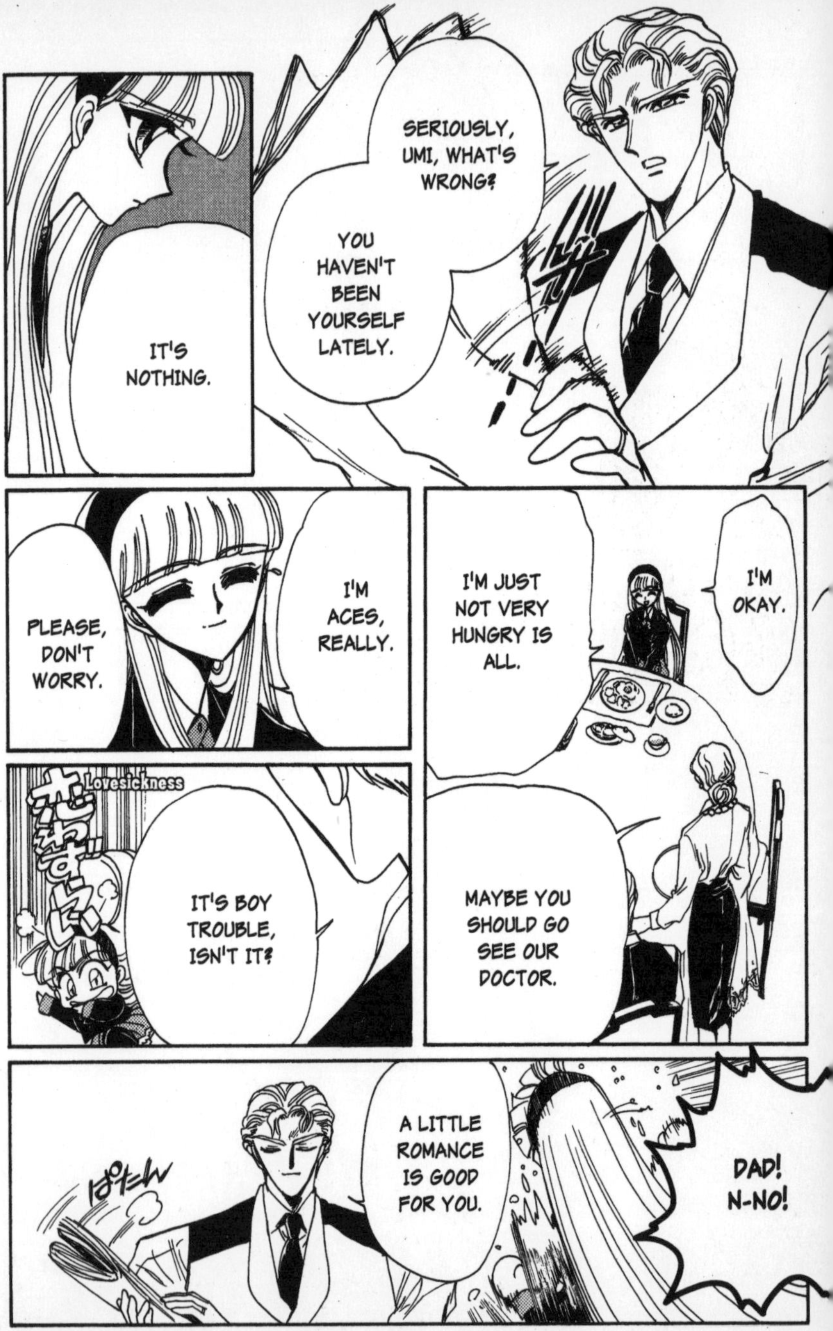
SERIOUSLY, UMI, WHAT'S WRONG?
YOU HAVEN'T BEEN YOURSELF LATELY.
IT'S NOTHING.
I'M OKAY.
I'M JUST NOT VERY HUNGRY IS ALL.
I'M ACES, REALLY.
PLEASE, DON'T WORRY.
MAYBE YOU SHOULD GO SEE OUR DOCTOR.
IT'S BOY TROUBLE, ISN'T IT?
Lovesickness
A LITTLE ROMANCE IS GOOD FOR YOU.
DAD! N-NO!
ぱたん

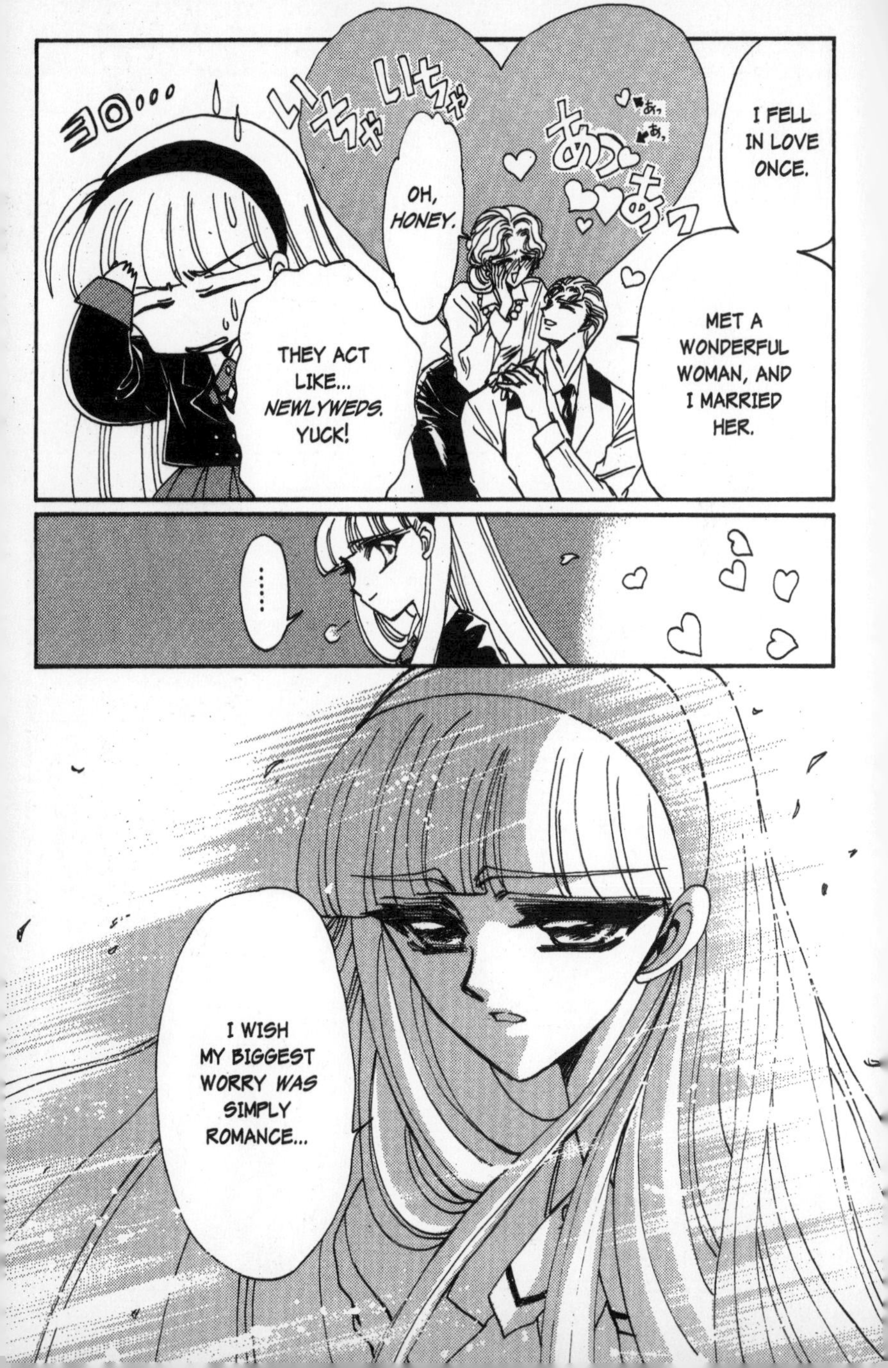
I FELL IN LOVE ONCE.
MET A WONDERFUL WOMAN, AND I MARRIED HER.
あっ
あっ
あっ あっ
OH, HONEY.
いちゃ いちゃ
ヨロ○○○
THEY ACT LIKE... NEWLYWEDS. YUCK!
......
I WISH MY BIGGEST WORRY WAS SIMPLY ROMANCE...

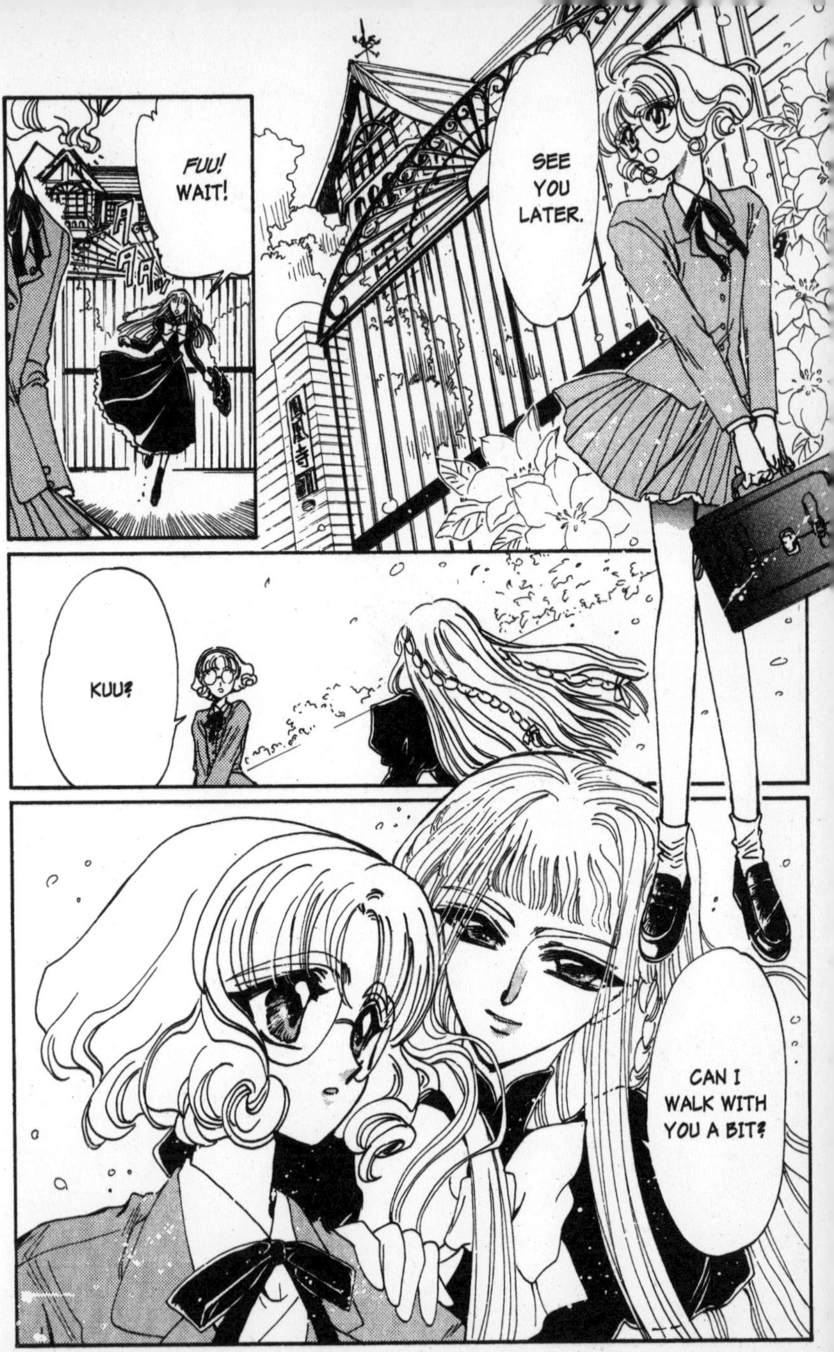
SEE YOU LATER.
FUU! WAIT!
KUU?
CAN I WALK WITH YOU A BIT?

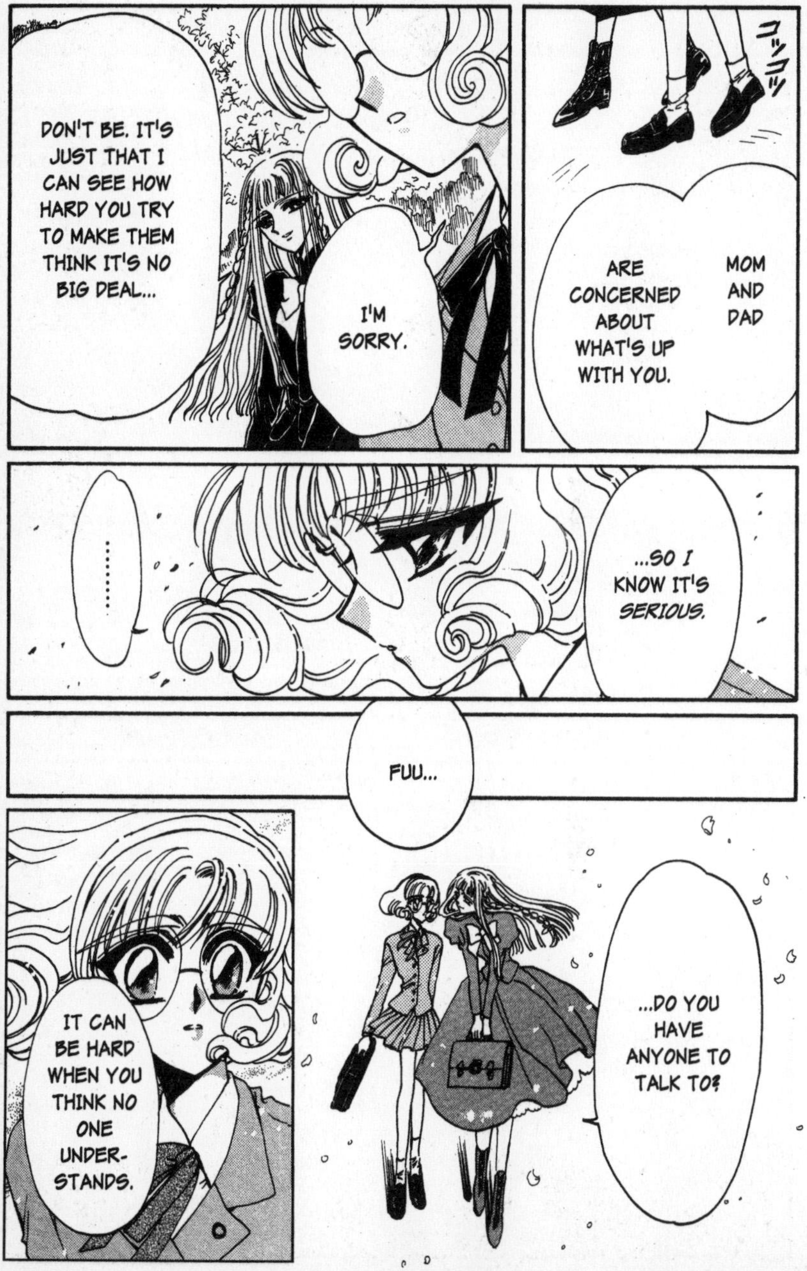
コッコッ
MOM AND DAD ARE CONCERNED ABOUT WHAT'S UP WITH YOU.
I'M SORRY.
DON'T BE. IT'S JUST THAT I CAN SEE HOW HARD YOU TRY TO MAKE THEM THINK IT'S NO BIG DEAL...
...SO I KNOW IT'S *SERIOUS.*
......
FUU...
...DO YOU HAVE ANYONE TO TALK TO?
IT CAN BE HARD WHEN YOU THINK NO ONE UNDER-STANDS.

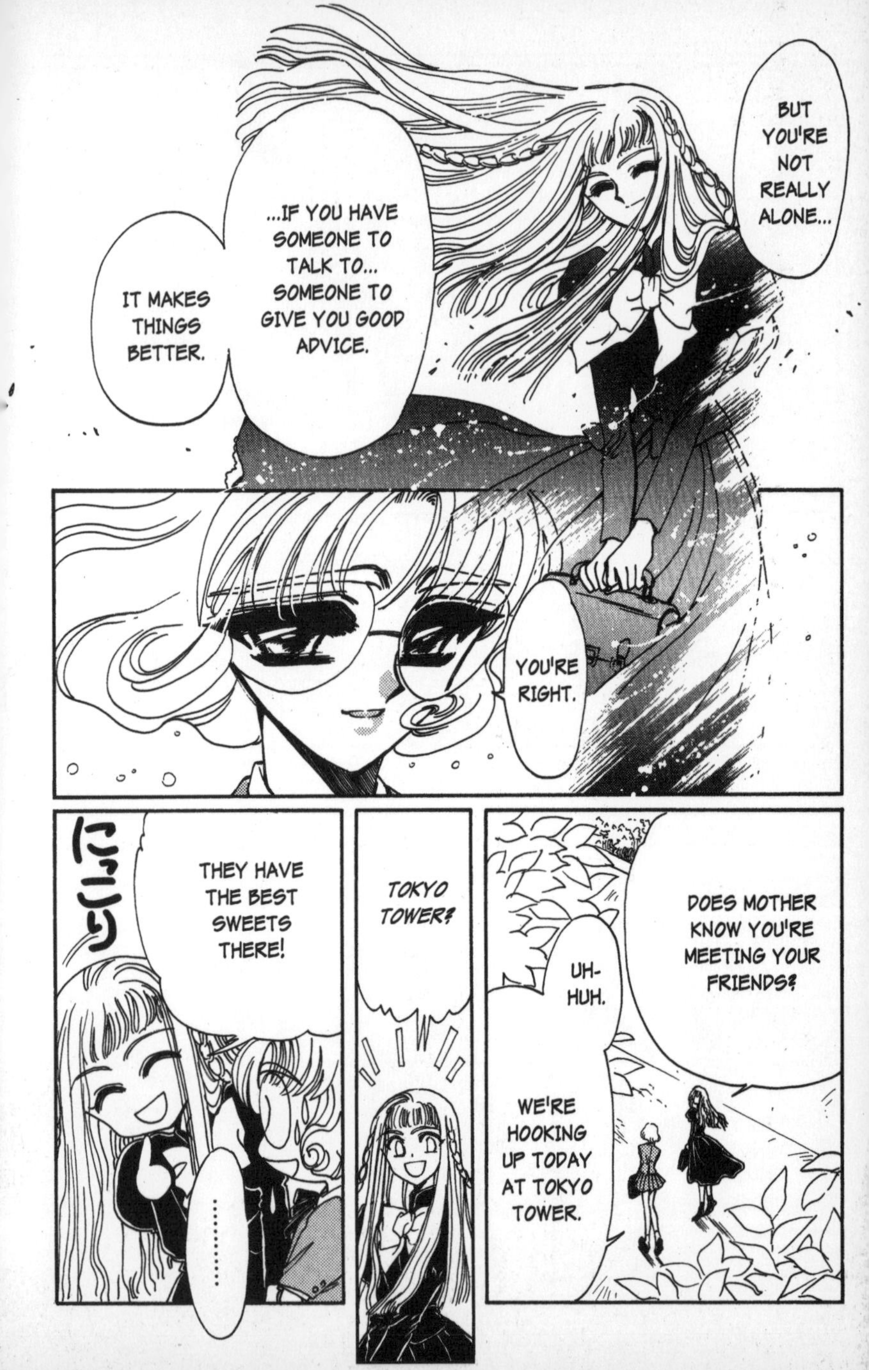
BUT YOU'RE NOT REALLY ALONE...
...IF YOU HAVE SOMEONE TO TALK TO... SOMEONE TO GIVE YOU GOOD ADVICE.
IT MAKES THINGS BETTER.
YOU'RE RIGHT.
DOES MOTHER KNOW YOU'RE MEETING YOUR FRIENDS?
UH-HUH.
WE'RE HOOKING UP TODAY AT TOKYO TOWER.
TOKYO TOWER?
THEY HAVE THE BEST SWEETS THERE!
にっこり
......

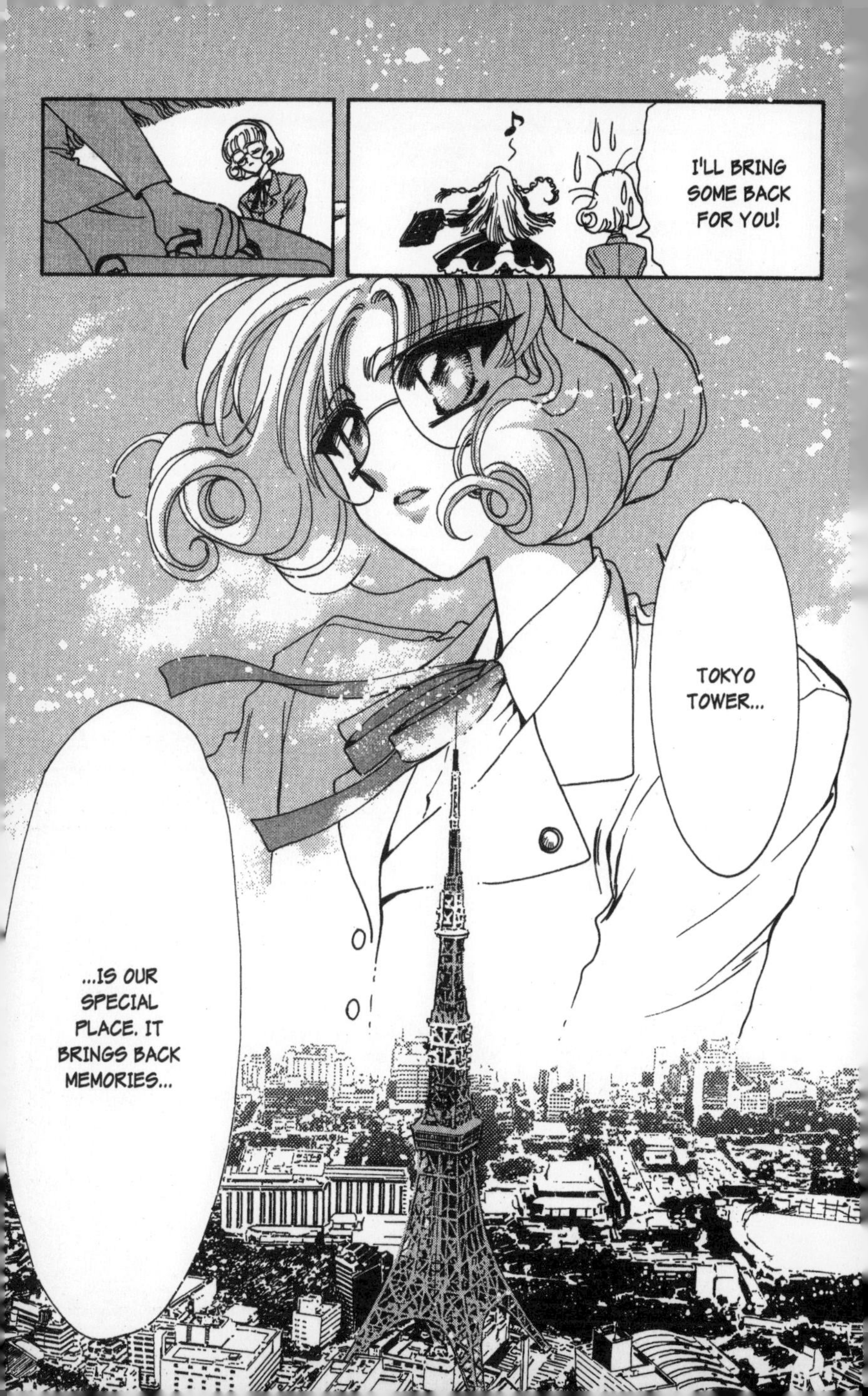
I'LL BRING SOME BACK FOR YOU!
TOKYO TOWER...
...IS OUR SPECIAL PLACE. IT BRINGS BACK MEMORIES...

PRINCESS EMERAUDE ...
AHHHHH!
GEEZ, YOU LOOK LIKE YOU'RE GONNA START BAWLIN'!
DON'T YOU DARE, OR YOU'LL GET *ME* STARTED.
UMI! FUU!
I DREAM ABOUT CEPHIRO.

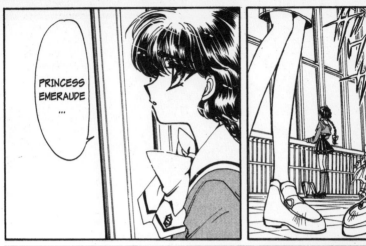

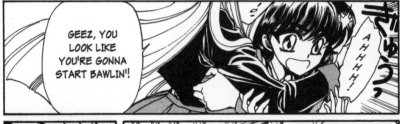

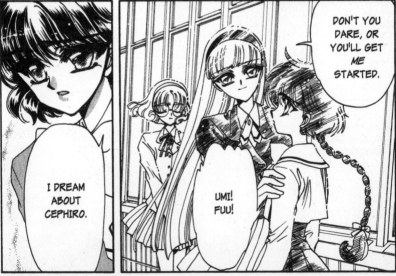

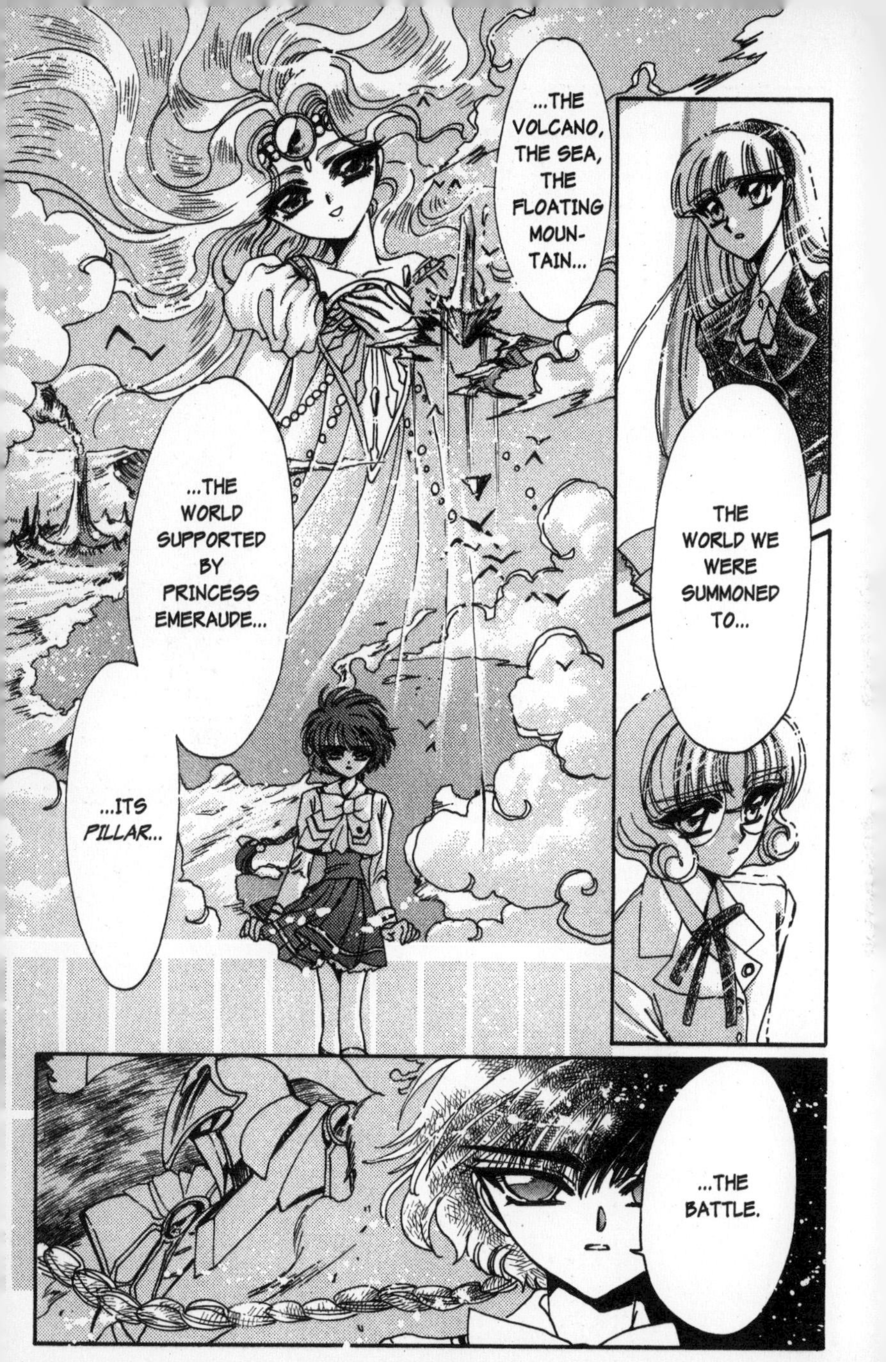
...THE VOLCANO, THE SEA, THE FLOATING MOUN-TAIN...
...THE WORLD SUPPORTED BY PRINCESS EMERAUDE...
...ITS *PILLAR*...
THE WORLD WE WERE SUMMONED TO...
...THE BATTLE.

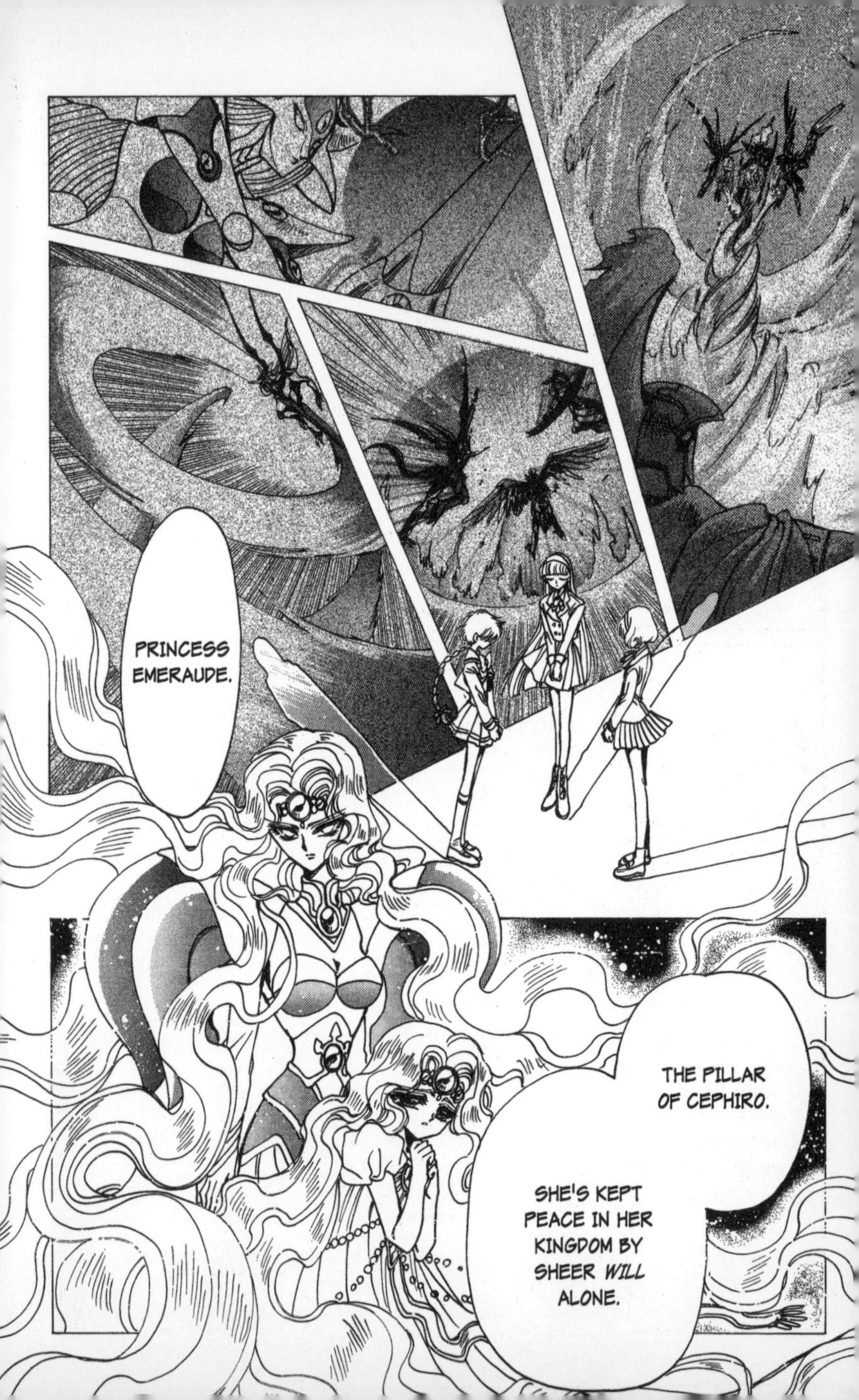
PRINCESS EMERAUDE.
THE PILLAR OF CEPHIRO.
SHE'S KEPT PEACE IN HER KINGDOM BY SHEER *WILL* ALONE.

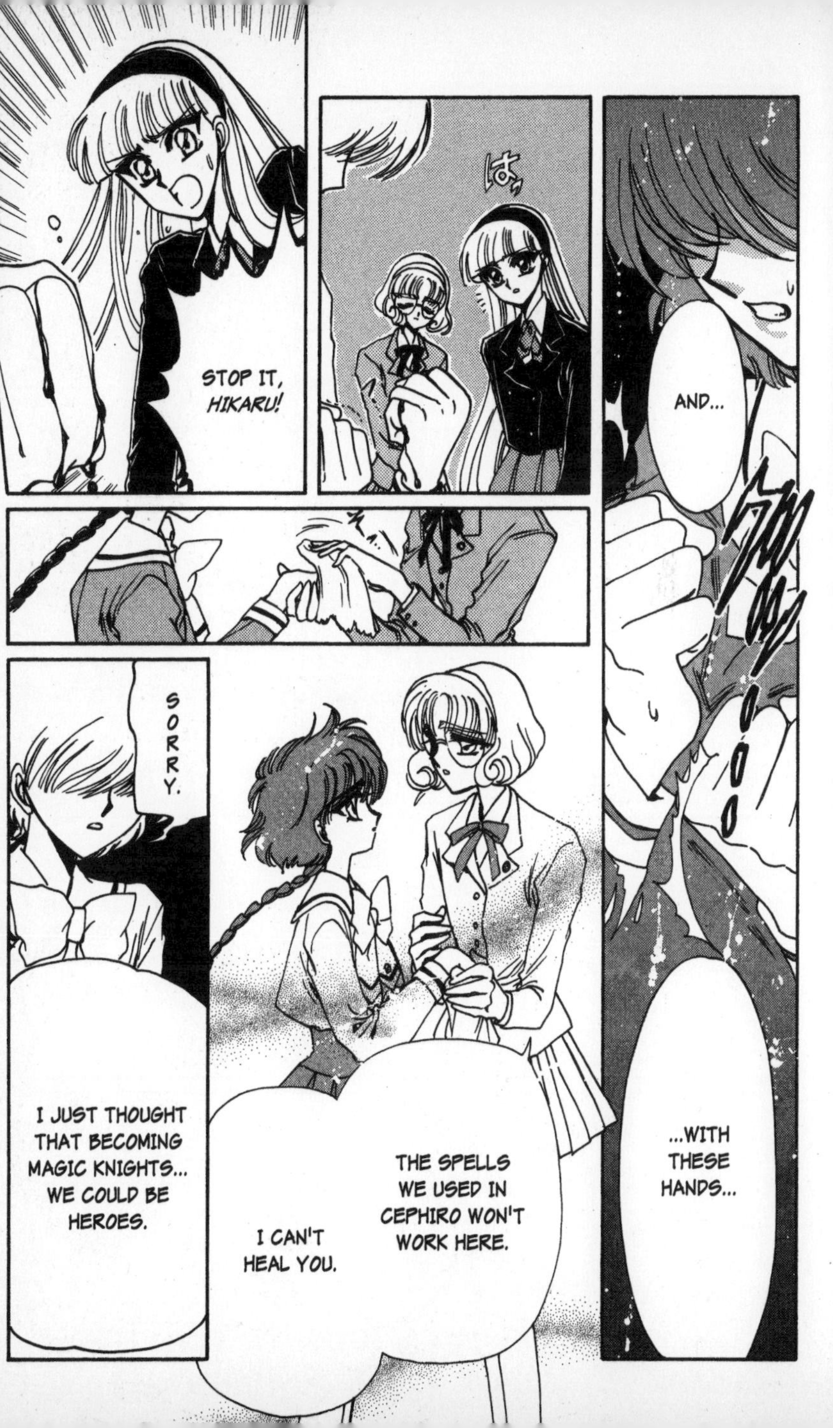
AND...
...WITH THESE HANDS...
は
STOP IT, HIKARU!
THE SPELLS WE USED IN CEPHIRO WON'T WORK HERE.
I CAN'T HEAL YOU.
SORRY.
I JUST THOUGHT THAT BECOMING MAGIC KNIGHTS... WE COULD BE HEROES.

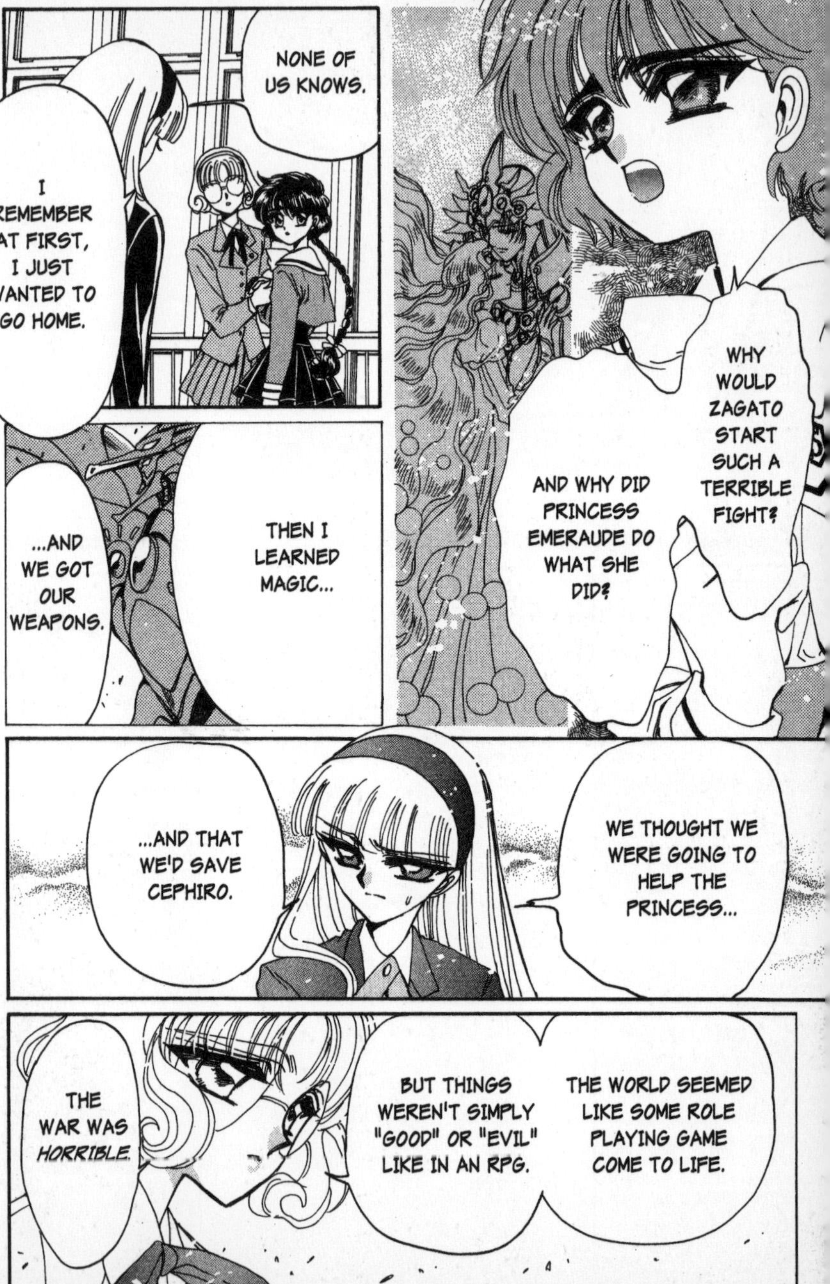

WHY WOULD ZAGATO START SUCH A TERRIBLE FIGHT?
AND WHY DID PRINCESS EMERAUDE DO WHAT SHE DID?
NONE OF US KNOWS.
I REMEMBER AT FIRST, I JUST WANTED TO GO HOME.
THEN I LEARNED MAGIC...
...AND WE GOT OUR WEAPONS.
WE THOUGHT WE WERE GOING TO HELP THE PRINCESS...
...AND THAT WE'D SAVE CEPHIRO.
THE WORLD SEEMED LIKE SOME ROLE PLAYING GAME COME TO LIFE.
BUT THINGS WEREN'T SIMPLY "GOOD" OR "EVIL" LIKE IN AN RPG.
THE WAR WAS *HORRIBLE*.

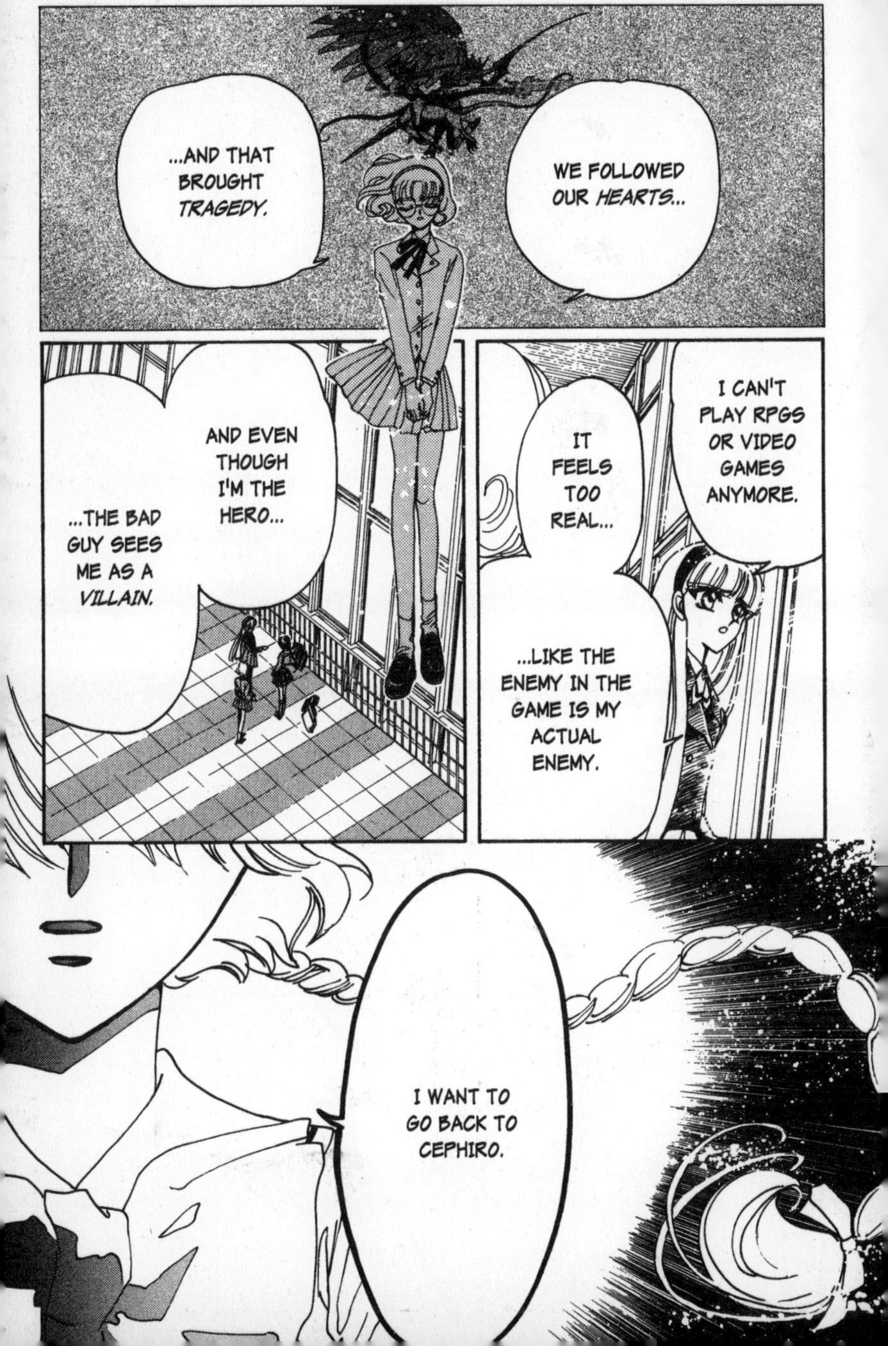
WE FOLLOWED OUR *HEARTS*...
...AND THAT BROUGHT *TRAGEDY.*
I CAN'T PLAY RPGS OR VIDEO GAMES ANYMORE.
IT FEELS TOO REAL...
...LIKE THE ENEMY IN THE GAME IS MY ACTUAL ENEMY.
AND EVEN THOUGH I'M THE HERO...
...THE BAD GUY SEES ME AS A *VILLAIN.*
I WANT TO GO BACK TO CEPHIRO.

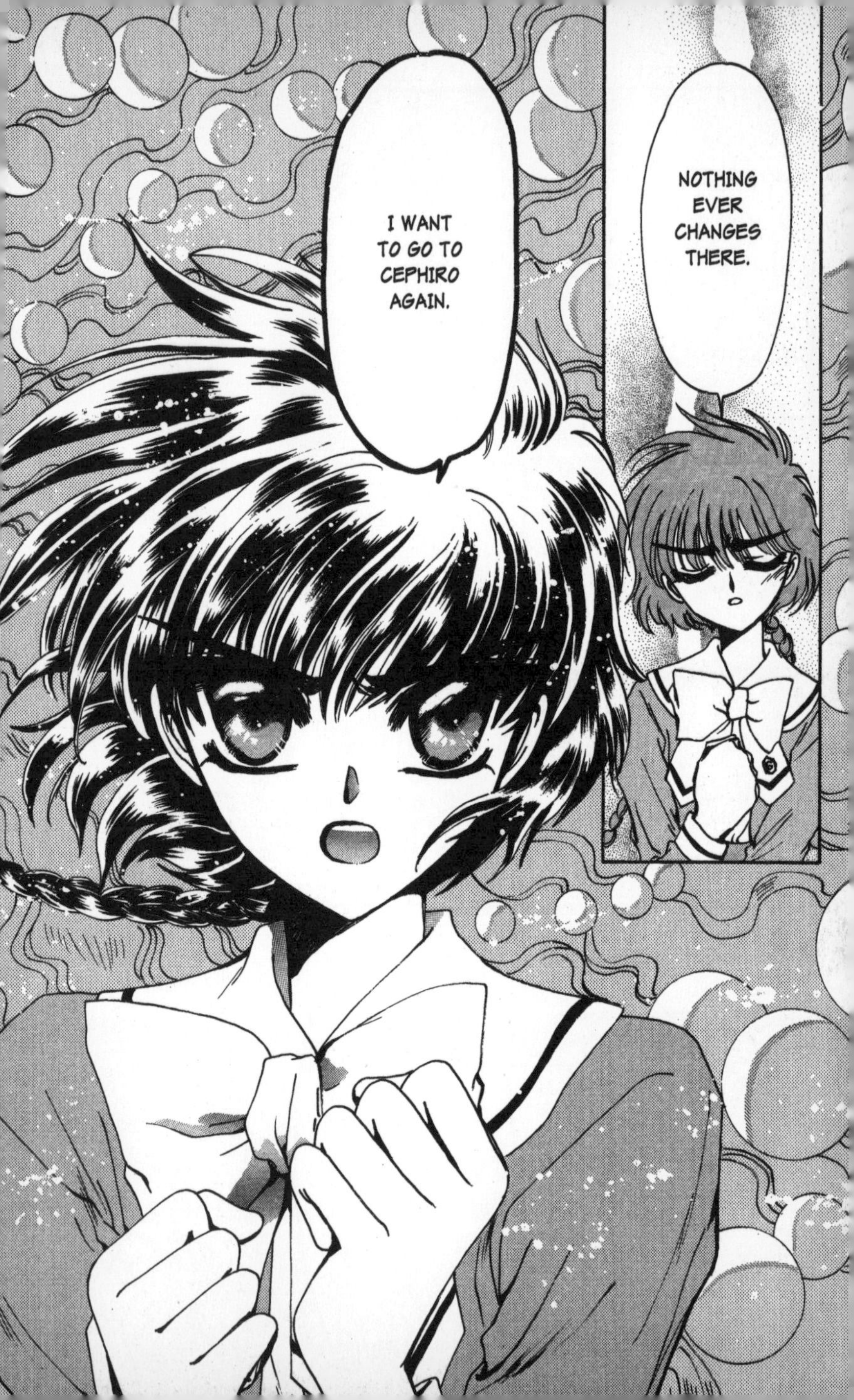
NOTHING EVER CHANGES THERE.
I WANT TO GO TO CEPHIRO AGAIN.

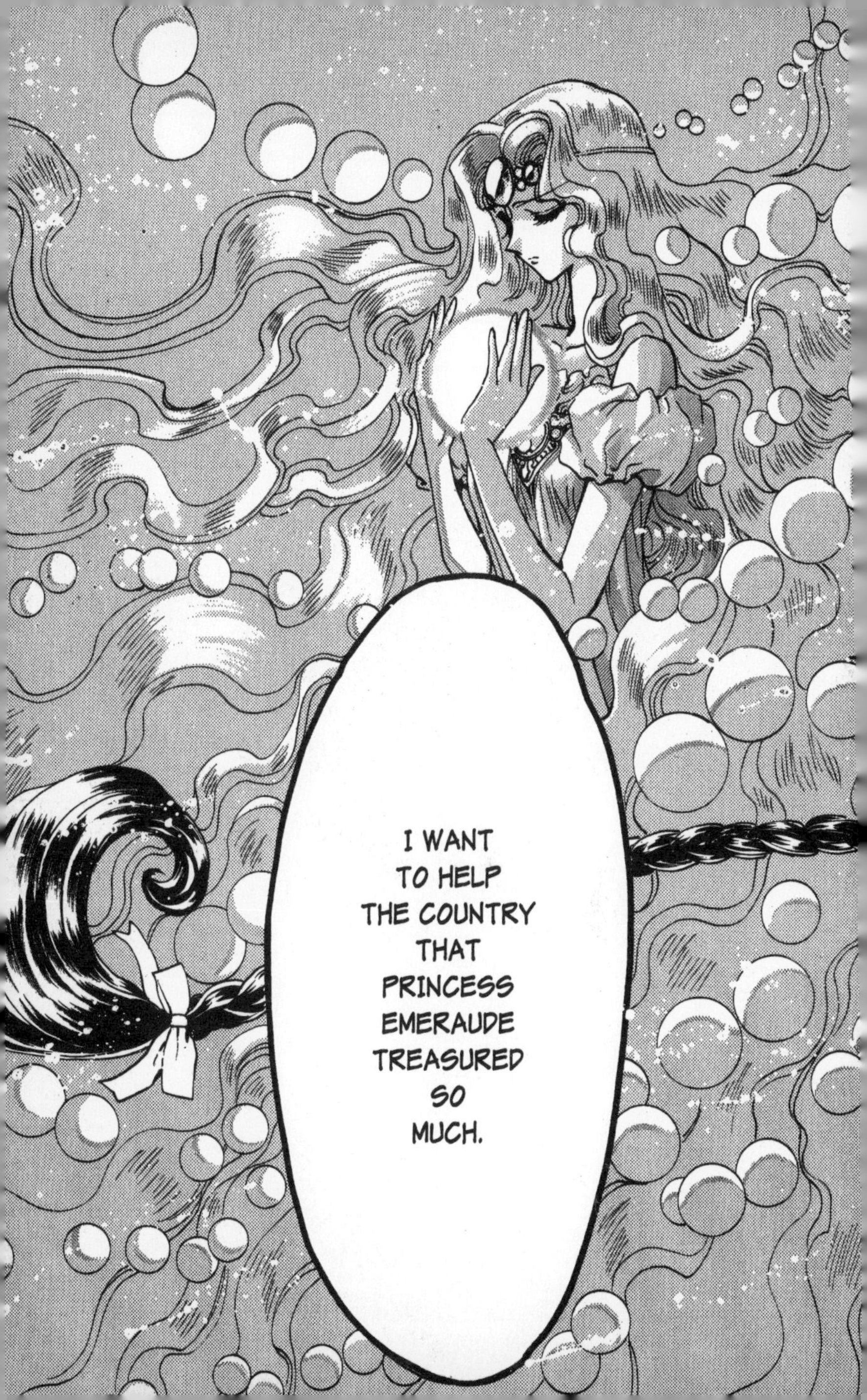
I WANT TO HELP THE COUNTRY THAT PRINCESS EMERAUDE TREASURED SO MUCH.

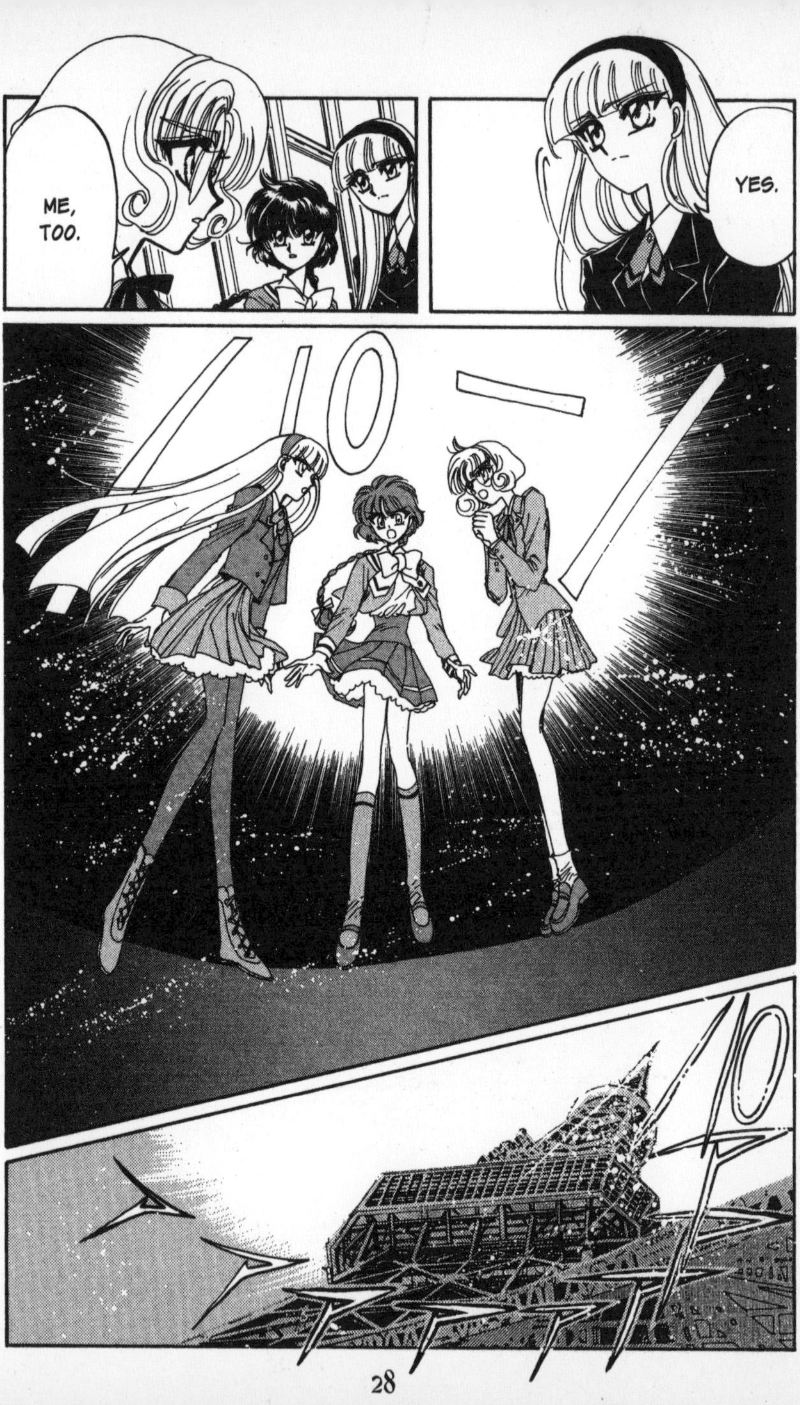
YES.
ME, TOO.

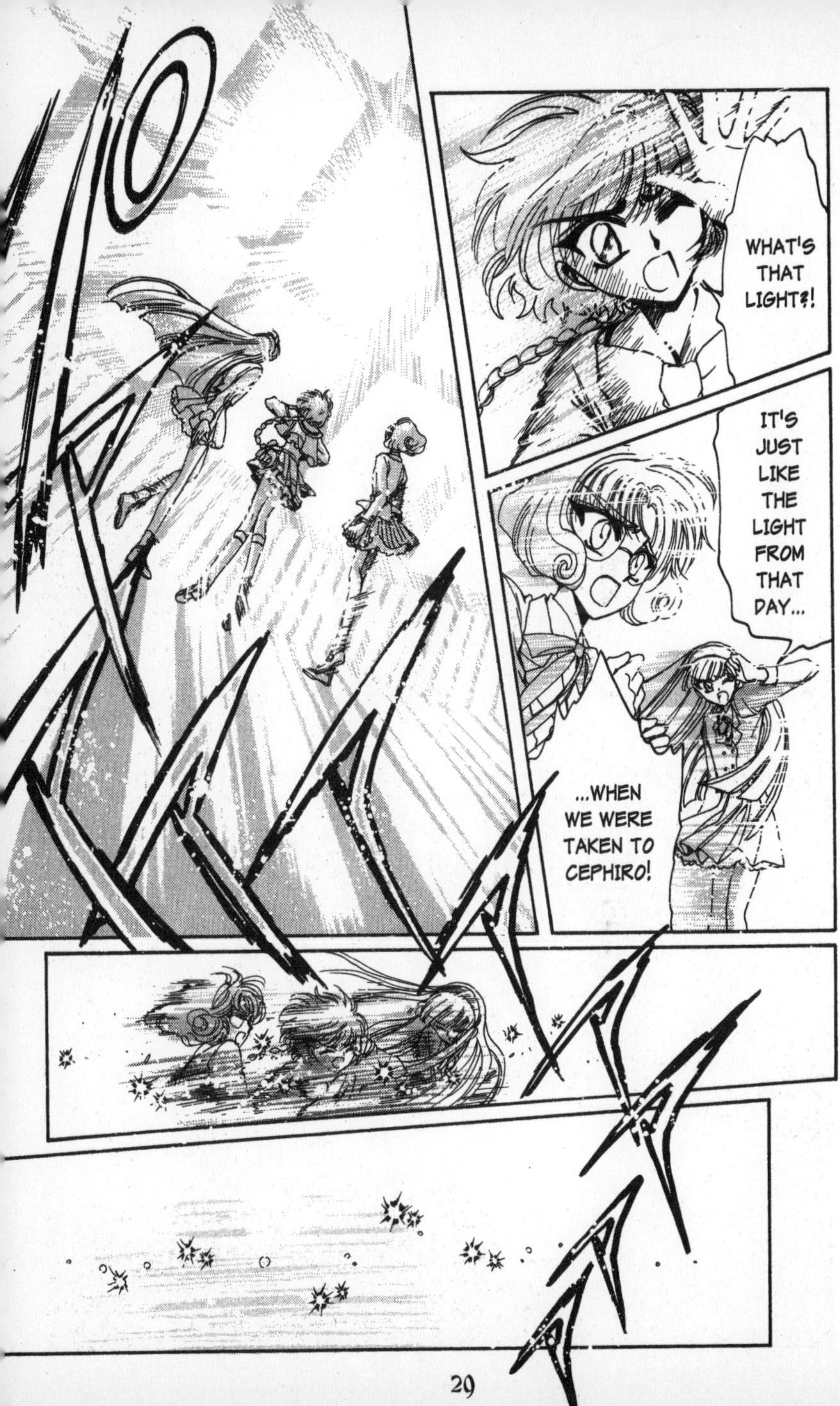
WHAT'S THAT LIGHT?!
IT'S JUST LIKE THE LIGHT FROM THAT DAY...
...WHEN WE WERE TAKEN TO CEPHIRO!

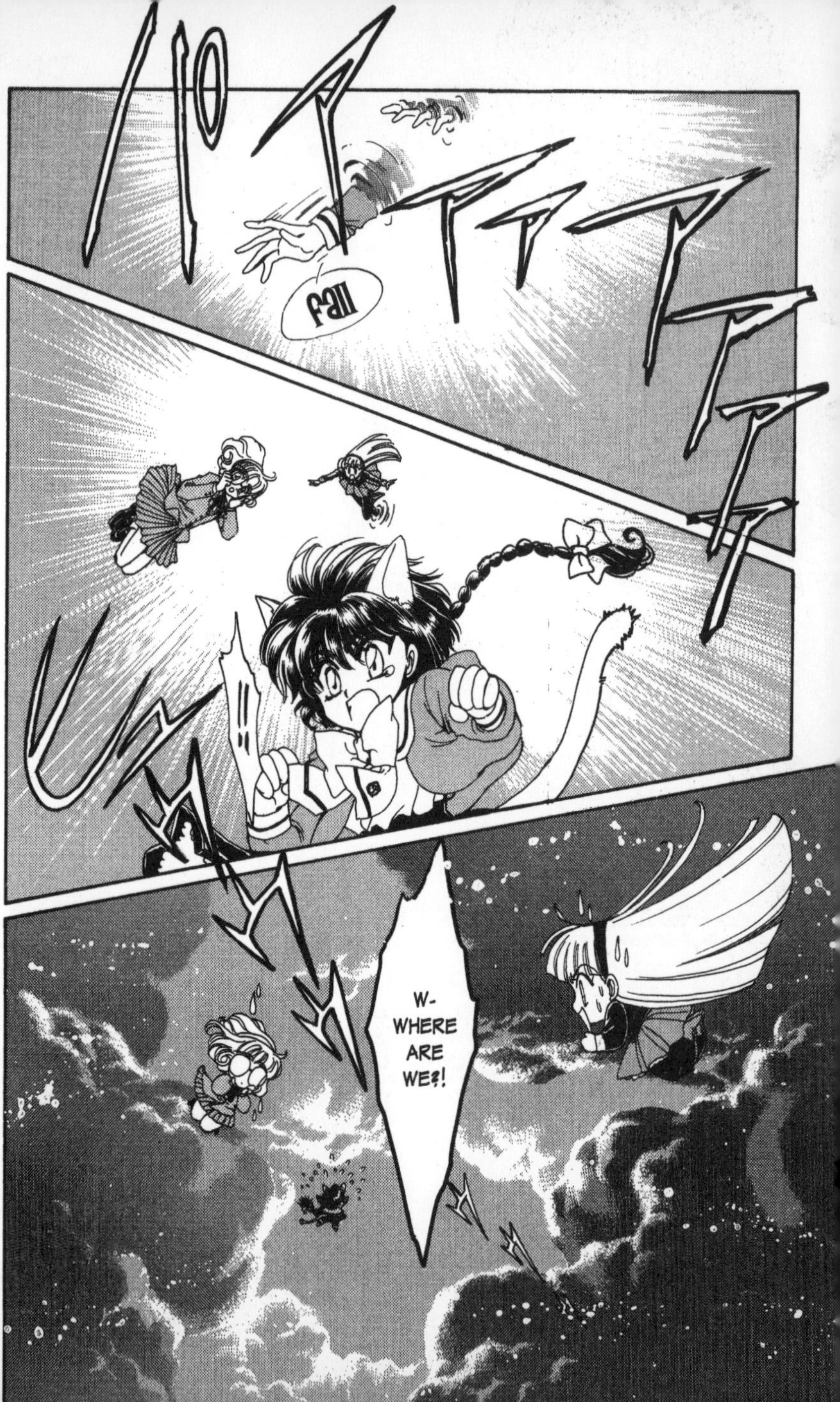
fall
W-
WHERE
ARE
WE?!

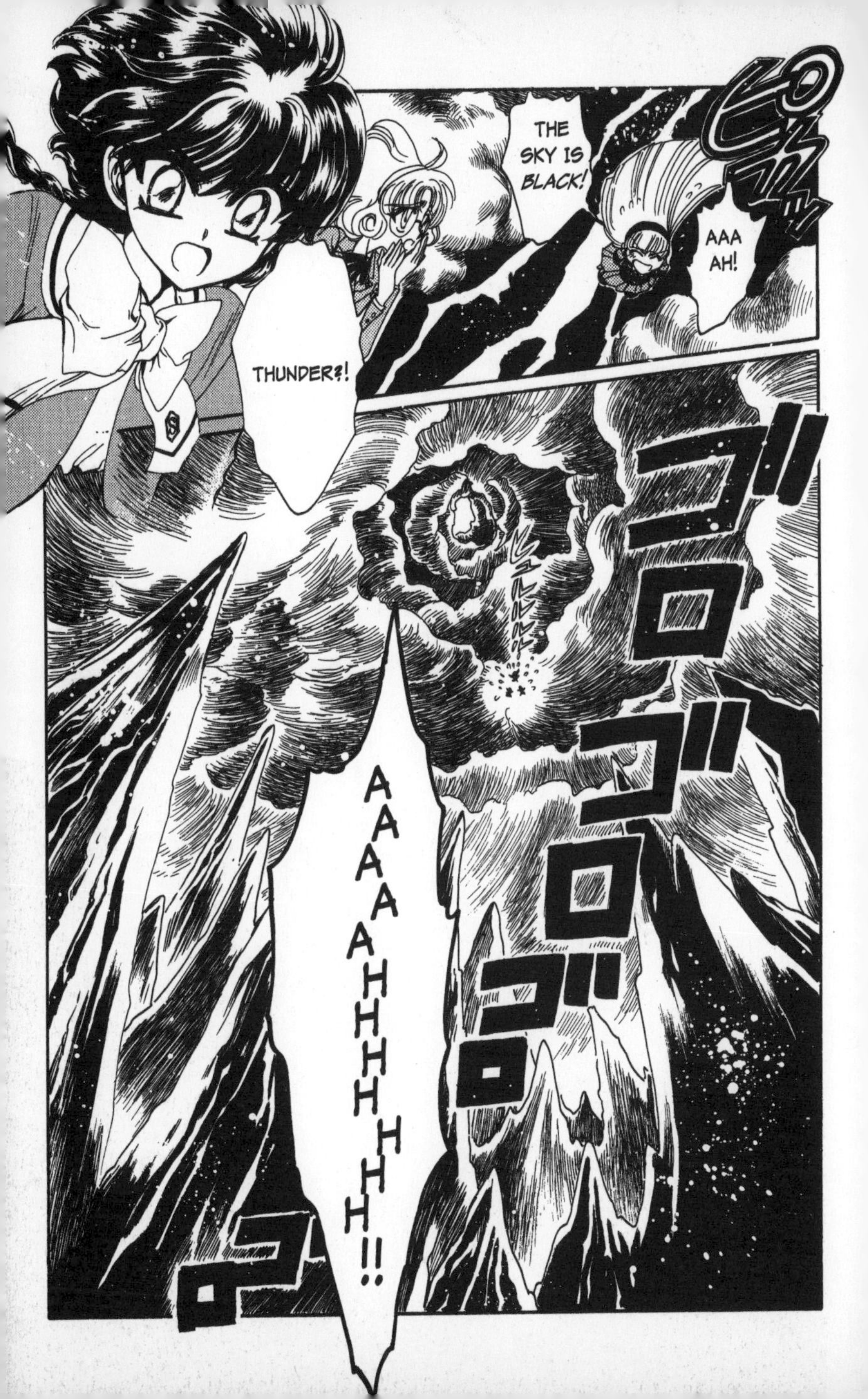
AAA AH!
THE SKY IS BLACK!
THUNDER?!
ゴロゴロゴロ
AAAAAHHHHHHH!!

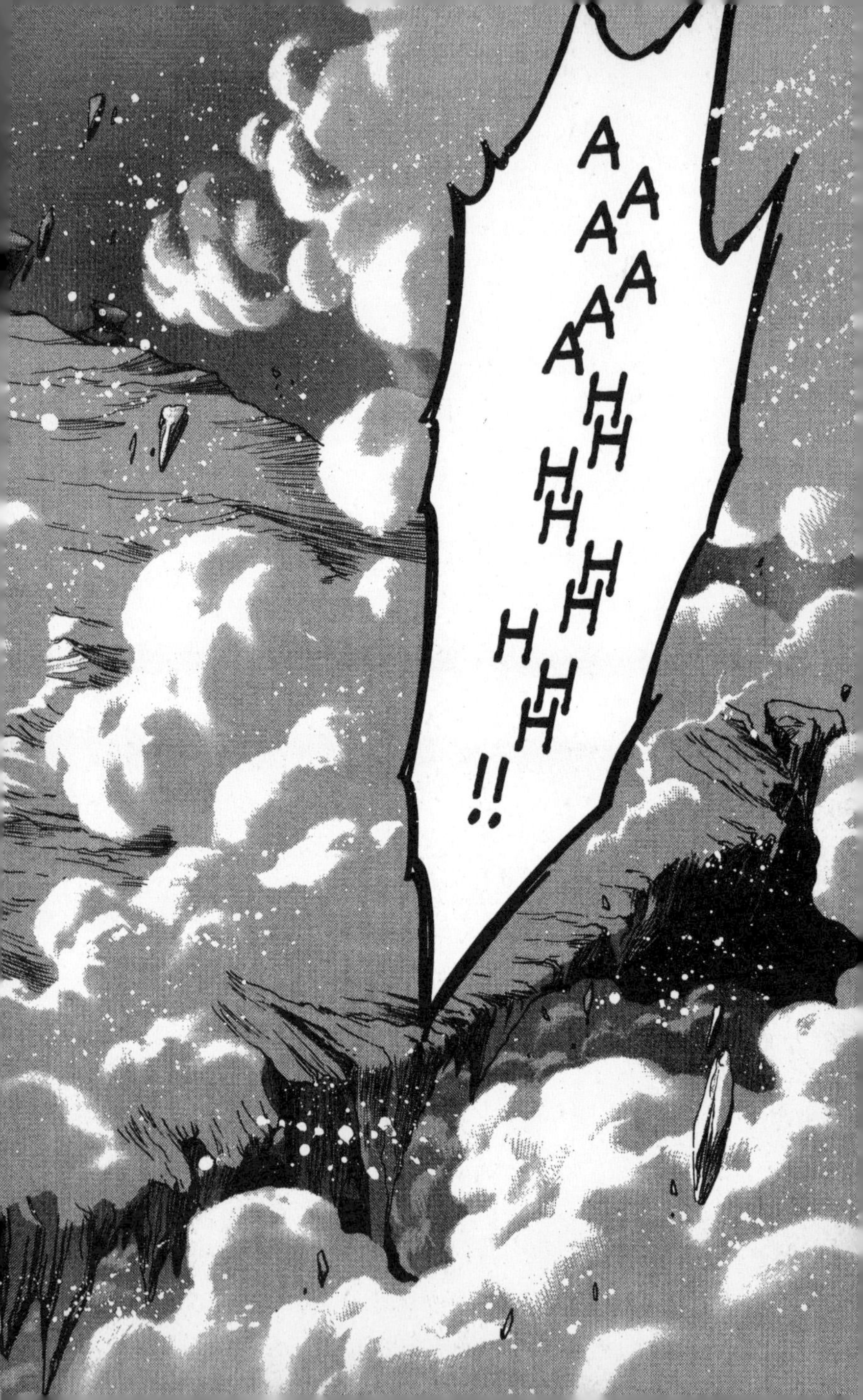
AAAAAAAHHHHHHHHH!!

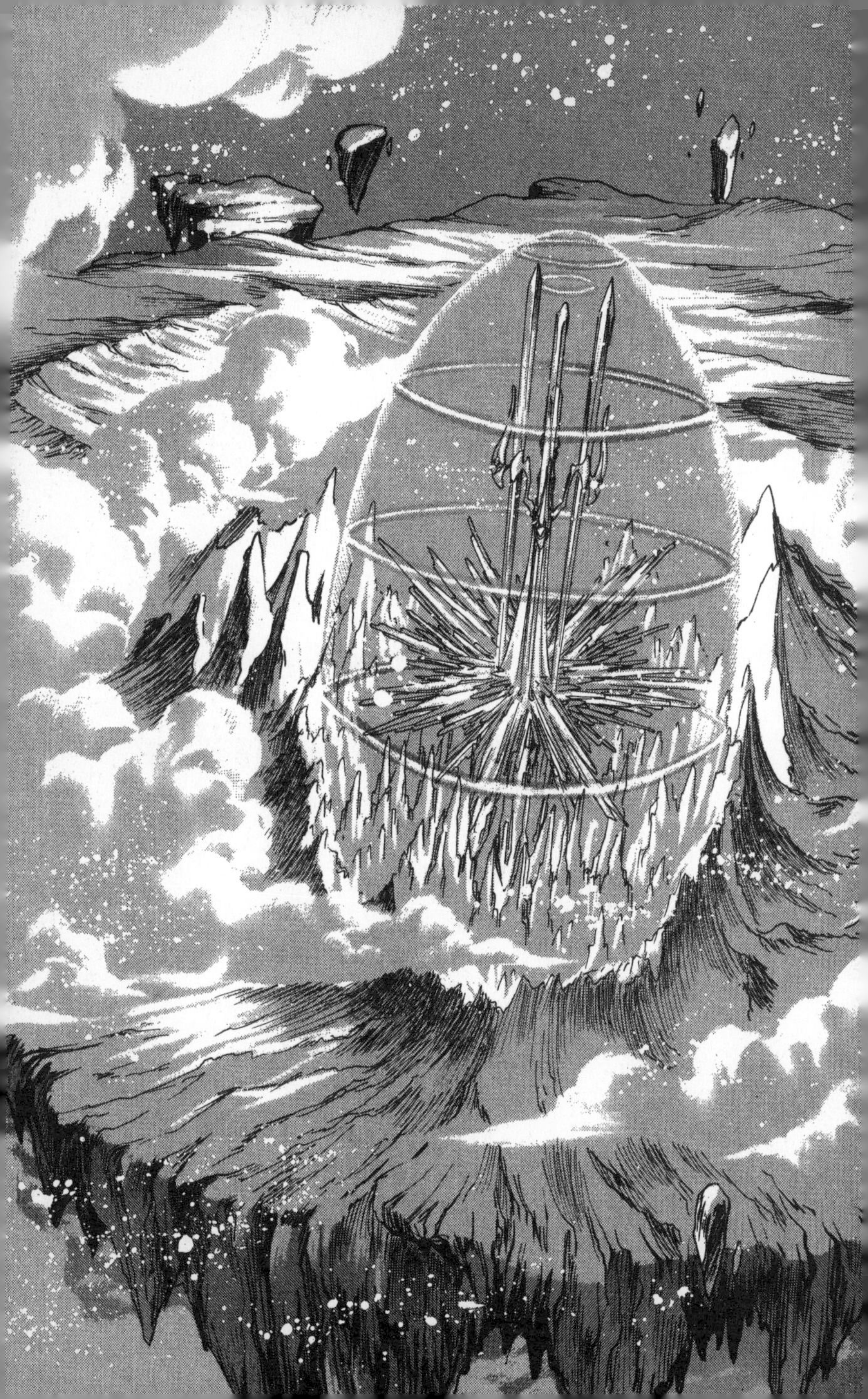

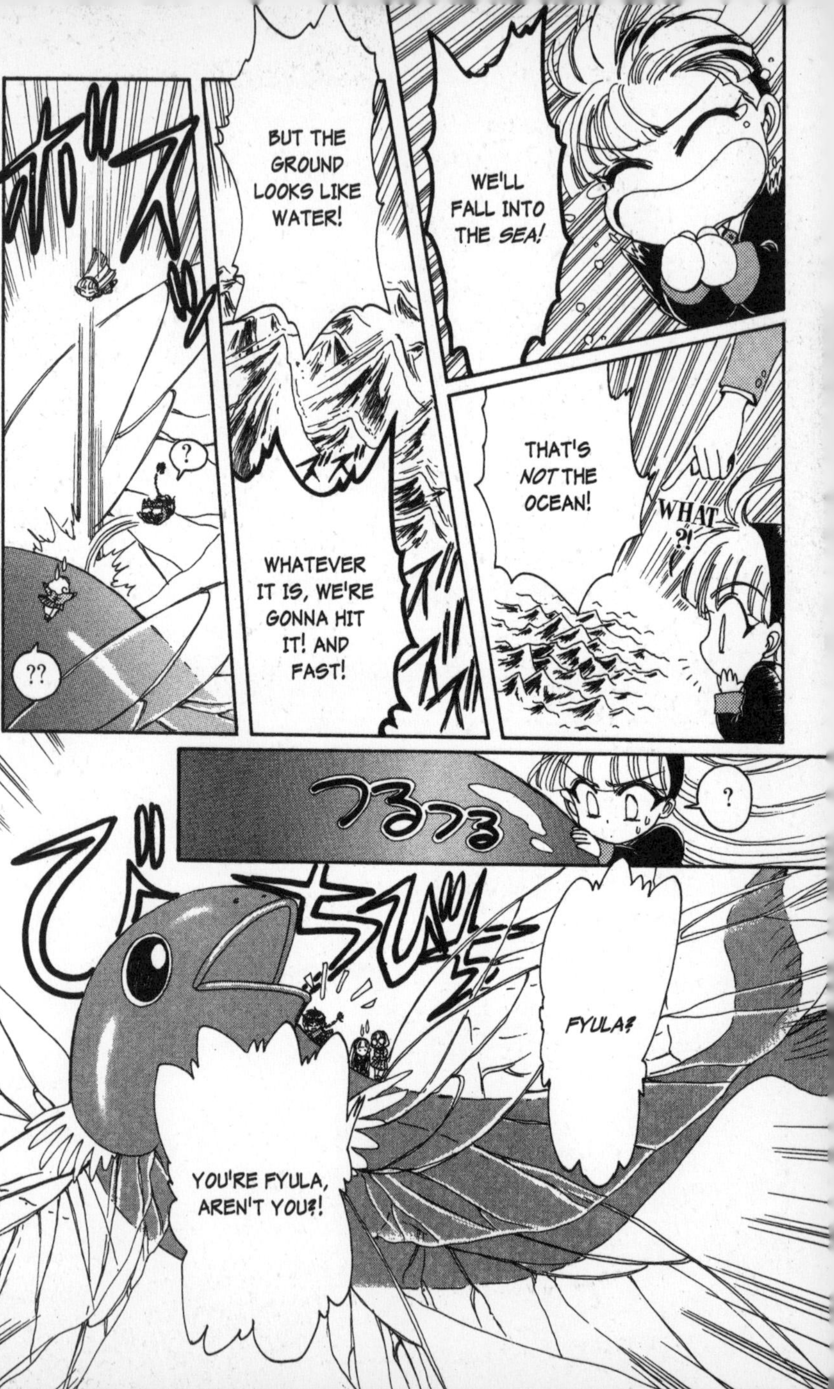
WE'LL FALL INTO THE SEA!
THAT'S NOT THE OCEAN!
WHAT?!
BUT THE GROUND LOOKS LIKE WATER!
WHATEVER IT IS, WE'RE GONNA HIT IT! AND FAST!
?
??
つるつる
?
FYULA?
YOU'RE FYULA, AREN'T YOU?!

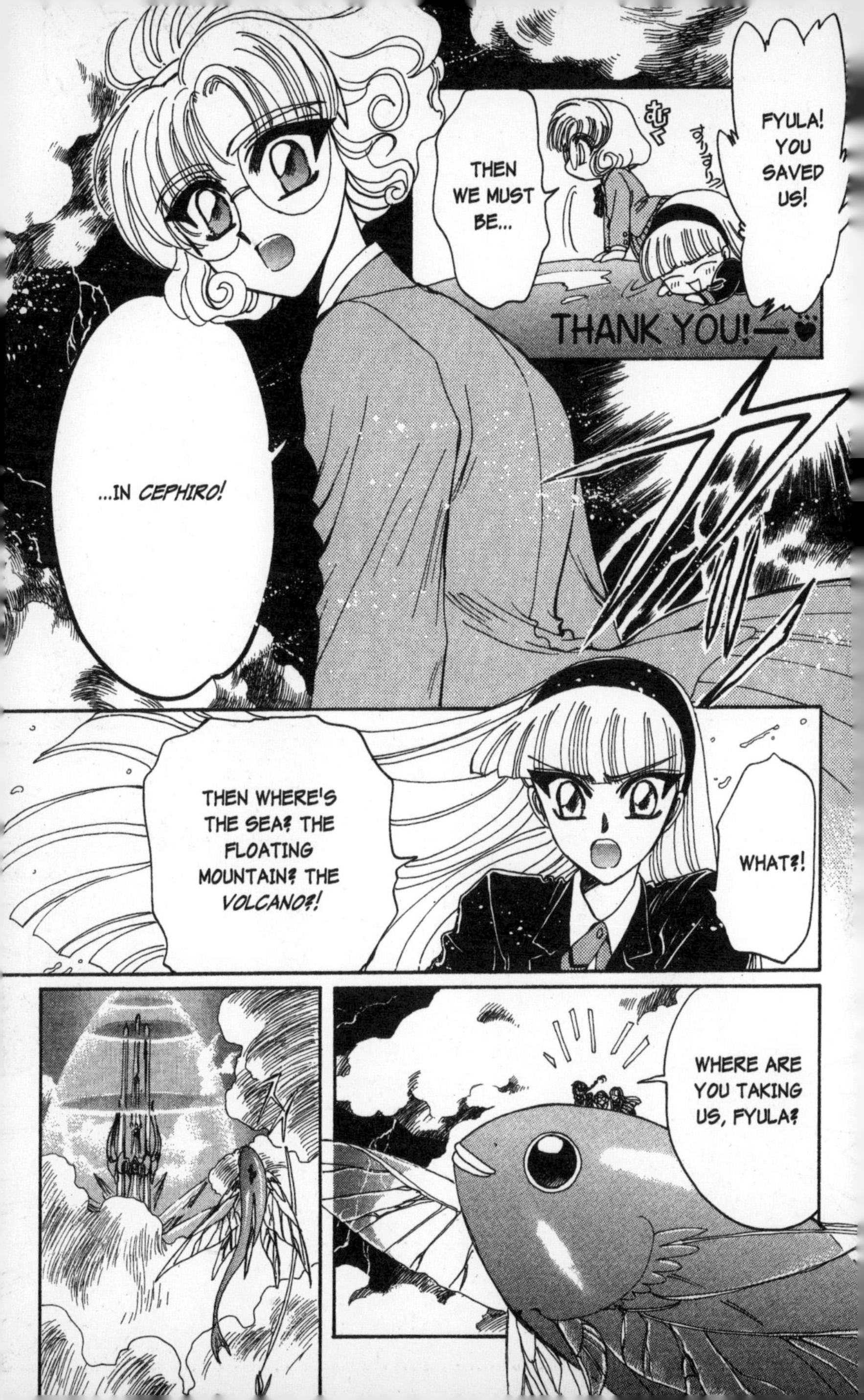
FYULA! YOU SAVED US!
THANK YOU!
THEN WE MUST BE...
...IN CEPHIRO!
WHAT?!
THEN WHERE'S THE SEA? THE FLOATING MOUNTAIN? THE VOLCANO?!
WHERE ARE YOU TAKING US, FYULA?

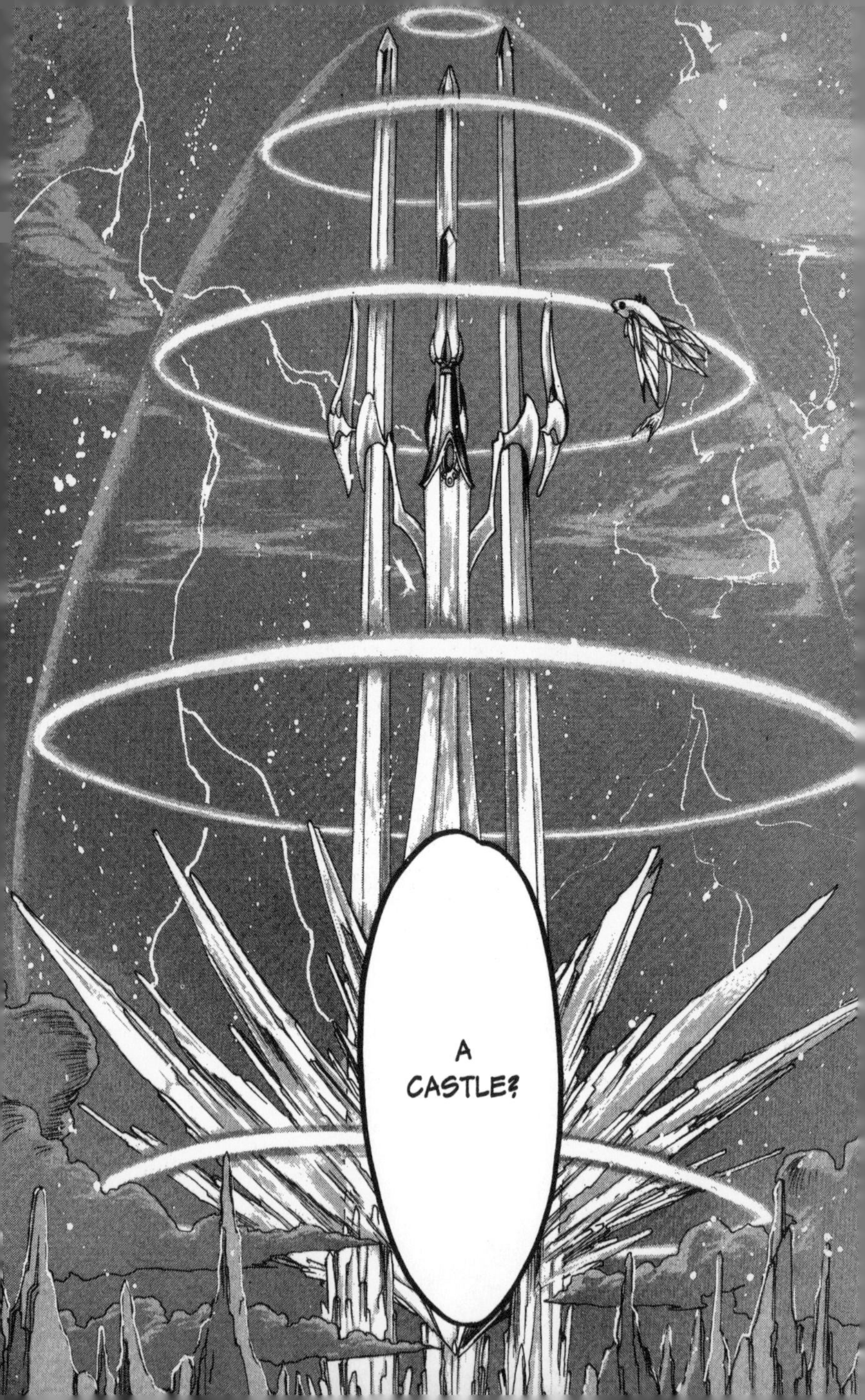
A CASTLE?

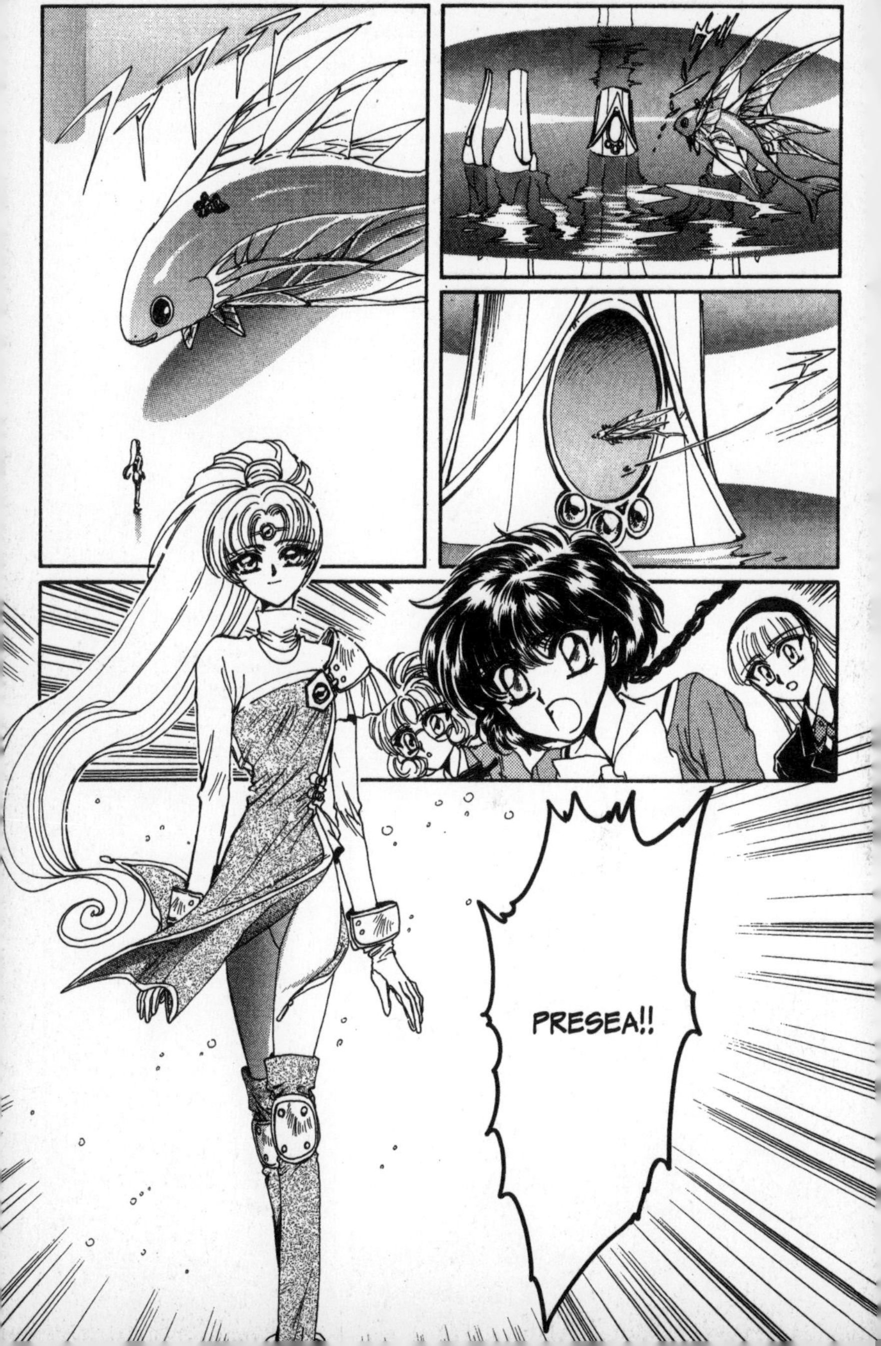
PRESEA!!

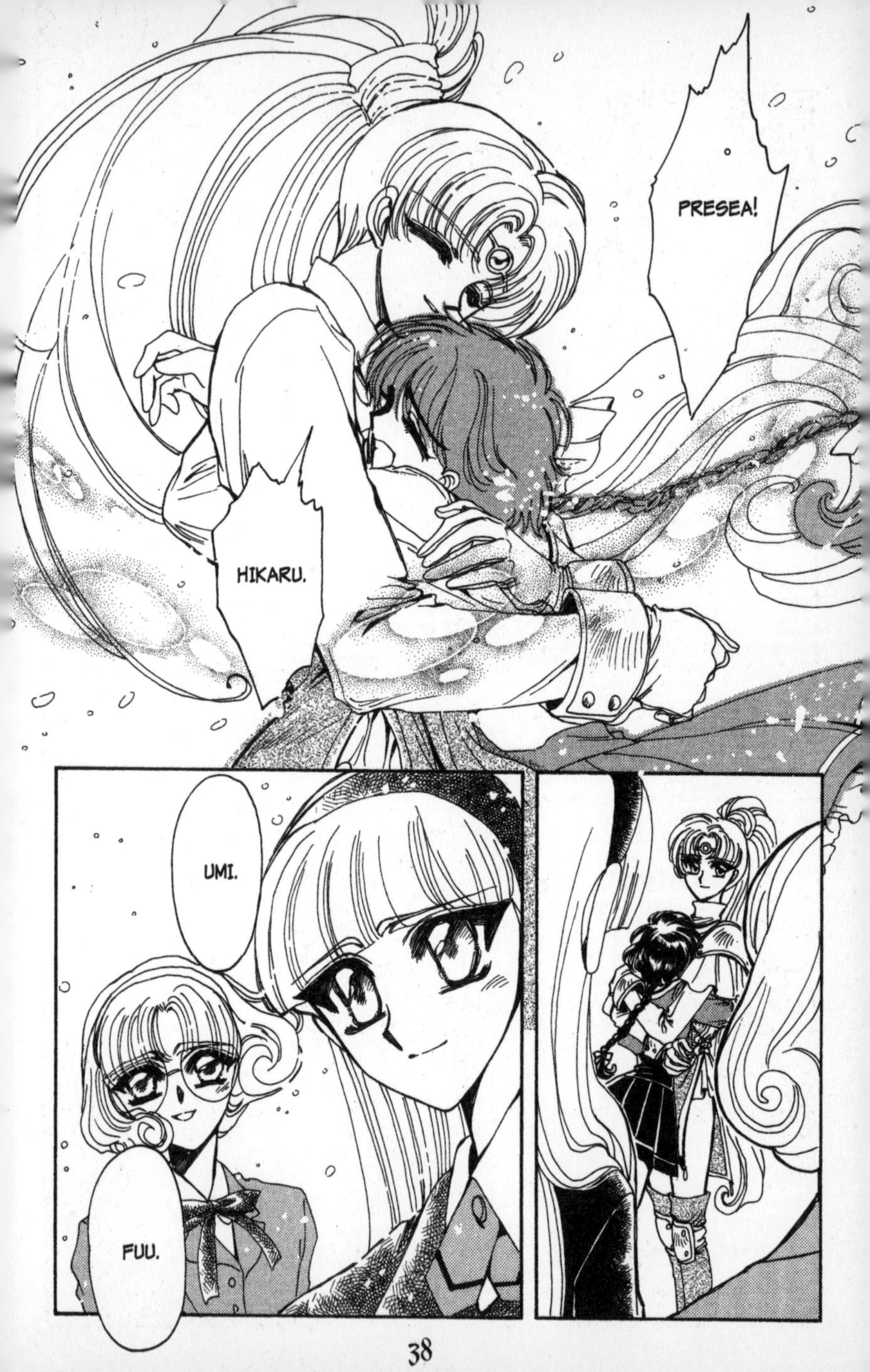
PRESEA!
HIKARU.
UMI.
FUU.

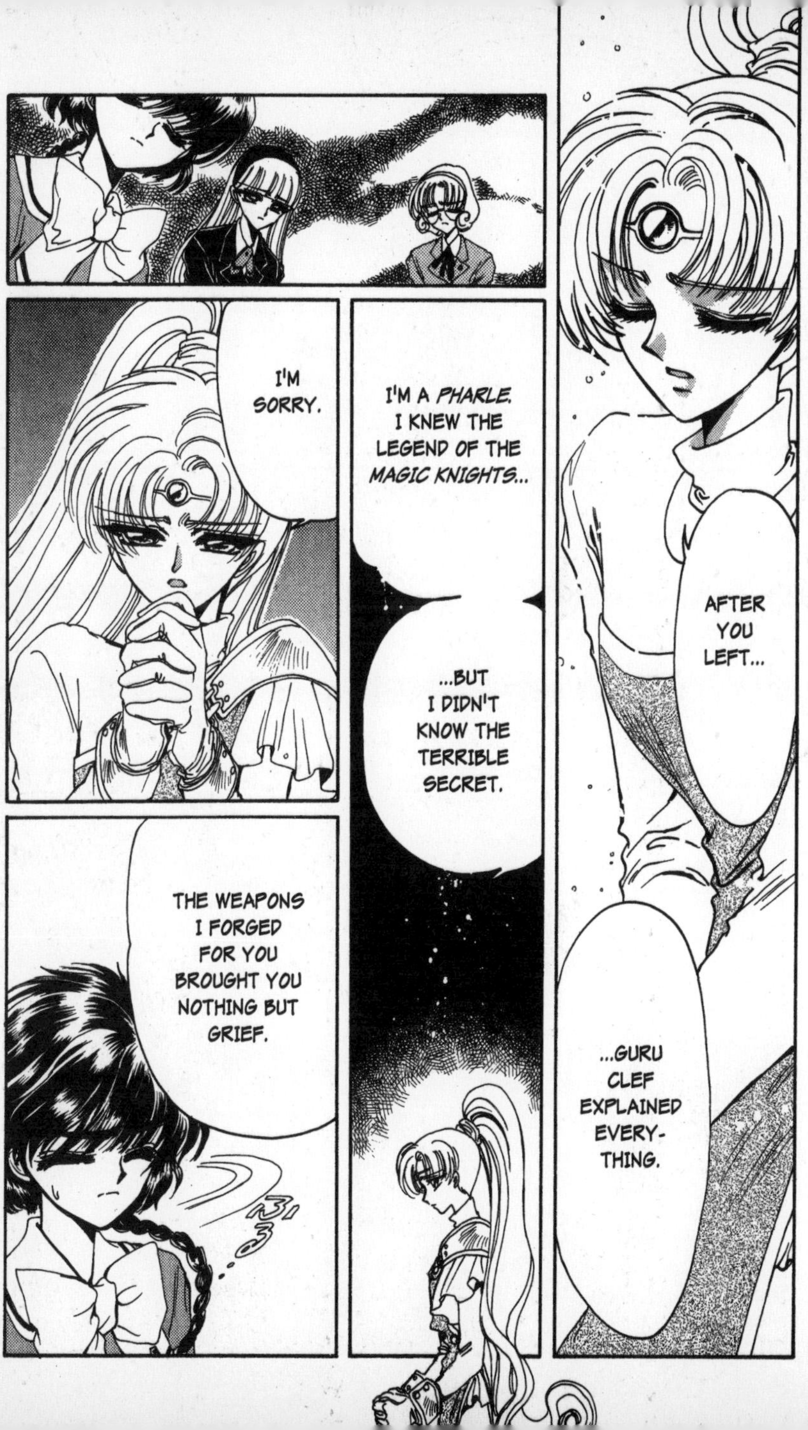
AFTER YOU LEFT...
...GURU CLEF EXPLAINED EVERY-THING.
I'M A *PHARLE.* I KNEW THE LEGEND OF THE *MAGIC KNIGHTS...*
...BUT I DIDN'T KNOW THE TERRIBLE SECRET.
I'M SORRY.
THE WEAPONS I FORGED FOR YOU BROUGHT YOU NOTHING BUT GRIEF.

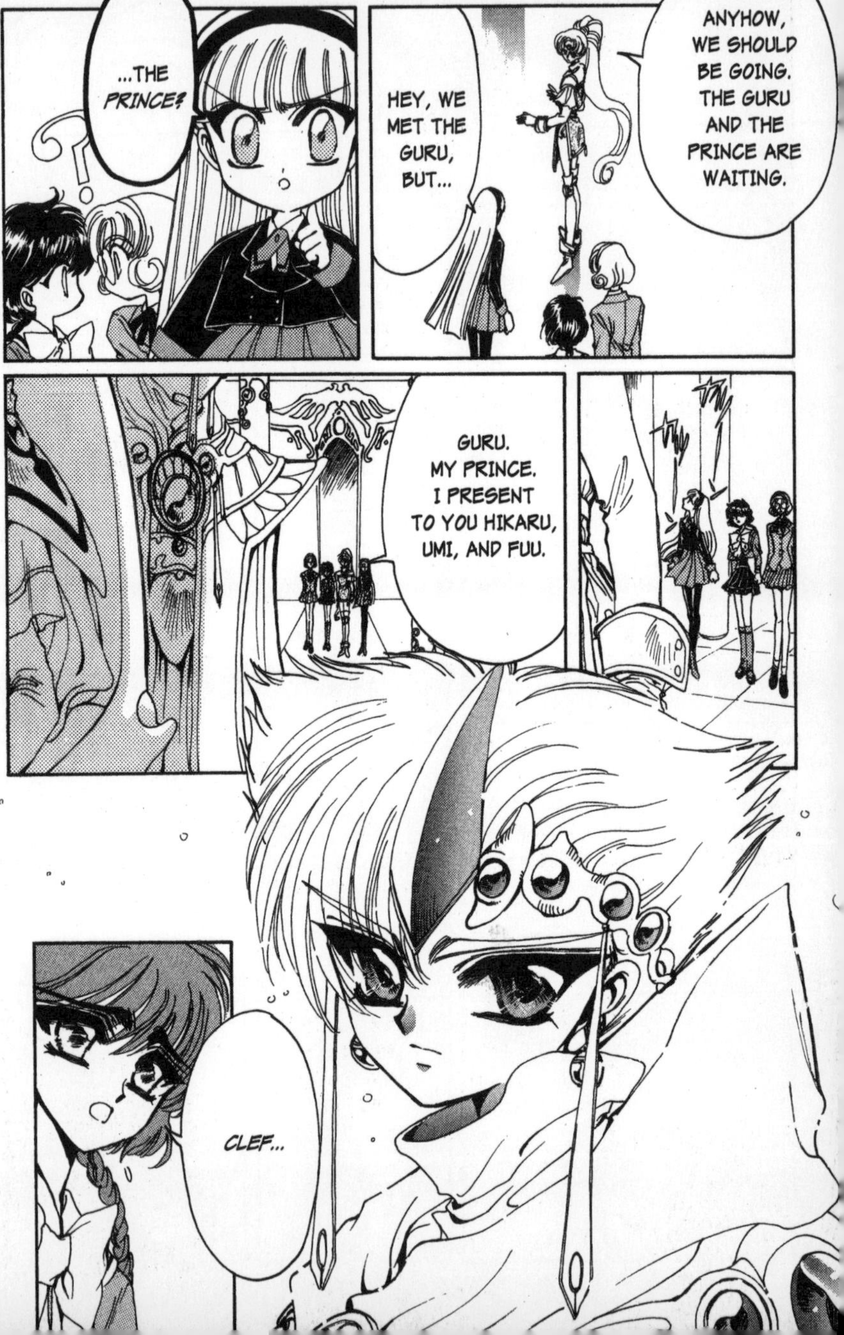
ANYHOW, WE SHOULD BE GOING. THE GURU AND THE PRINCE ARE WAITING.
HEY, WE MET THE GURU, BUT...
...THE PRINCE?
GURU. MY PRINCE. I PRESENT TO YOU HIKARU, UMI, AND FUU.
CLEF...

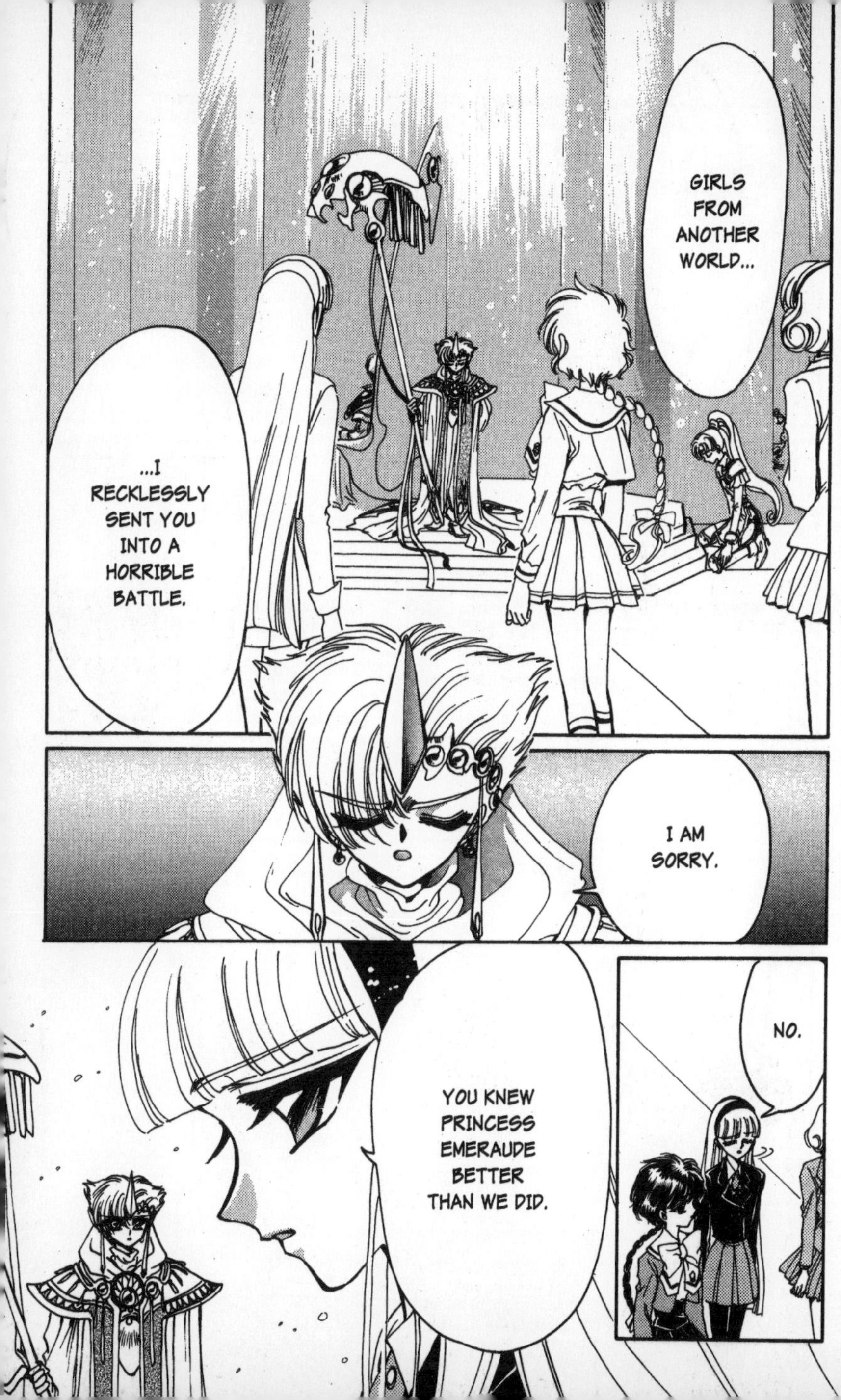
GIRLS FROM ANOTHER WORLD...
...I RECKLESSLY SENT YOU INTO A HORRIBLE BATTLE.
I AM SORRY.
NO.
YOU KNEW PRINCESS EMERAUDE BETTER THAN WE DID.

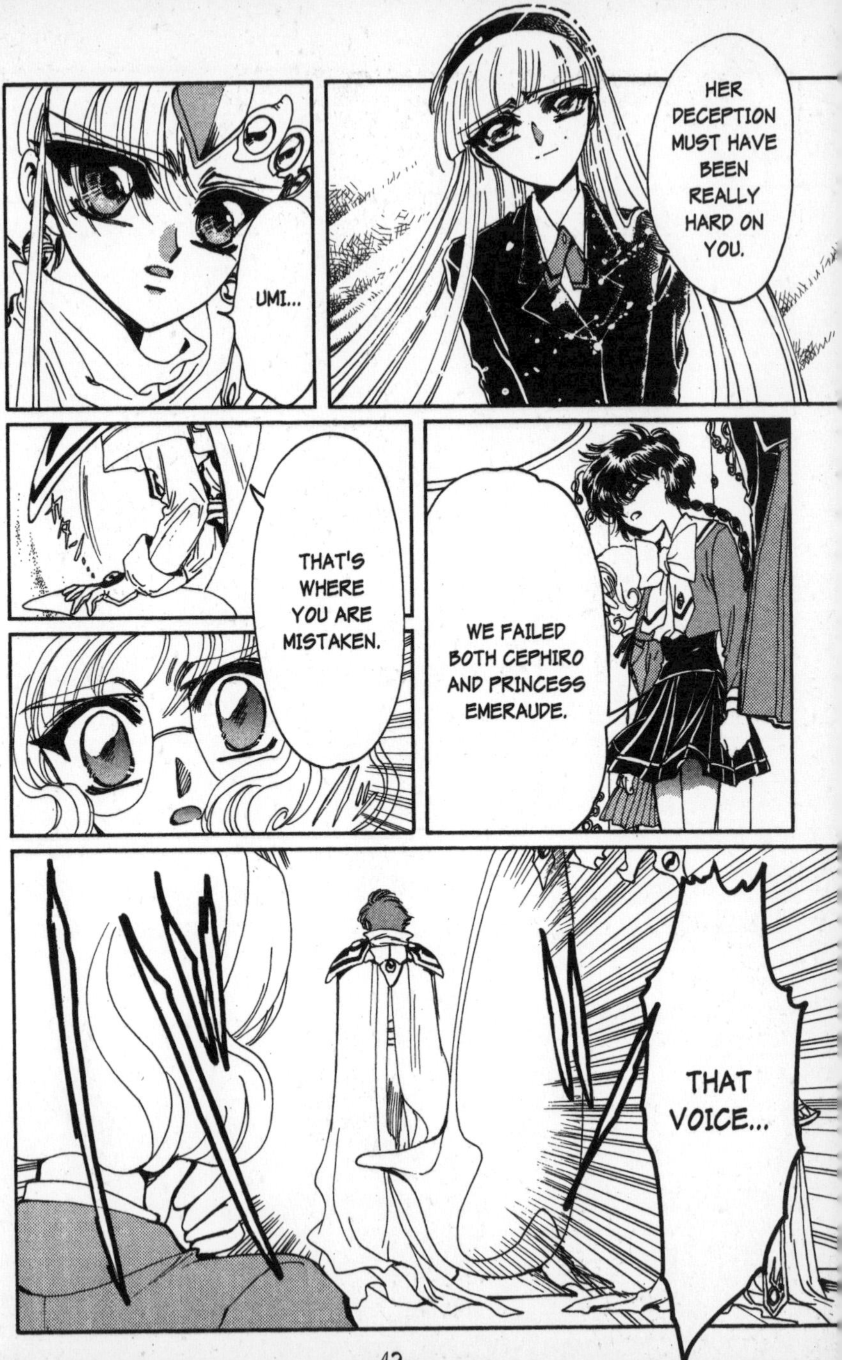
HER DECEPTION MUST HAVE BEEN REALLY HARD ON YOU.
UMI...
WE FAILED BOTH CEPHIRO AND PRINCESS EMERAUDE.
THAT'S WHERE YOU ARE MISTAKEN.
THAT VOICE...

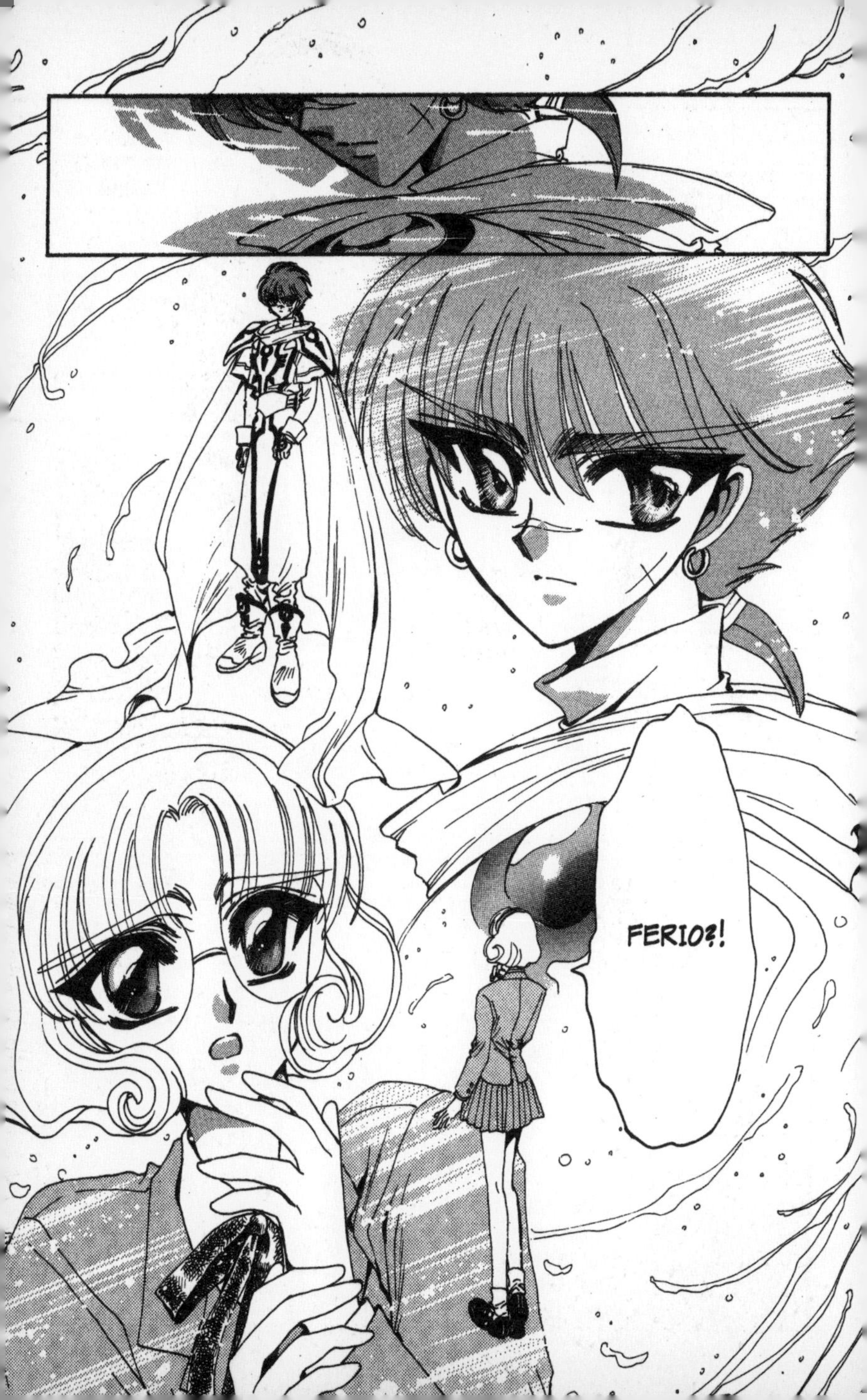
FERIO?!

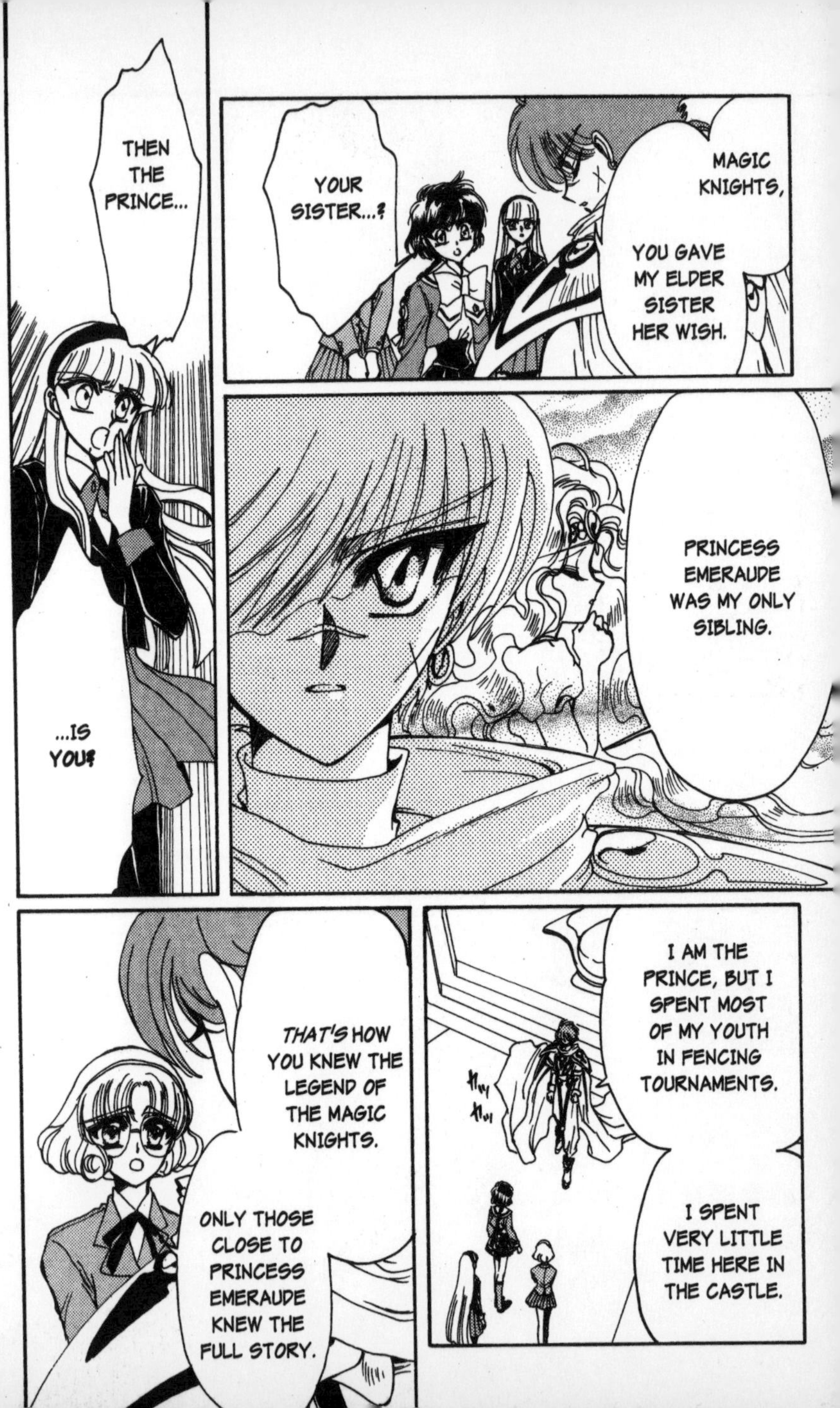
MAGIC KNIGHTS,
YOU GAVE MY ELDER SISTER HER WISH.
YOUR SISTER...?
PRINCESS EMERAUDE WAS MY ONLY SIBLING.
THEN THE PRINCE...
...IS YOU?
I AM THE PRINCE, BUT I SPENT MOST OF MY YOUTH IN FENCING TOURNAMENTS.
I SPENT VERY LITTLE TIME HERE IN THE CASTLE.
THAT'S HOW YOU KNEW THE LEGEND OF THE MAGIC KNIGHTS.
ONLY THOSE CLOSE TO PRINCESS EMERAUDE KNEW THE FULL STORY.

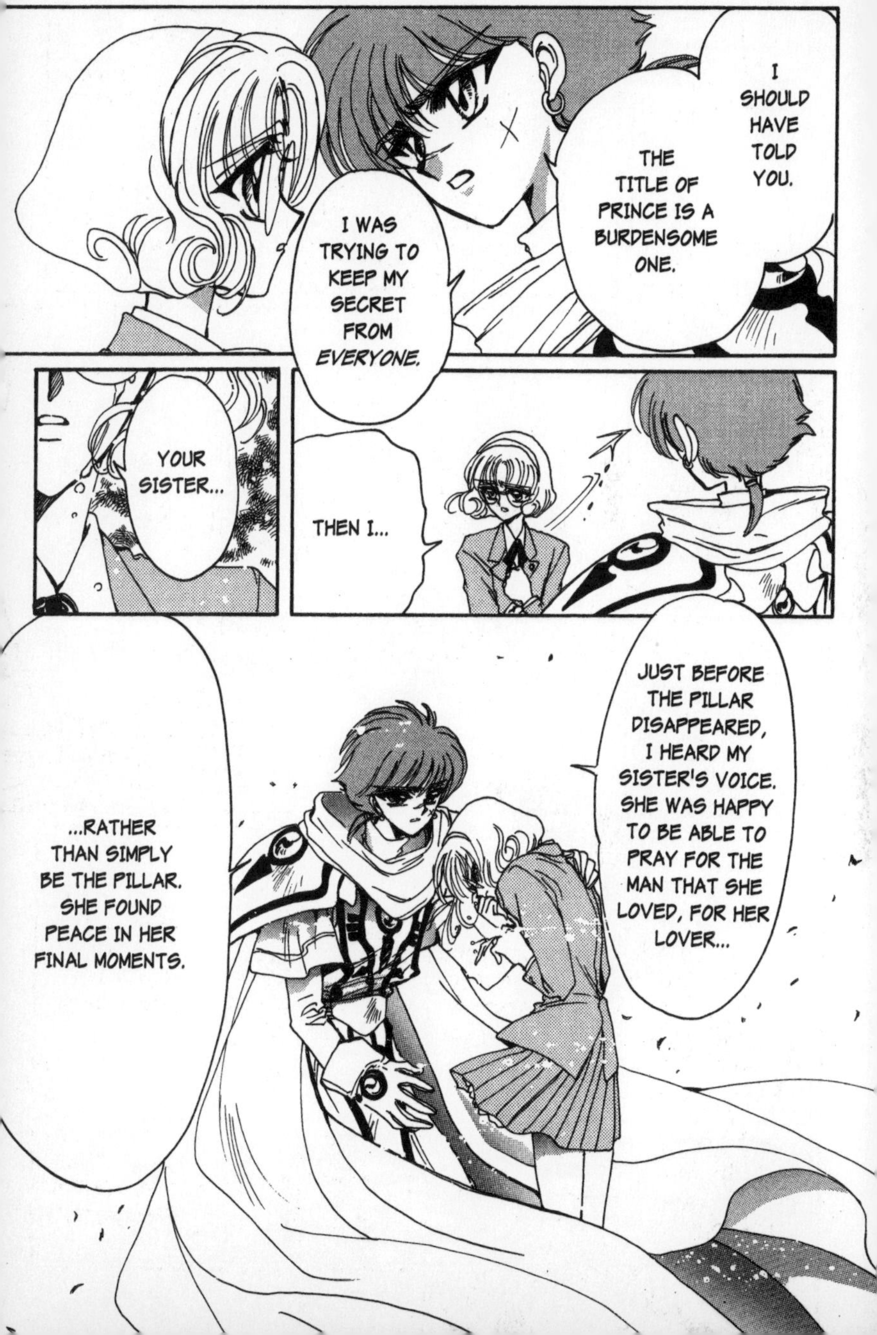
I SHOULD HAVE TOLD YOU.
THE TITLE OF PRINCE IS A BURDENSOME ONE.
I WAS TRYING TO KEEP MY SECRET FROM *EVERYONE.*
THEN I...
YOUR SISTER...
JUST BEFORE THE PILLAR DISAPPEARED, I HEARD MY SISTER'S VOICE. SHE WAS HAPPY TO BE ABLE TO PRAY FOR THE MAN THAT SHE LOVED, FOR HER LOVER...
...RATHER THAN SIMPLY BE THE PILLAR. SHE FOUND PEACE IN HER FINAL MOMENTS.

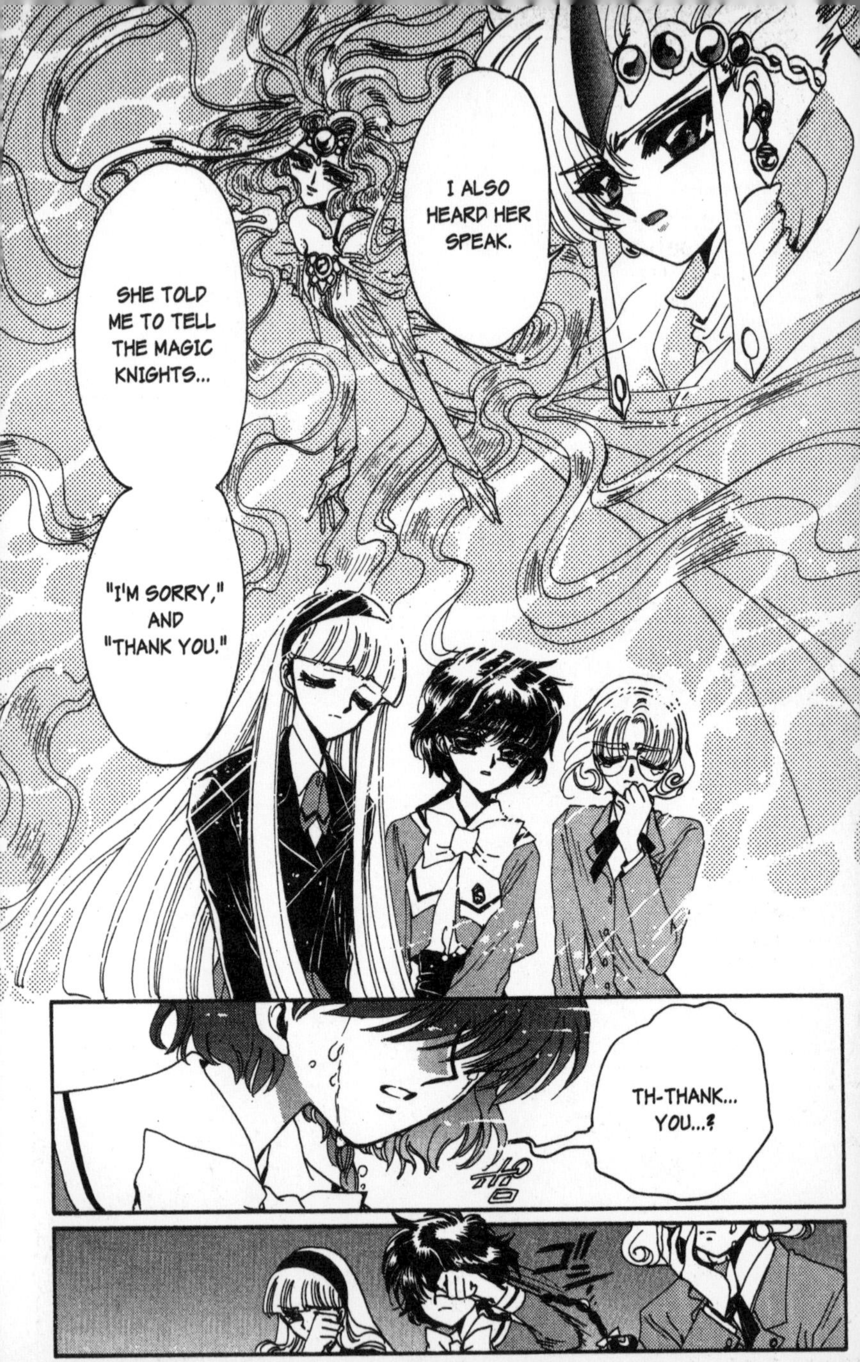
I ALSO HEARD HER SPEAK.
SHE TOLD ME TO TELL THE MAGIC KNIGHTS...
"I'M SORRY," AND "THANK YOU."
TH-THANK... YOU...?

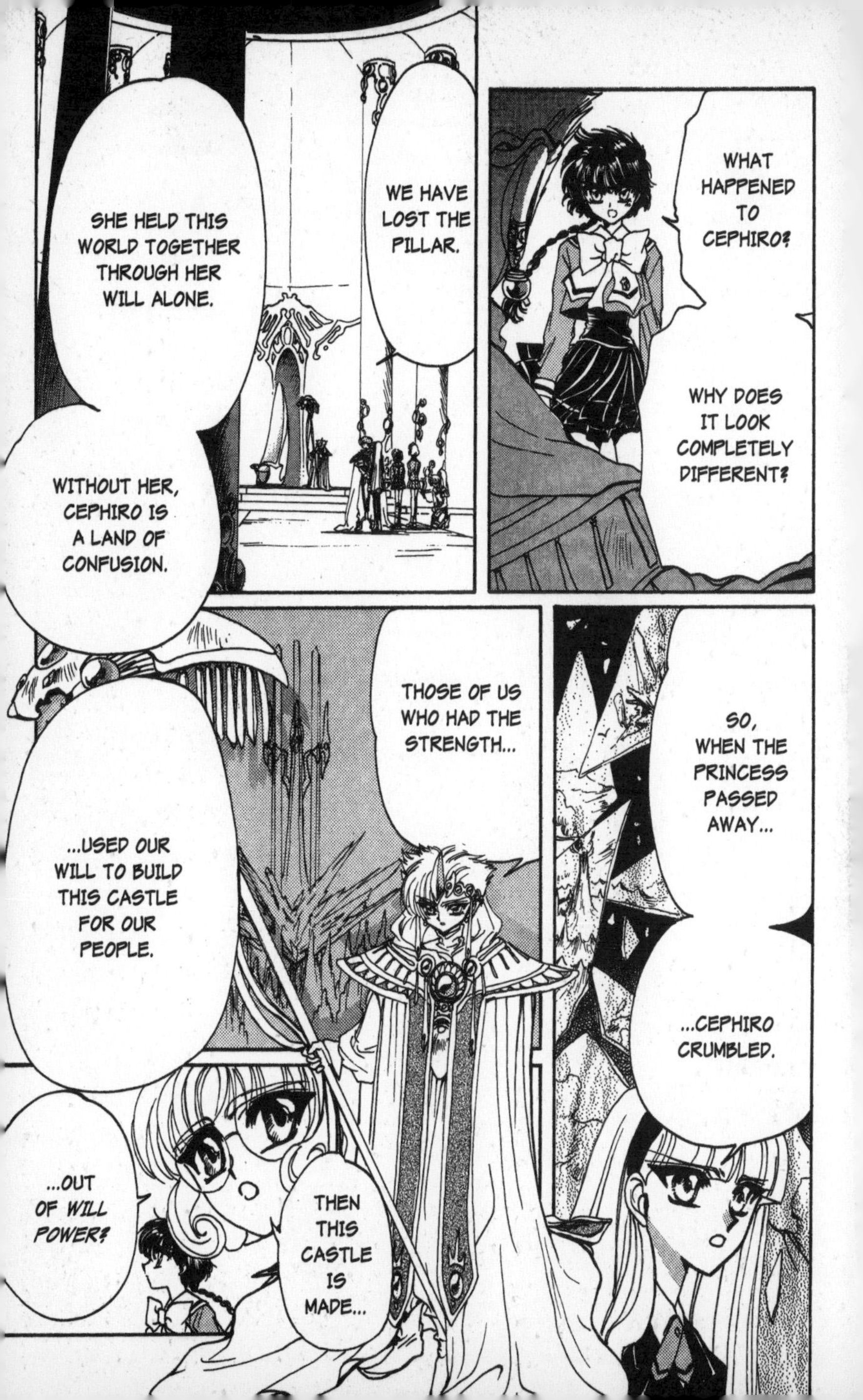
WHAT HAPPENED TO CEPHIRO?
WHY DOES IT LOOK COMPLETELY DIFFERENT?
WE HAVE LOST THE PILLAR.
SHE HELD THIS WORLD TOGETHER THROUGH HER WILL ALONE.
WITHOUT HER, CEPHIRO IS A LAND OF CONFUSION.
SO, WHEN THE PRINCESS PASSED AWAY...
...CEPHIRO CRUMBLED.
THOSE OF US WHO HAD THE STRENGTH...
...USED OUR WILL TO BUILD THIS CASTLE FOR OUR PEOPLE.
THEN THIS CASTLE IS MADE...
...OUT OF WILL POWER?

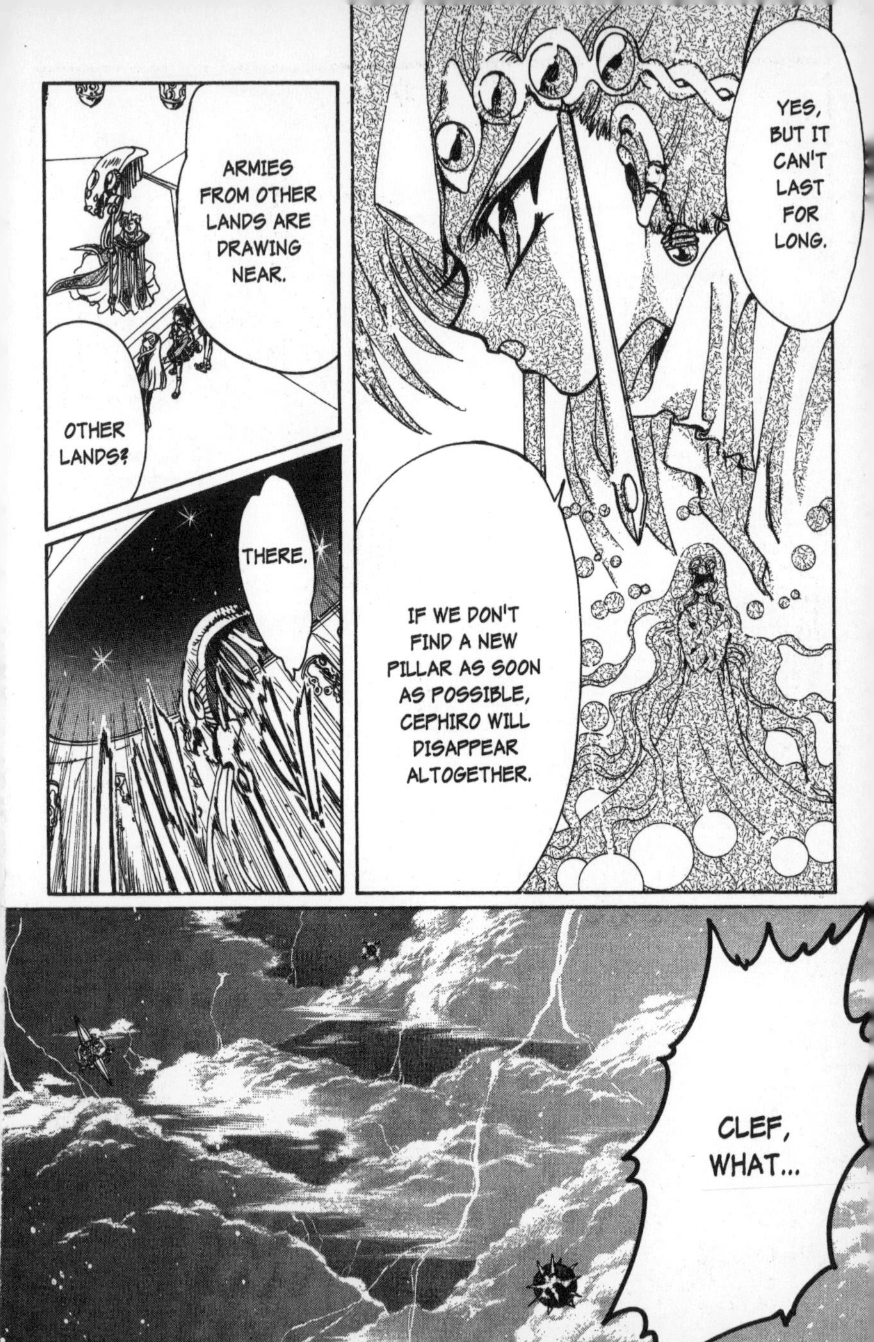
YES, BUT IT CAN'T LAST FOR LONG.
IF WE DON'T FIND A NEW PILLAR AS SOON AS POSSIBLE, CEPHIRO WILL DISAPPEAR ALTOGETHER.
ARMIES FROM OTHER LANDS ARE DRAWING NEAR.
OTHER LANDS?
THERE.
CLEF, WHAT...

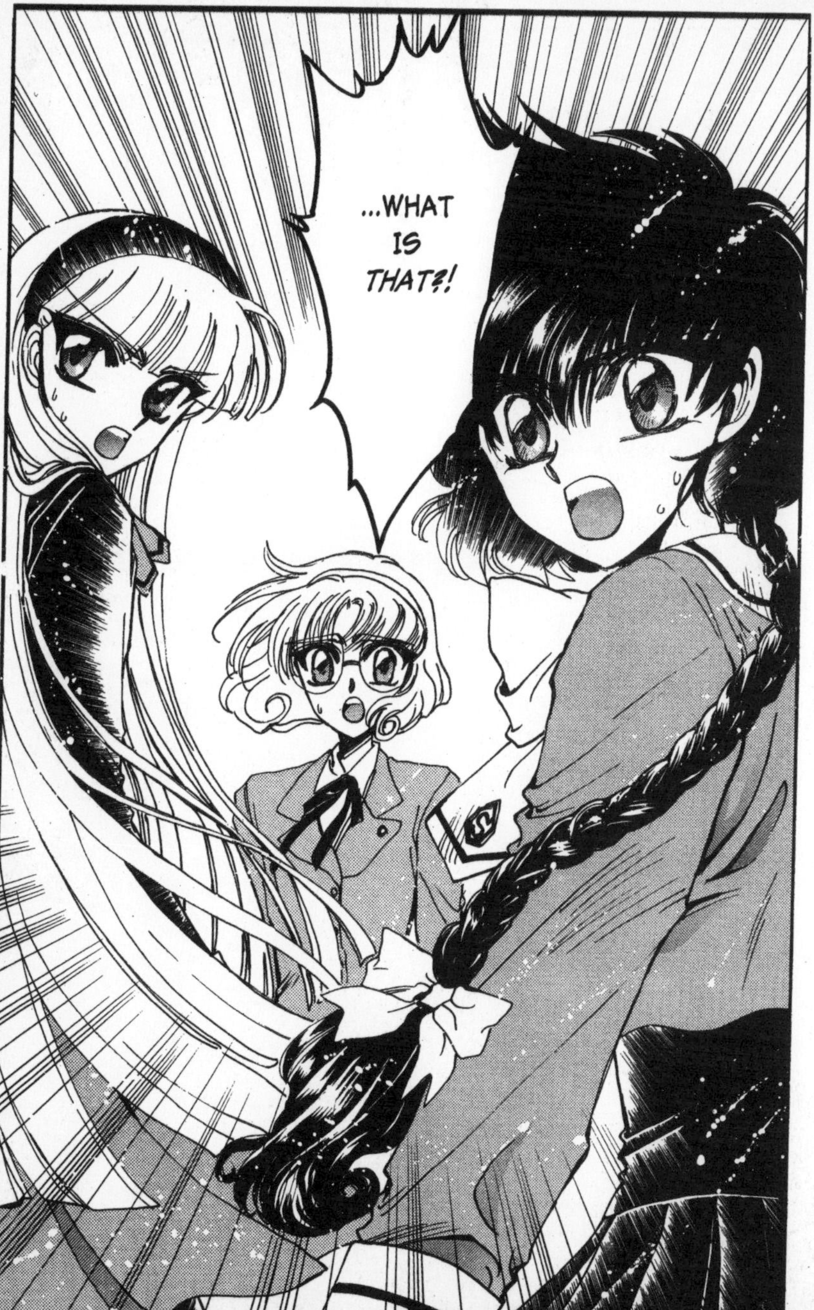
...WHAT IS THAT?!

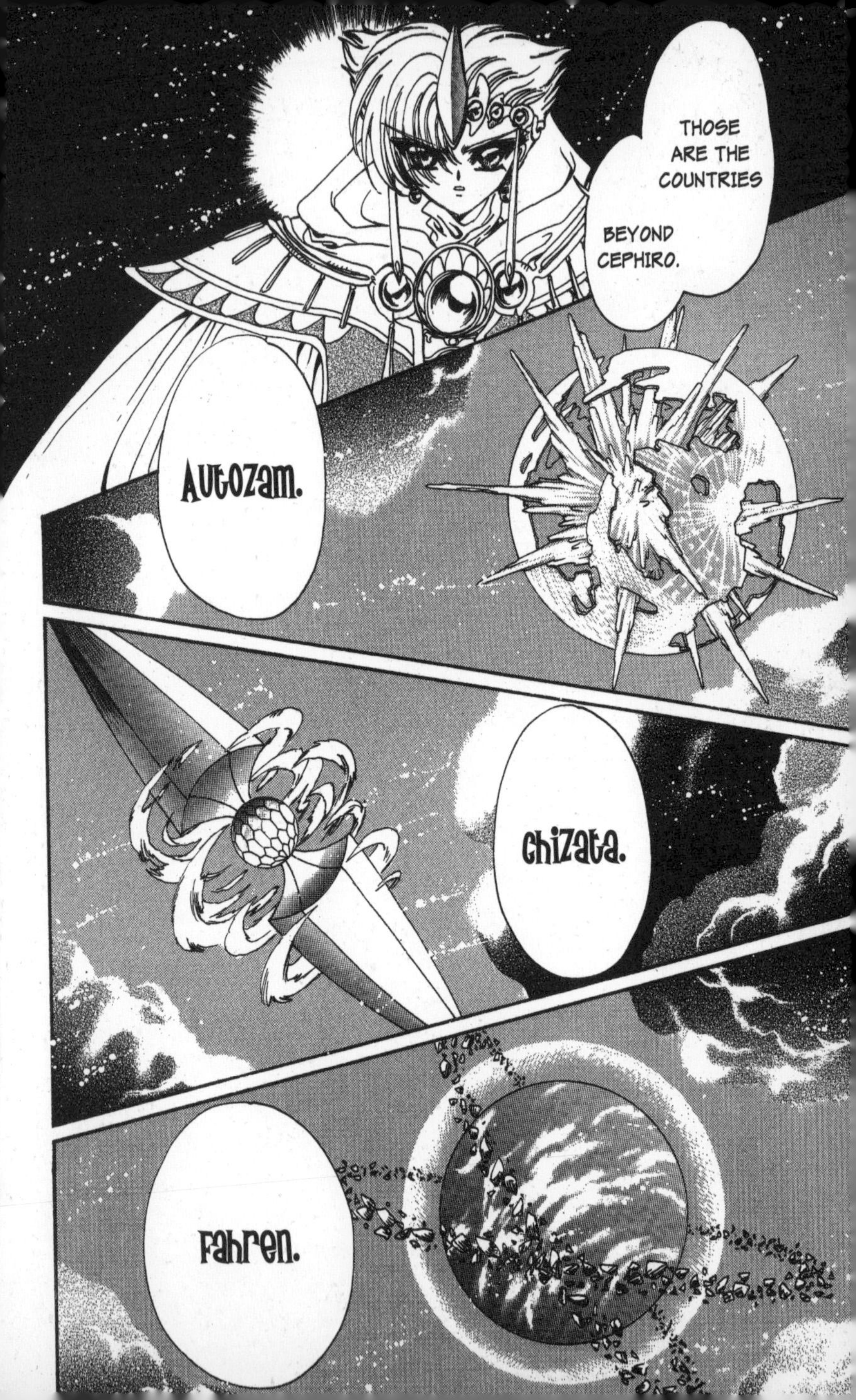
THOSE ARE THE COUNTRIES
BEYOND CEPHIRO.
Autozam.
Chizata.
Fahren.

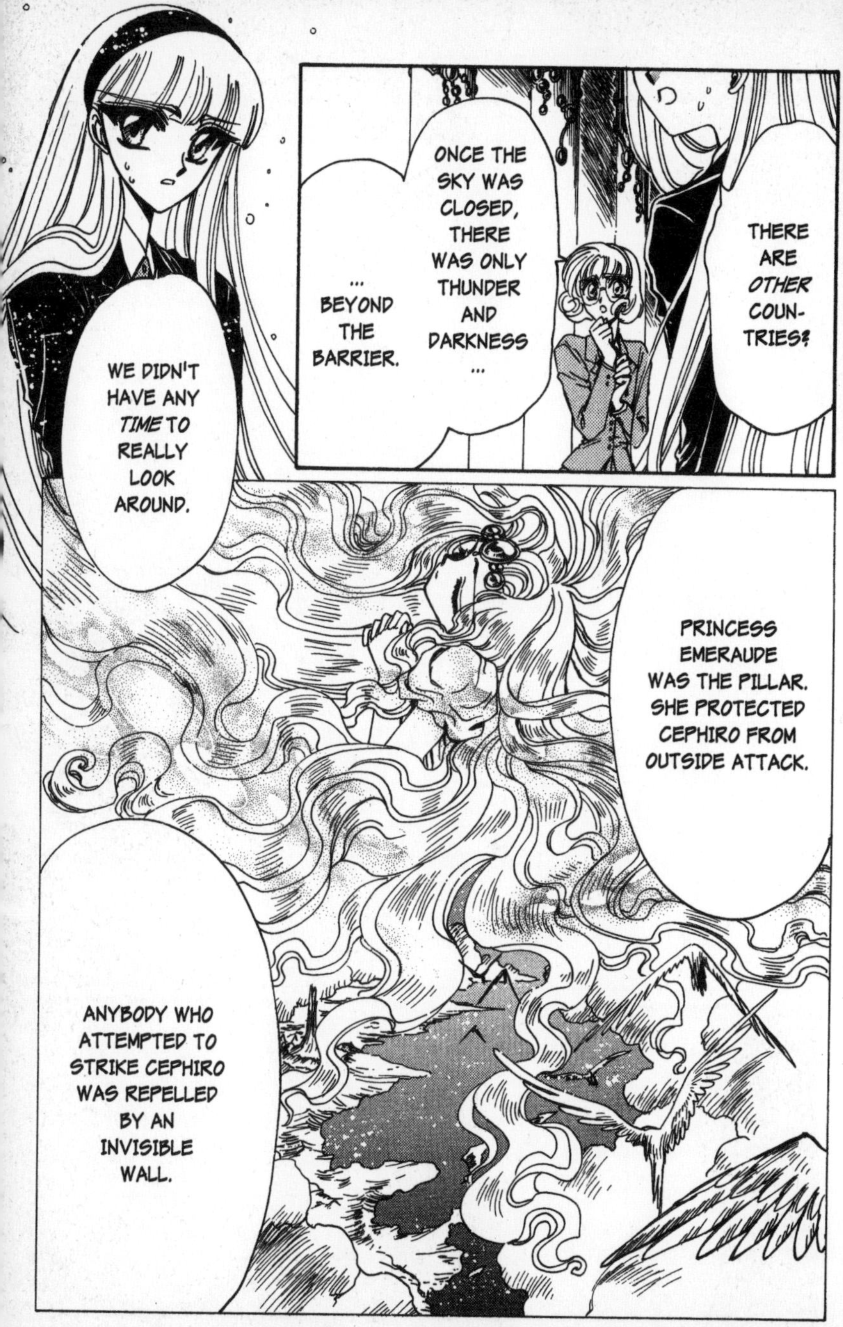
THERE ARE OTHER COUNTRIES?
ONCE THE SKY WAS CLOSED, THERE WAS ONLY THUNDER AND DARKNESS ...
... BEYOND THE BARRIER.
WE DIDN'T HAVE ANY TIME TO REALLY LOOK AROUND.
PRINCESS EMERAUDE WAS THE PILLAR. SHE PROTECTED CEPHIRO FROM OUTSIDE ATTACK.
ANYBODY WHO ATTEMPTED TO STRIKE CEPHIRO WAS REPELLED BY AN INVISIBLE WALL.

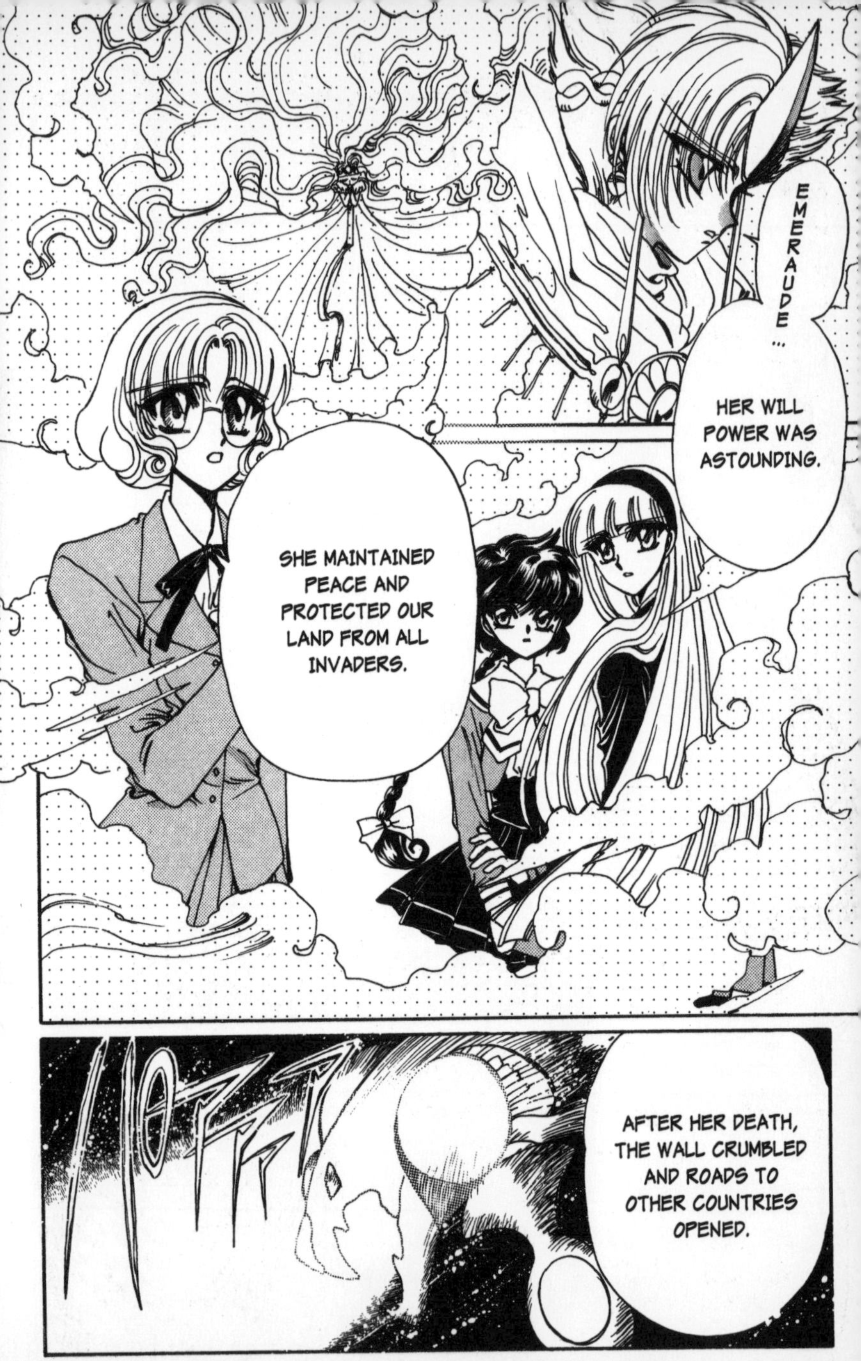
EMERAUDE...
HER WILL POWER WAS ASTOUNDING.
SHE MAINTAINED PEACE AND PROTECTED OUR LAND FROM ALL INVADERS.
AFTER HER DEATH, THE WALL CRUMBLED AND ROADS TO OTHER COUNTRIES OPENED.

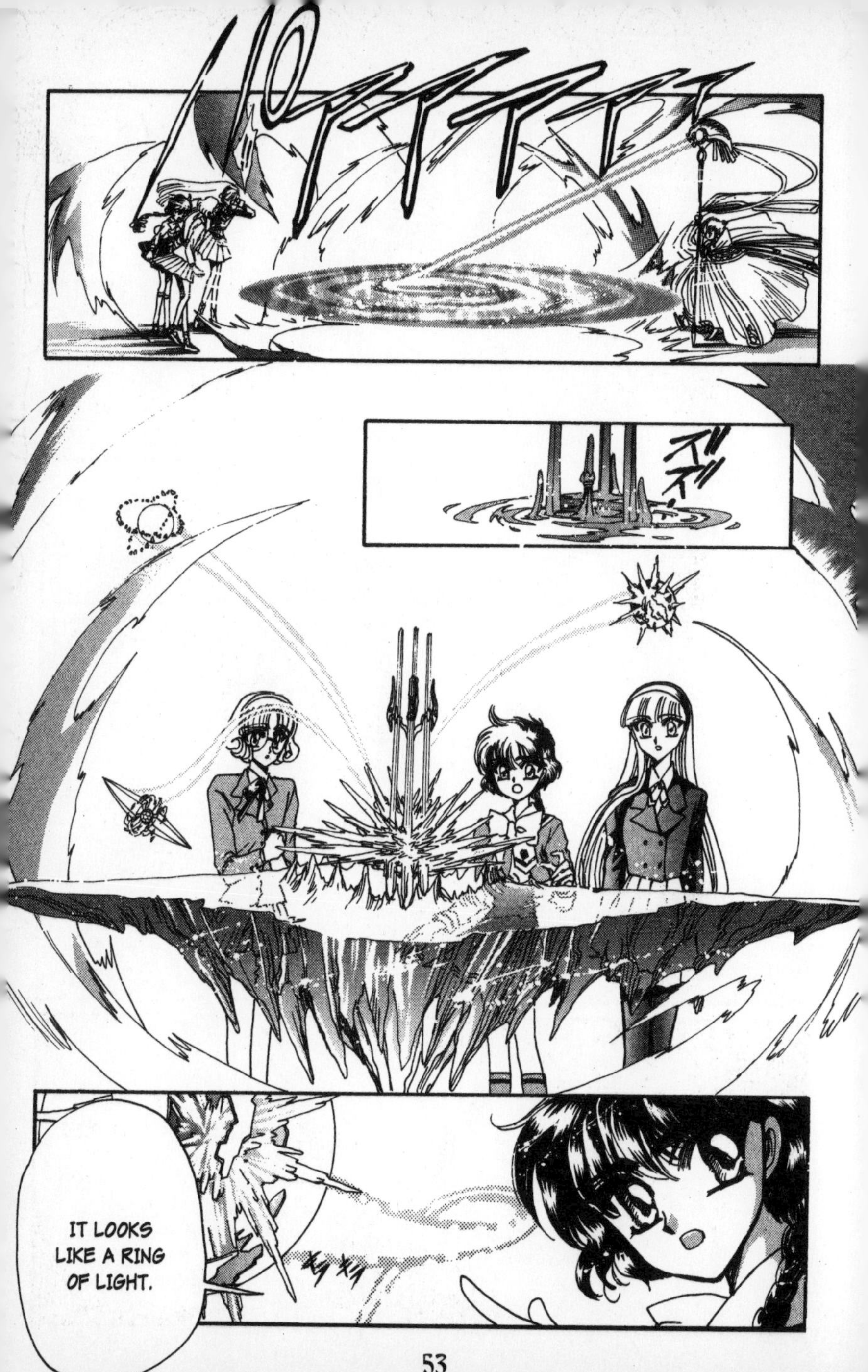
IT LOOKS LIKE A RING OF LIGHT.

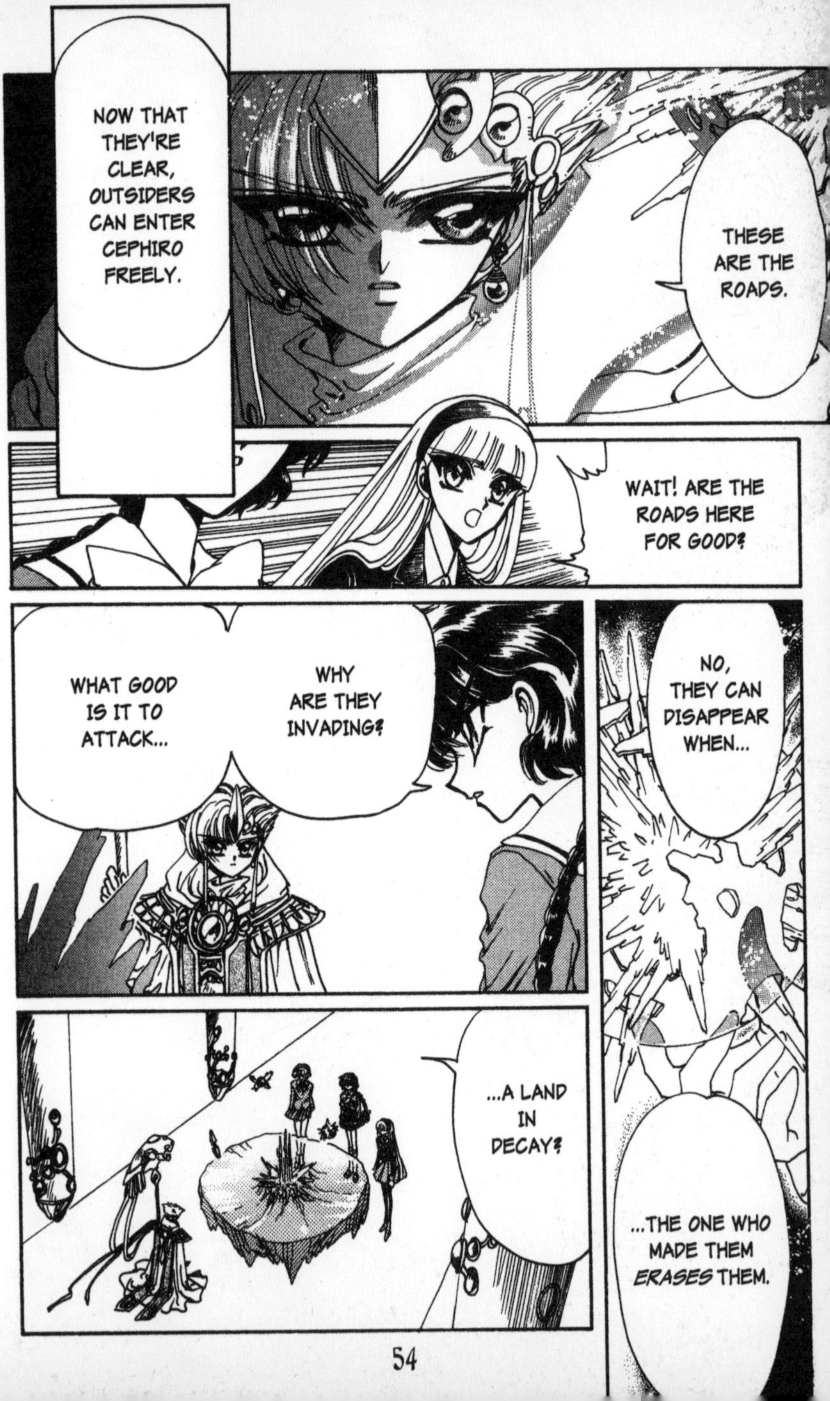
THESE ARE THE ROADS.
NOW THAT THEY'RE CLEAR, OUTSIDERS CAN ENTER CEPHIRO FREELY.
WAIT! ARE THE ROADS HERE FOR GOOD?
NO, THEY CAN DISAPPEAR WHEN...
...THE ONE WHO MADE THEM *ERASES* THEM.
WHY ARE THEY INVADING?
WHAT GOOD IS IT TO ATTACK...
...A LAND IN DECAY?

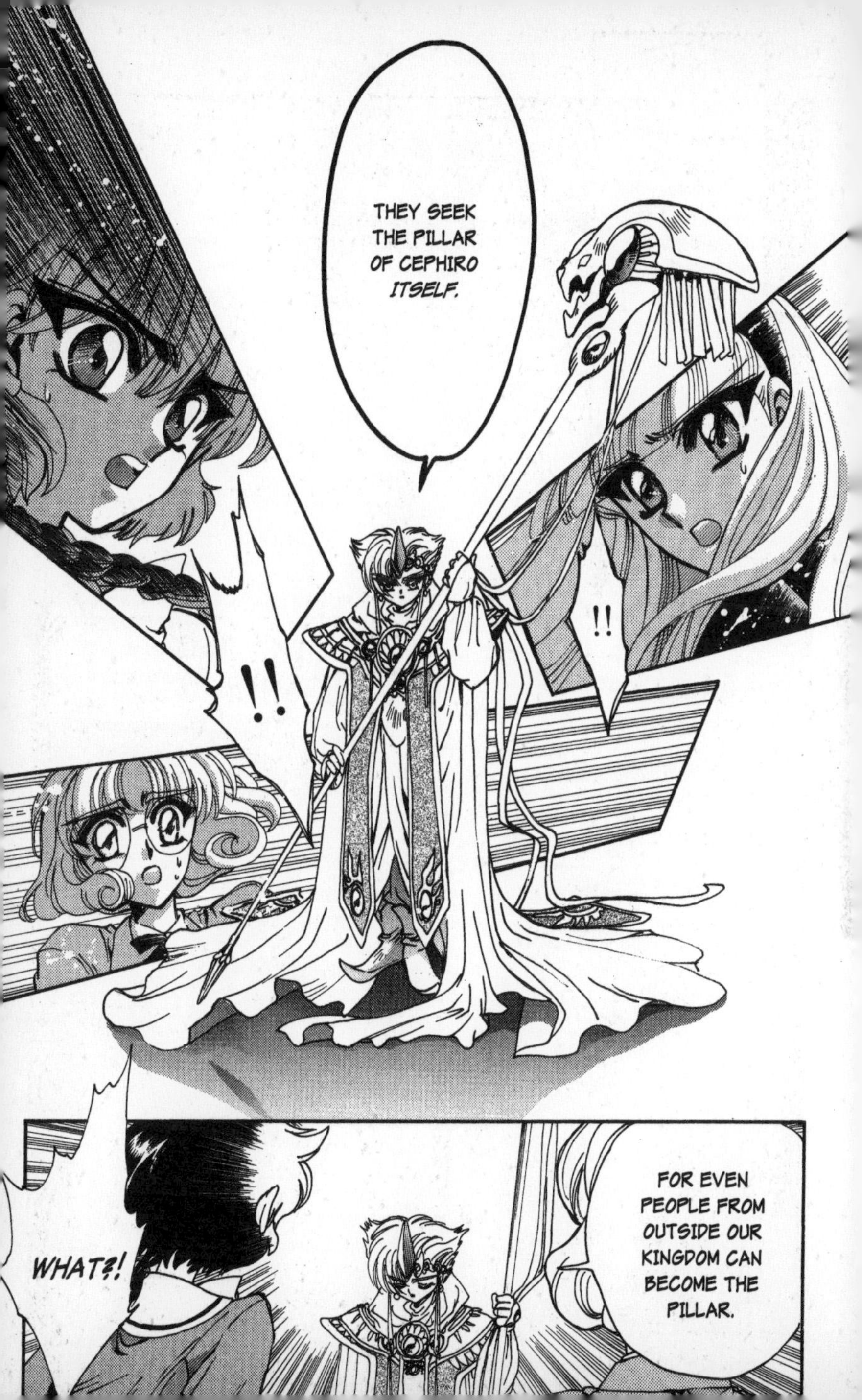
THEY SEEK THE PILLAR OF CEPHIRO *ITSELF.*
!!
!!
FOR EVEN PEOPLE FROM OUTSIDE OUR KINGDOM CAN BECOME THE PILLAR.
WHAT?!

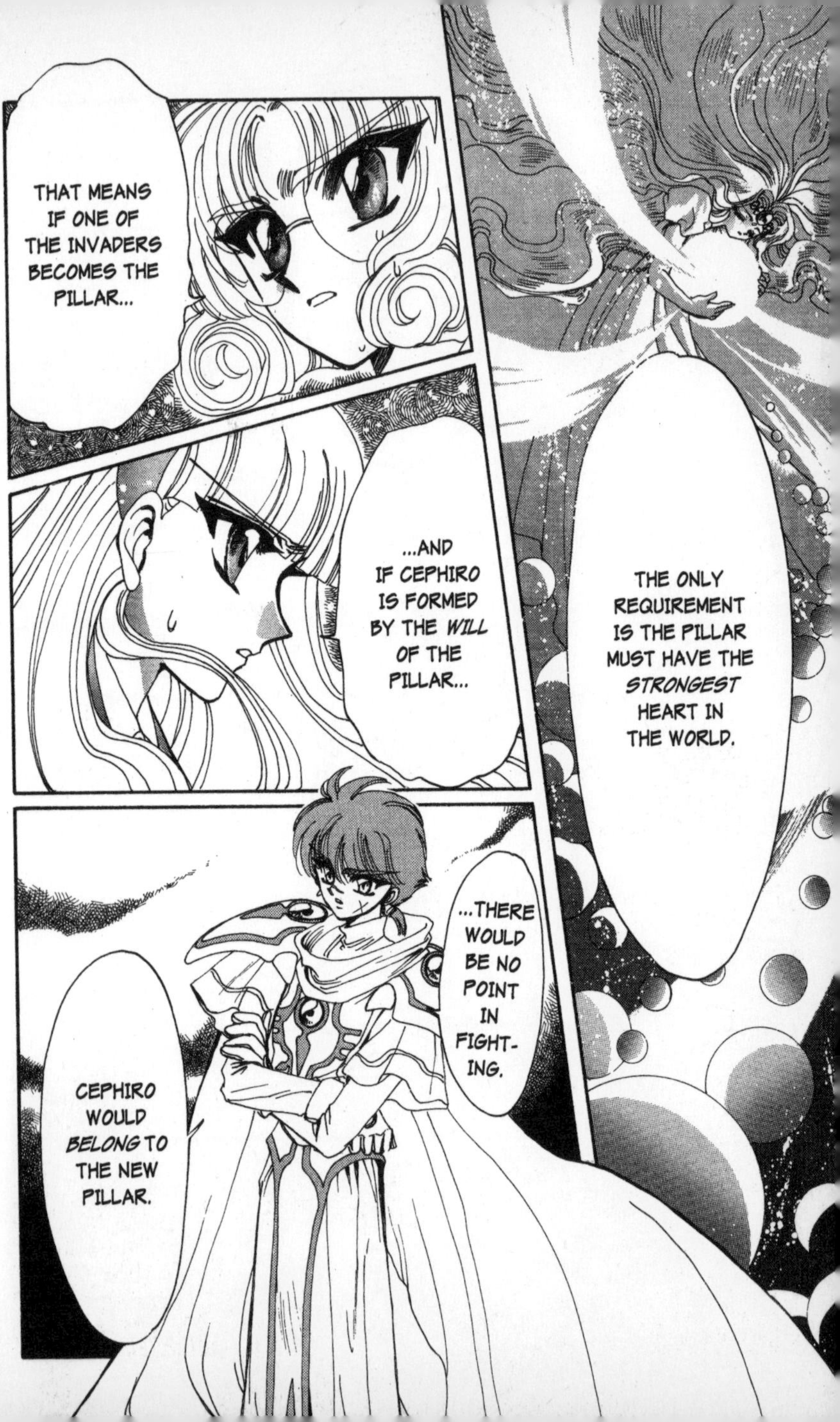
THE ONLY REQUIREMENT IS THE PILLAR MUST HAVE THE *STRONGEST* HEART IN THE WORLD.
THAT MEANS IF ONE OF THE INVADERS BECOMES THE PILLAR...
...AND IF CEPHIRO IS FORMED BY THE *WILL* OF THE PILLAR...
CEPHIRO WOULD *BELONG* TO THE NEW PILLAR.
...THERE WOULD BE NO POINT IN FIGHT-ING.

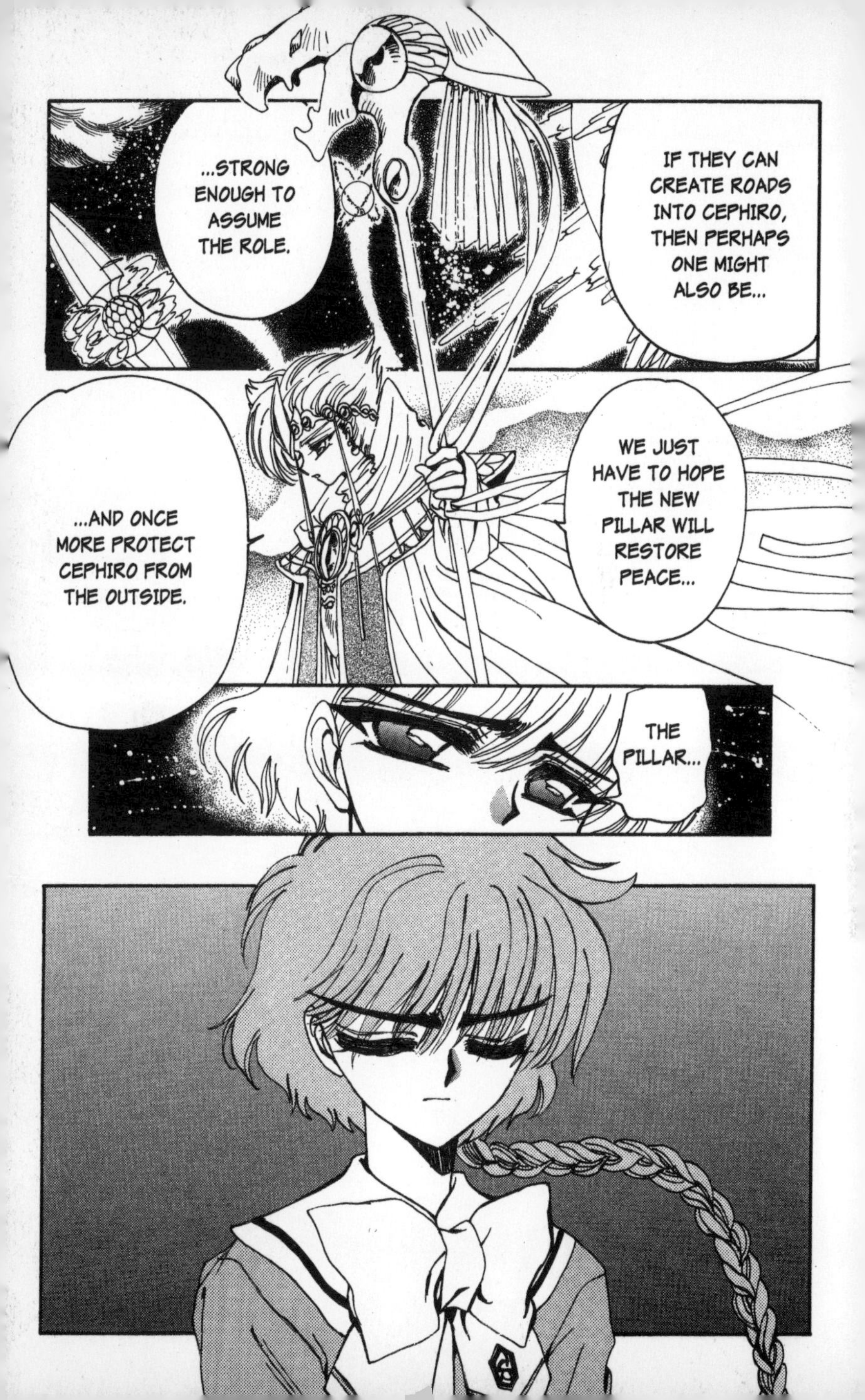
IF THEY CAN CREATE ROADS INTO CEPHIRO, THEN PERHAPS ONE MIGHT ALSO BE...
...STRONG ENOUGH TO ASSUME THE ROLE.
WE JUST HAVE TO HOPE THE NEW PILLAR WILL RESTORE PEACE...
...AND ONCE MORE PROTECT CEPHIRO FROM THE OUTSIDE.
THE PILLAR...

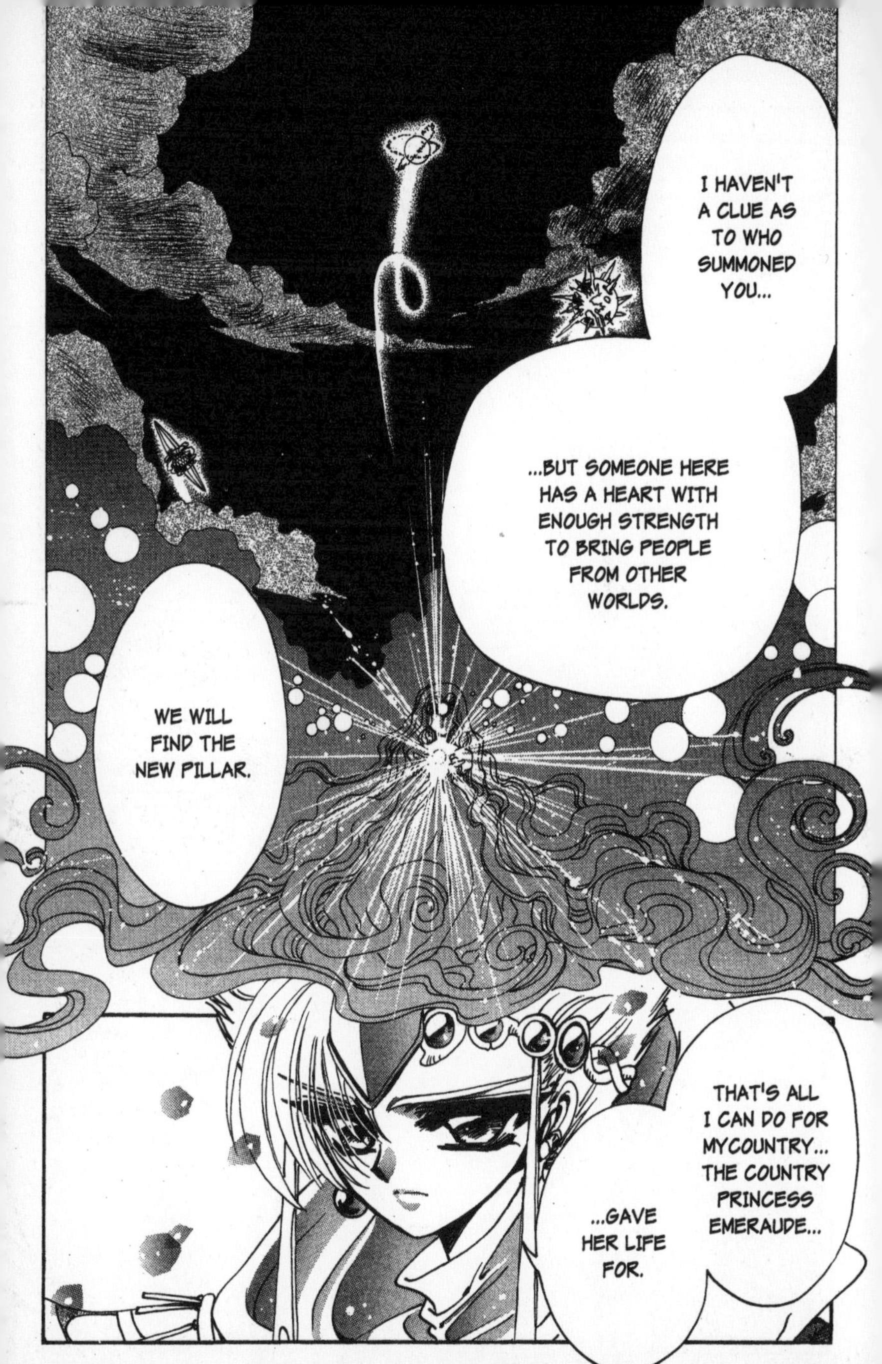
I HAVEN'T A CLUE AS TO WHO SUMMONED YOU...
...BUT SOMEONE HERE HAS A HEART WITH ENOUGH STRENGTH TO BRING PEOPLE FROM OTHER WORLDS.
WE WILL FIND THE NEW PILLAR.
THAT'S ALL I CAN DO FOR MYCOUNTRY... THE COUNTRY PRINCESS EMERAUDE...
...GAVE HER LIFE FOR.

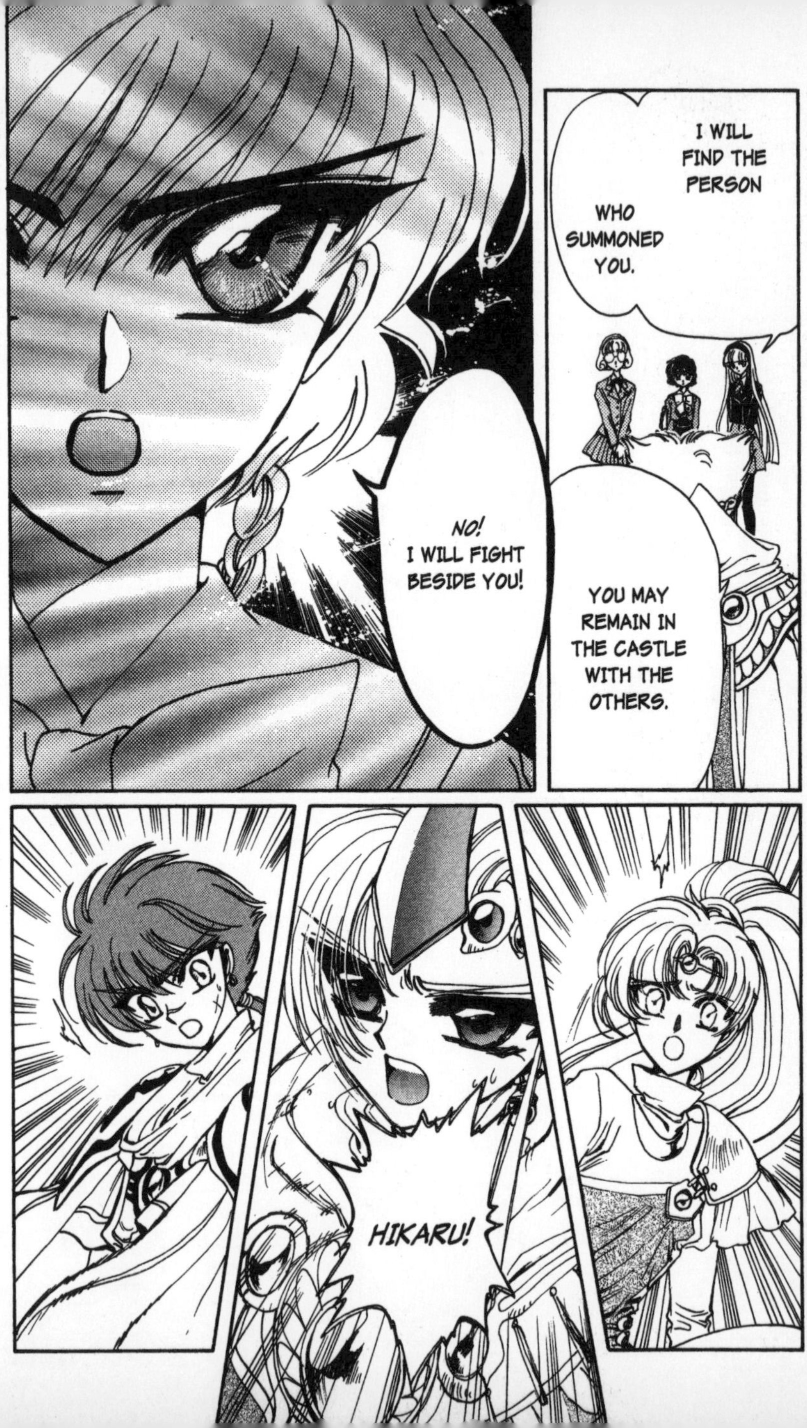
I WILL FIND THE PERSON WHO SUMMONED YOU.
YOU MAY REMAIN IN THE CASTLE WITH THE OTHERS.
NO! I WILL FIGHT BESIDE YOU!
HIKARU!

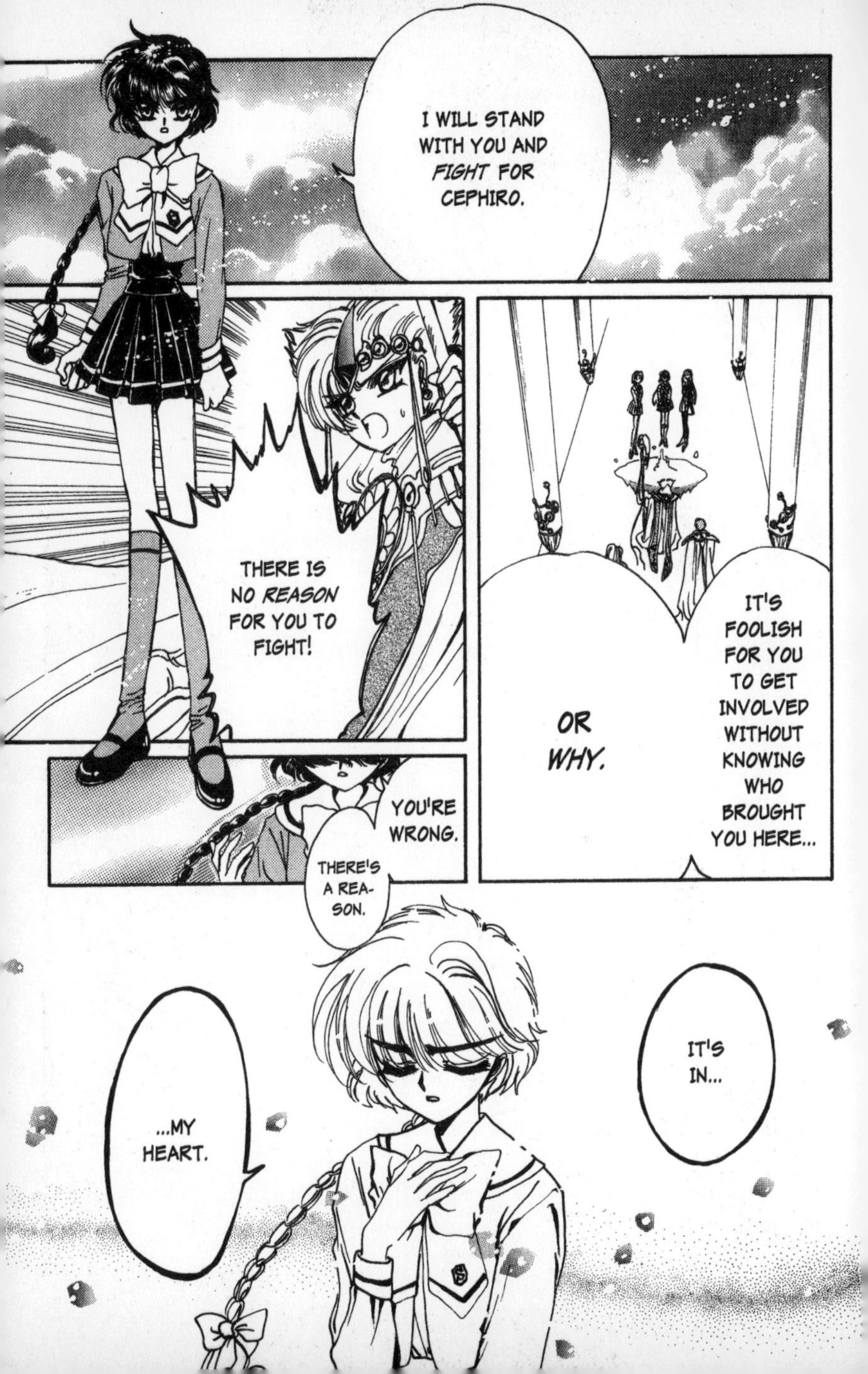
I WILL STAND WITH YOU AND *FIGHT* FOR CEPHIRO.
IT'S FOOLISH FOR YOU TO GET INVOLVED WITHOUT KNOWING WHO BROUGHT YOU HERE...
OR *WHY.*
THERE IS NO *REASON* FOR YOU TO FIGHT!
YOU'RE WRONG.
THERE'S A REA-SON.
IT'S IN...
...MY HEART.

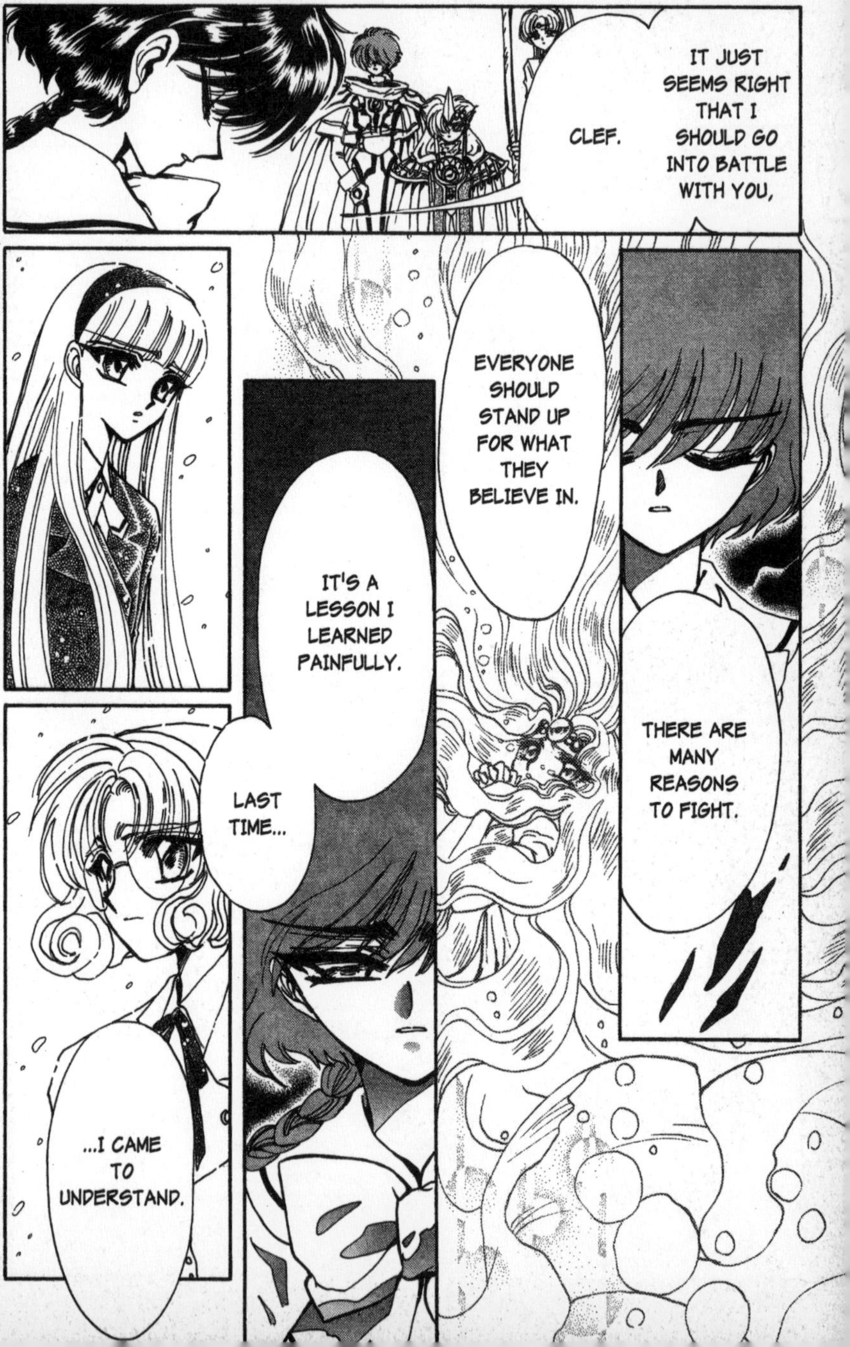
IT JUST SEEMS RIGHT THAT I SHOULD GO INTO BATTLE WITH YOU, CLEF.
THERE ARE MANY REASONS TO FIGHT.
EVERYONE SHOULD STAND UP FOR WHAT THEY BELIEVE IN.
IT'S A LESSON I LEARNED PAINFULLY.
LAST TIME...
...I CAME TO UNDERSTAND.

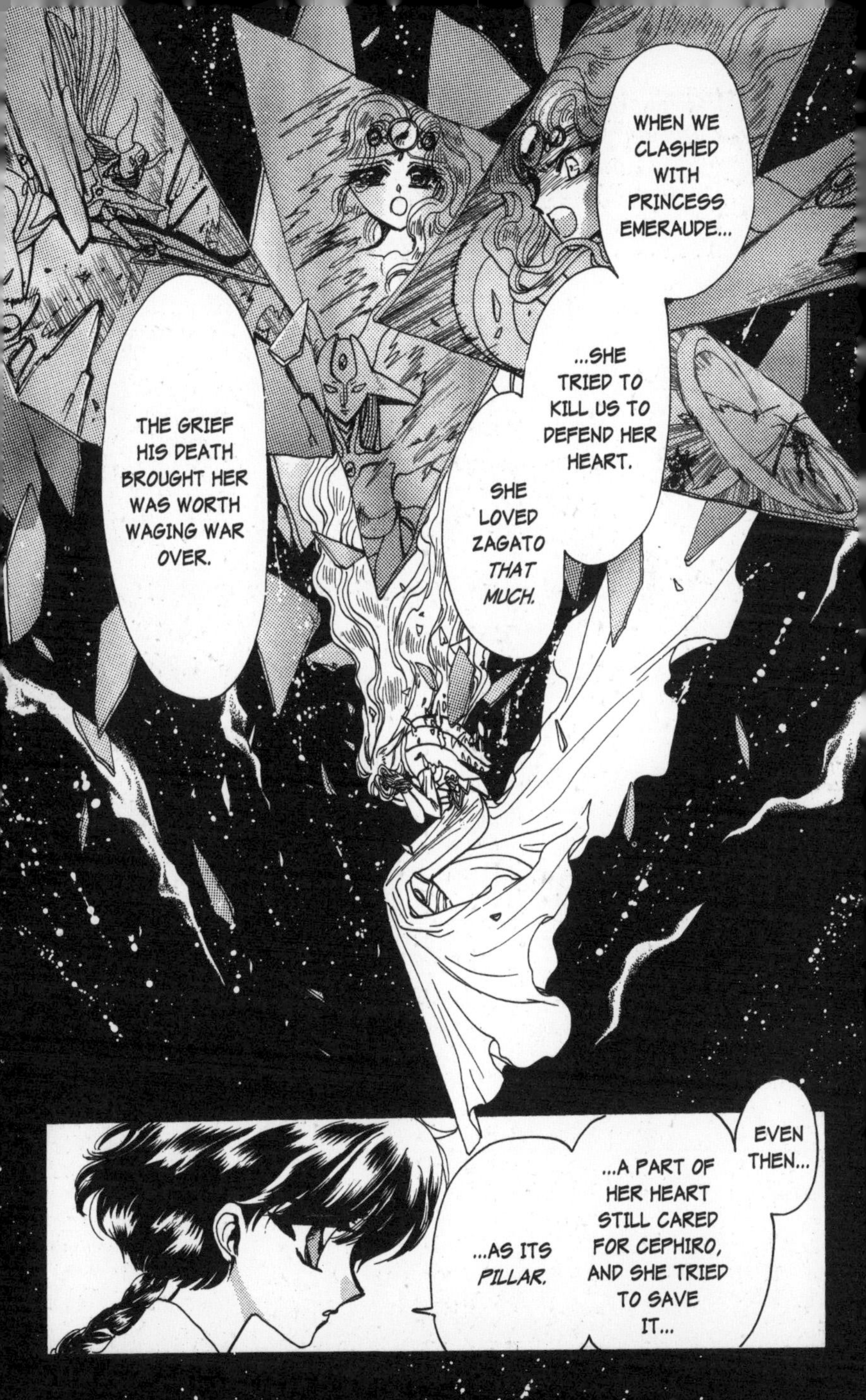
WHEN WE CLASHED WITH PRINCESS EMERAUDE...
...SHE TRIED TO KILL US TO DEFEND HER HEART.
SHE LOVED ZAGATO *THAT* MUCH.
THE GRIEF HIS DEATH BROUGHT HER WAS WORTH WAGING WAR OVER.
EVEN THEN...
...A PART OF HER HEART STILL CARED FOR CEPHIRO, AND SHE TRIED TO SAVE IT...
...AS ITS *PILLAR*.

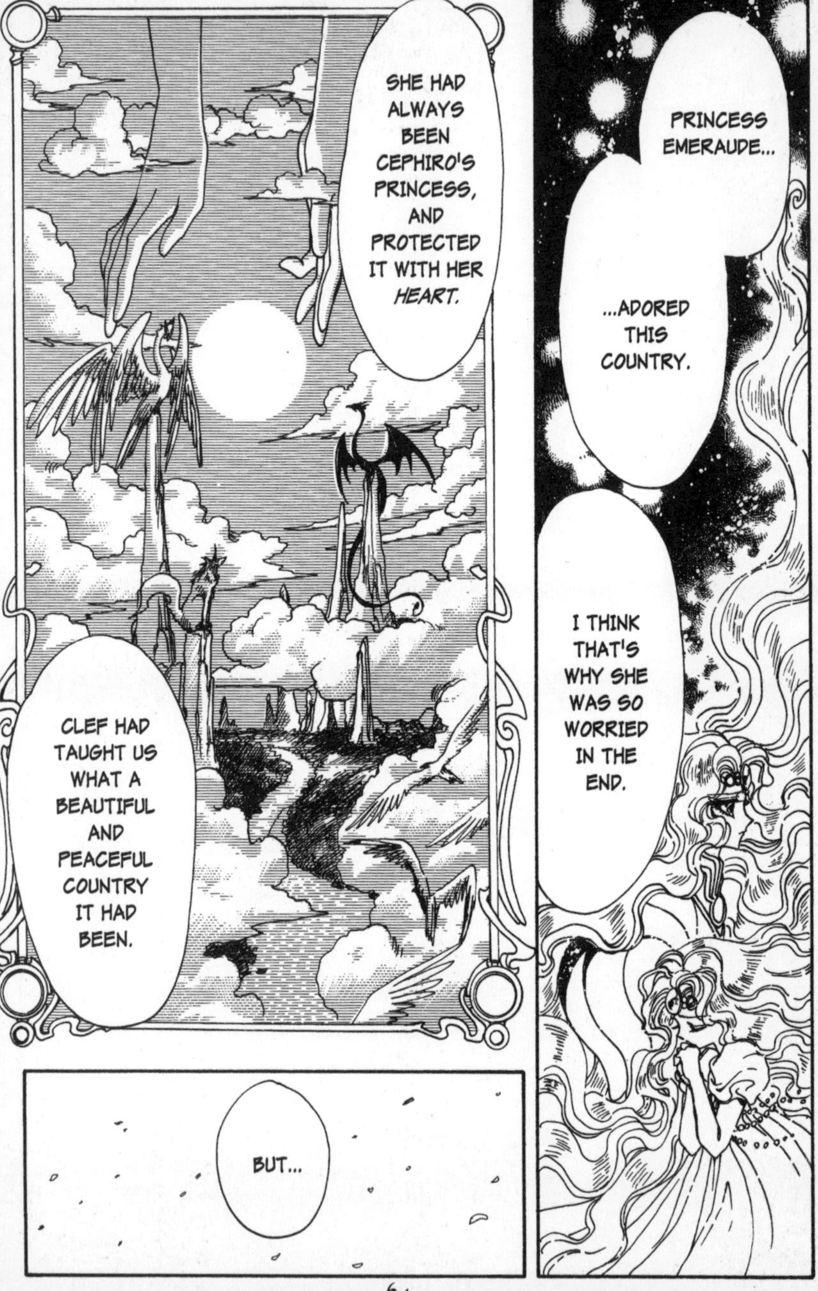
PRINCESS EMERAUDE...
...ADORED THIS COUNTRY.
I THINK THAT'S WHY SHE WAS SO WORRIED IN THE END.
SHE HAD ALWAYS BEEN CEPHIRO'S PRINCESS, AND PROTECTED IT WITH HER *HEART.*
CLEF HAD TAUGHT US WHAT A BEAUTIFUL AND PEACEFUL COUNTRY IT HAD BEEN.
BUT...

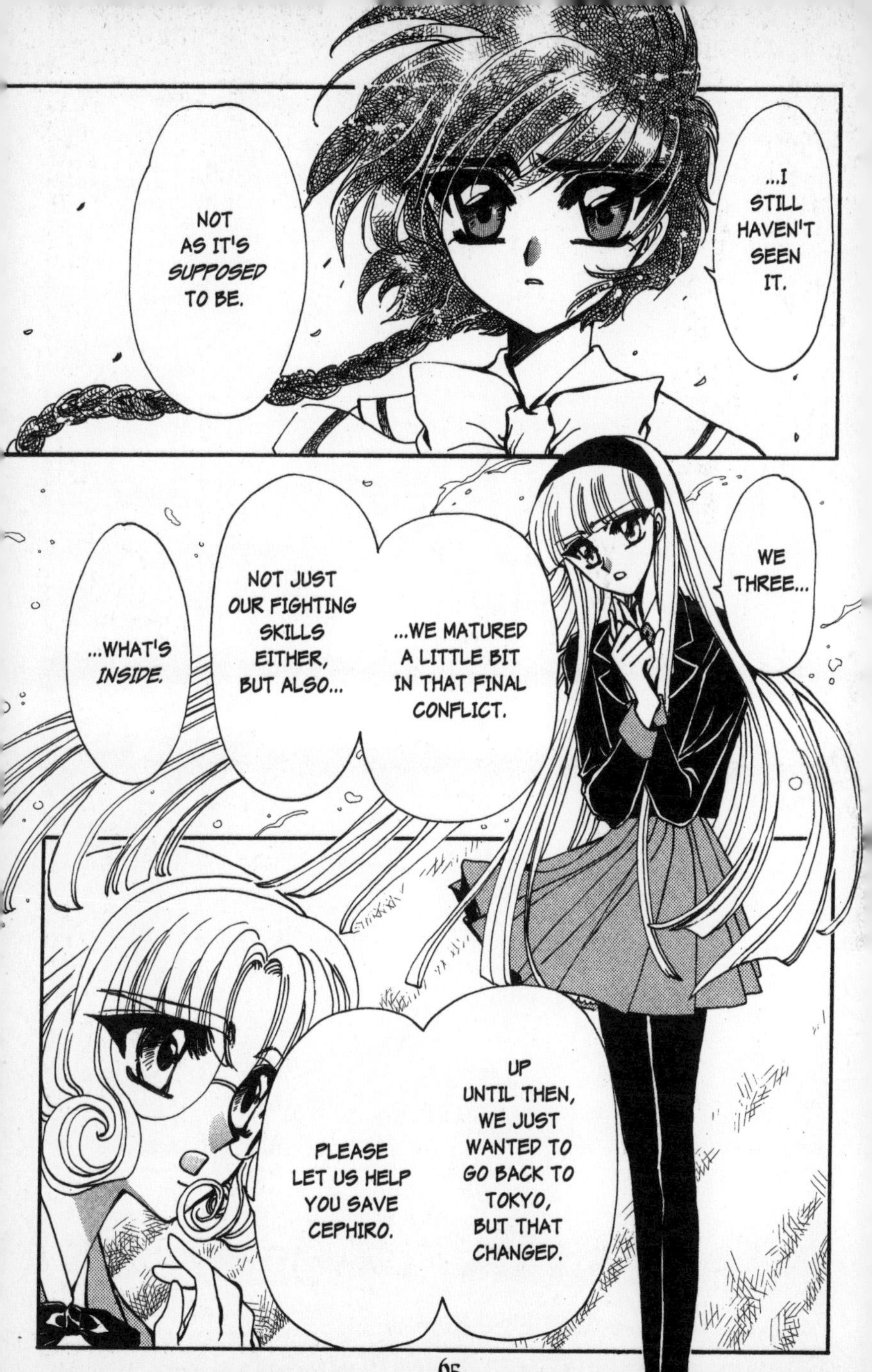
...I STILL HAVEN'T SEEN IT.
NOT AS IT'S *SUPPOSED* TO BE.
WE THREE...
...WE MATURED A LITTLE BIT IN THAT FINAL CONFLICT.
NOT JUST OUR FIGHTING SKILLS EITHER, BUT ALSO...
...WHAT'S *INSIDE.*
UP UNTIL THEN, WE JUST WANTED TO GO BACK TO TOKYO, BUT THAT CHANGED.
PLEASE LET US HELP YOU SAVE CEPHIRO.

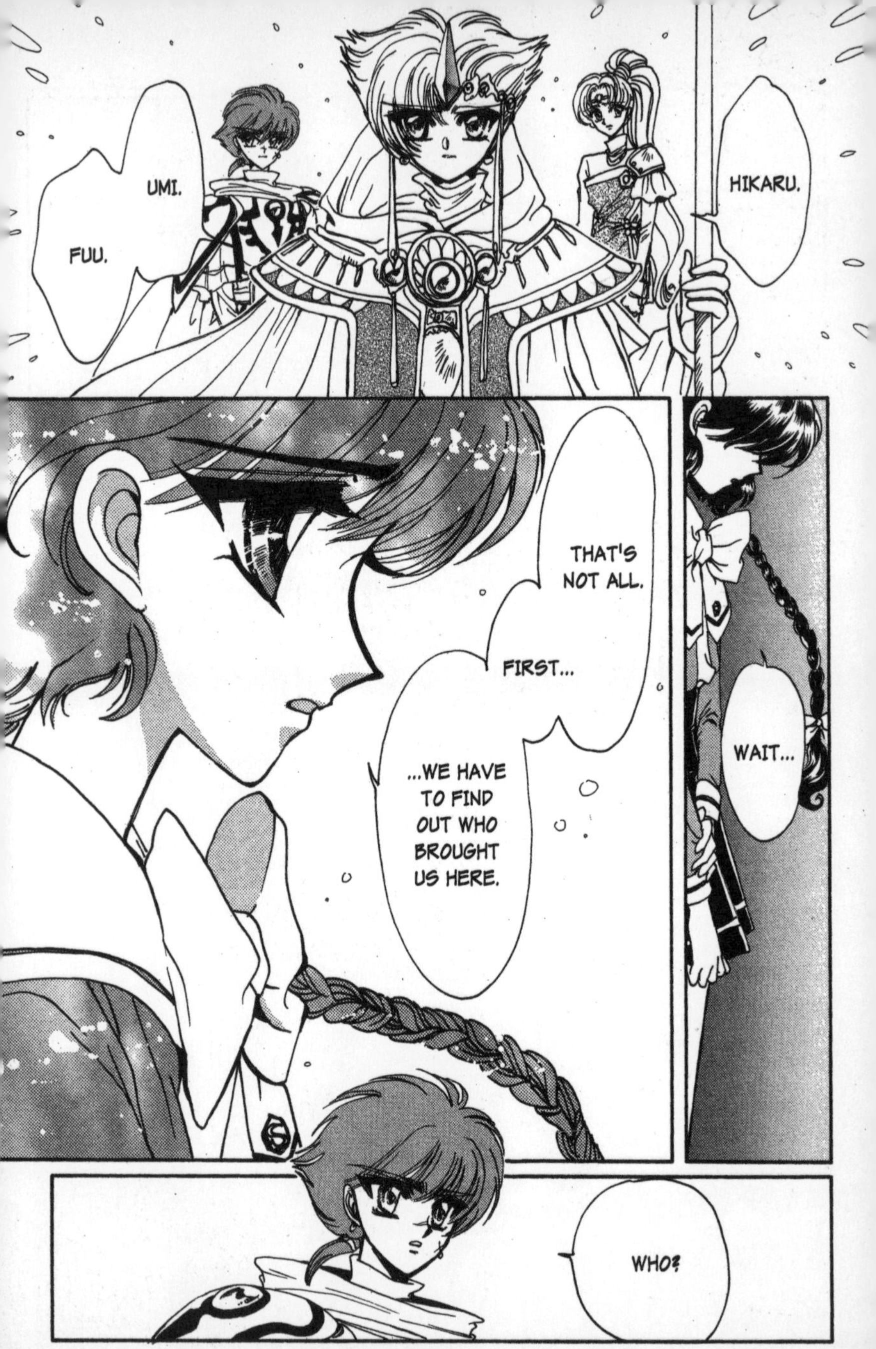
HIKARU.
UMI.
FUU.
WAIT...
THAT'S NOT ALL.
FIRST...
...WE HAVE TO FIND OUT WHO BROUGHT US HERE.
WHO?

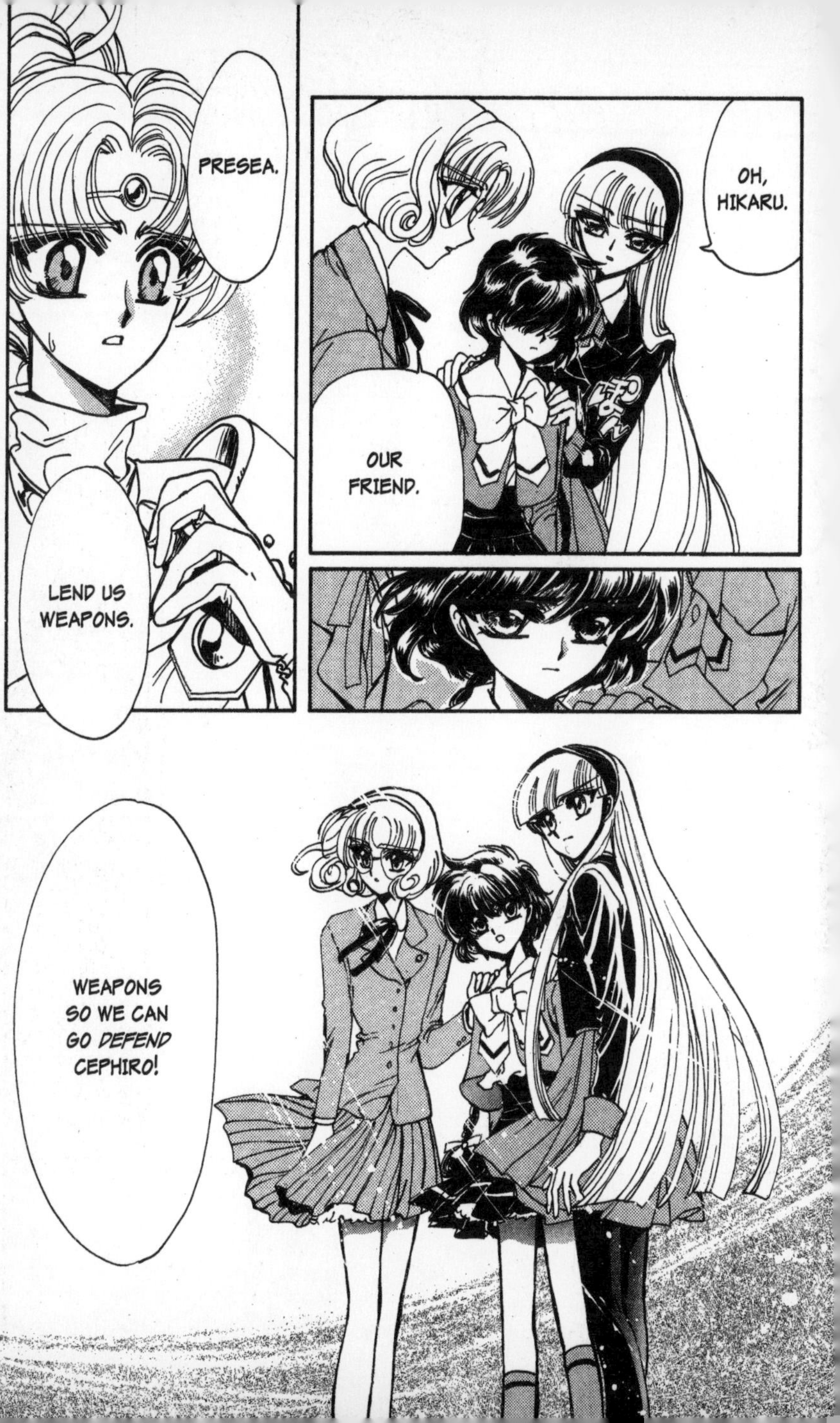
OH, HIKARU.
OUR FRIEND.
PRESEA.
LEND US WEAPONS.
WEAPONS SO WE CAN GO *DEFEND* CEPHIRO!

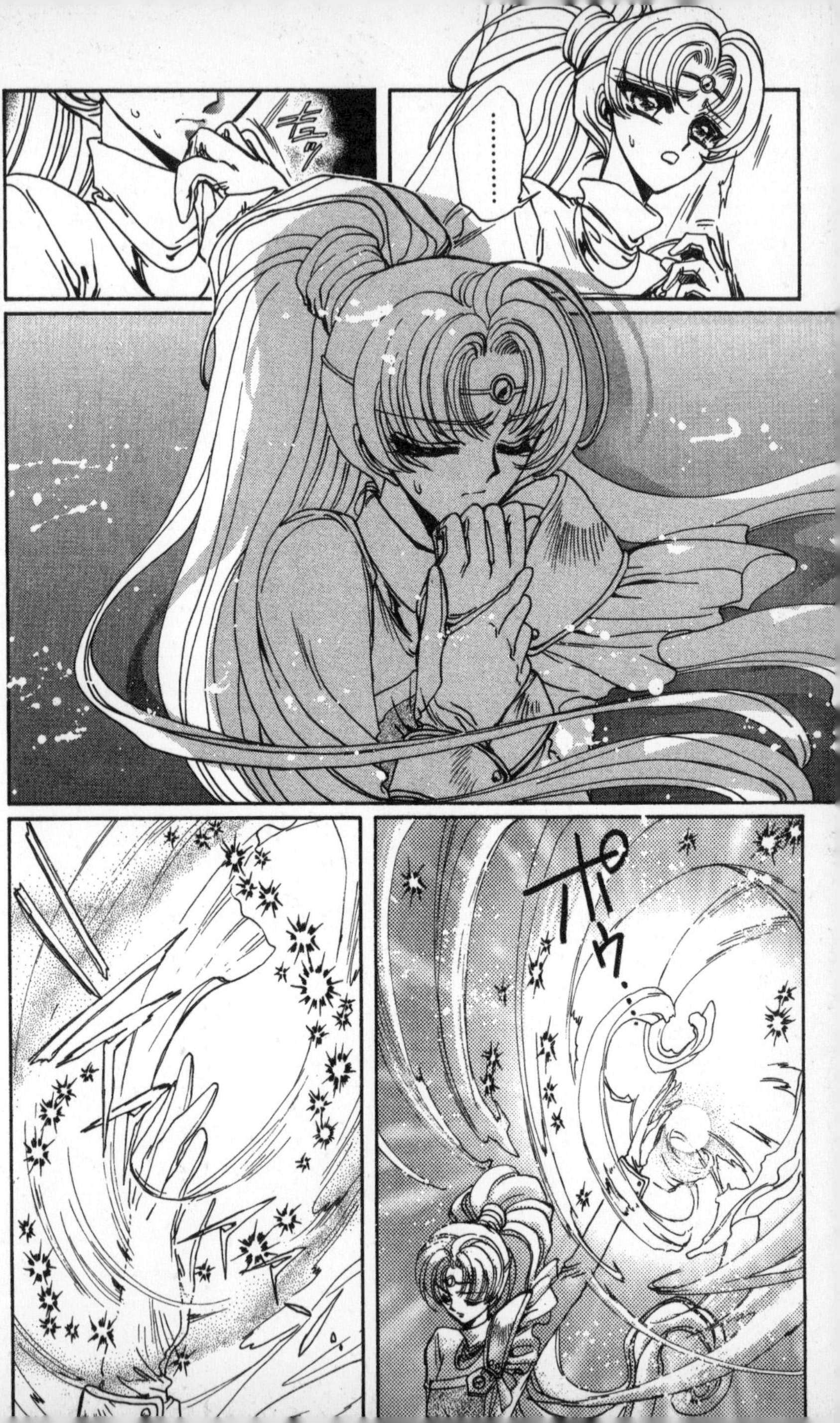
……
ギュッ
ポウ…

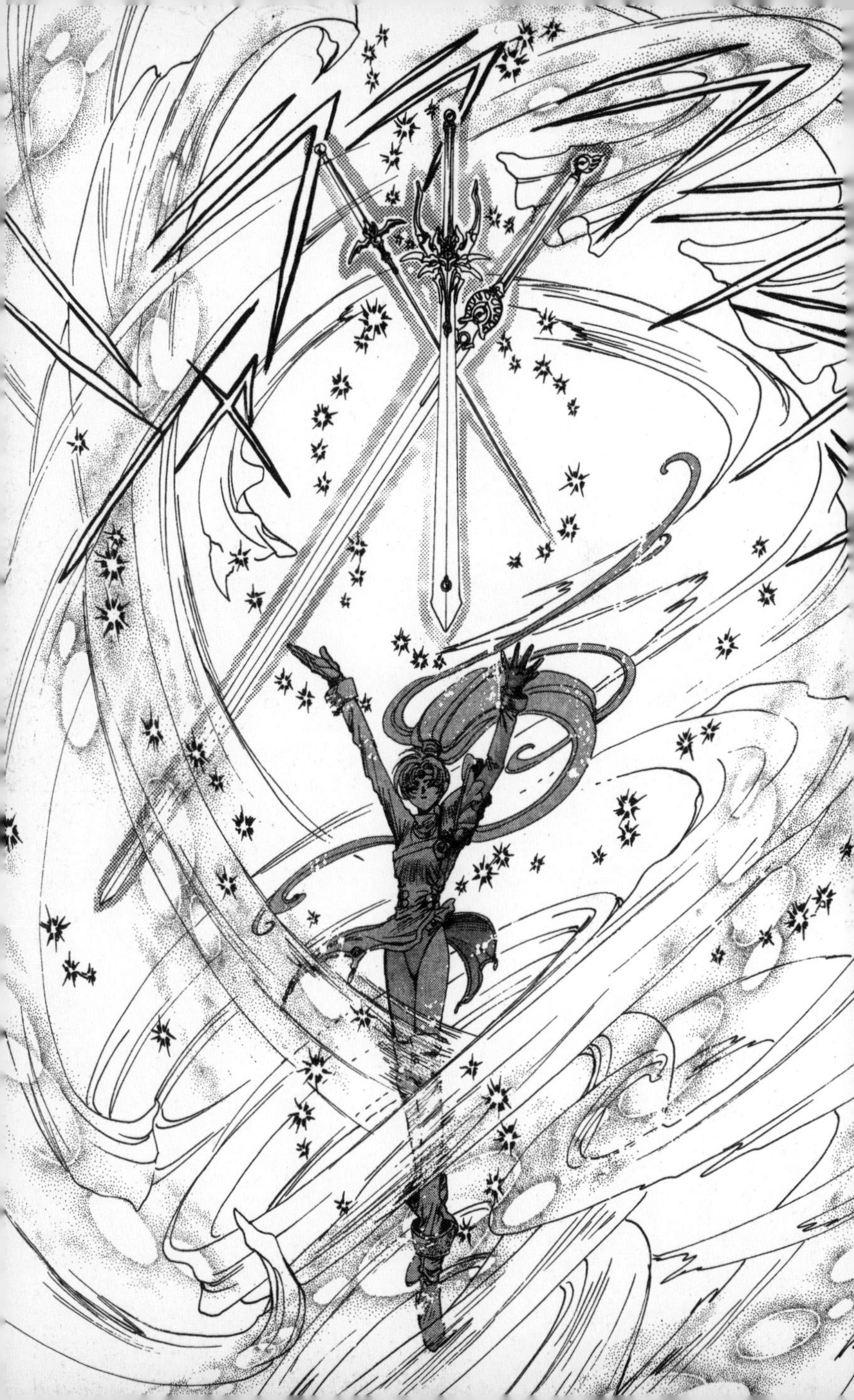

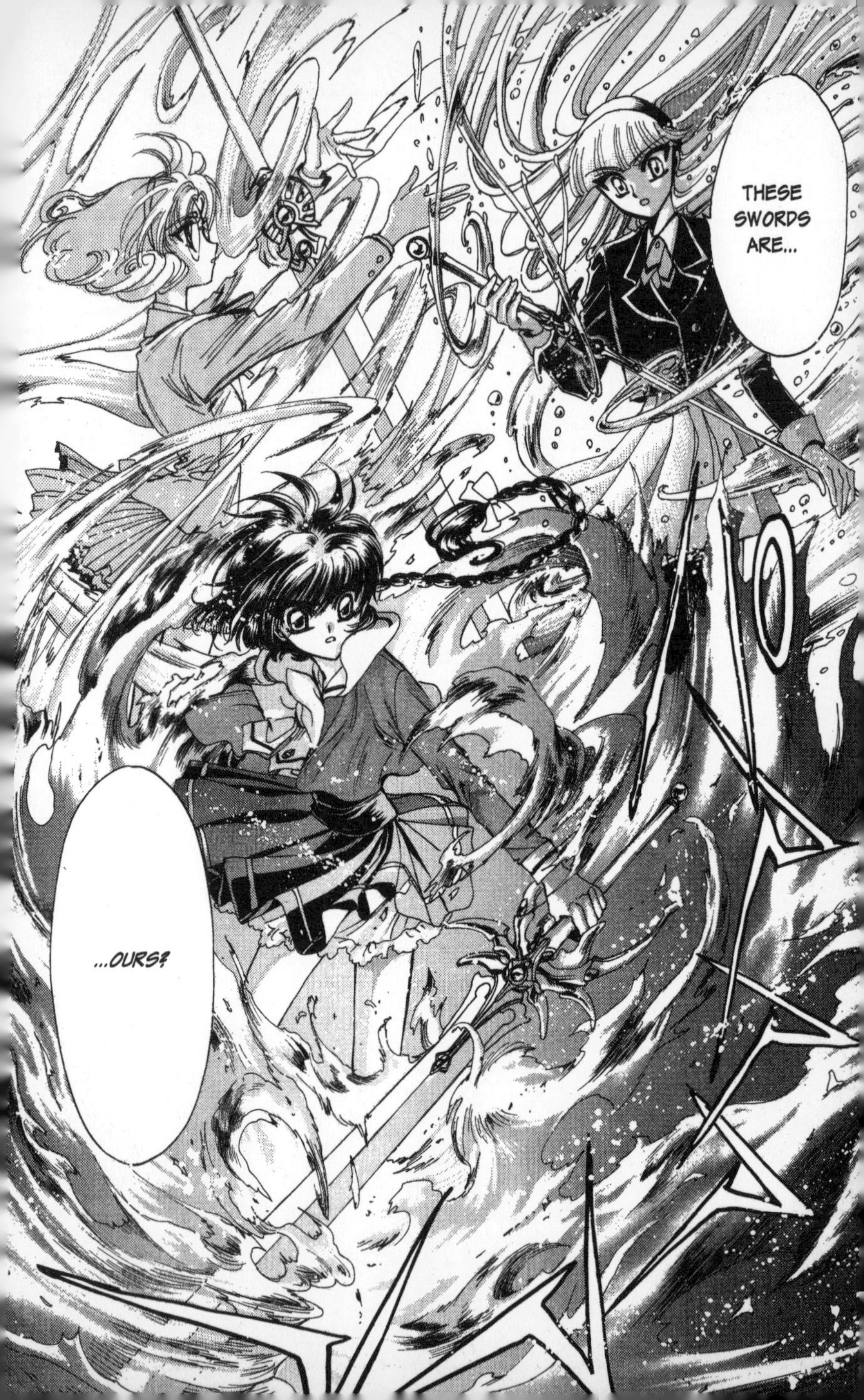
THESE SWORDS ARE...
...OURS?

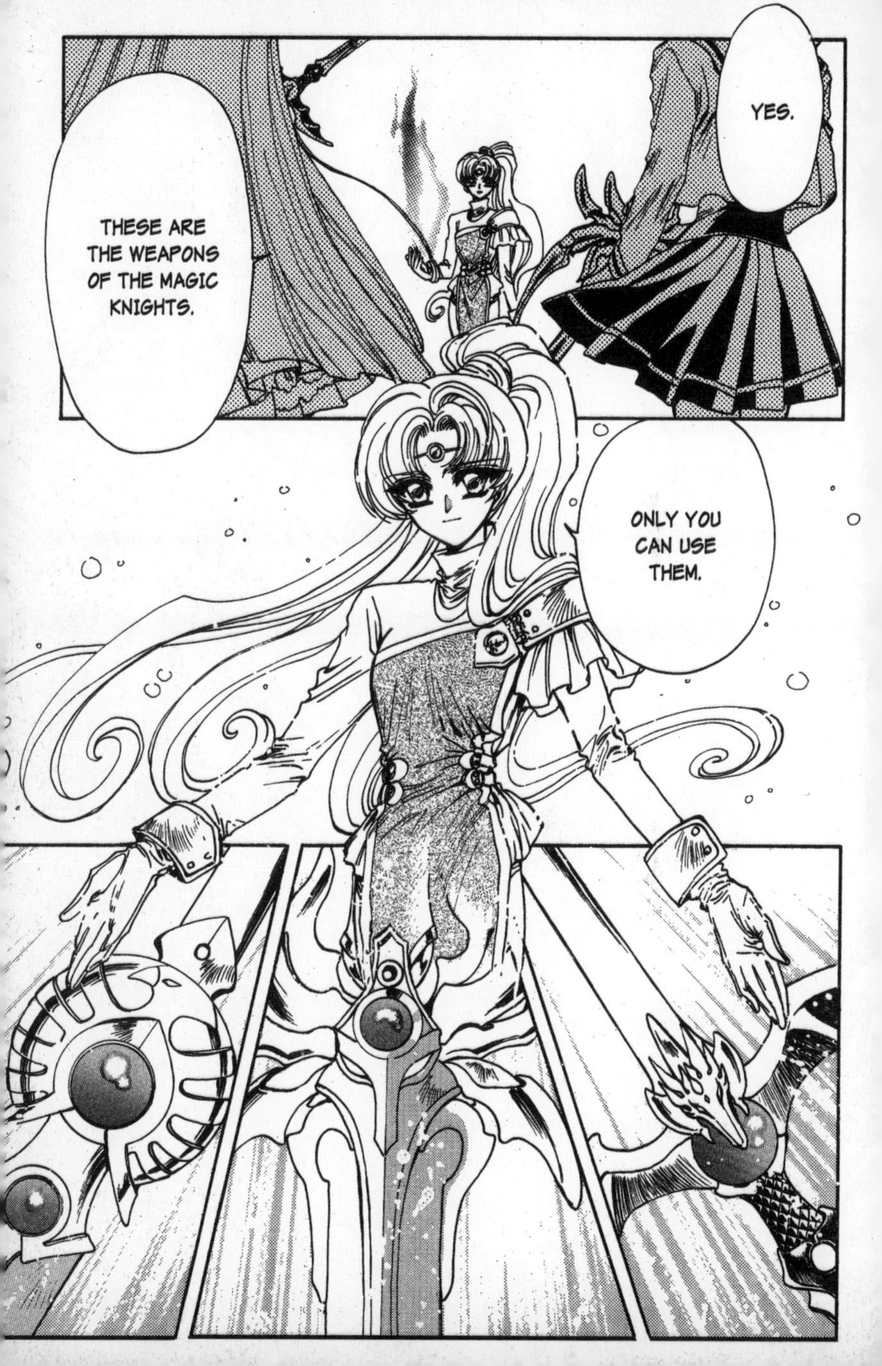
YES.
THESE ARE THE WEAPONS OF THE MAGIC KNIGHTS.
ONLY YOU CAN USE THEM.

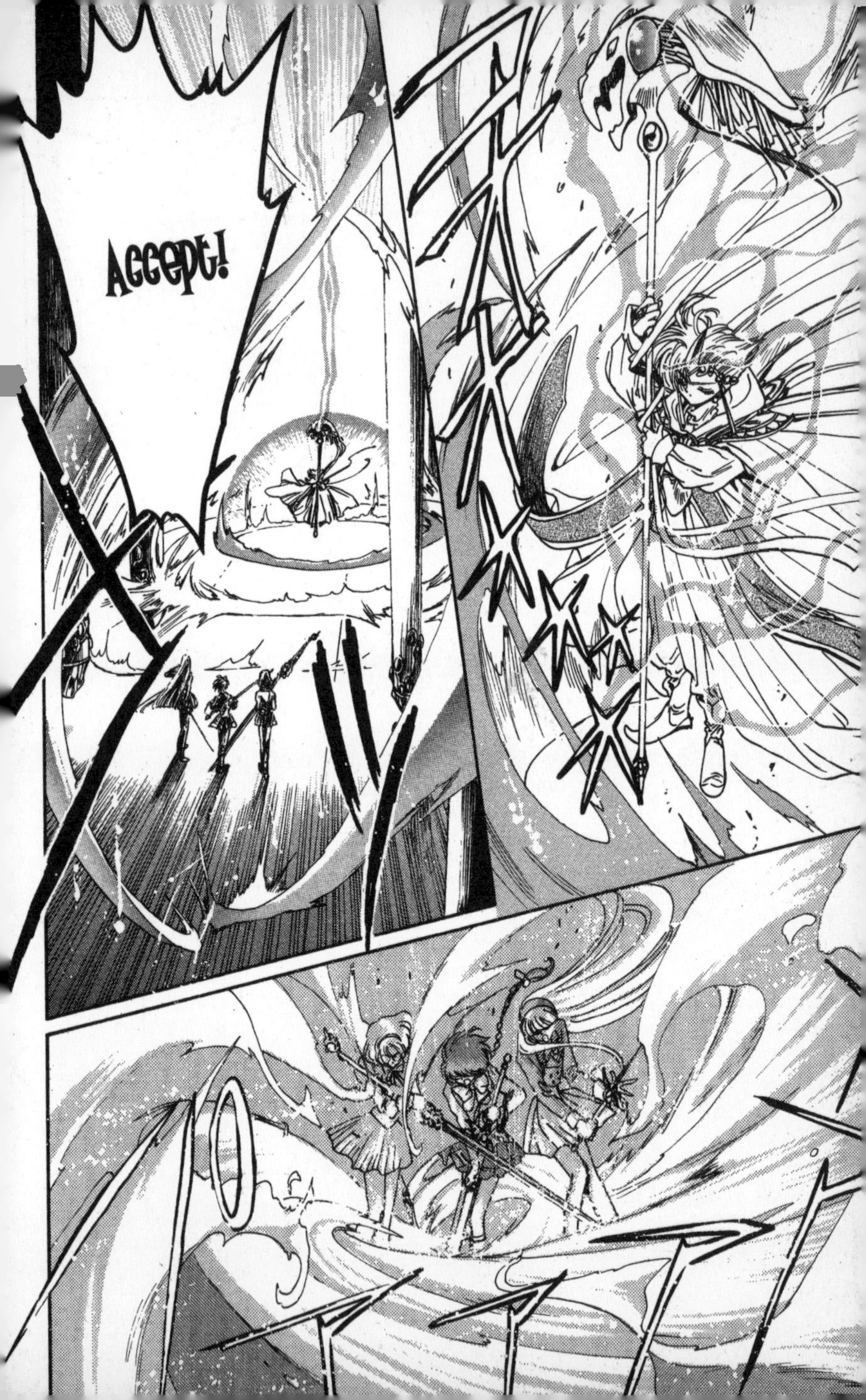
Accept!

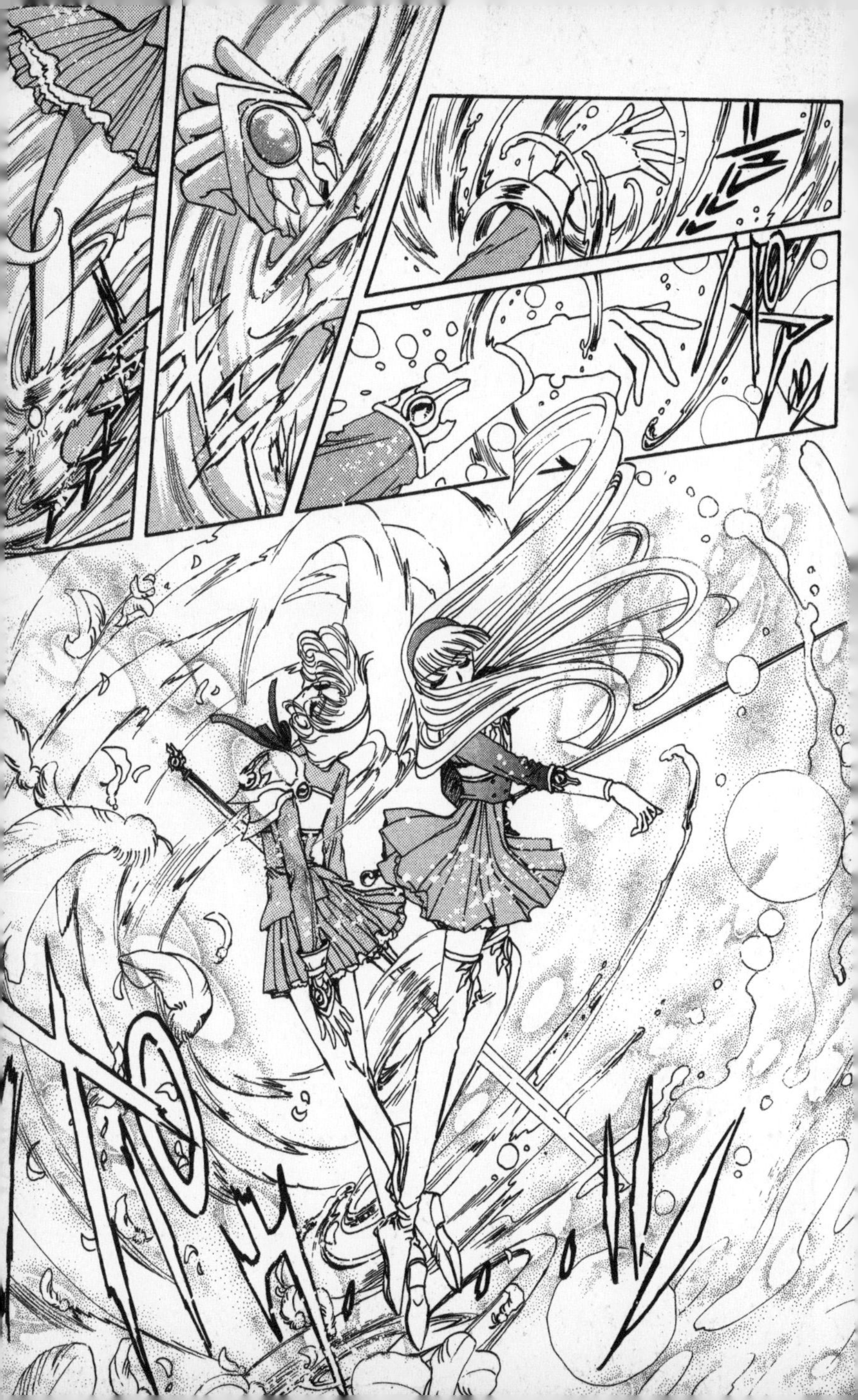

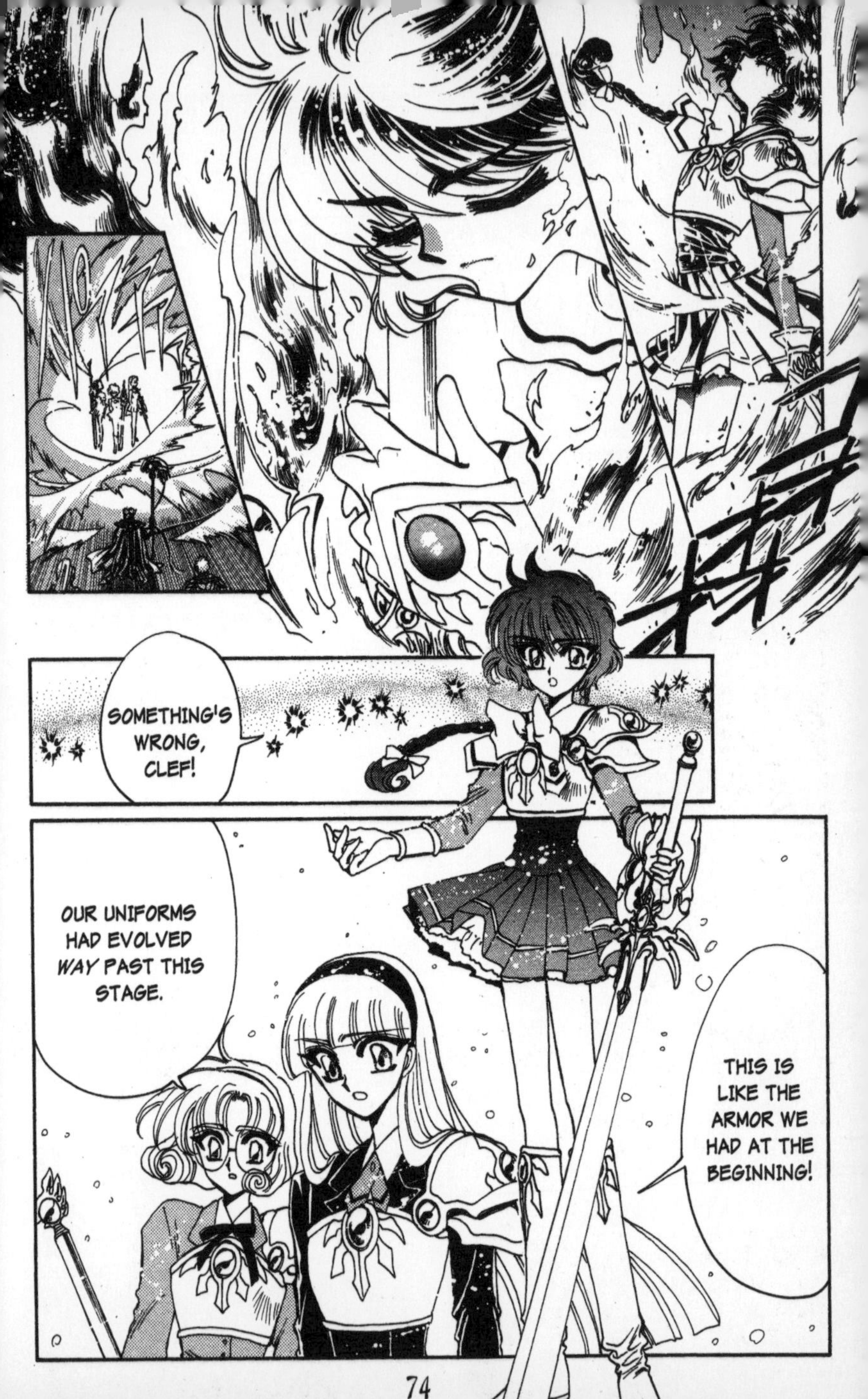
SOMETHING'S WRONG, CLEF!
THIS IS LIKE THE ARMOR WE HAD AT THE BEGINNING!
OUR UNIFORMS HAD EVOLVED *WAY* PAST THIS STAGE.

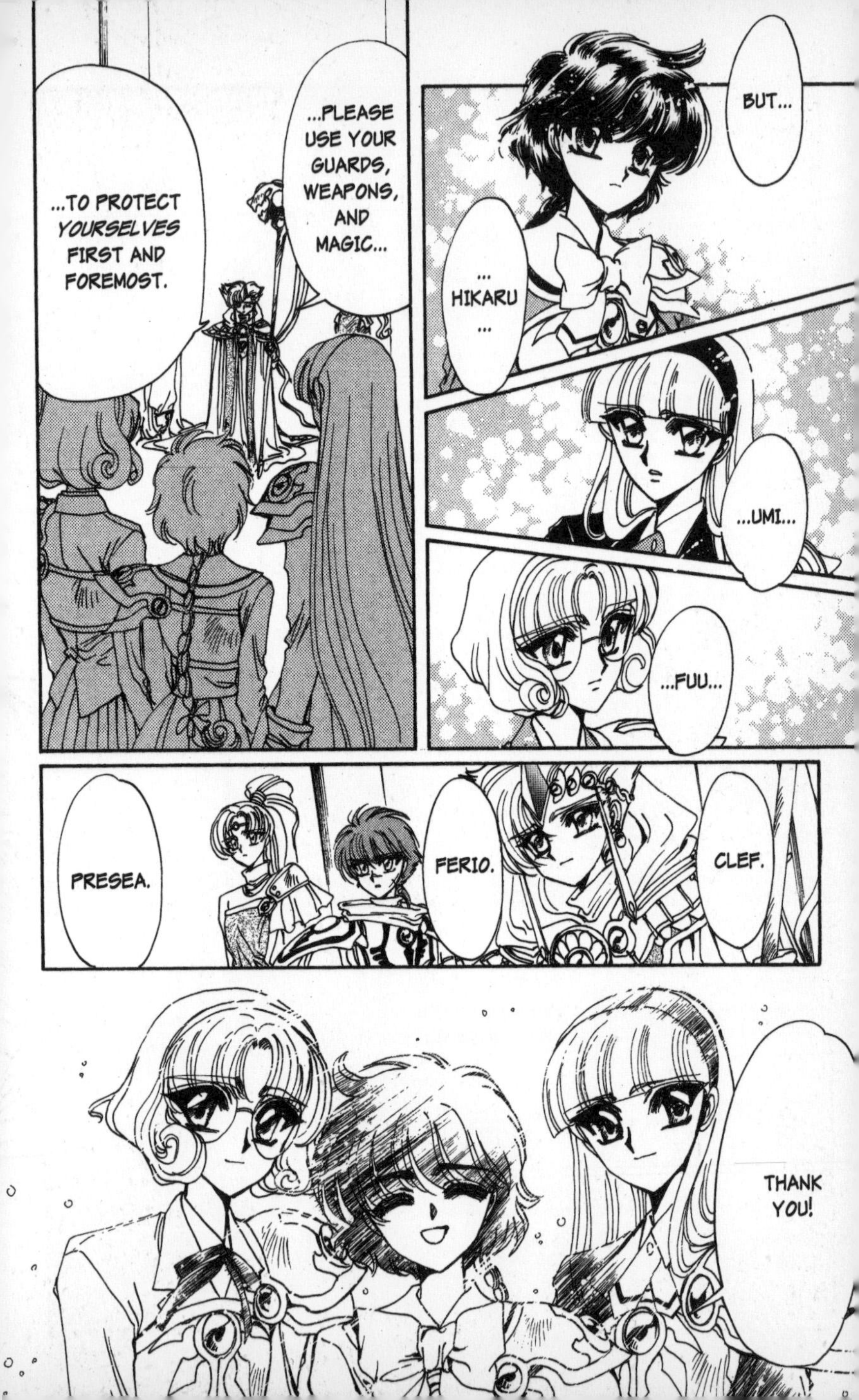
BUT...
...
HIKARU
...
...UMI...
...FUU...
...PLEASE USE YOUR GUARDS, WEAPONS, AND MAGIC...
...TO PROTECT YOURSELVES FIRST AND FOREMOST.
CLEF.
FERIO.
PRESEA.
THANK YOU!

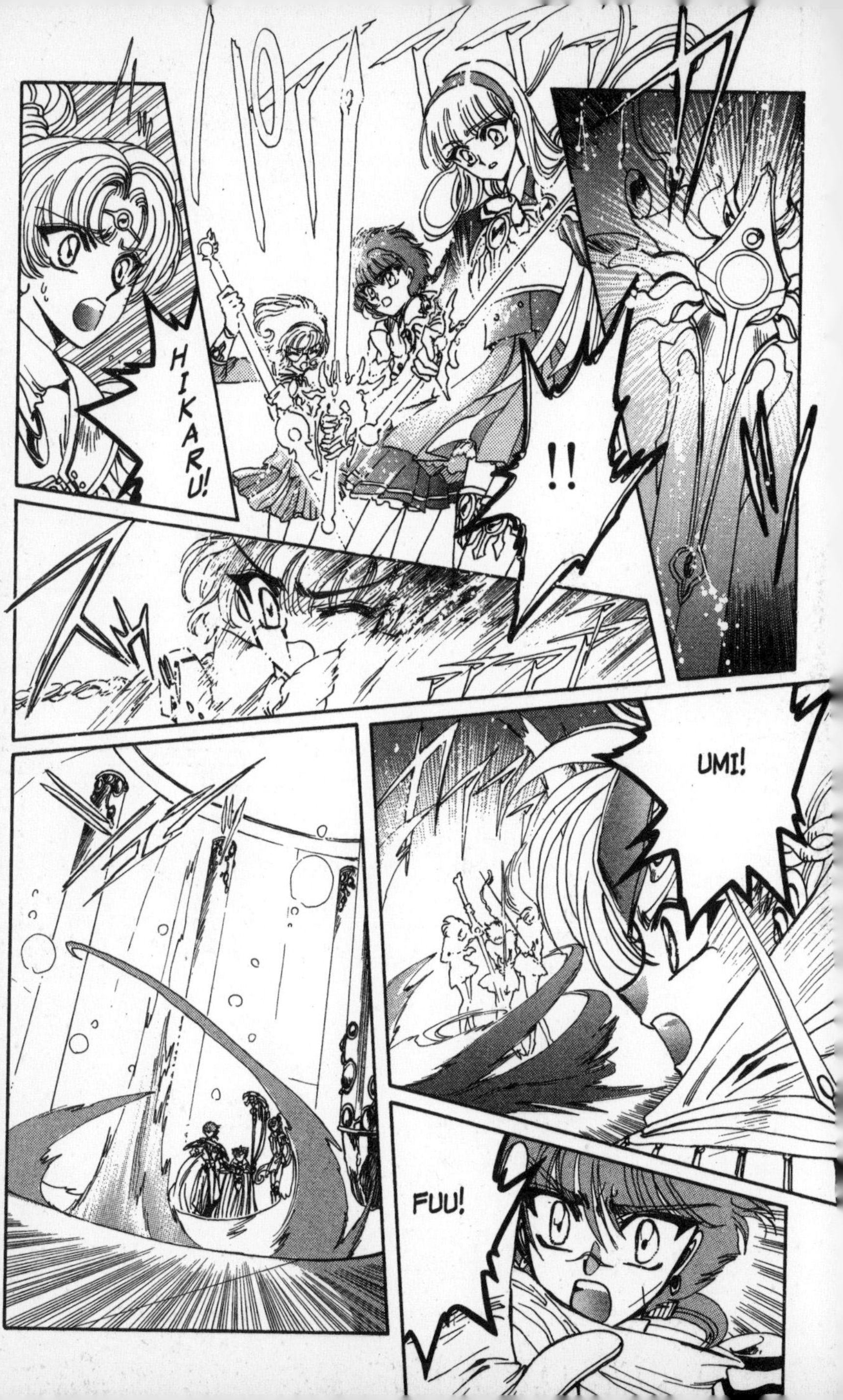
!!
HIKARU!
UMI!
FUU!

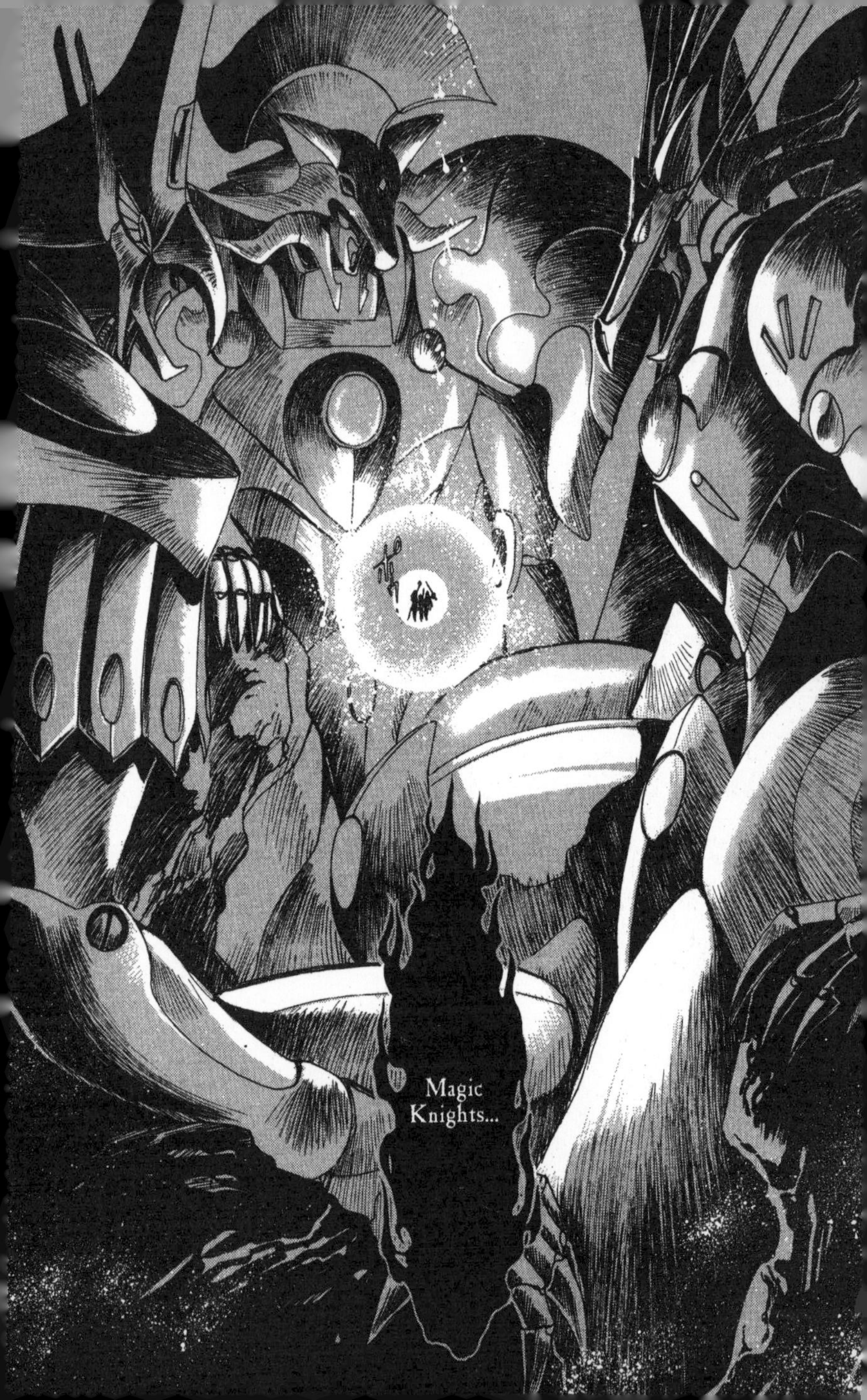
Magic Knights...

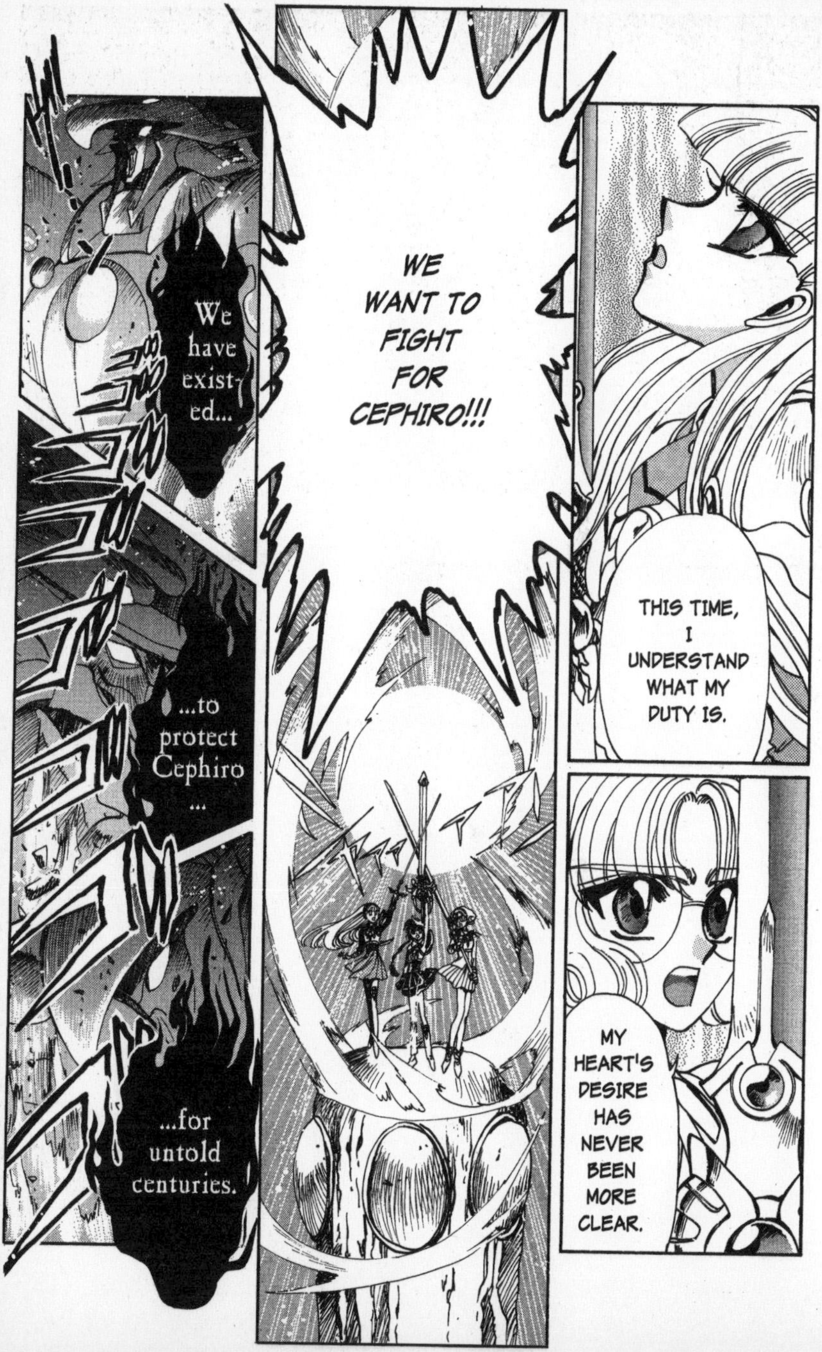
THIS TIME, I UNDERSTAND WHAT MY DUTY IS.
MY HEART'S DESIRE HAS NEVER BEEN MORE CLEAR.
WE WANT TO FIGHT FOR CEPHIRO!!!
We have exist-ed...
...to protect Cephiro ...
...for untold centuries.

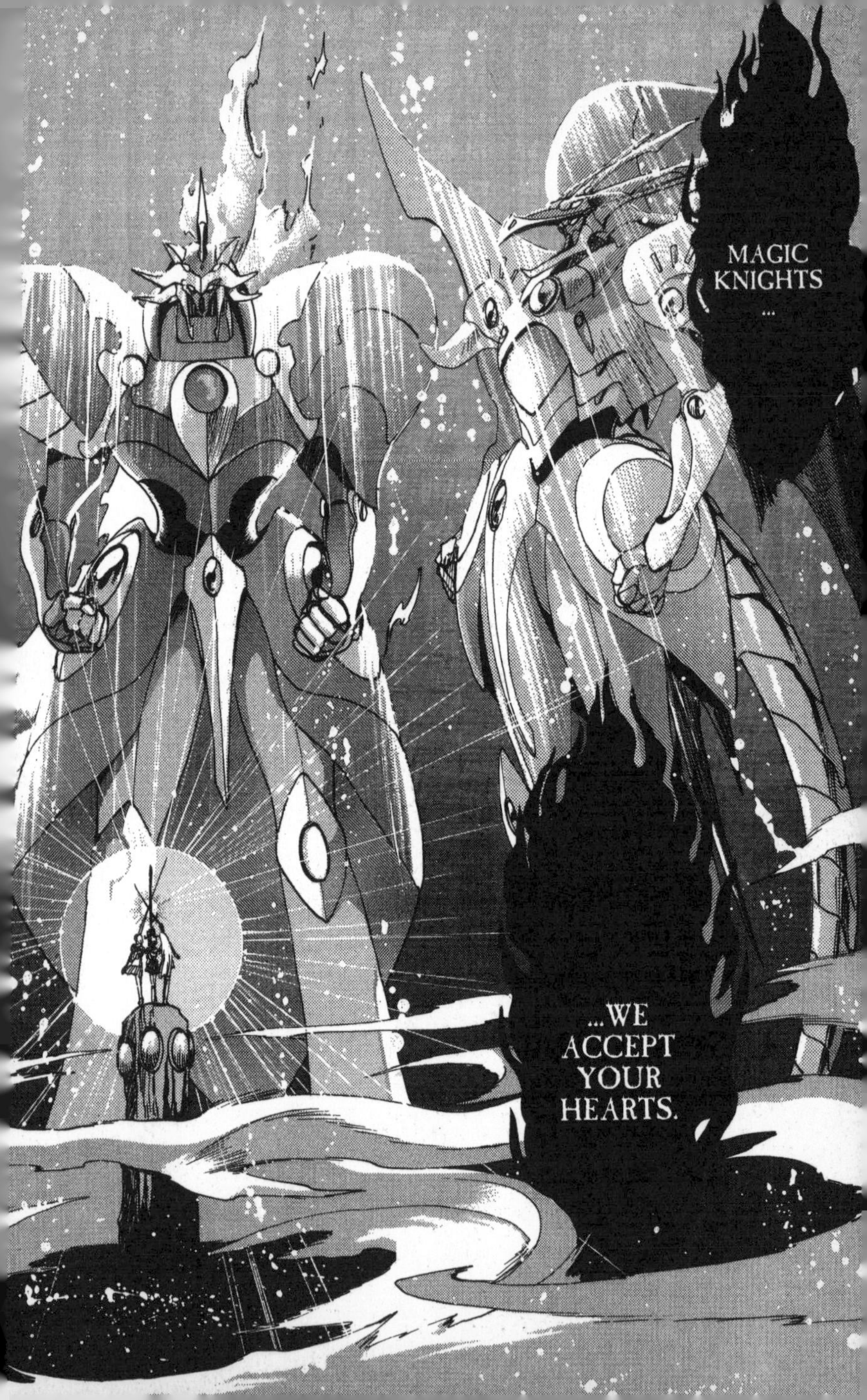
MAGIC KNIGHTS ...
...WE ACCEPT YOUR HEARTS.

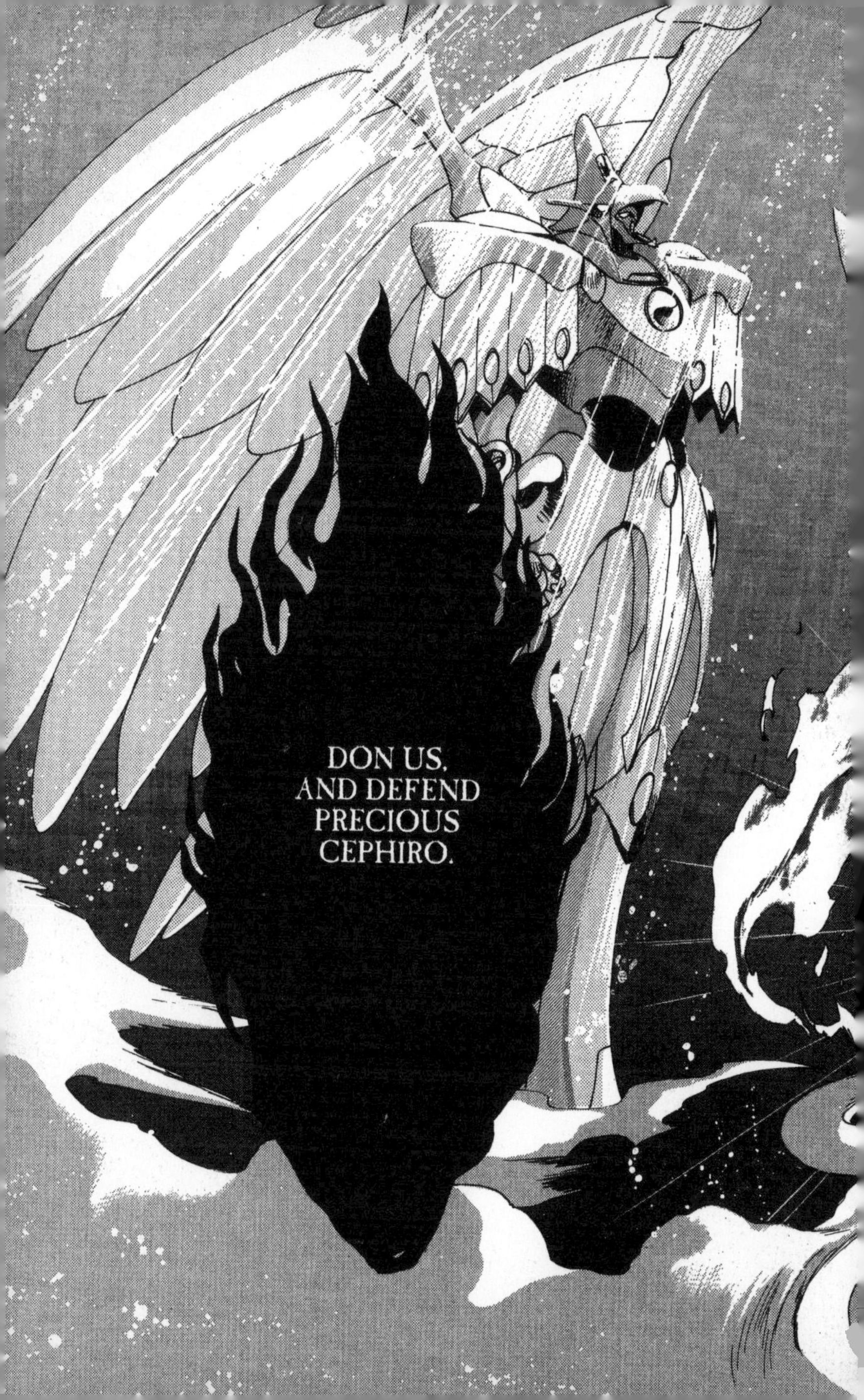
DON US, AND DEFEND PRECIOUS CEPHIRO.

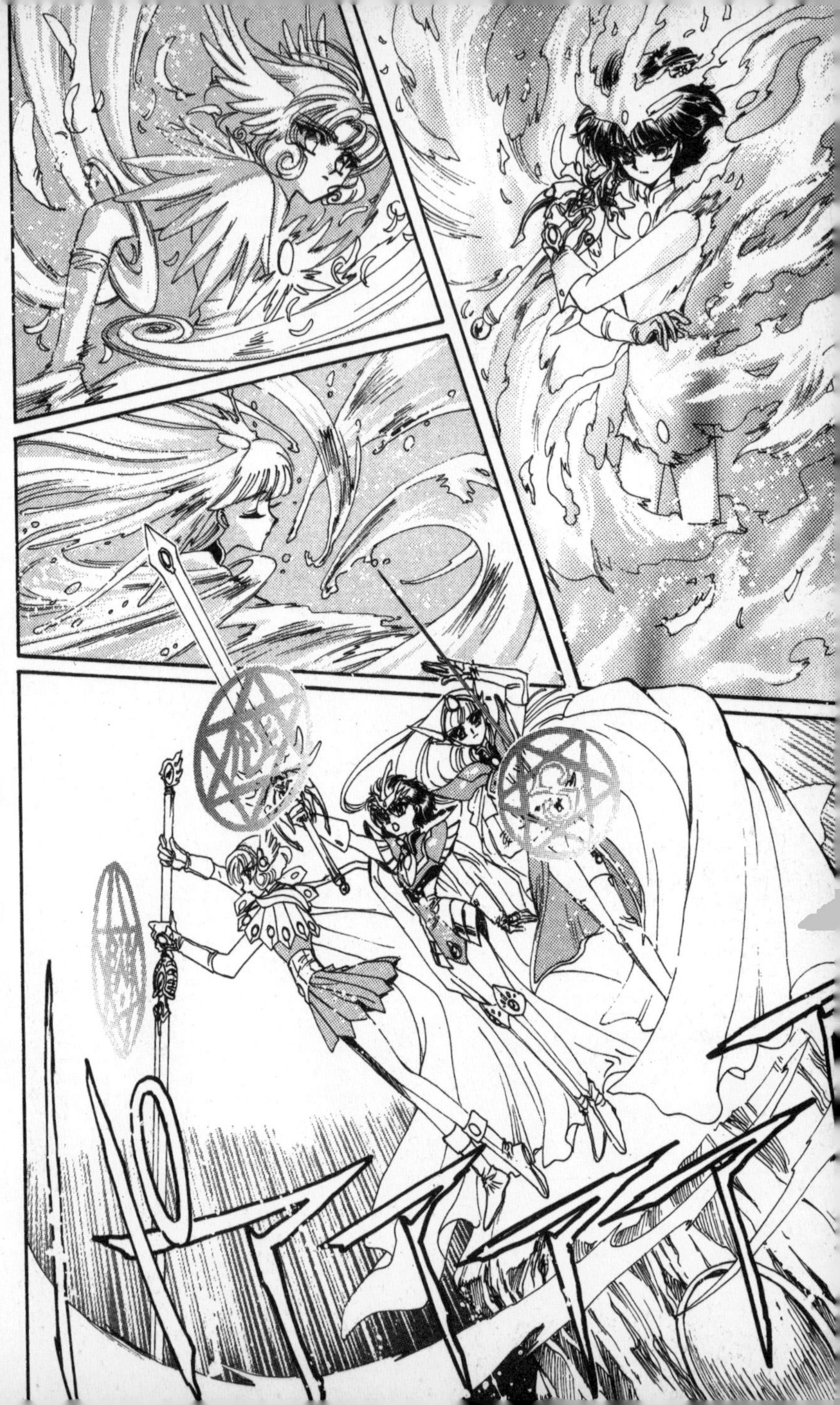

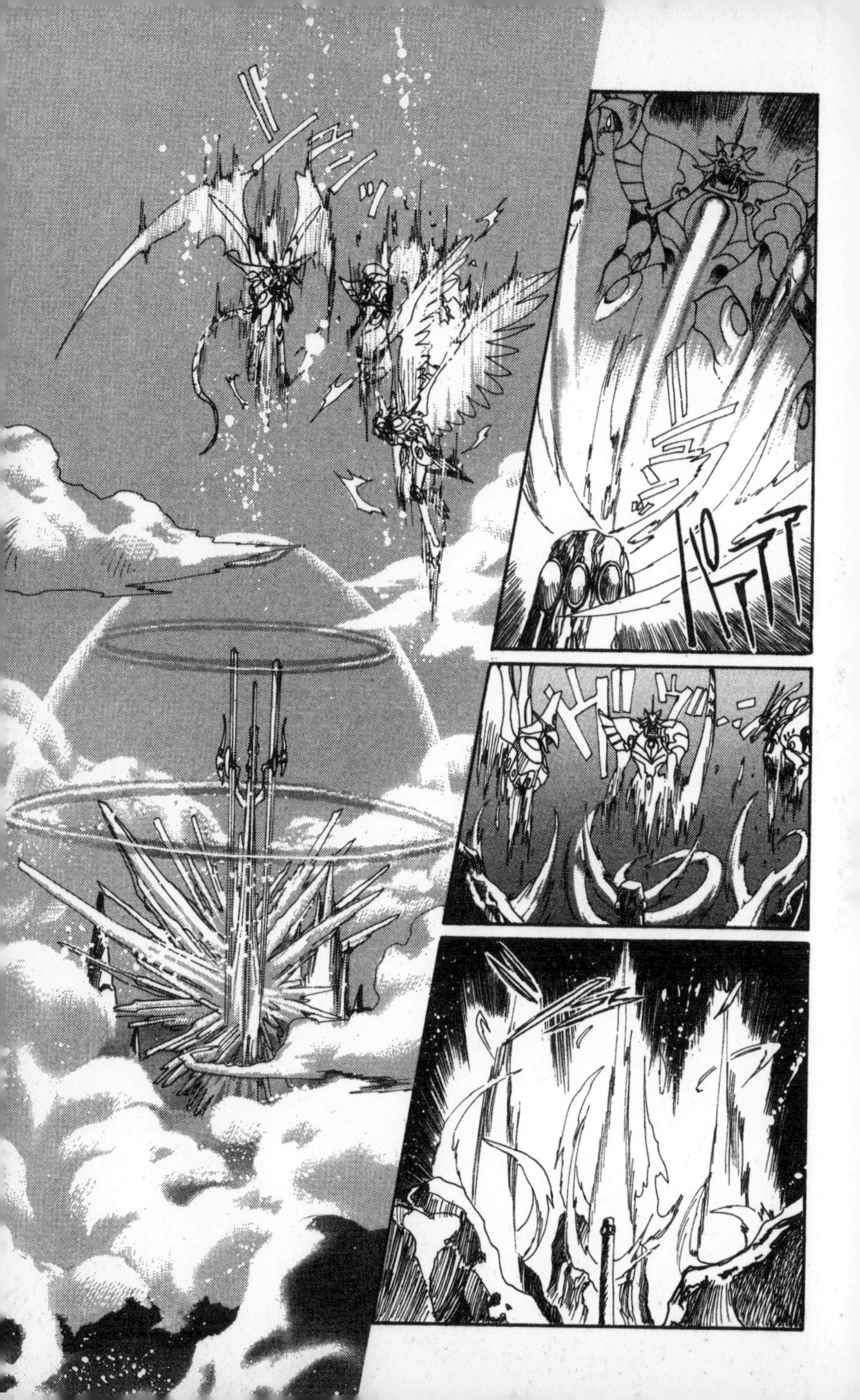
パァァァ

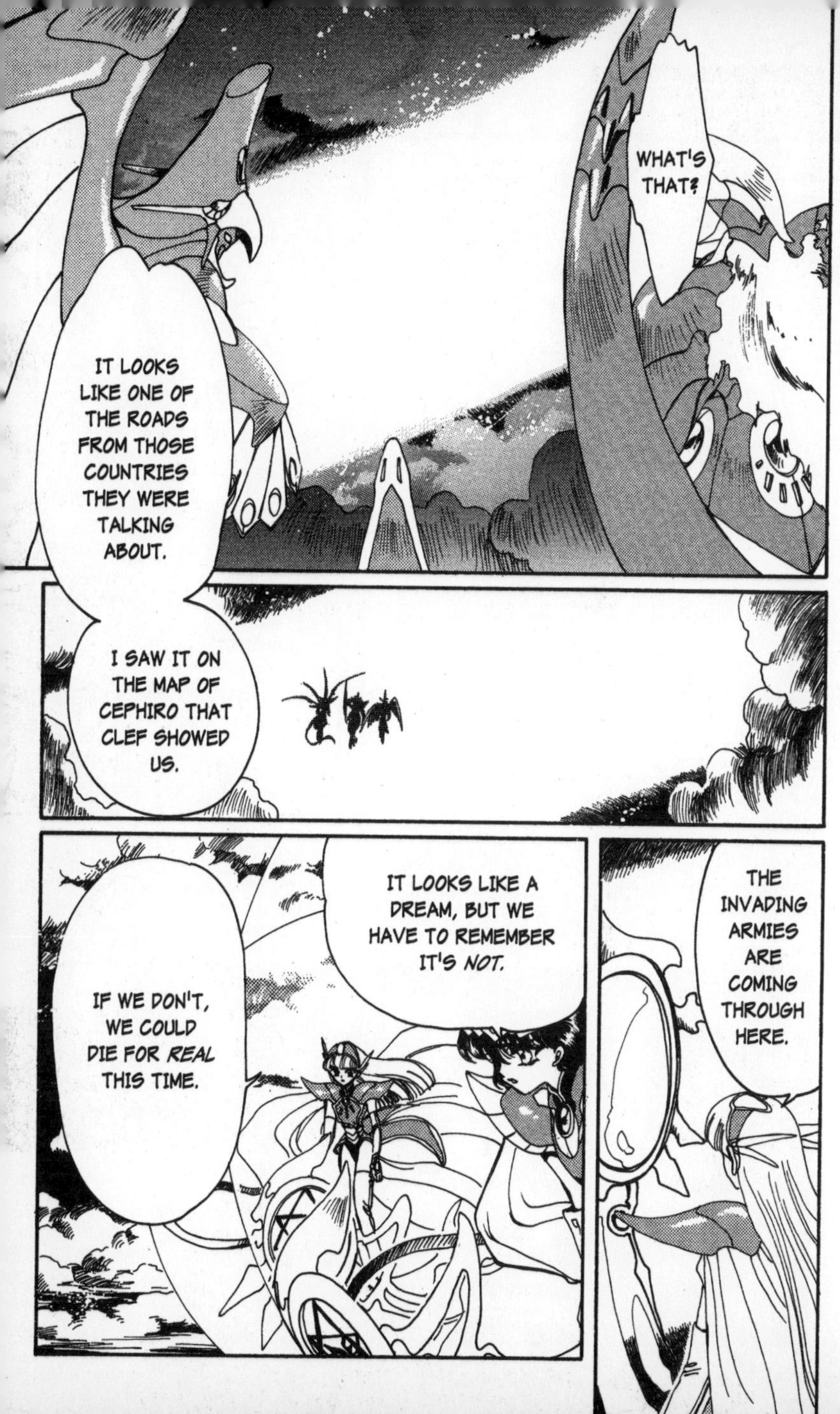
WHAT'S THAT?
IT LOOKS LIKE ONE OF THE ROADS FROM THOSE COUNTRIES THEY WERE TALKING ABOUT.
I SAW IT ON THE MAP OF CEPHIRO THAT CLEF SHOWED US.
THE INVADING ARMIES ARE COMING THROUGH HERE.
IT LOOKS LIKE A DREAM, BUT WE HAVE TO REMEMBER IT'S *NOT*.
IF WE DON'T, WE COULD DIE FOR *REAL* THIS TIME.

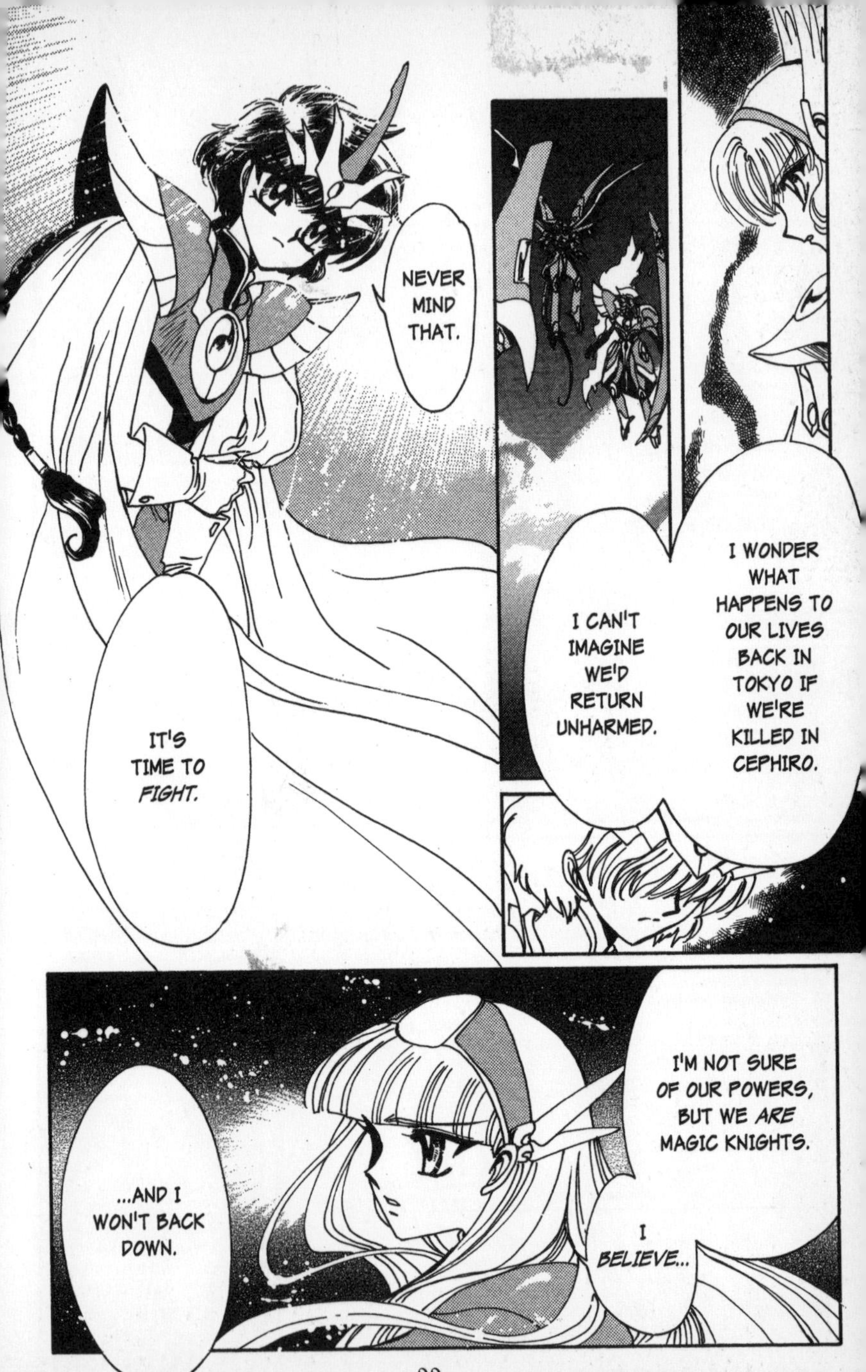
I WONDER WHAT HAPPENS TO OUR LIVES BACK IN TOKYO IF WE'RE KILLED IN CEPHIRO.
I CAN'T IMAGINE WE'D RETURN UNHARMED.
NEVER MIND THAT.
IT'S TIME TO *FIGHT.*
I'M NOT SURE OF OUR POWERS, BUT WE *ARE* MAGIC KNIGHTS.
I *BELIEVE...*
...AND I WON'T BACK DOWN.

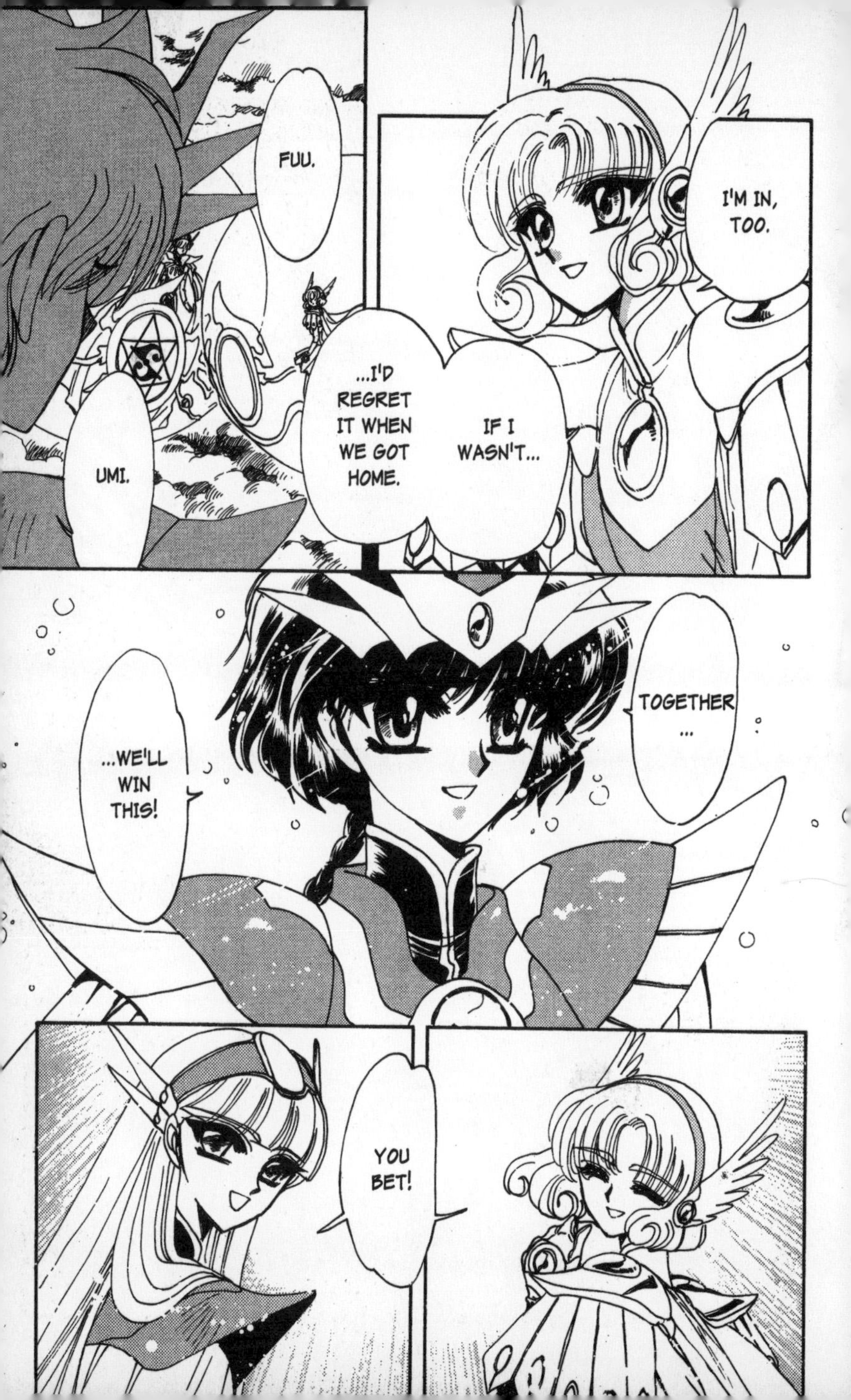
I'M IN, TOO.
IF I WASN'T...
...I'D REGRET IT WHEN WE GOT HOME.
FUU.
UMI.
TOGETHER...
...WE'LL WIN THIS!
YOU BET!

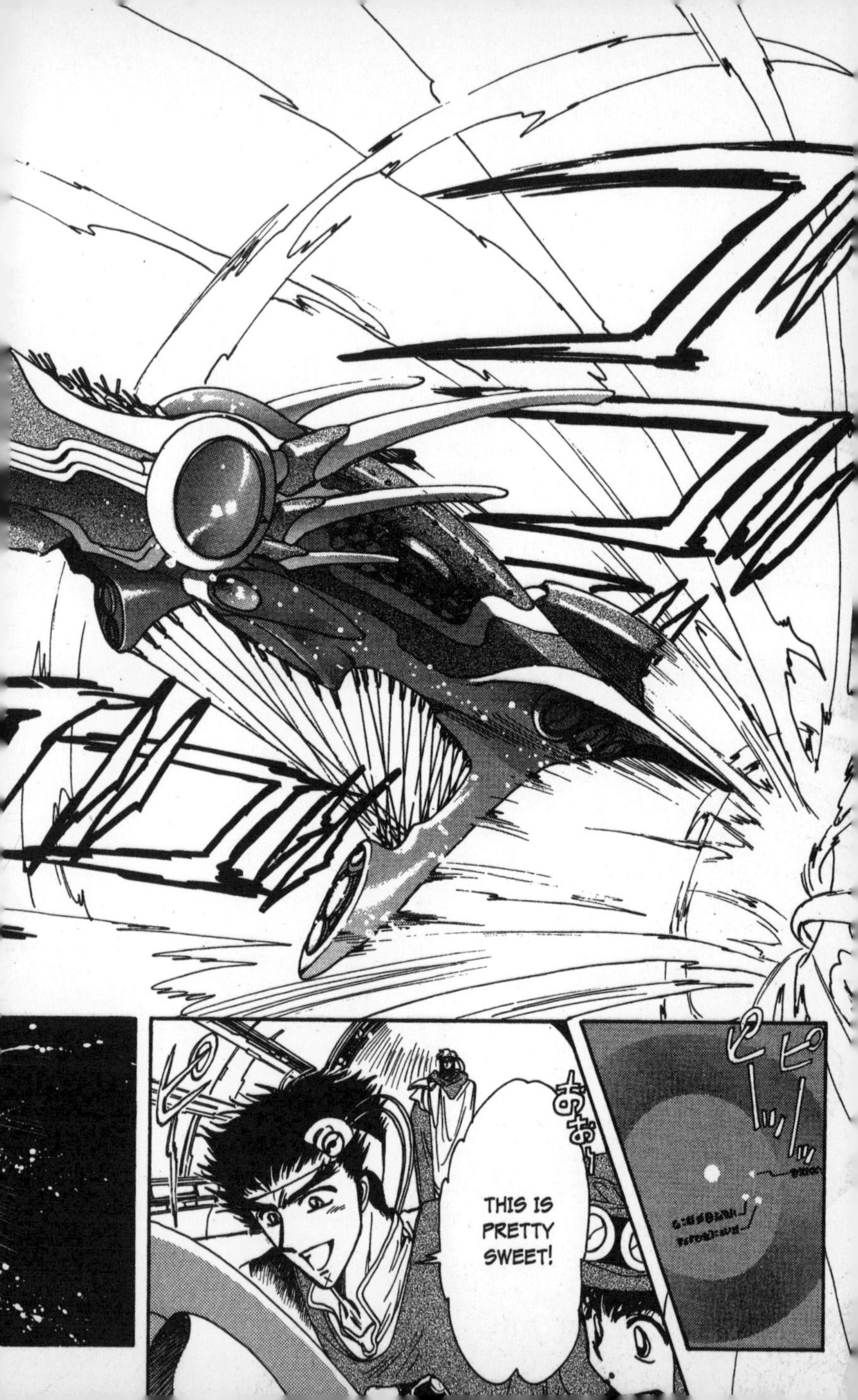
ピーッ ピーッ
おお
THIS IS PRETTY SWEET!

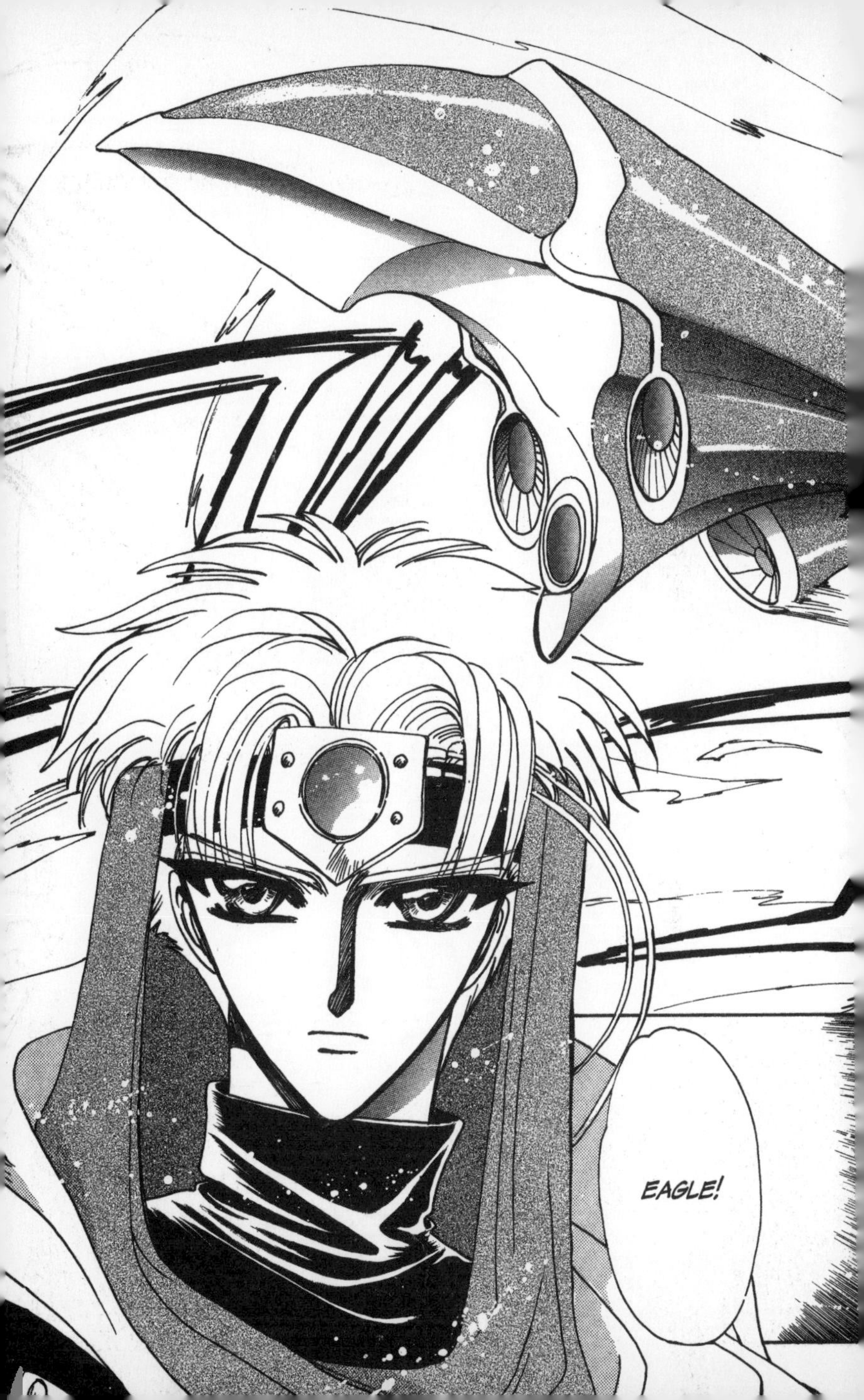
EAGLE!

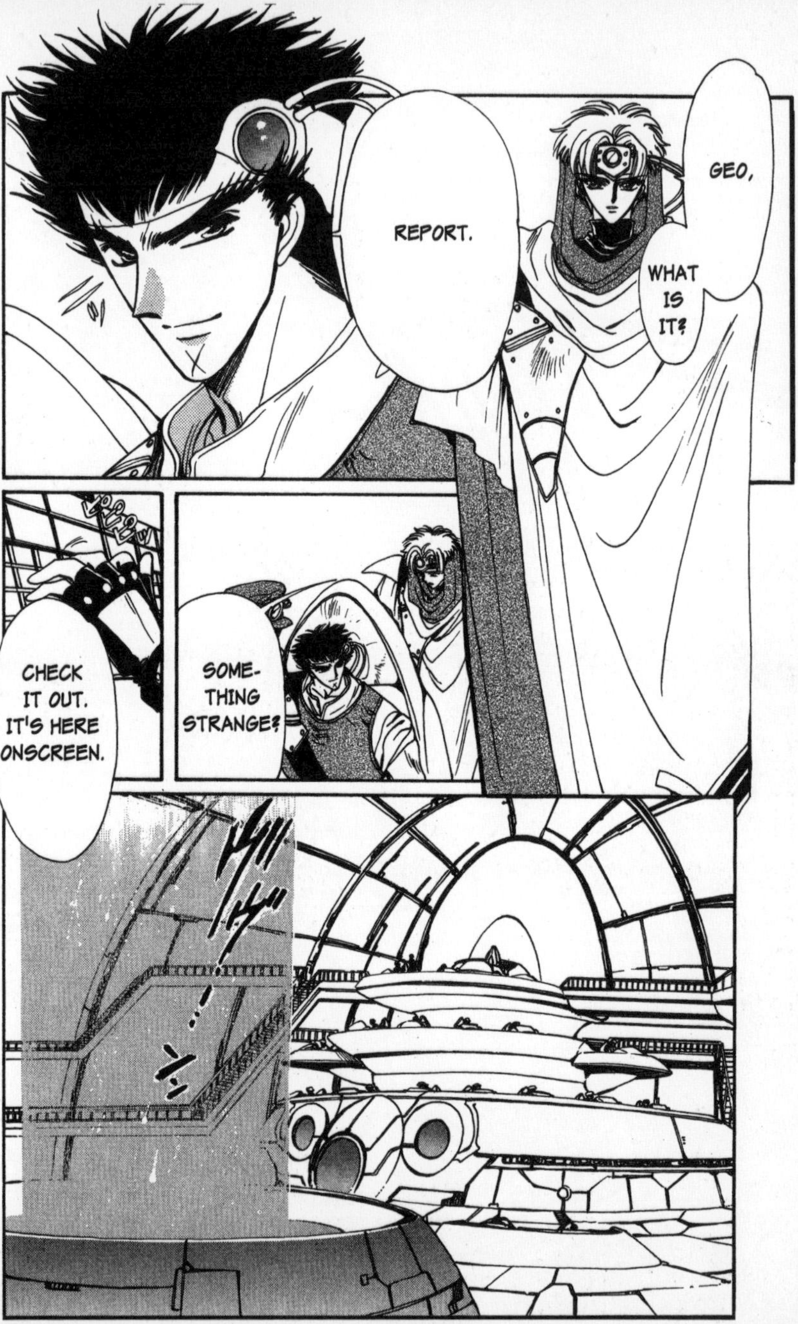
GEO,
WHAT IS IT?
REPORT.
SOME-THING STRANGE?
CHECK IT OUT. IT'S HERE ONSCREEN.

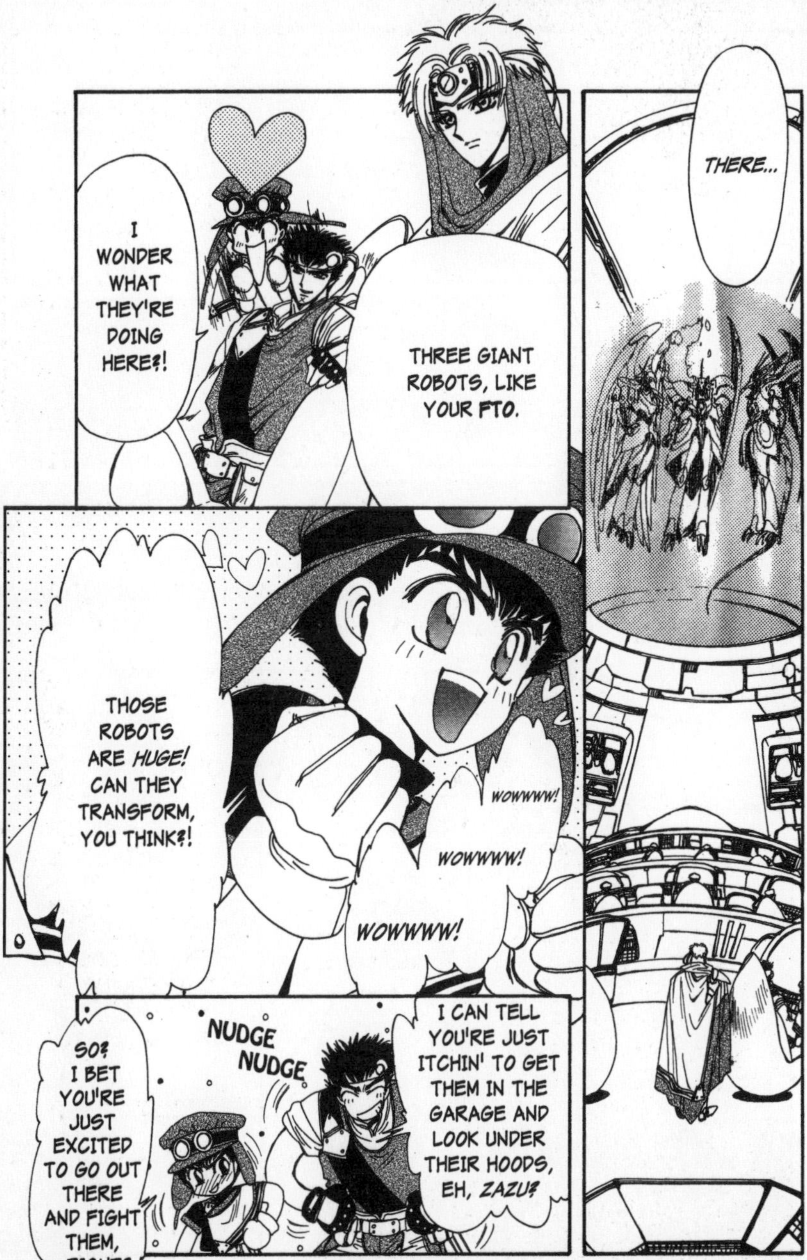
THERE...
THREE GIANT ROBOTS, LIKE YOUR FTO.
I WONDER WHAT THEY'RE DOING HERE?!
WOWWWW!
WOWWWW!
WOWWWW!
THOSE ROBOTS ARE *HUGE!* CAN THEY TRANSFORM, YOU THINK?!
I CAN TELL YOU'RE JUST ITCHIN' TO GET THEM IN THE GARAGE AND LOOK UNDER THEIR HOODS, EH, *ZAZU?*
NUDGE NUDGE
SO? I BET YOU'RE JUST EXCITED TO GO OUT THERE AND FIGHT THEM, RIGHT?

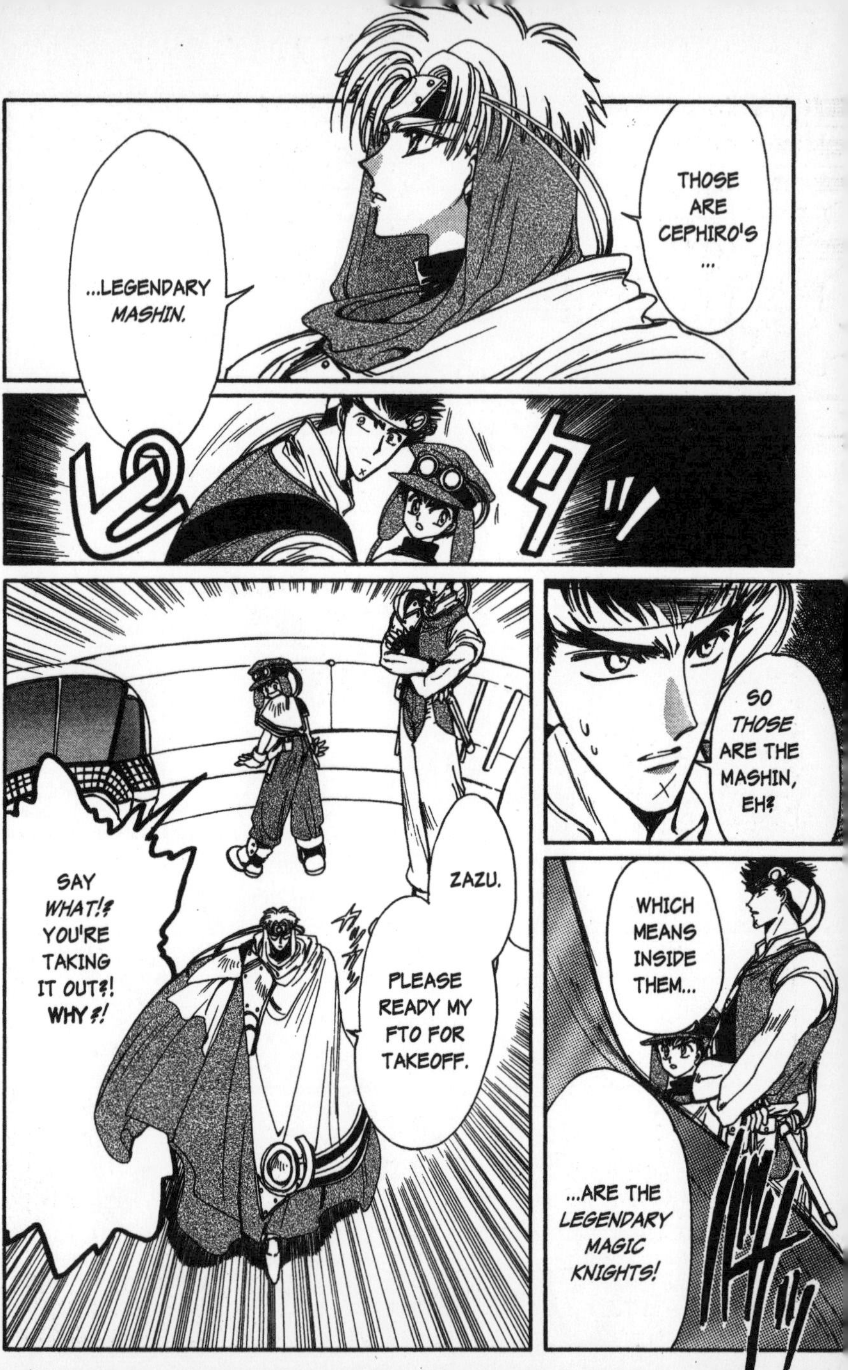
THOSE ARE CEPHIRO'S ...
...LEGENDARY MASHIN.
SO THOSE ARE THE MASHIN, EH?
WHICH MEANS INSIDE THEM...
...ARE THE LEGENDARY MAGIC KNIGHTS!
ZAZU.
PLEASE READY MY FTO FOR TAKEOFF.
SAY WHAT!? YOU'RE TAKING IT OUT?! WHY?!

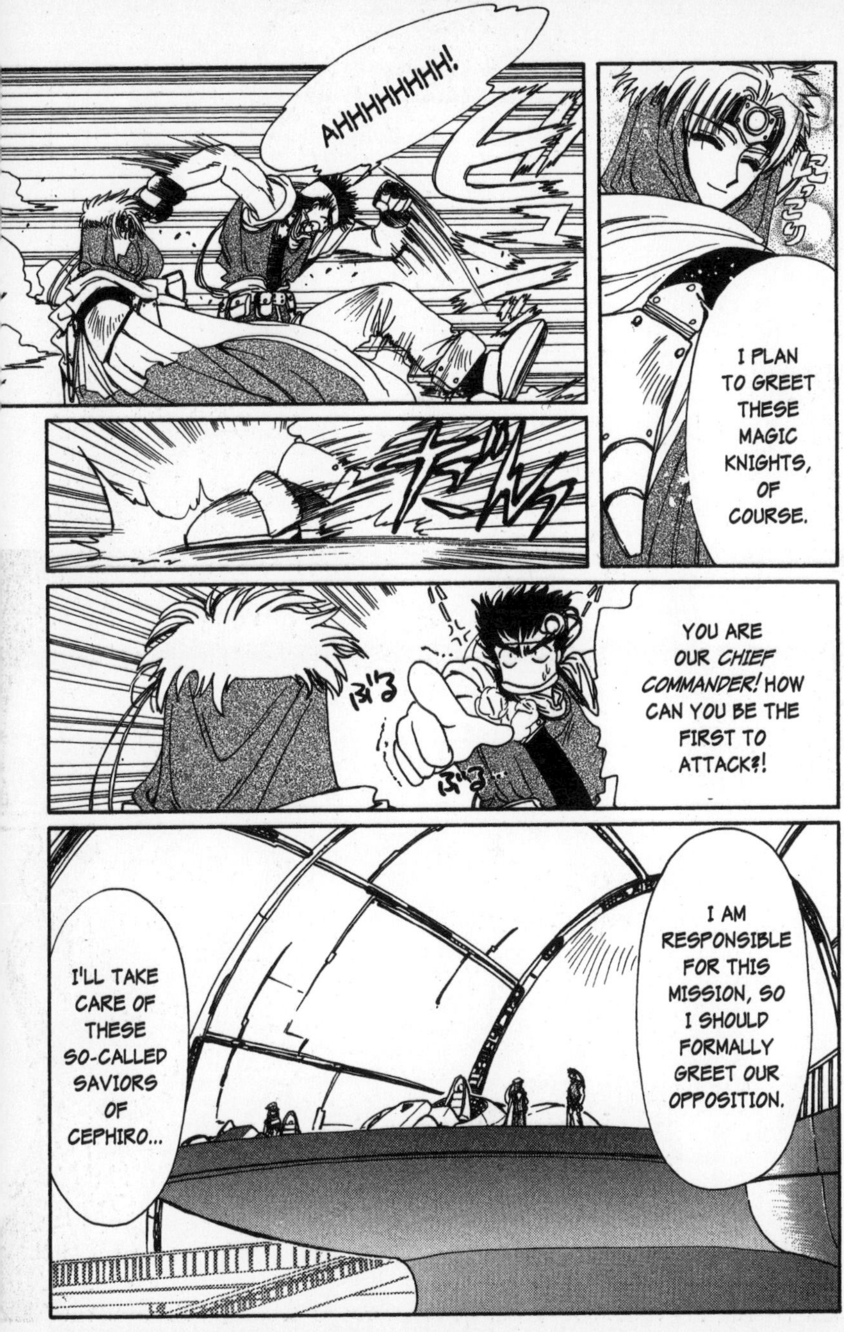
I PLAN TO GREET THESE MAGIC KNIGHTS, OF COURSE.
AHHHHHHHH!
YOU ARE OUR *CHIEF COMMANDER!* HOW CAN YOU BE THE FIRST TO ATTACK?!
I AM RESPONSIBLE FOR THIS MISSION, SO I SHOULD FORMALLY GREET OUR OPPOSITION.
I'LL TAKE CARE OF THESE SO-CALLED SAVIORS OF CEPHIRO...

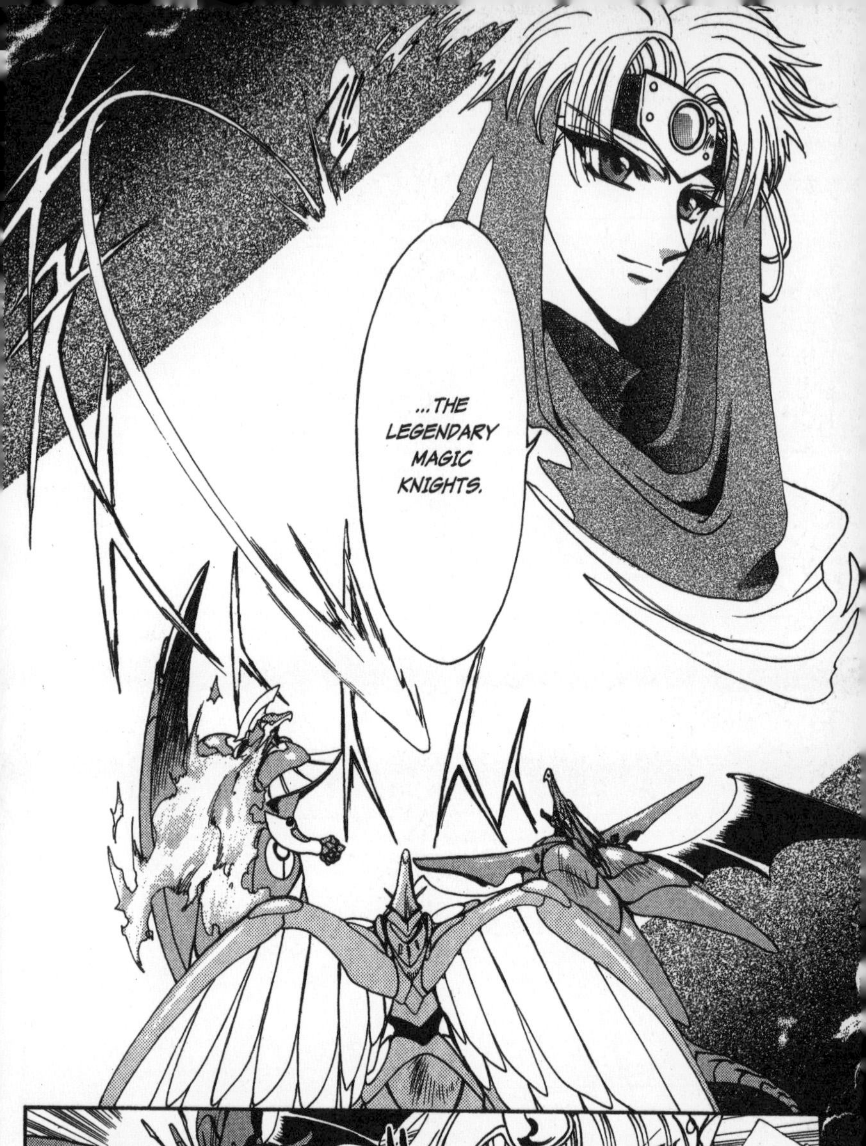
...THE LEGENDARY MAGIC KNIGHTS.
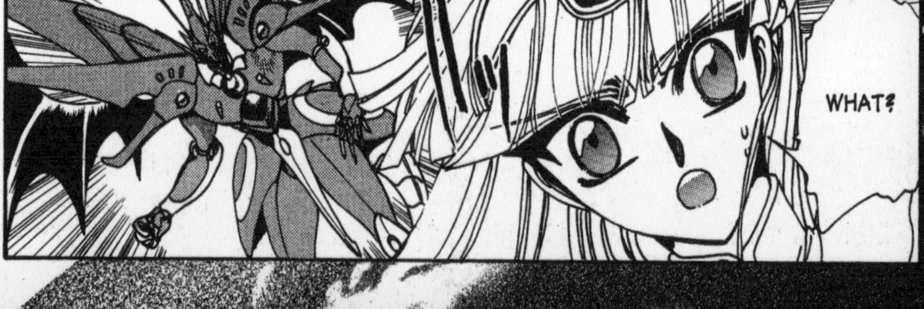
WHAT?

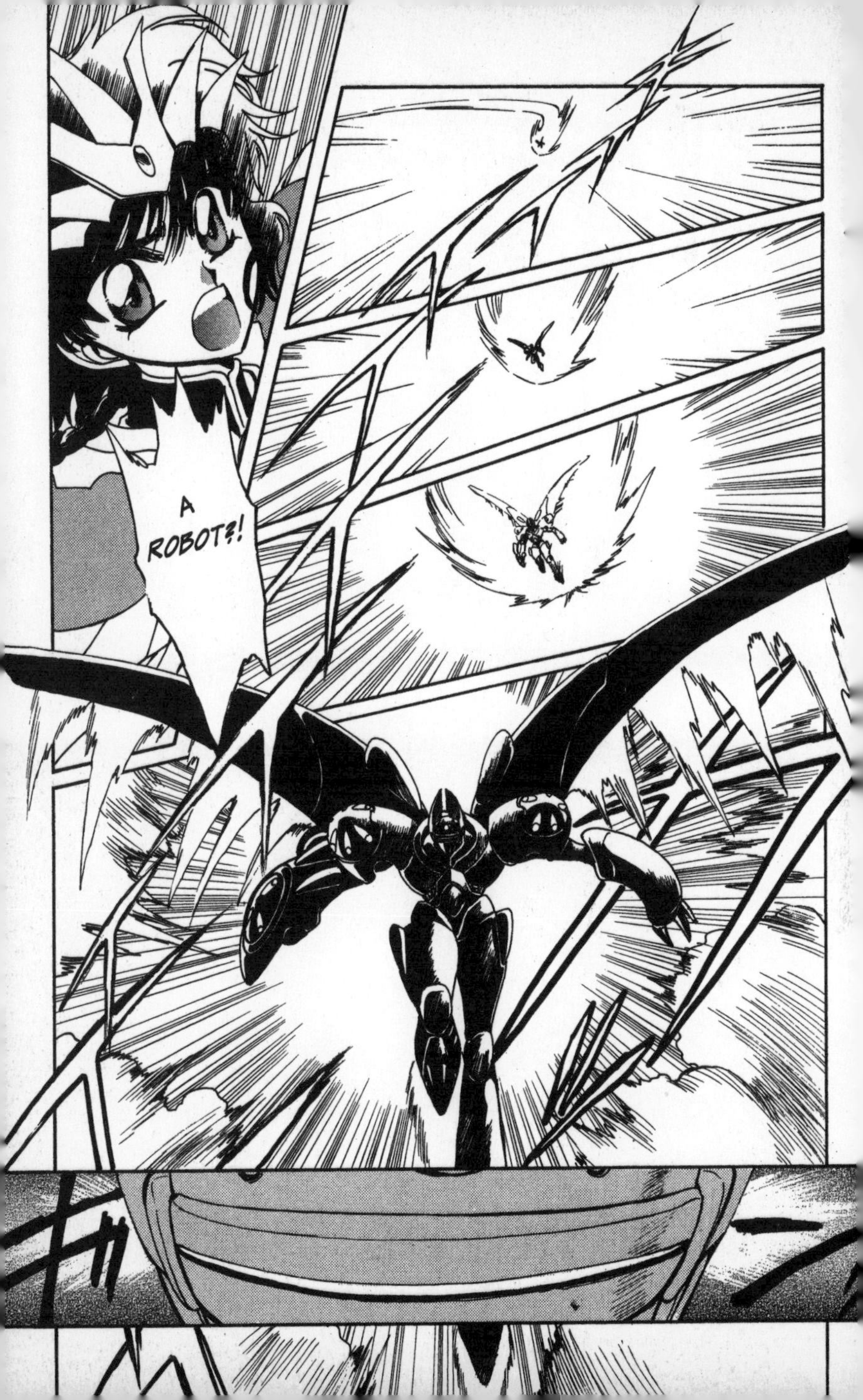
A ROBOT?!

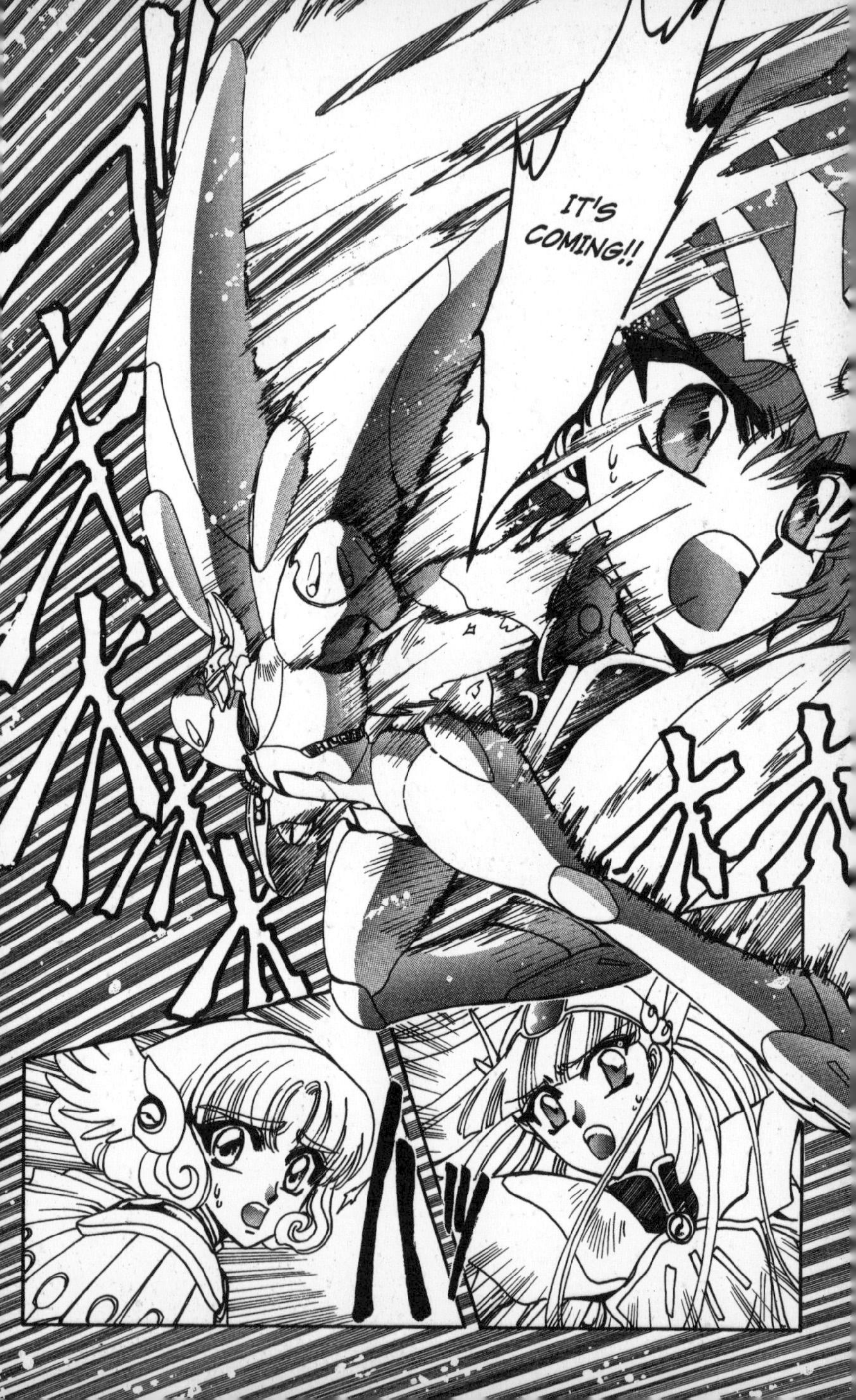
IT'S COMING!!

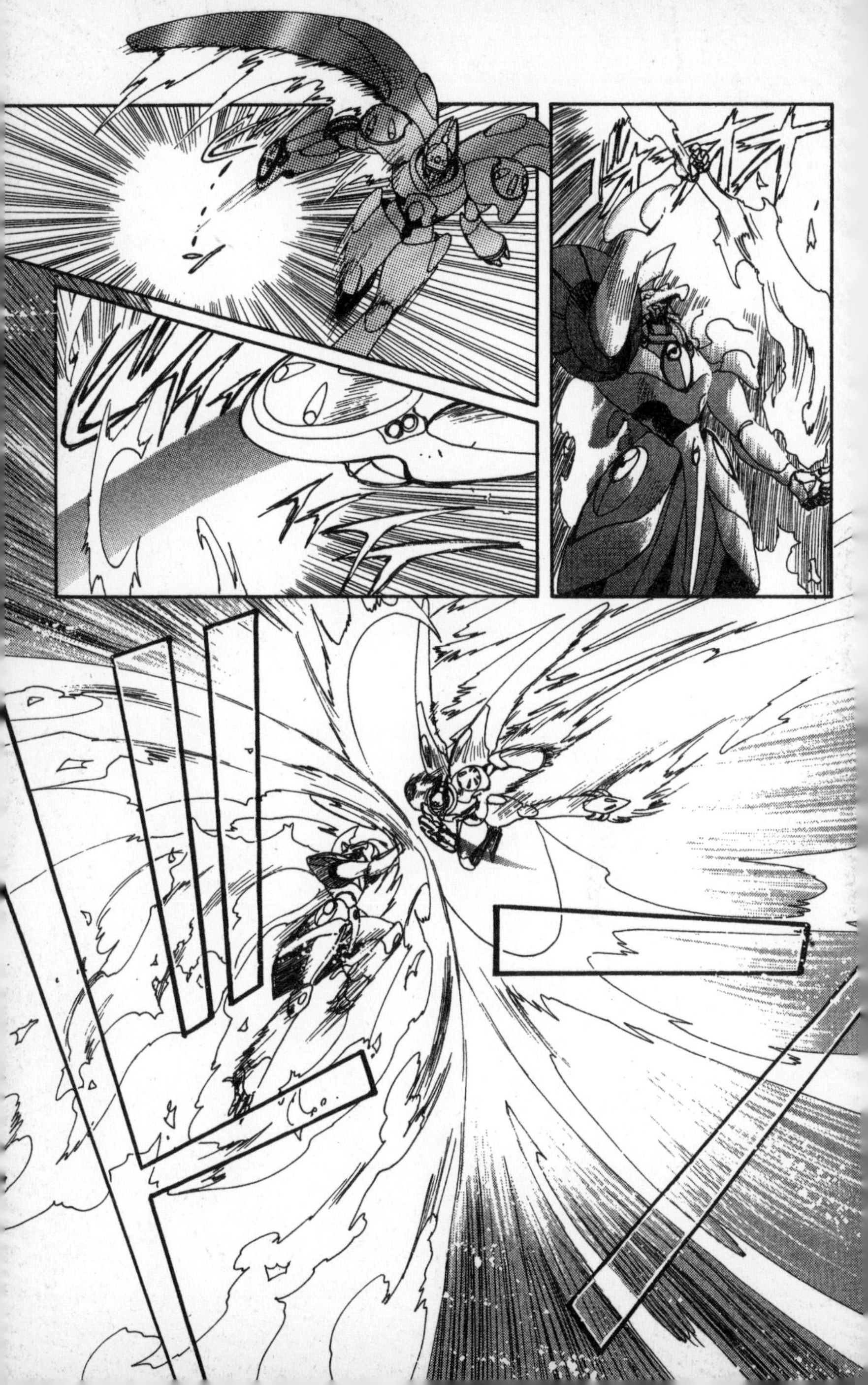

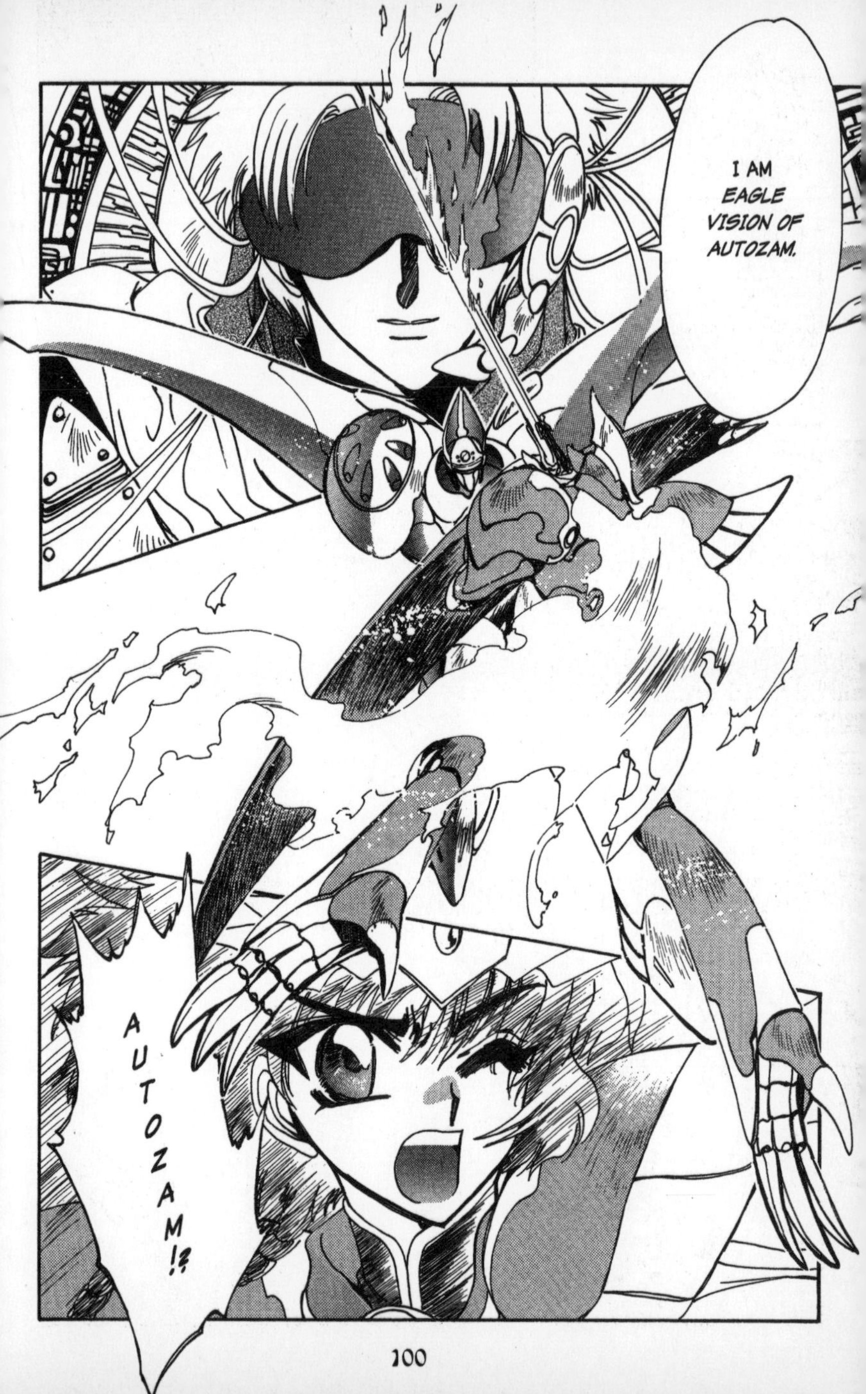
I AM EAGLE VISION OF AUTOZAM.
AUTOZAM!?

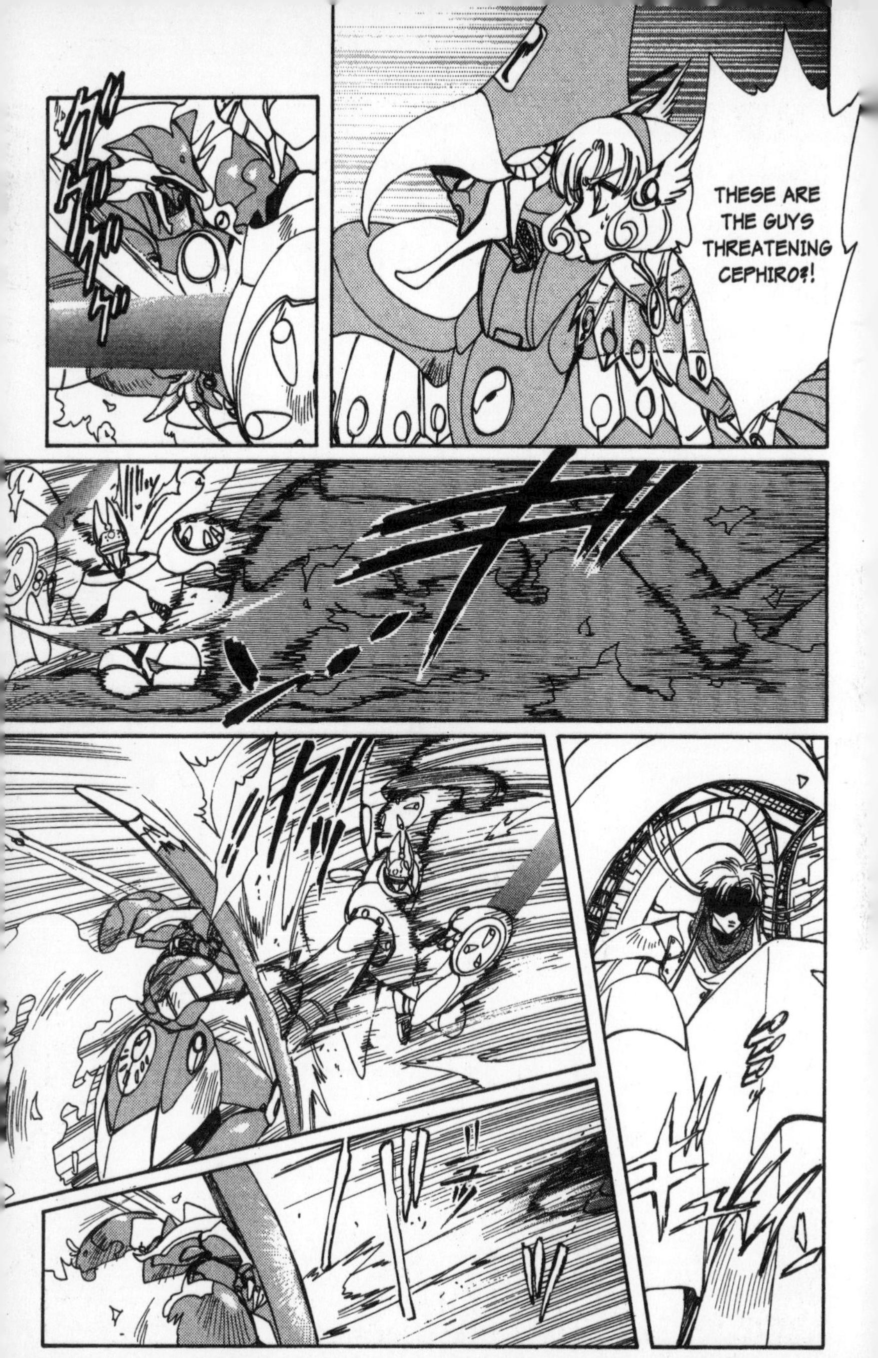
THESE ARE THE GUYS THREATENING CEPHIRO?!

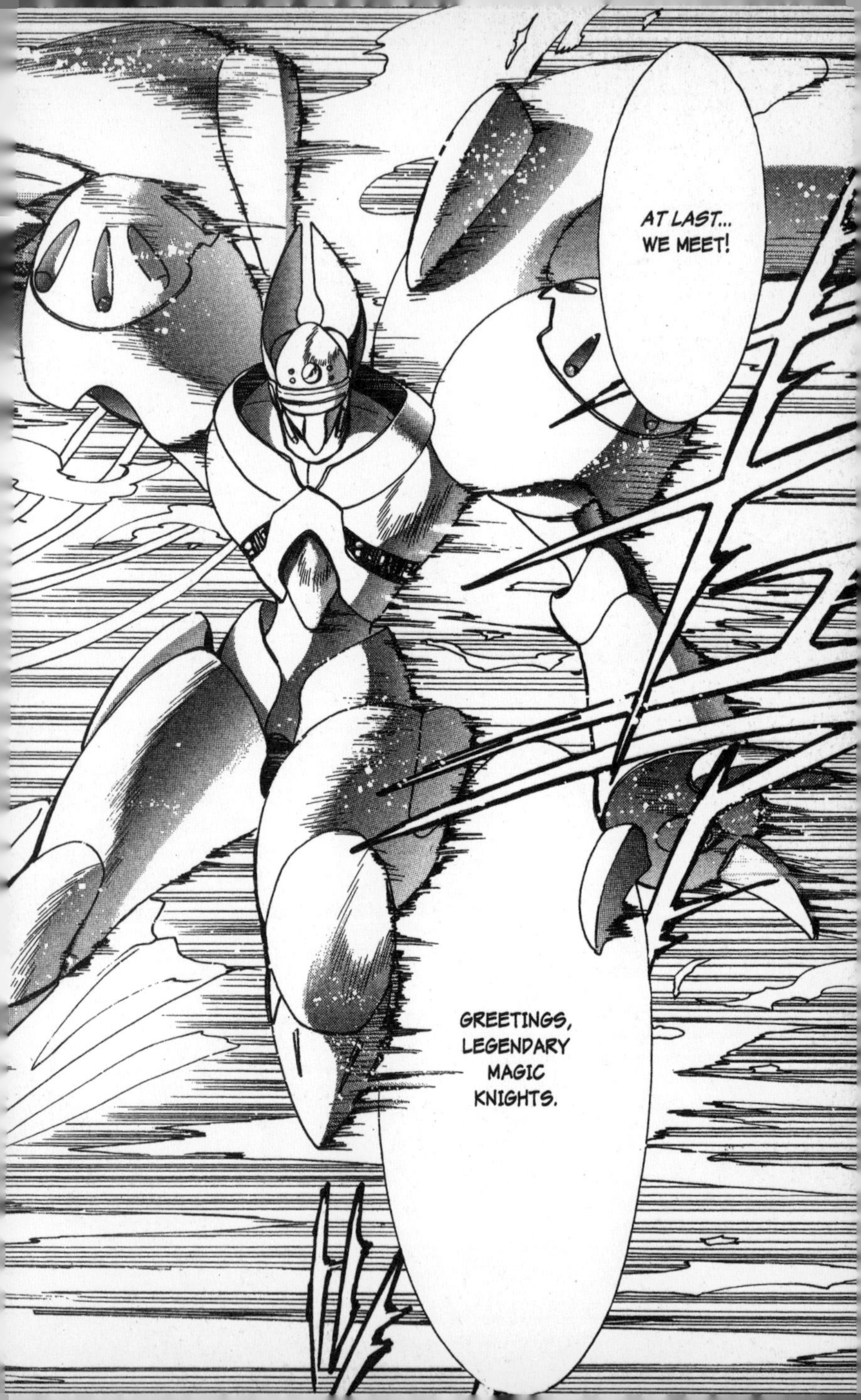
AT LAST... WE MEET!
GREETINGS, LEGENDARY MAGIC KNIGHTS.

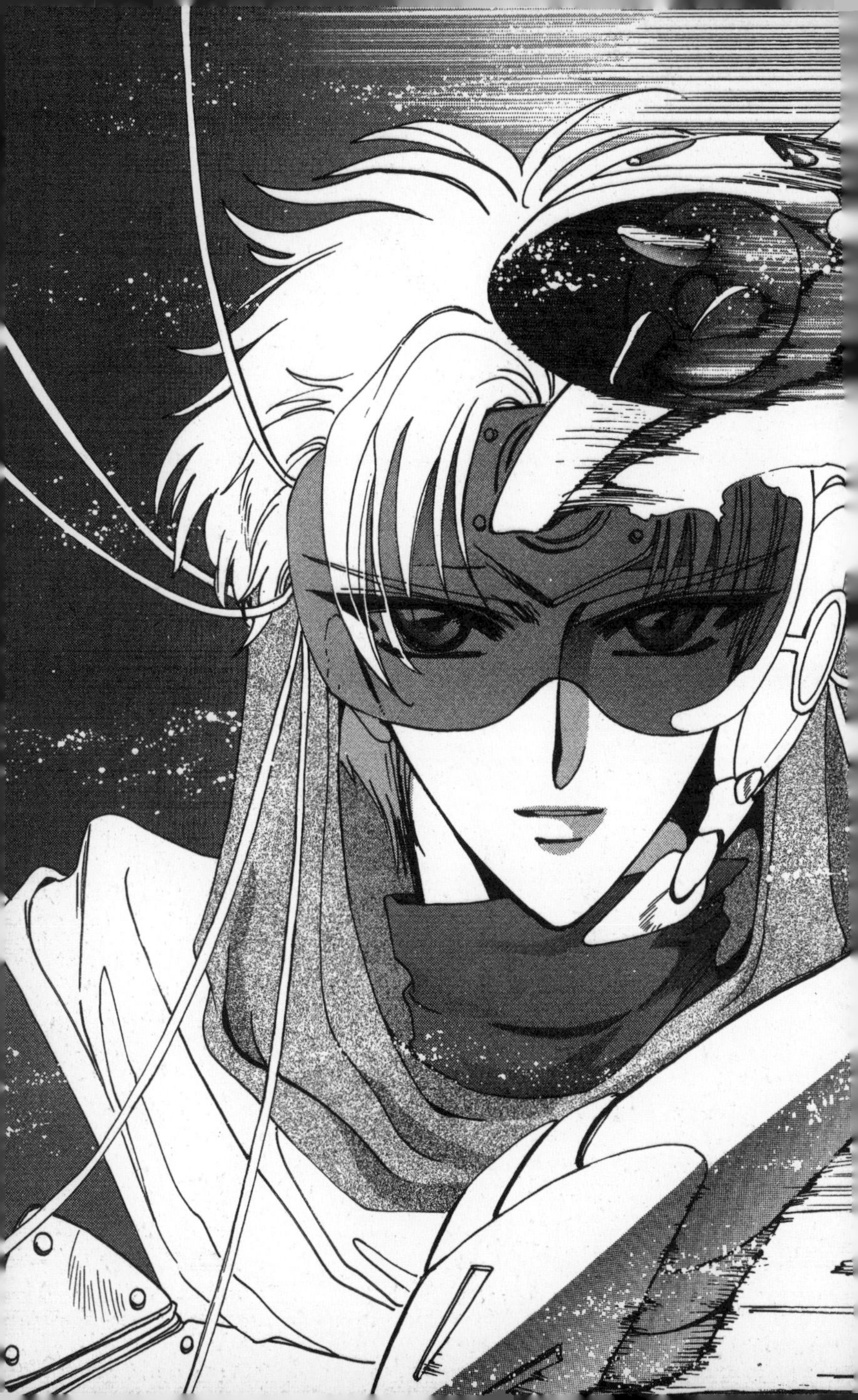

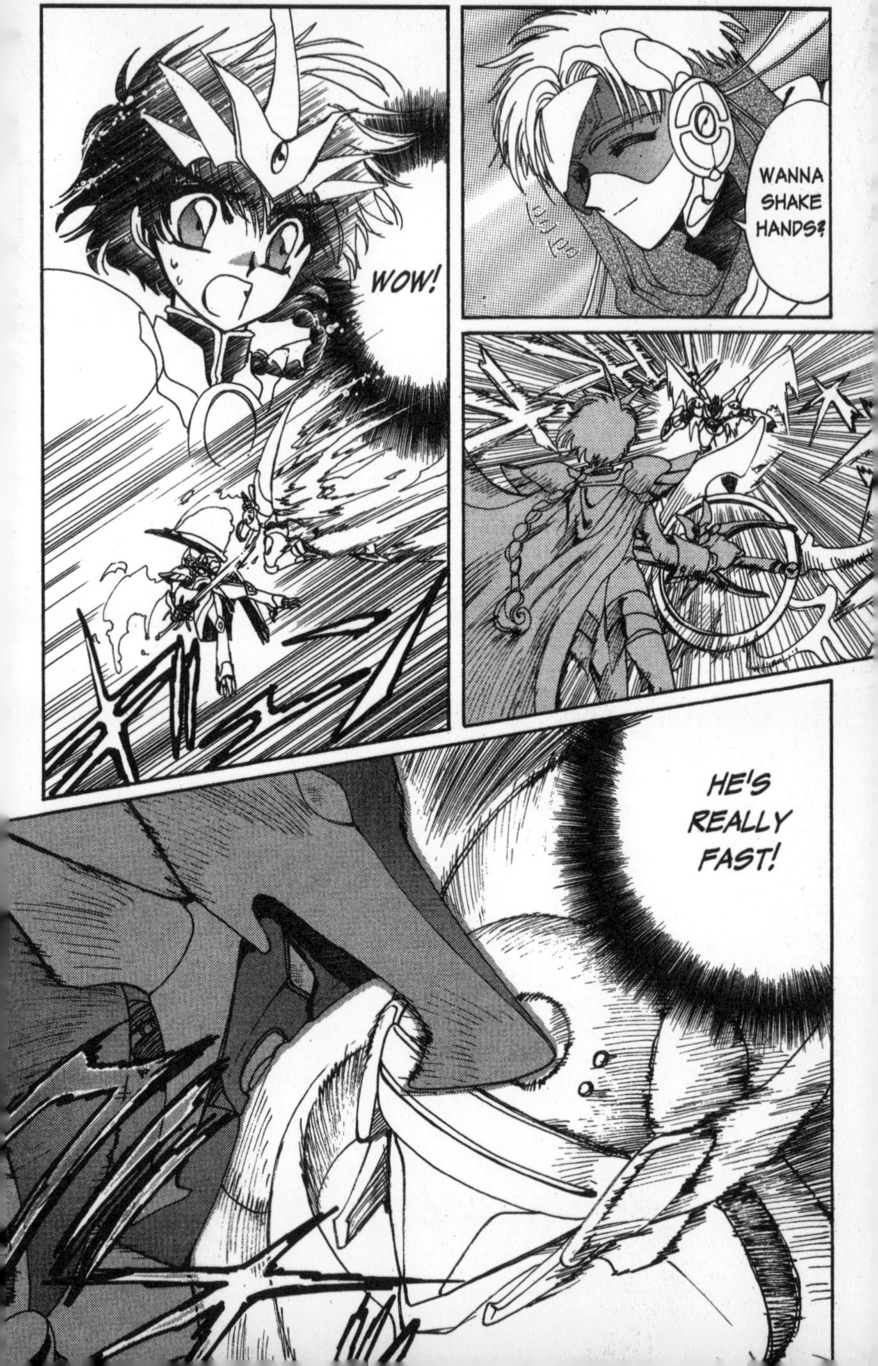
WANNA SHAKE HANDS?
WOW!
HE'S REALLY FAST!

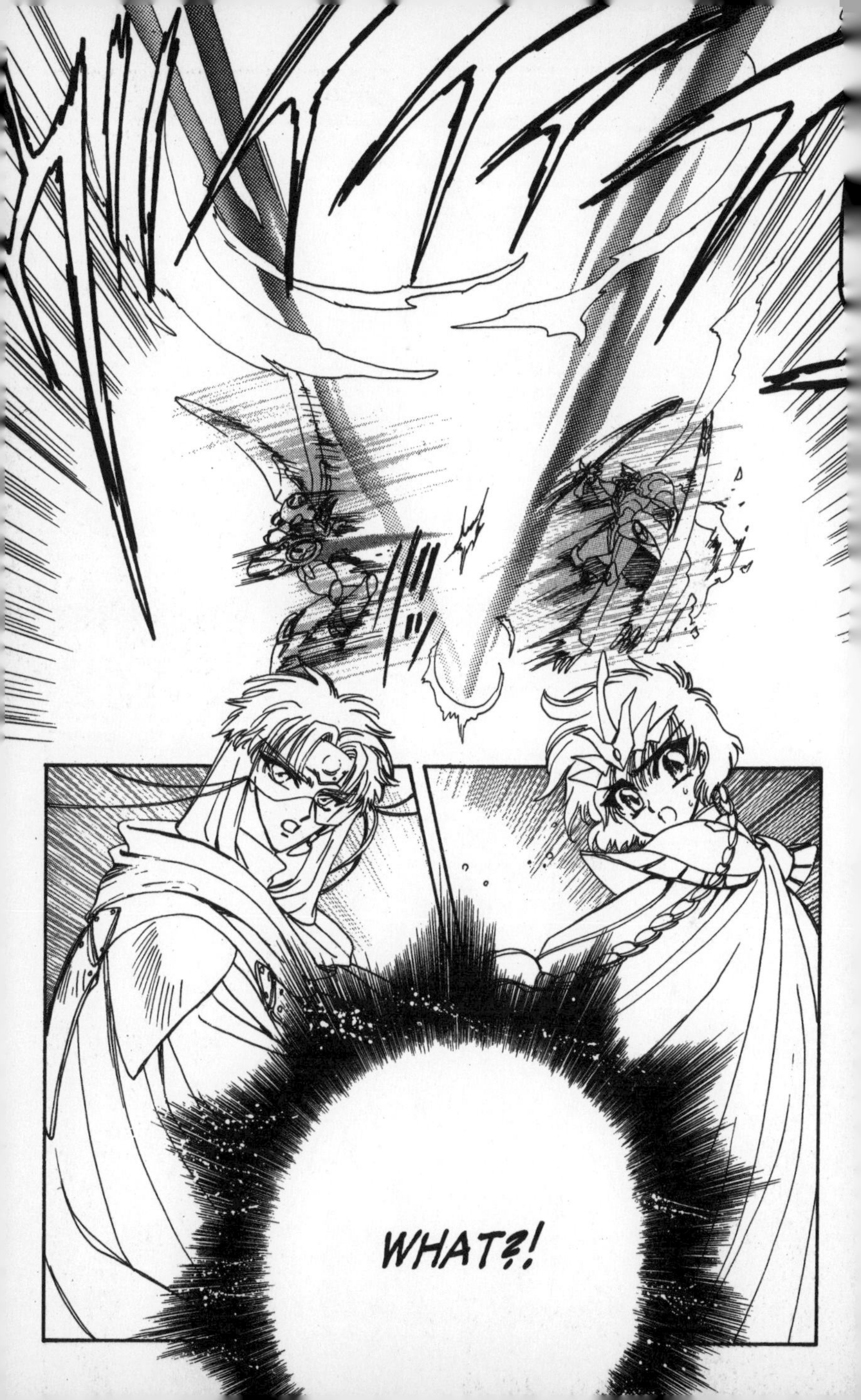
WHAT?!

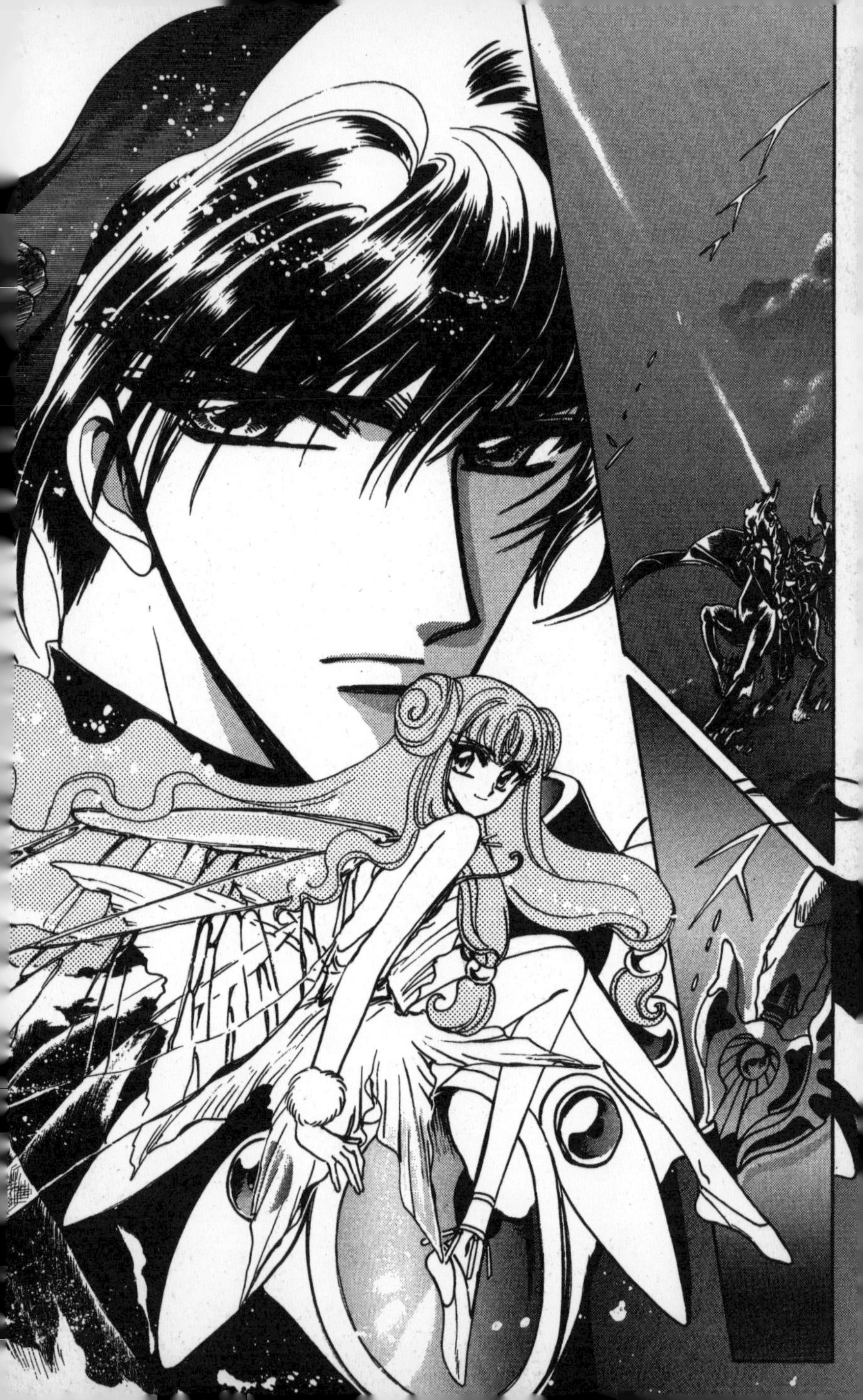

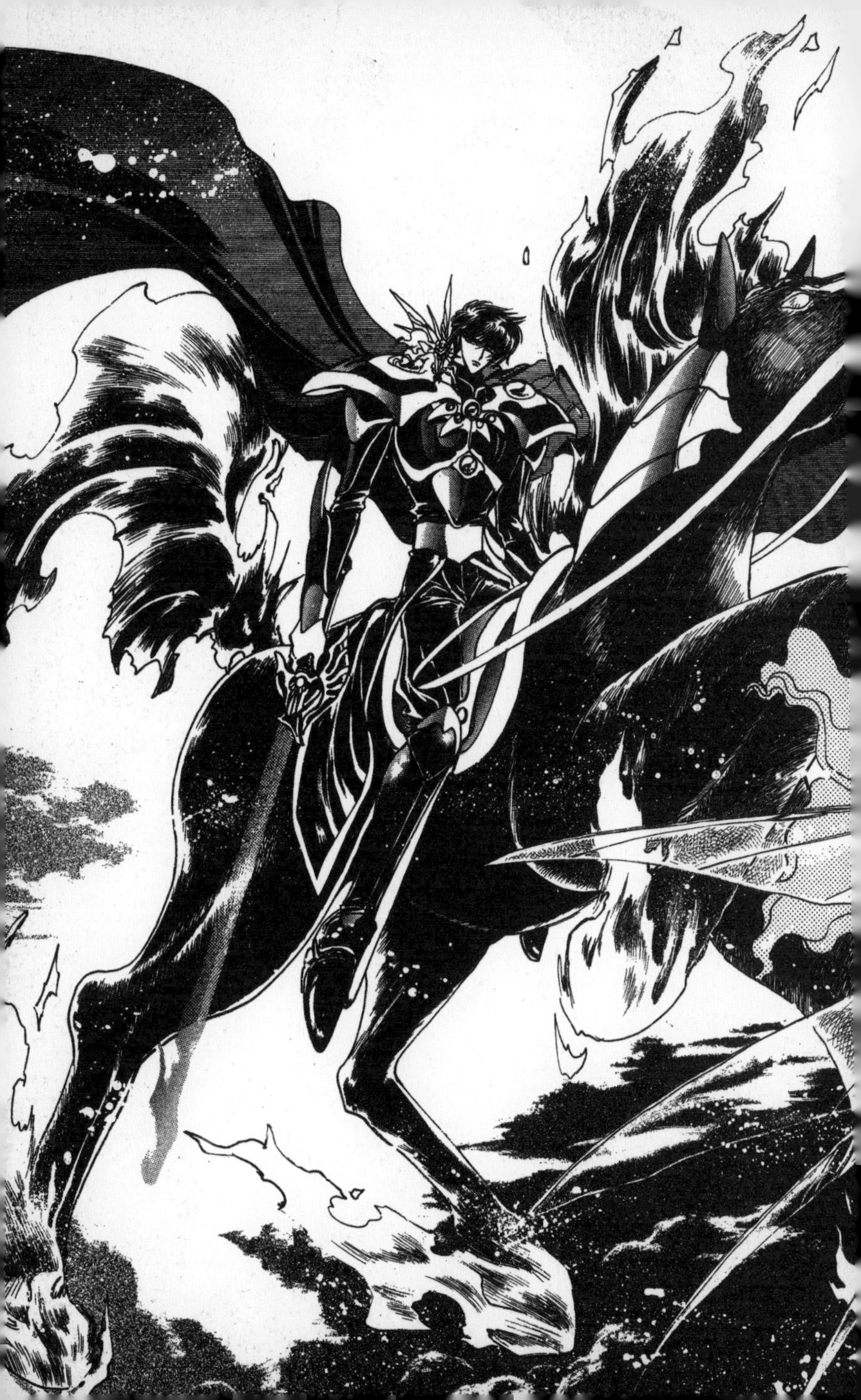

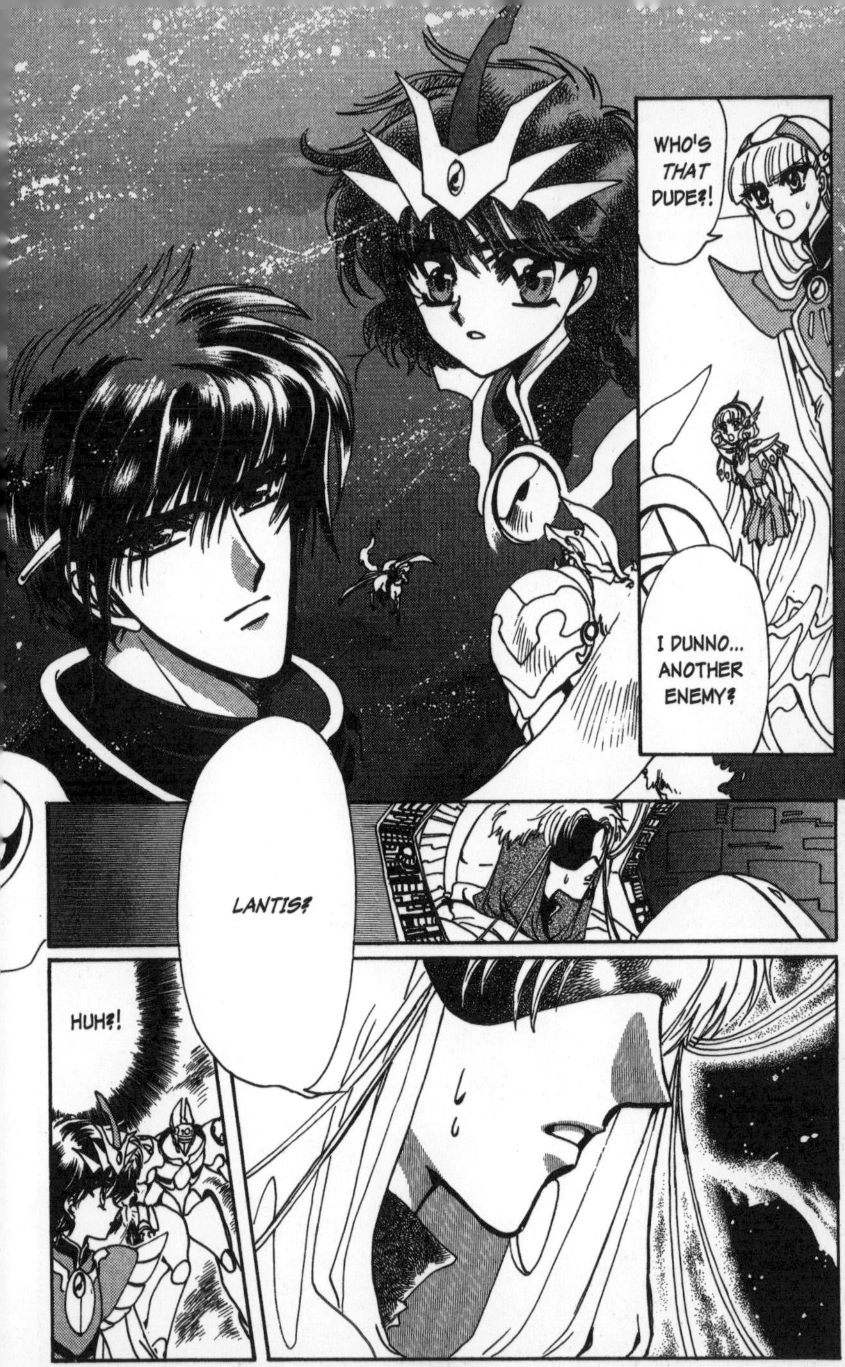
WHO'S *THAT* DUDE?!
I DUNNO... ANOTHER ENEMY?
LANTIS?
HUH?!

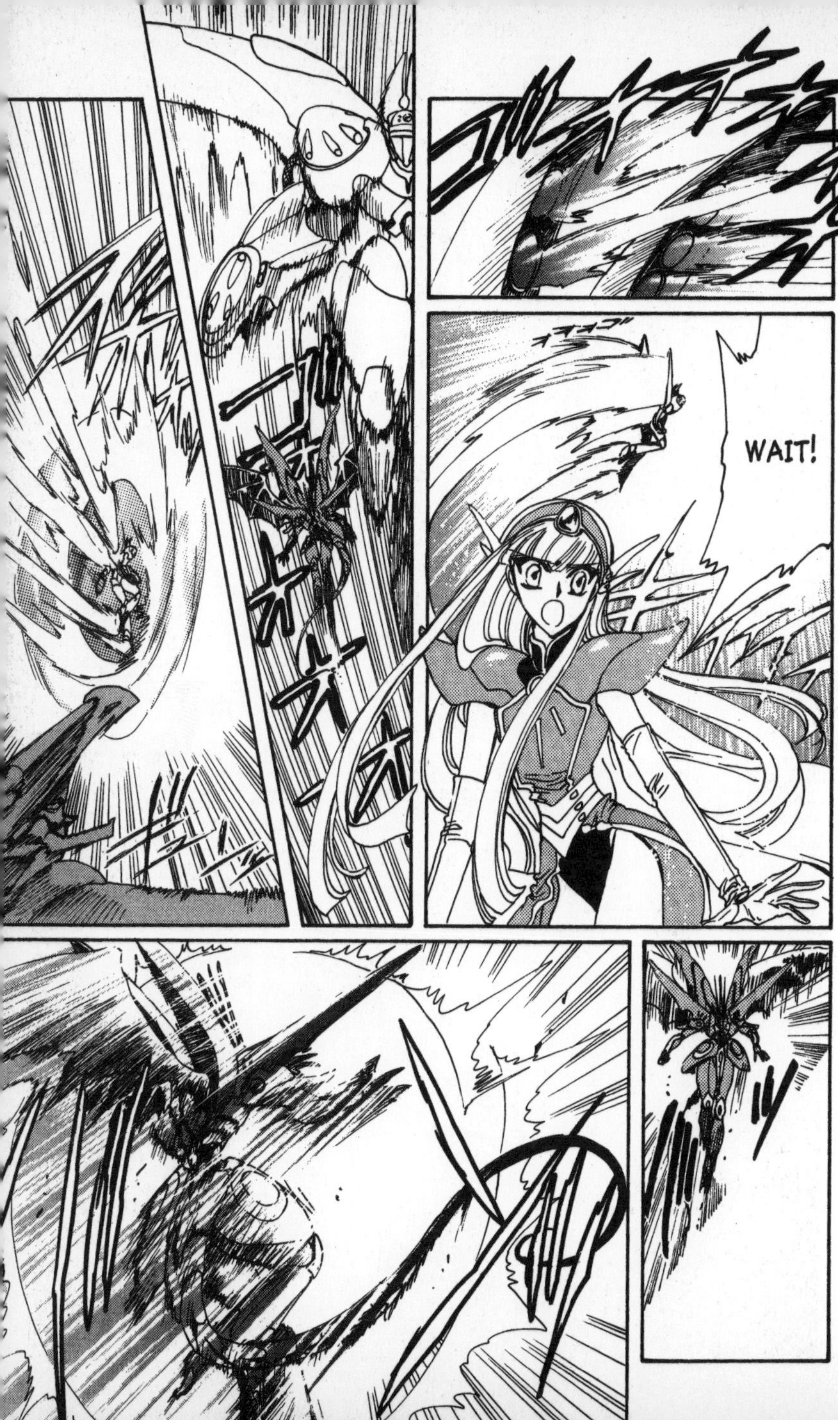
WAIT!

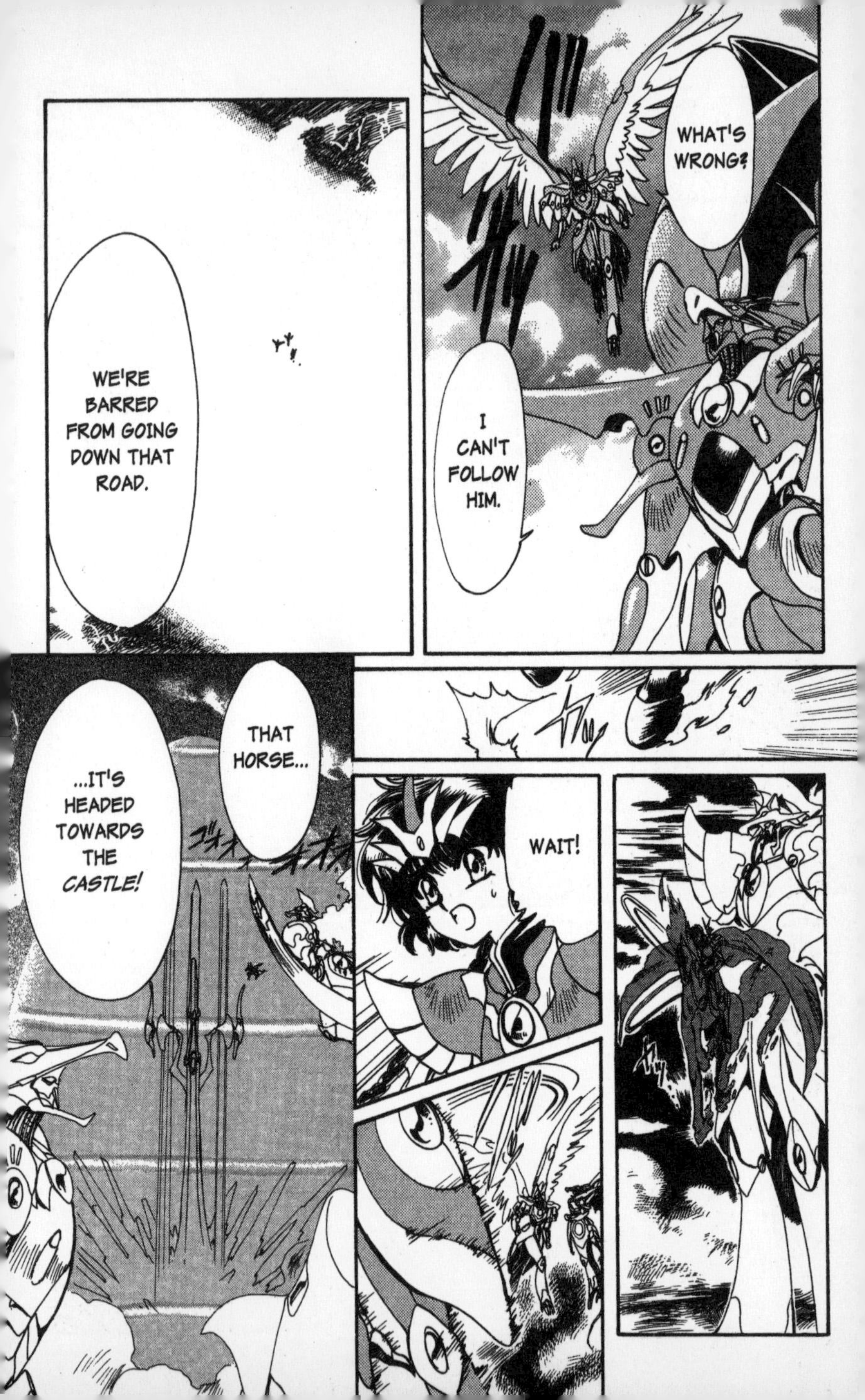
WHAT'S WRONG?
I CAN'T FOLLOW HIM.
WE'RE BARRED FROM GOING DOWN THAT ROAD.
WAIT!
THAT HORSE...
...IT'S HEADED TOWARDS THE *CASTLE!*

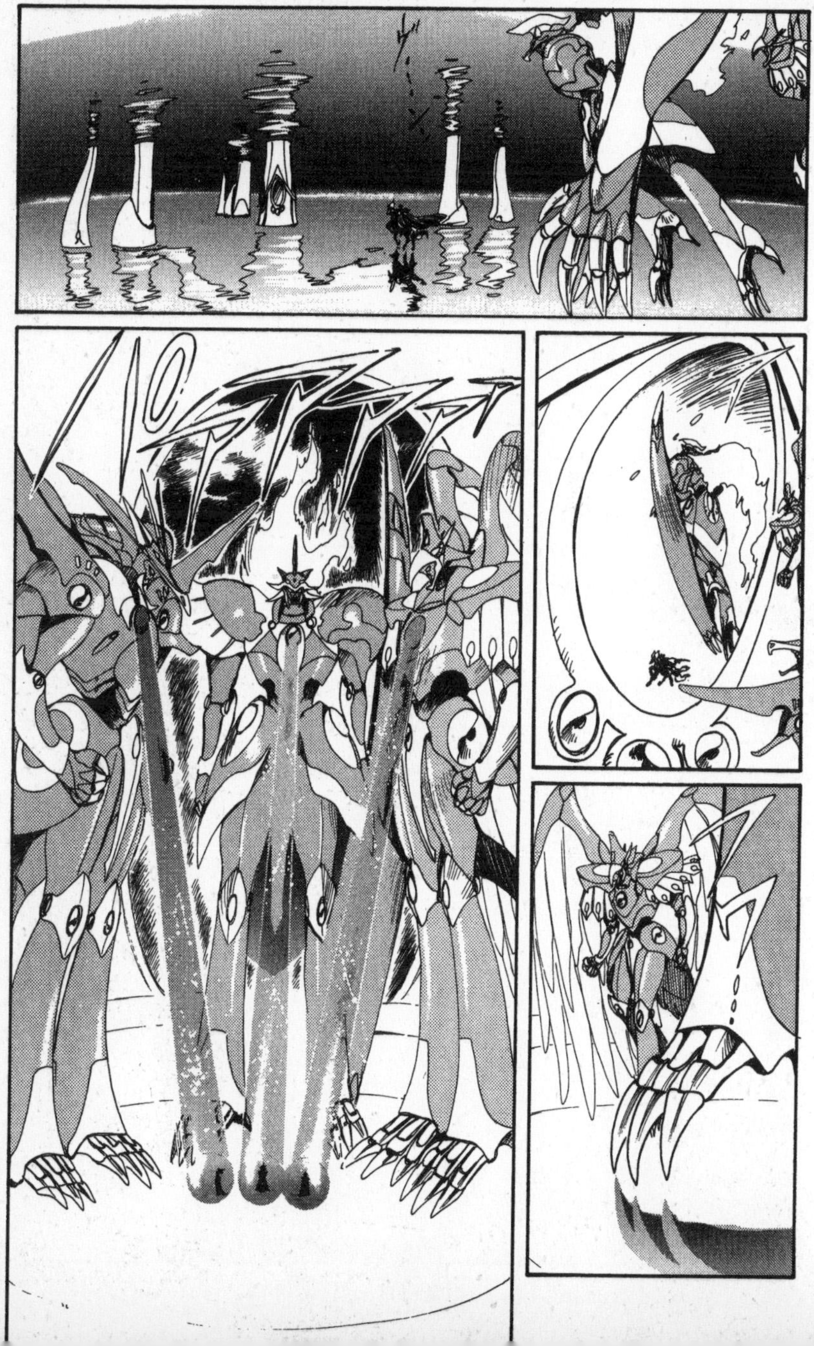

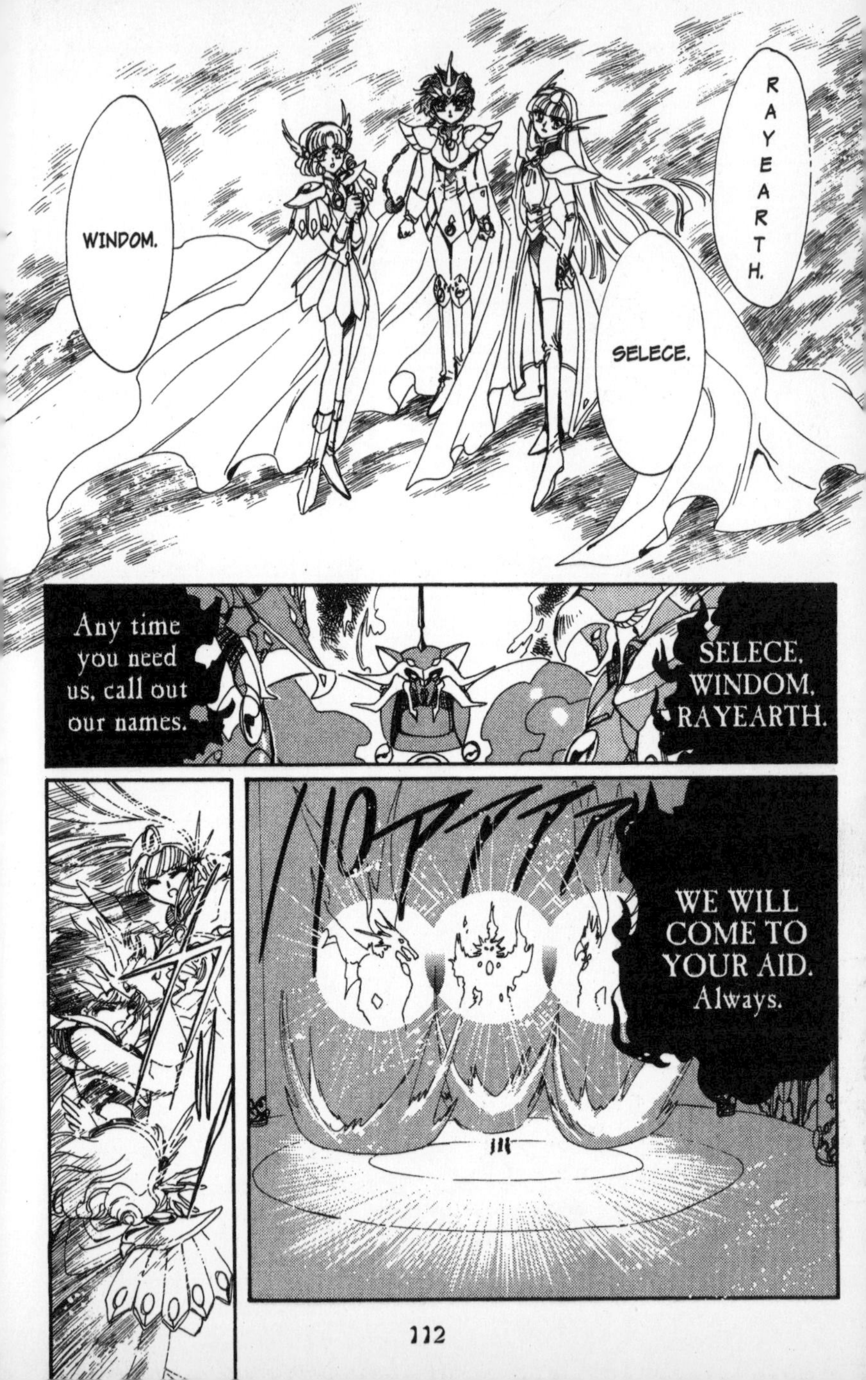
RAYEARTH.
SELECE.
WINDOM.
SELECE, WINDOM, RAYEARTH.
Any time you need us, call out our names.
WE WILL COME TO YOUR AID. Always.

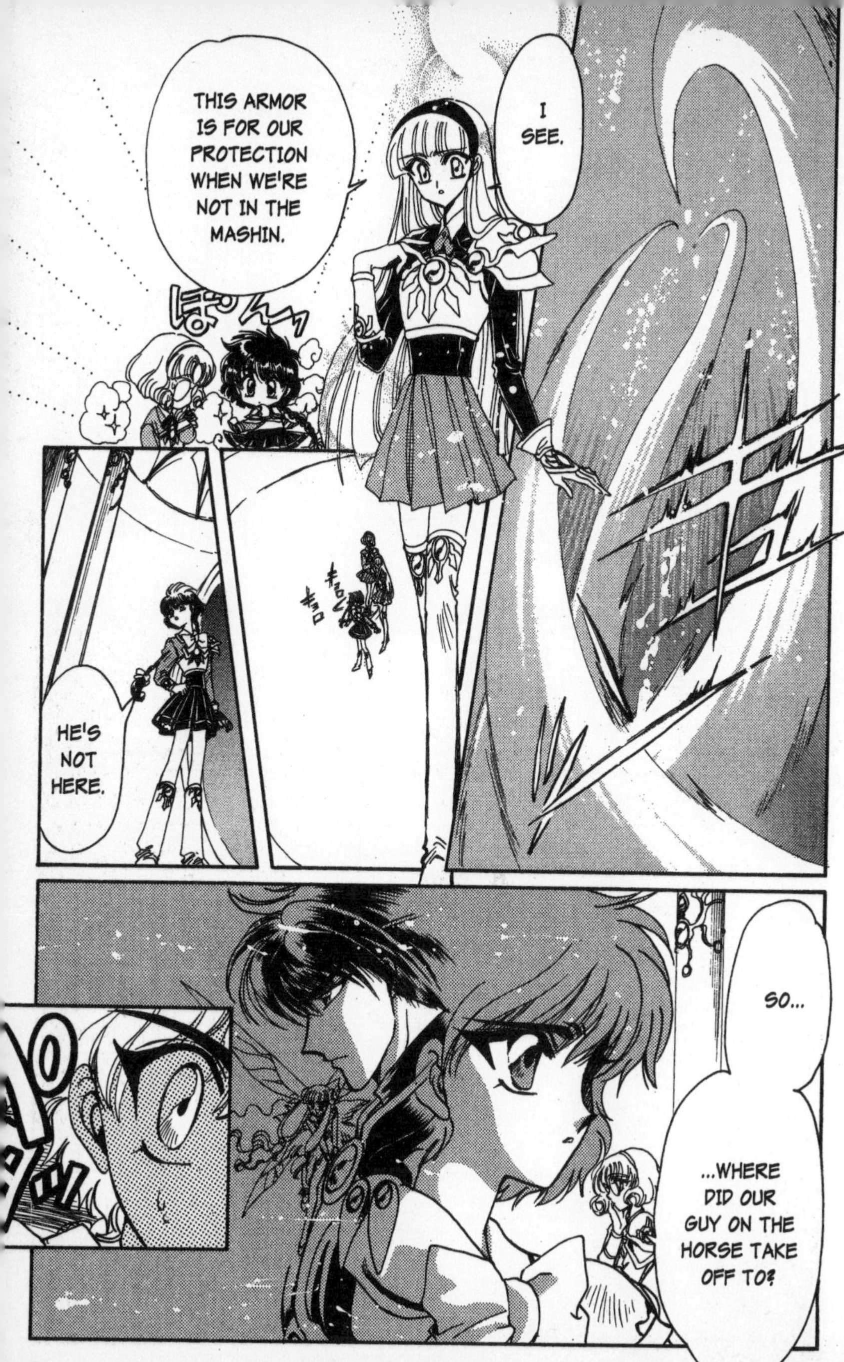
THIS ARMOR IS FOR OUR PROTECTION WHEN WE'RE NOT IN THE MASHIN.
I SEE.
HE'S NOT HERE.
SO...
...WHERE DID OUR GUY ON THE HORSE TAKE OFF TO?

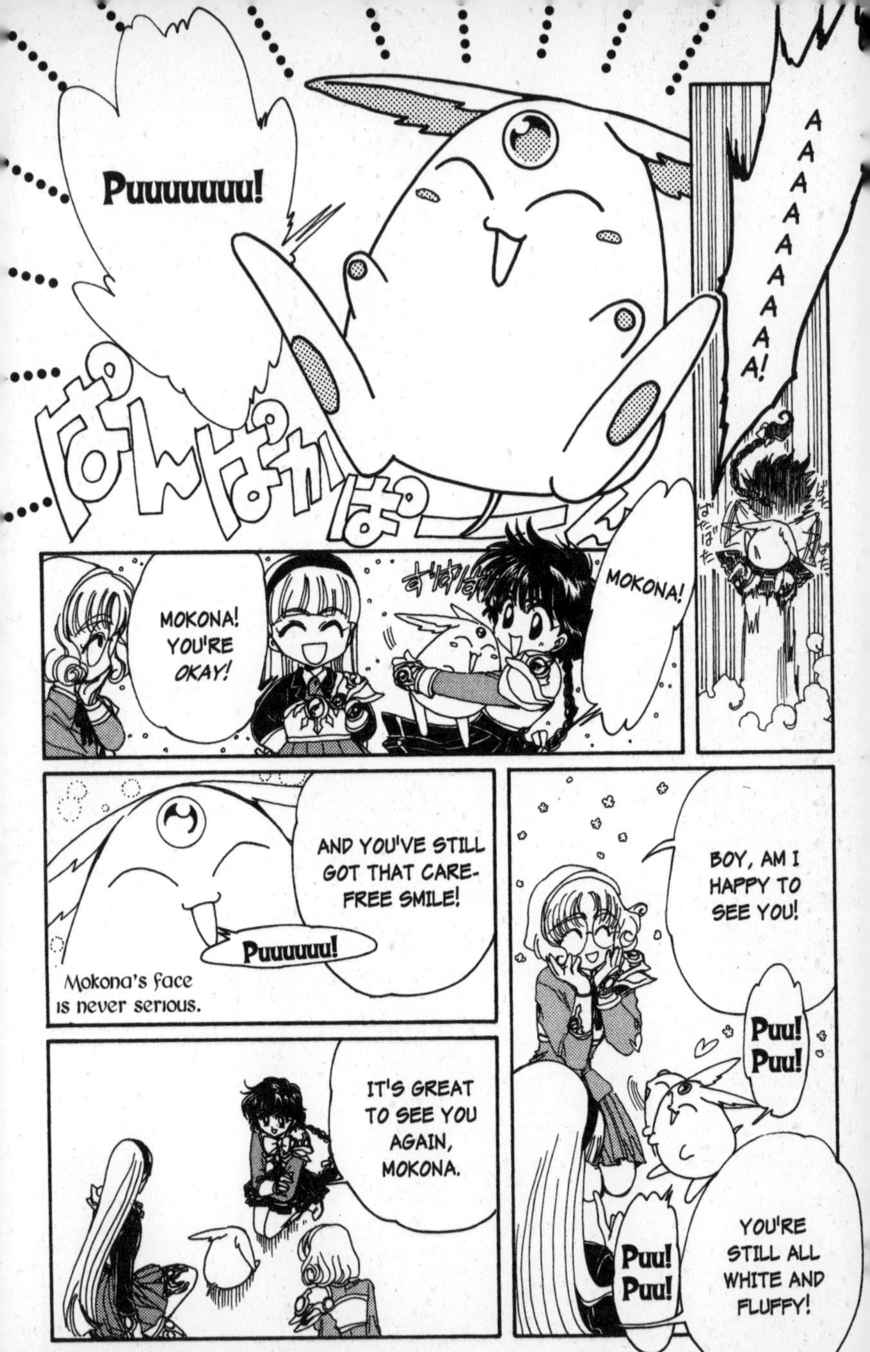
AAAAAAAAAAA!
Puuuuuuu!
ぱんぱかぱーん
MOKONA!
MOKONA! YOU'RE OKAY!
BOY, AM I HAPPY TO SEE YOU!
Puu! Puu!
YOU'RE STILL ALL WHITE AND FLUFFY!
Puu! Puu!
AND YOU'VE STILL GOT THAT CARE-FREE SMILE!
Puuuuuu!
Mokona's face is never serious.
IT'S GREAT TO SEE YOU AGAIN, MOKONA.

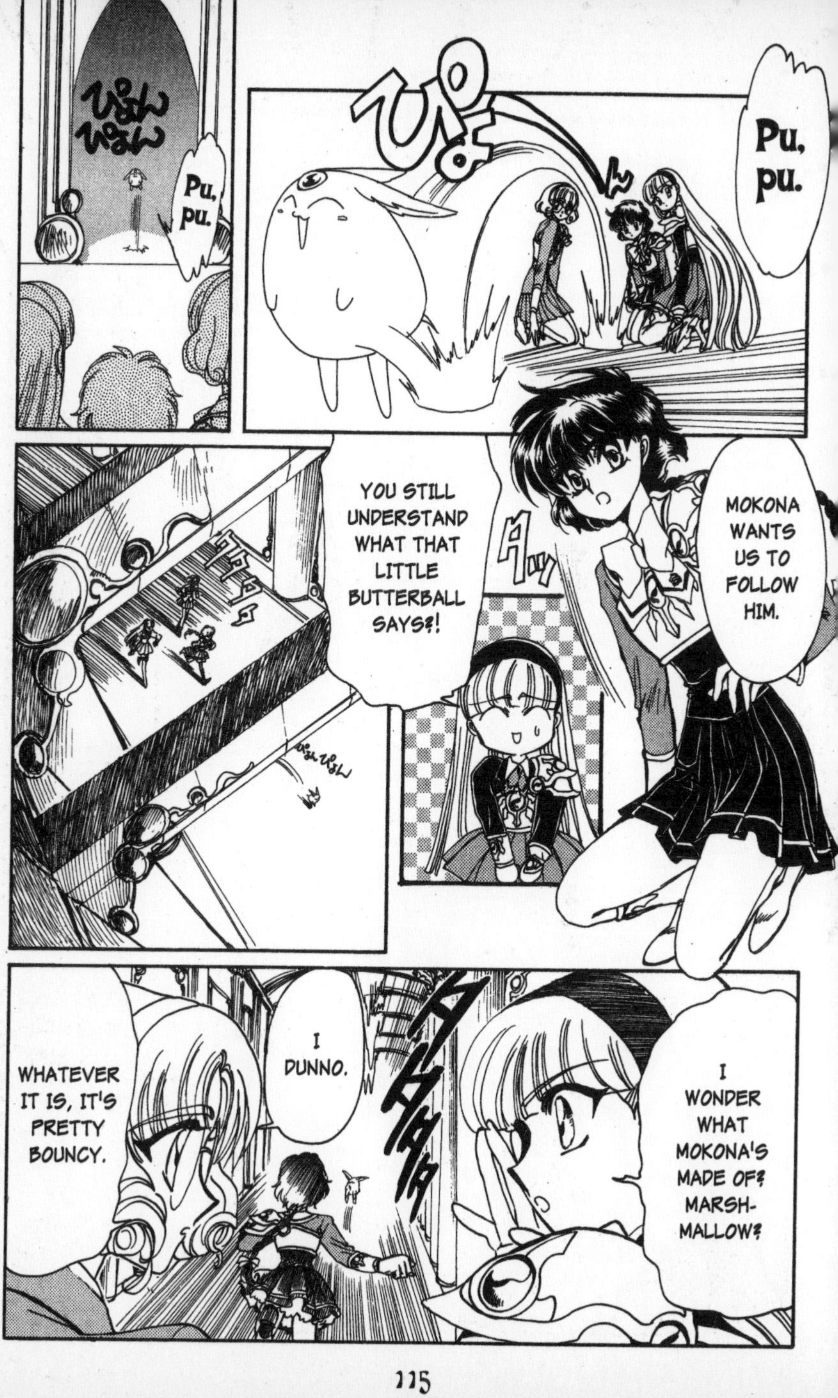
Pu, pu.
ぴょんぴょん
Pu, pu.
MOKONA WANTS US TO FOLLOW HIM.
YOU STILL UNDERSTAND WHAT THAT LITTLE BUTTERBALL SAYS?!
I WONDER WHAT MOKONA'S MADE OF? MARSH-MALLOW?
I DUNNO.
WHATEVER IT IS, IT'S PRETTY BOUNCY.

IT LOOKS LIKE IT COULD BE WHIPPED CREAM, OR THOSE NASTY EASTER CHICK CANDIES.
HEY, THAT SOUNDS TASTY!
Puu! Puu!
DO WE OPEN IT?
Puu, puu.
カチャ
WAAAAAAA!

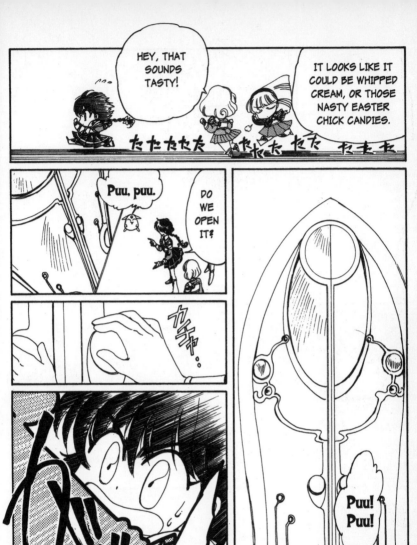

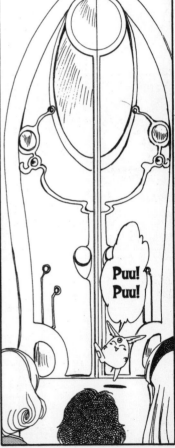

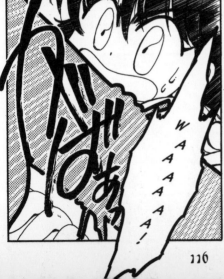

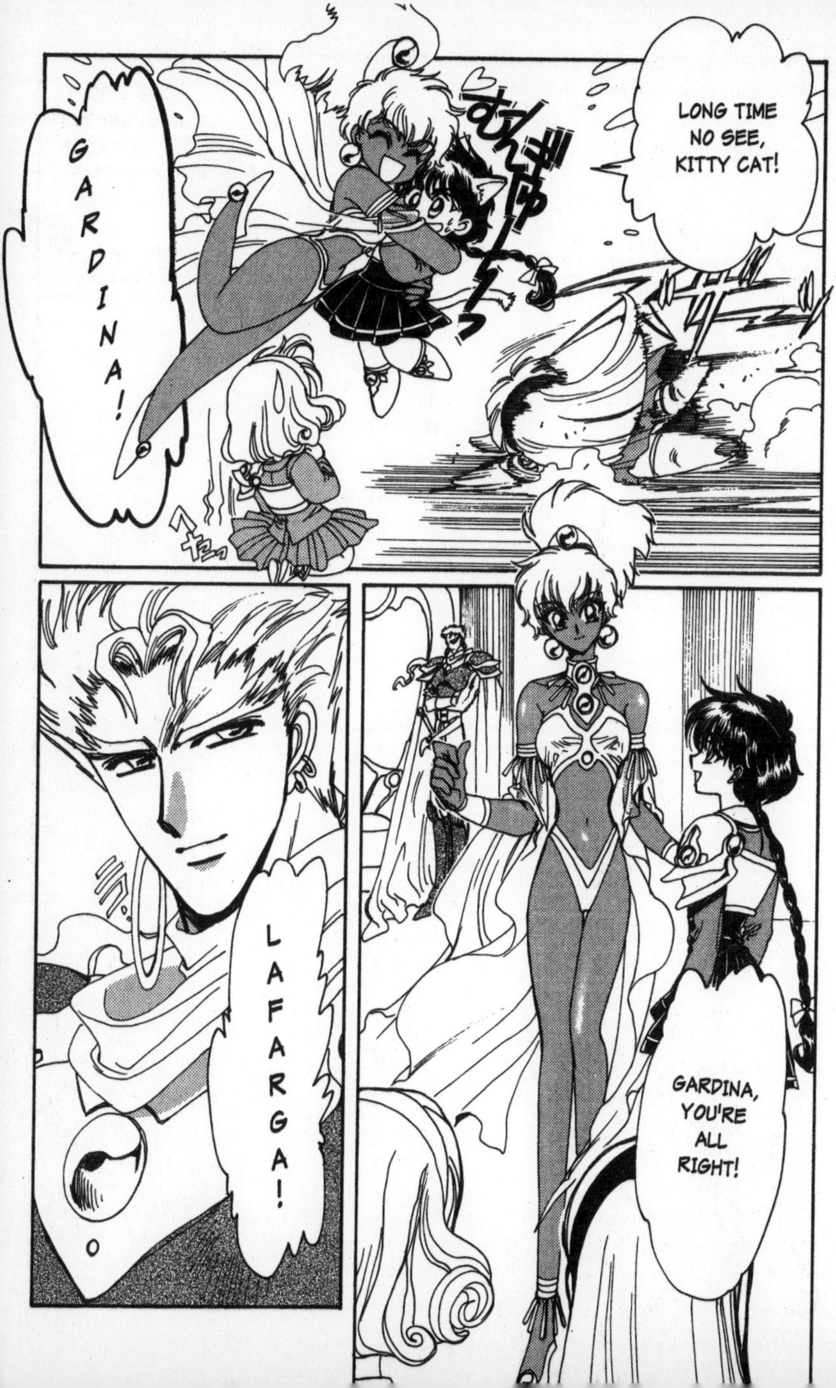
LONG TIME NO SEE, KITTY CAT!
GARDINA!
GARDINA, YOU'RE ALL RIGHT!
LAFARGA!

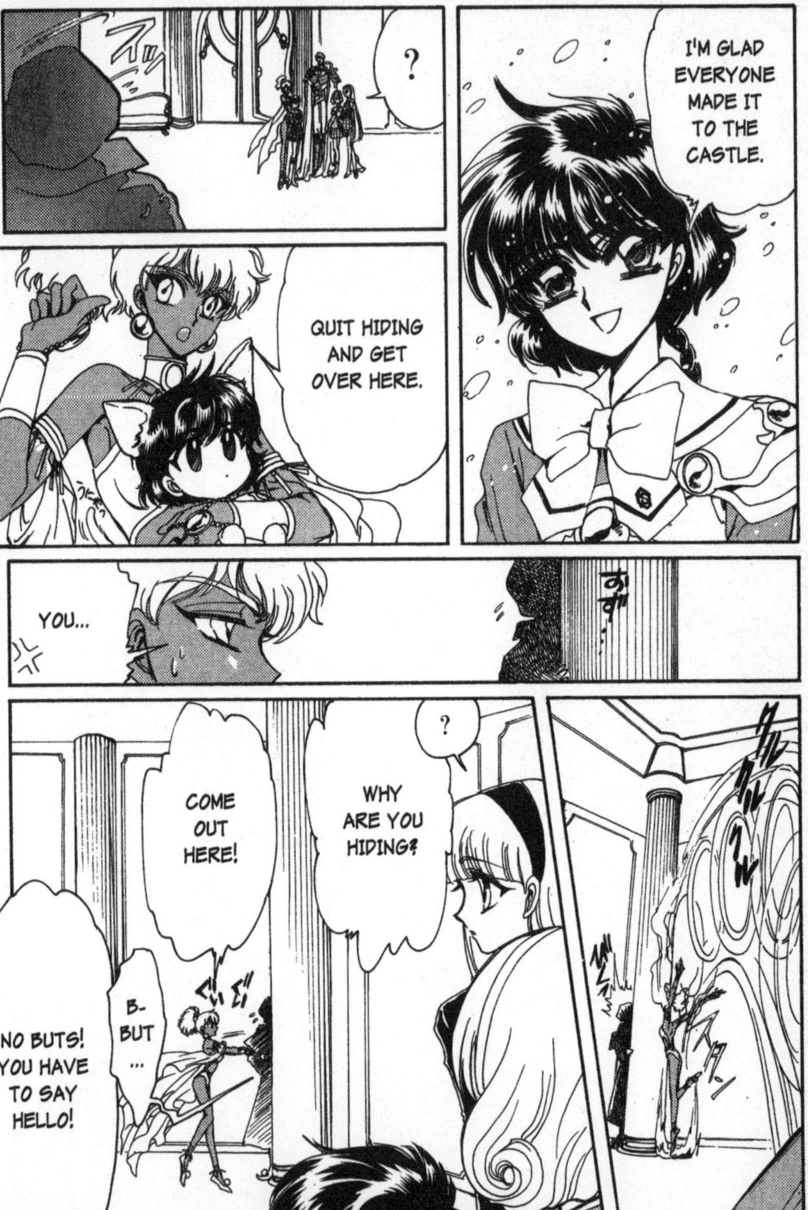
I'M GLAD EVERYONE MADE IT TO THE CASTLE.
?
QUIT HIDING AND GET OVER HERE.
YOU...
?
WHY ARE YOU HIDING?
COME OUT HERE!
B-BUT...
NO BUTS! YOU HAVE TO SAY HELLO!

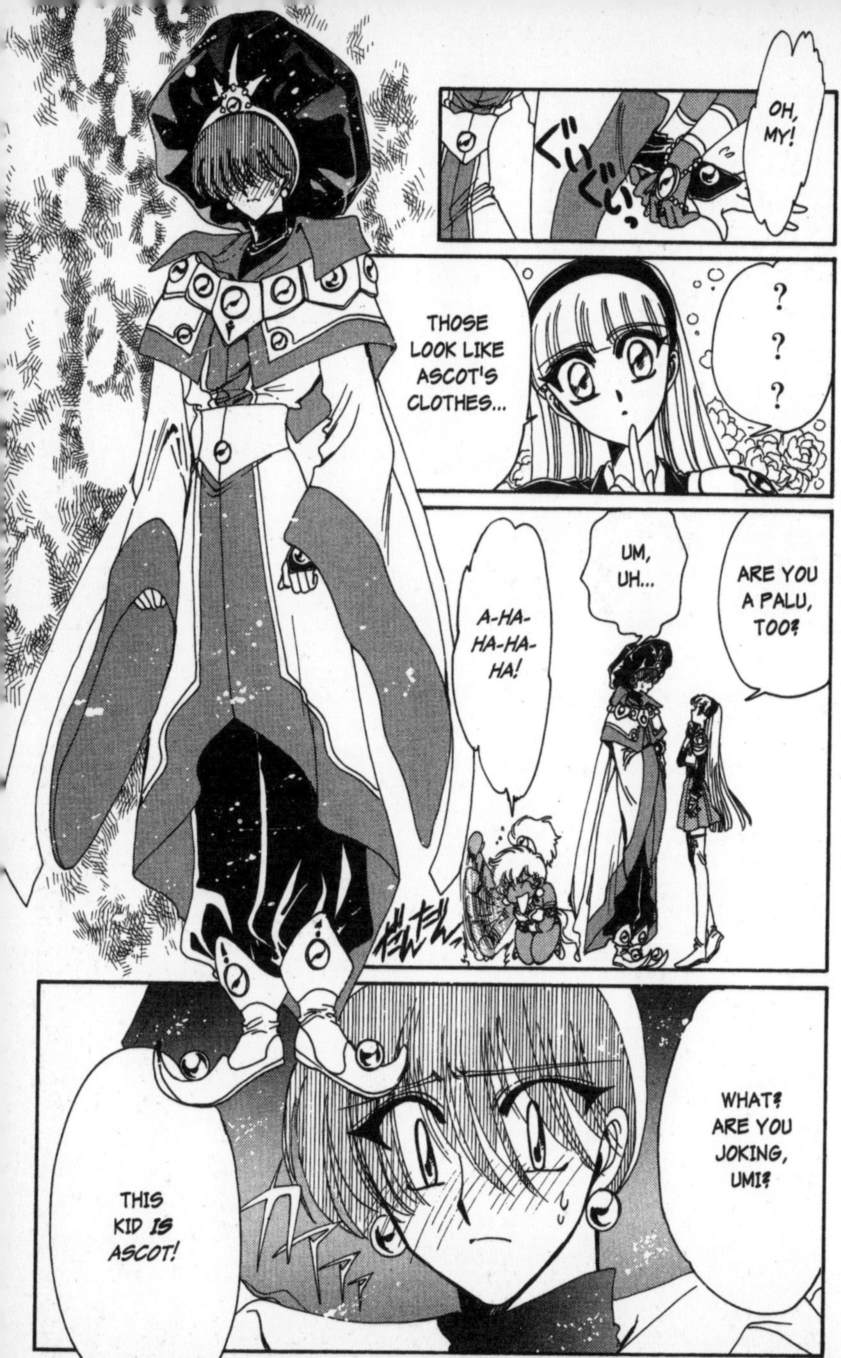
OH, MY!
ぐいぐいっ
???
THOSE LOOK LIKE ASCOT'S CLOTHES...
ARE YOU A PALU, TOO?
UM, UH...
A-HA-HA-HA-HA!
WHAT? ARE YOU JOKING, UMI?
THIS KID IS ASCOT!

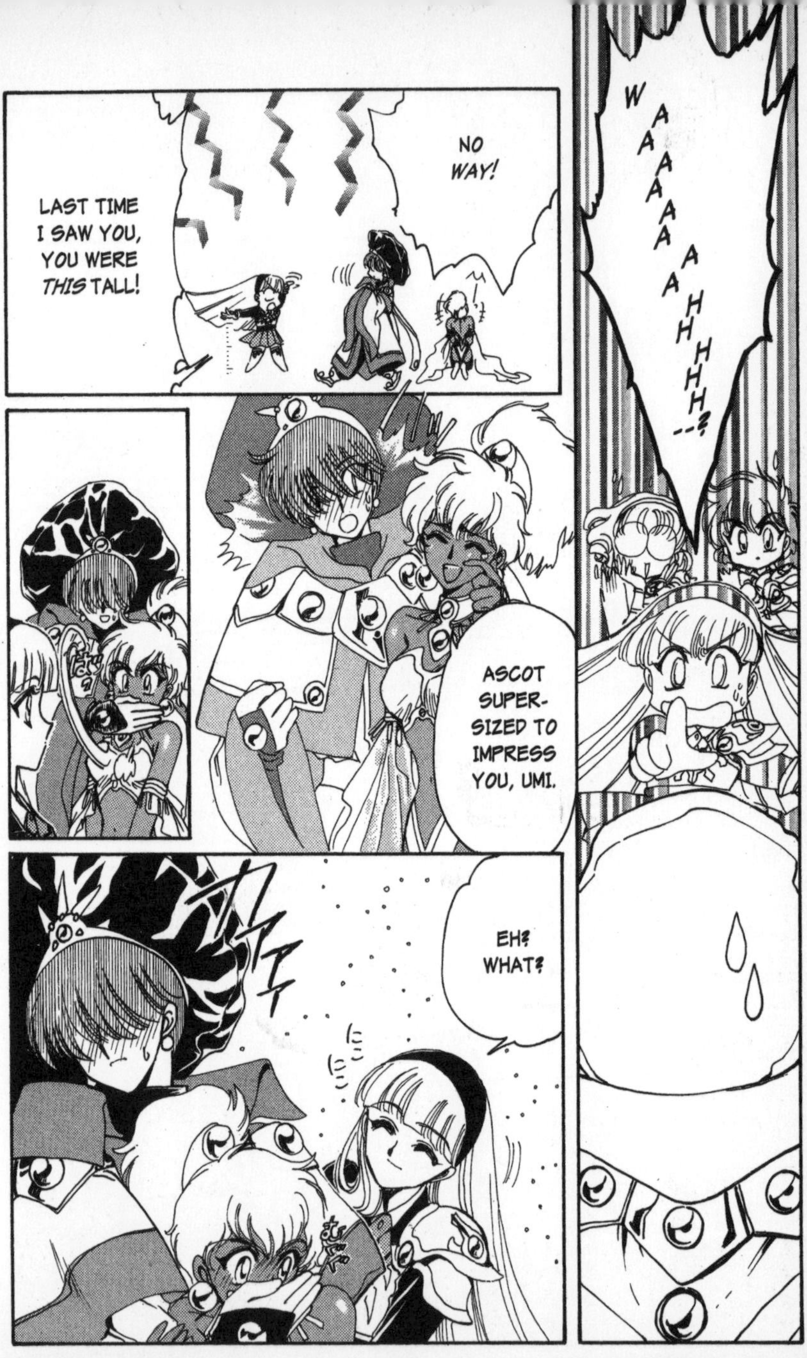
WAAAAAAAAAHHHHH--?
NO WAY!
LAST TIME I SAW YOU, YOU WERE *THIS* TALL!
ASCOT SUPER-SIZED TO IMPRESS YOU, UMI.
EH? WHAT?

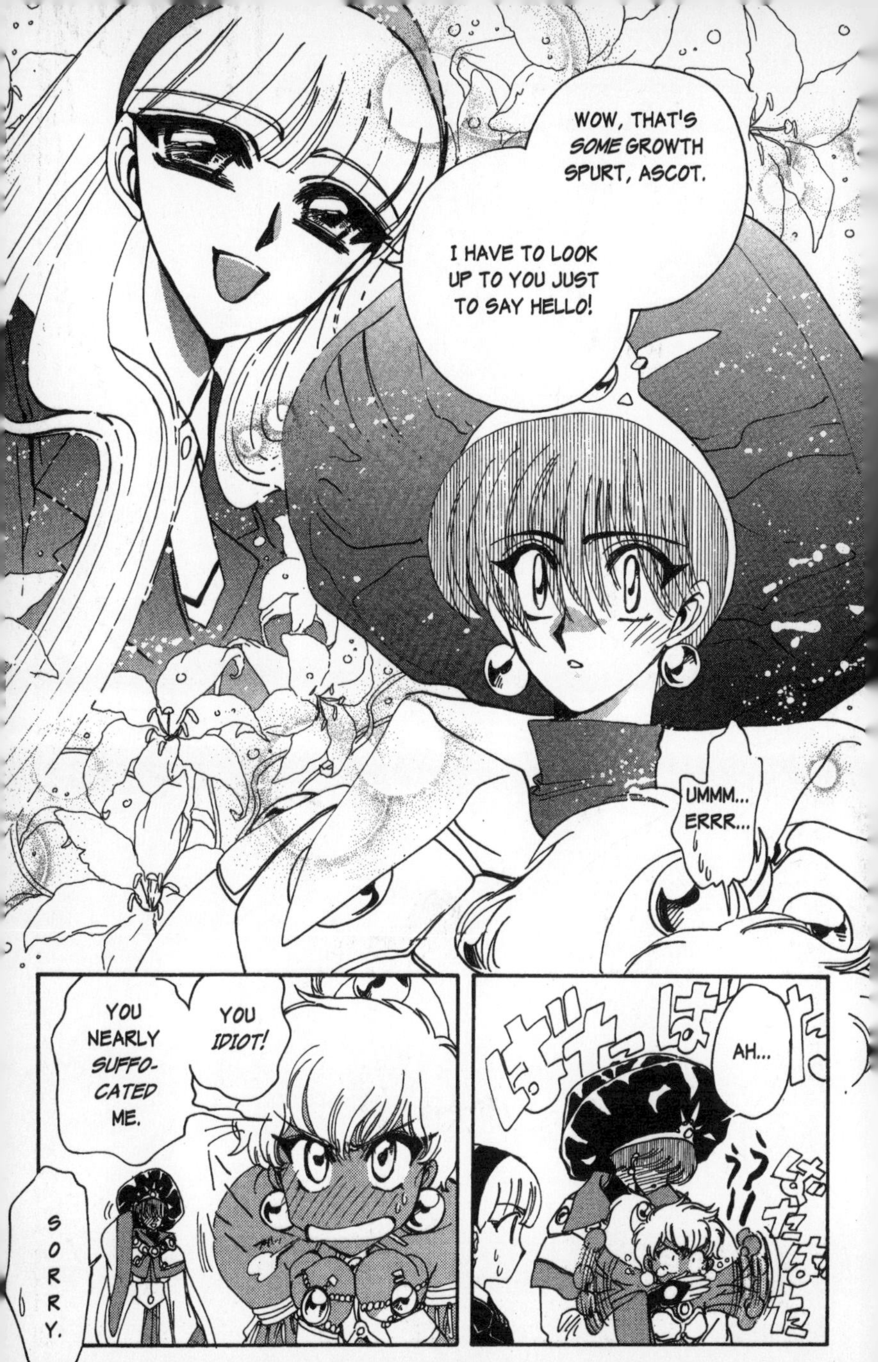
WOW, THAT'S *SOME* GROWTH SPURT, ASCOT.
I HAVE TO LOOK UP TO YOU JUST TO SAY HELLO!
UMMM... ERRR...
AH...
YOU *IDIOT!*
YOU NEARLY *SUFFOCATED* ME.
SORRY.

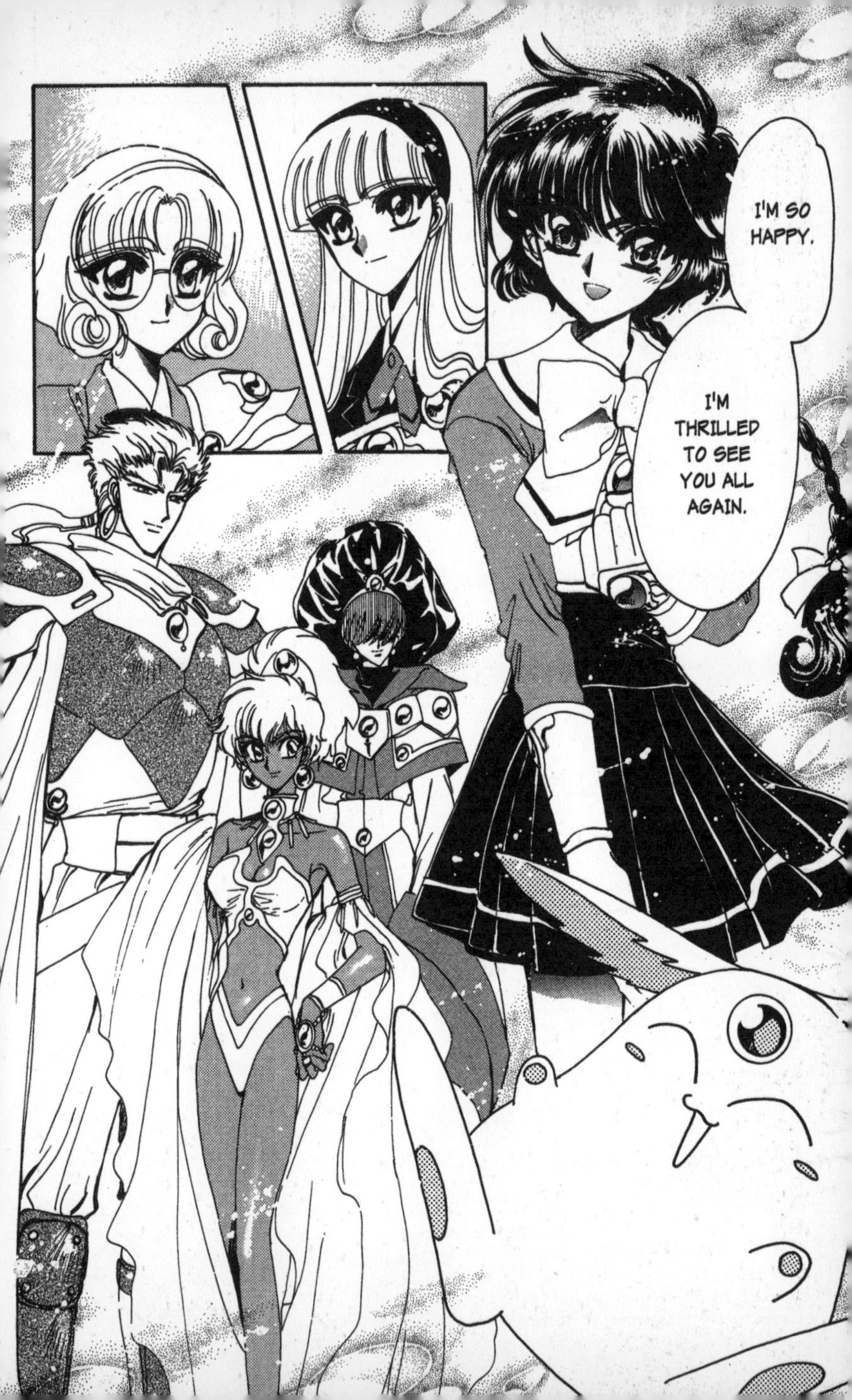
I'M SO HAPPY.
I'M THRILLED TO SEE YOU ALL AGAIN.

NOW THEY'RE *WELCOME* IN THE CASTLE!

YOU THREE TAUGHT ME TO STICK UP FOR MY FRIENDS.

I'VE SWORN TO NEVER RAISE MY SWORD AGAINST ALLIES OF CEPHIRO AGAIN.

WE WEREN'T ACTING FOR THE GOOD OF CEPHIRO BEFORE.

WE REALLY WANTED TO APOLOGIZE.

GASP YOU *WERE?* DID HE HURT YOU?

NAH, WE'RE FINE.

HEY, MAYBE *YOU* CAN HELP US WITH SOMETHING.

WHILE WE WERE IN OUR MASHIN, WE WERE ATTACKED BY A GIANT ROBOT, OR SOME KIND OF POWER SUIT, AND IT WAS FROM AUTOZAM.

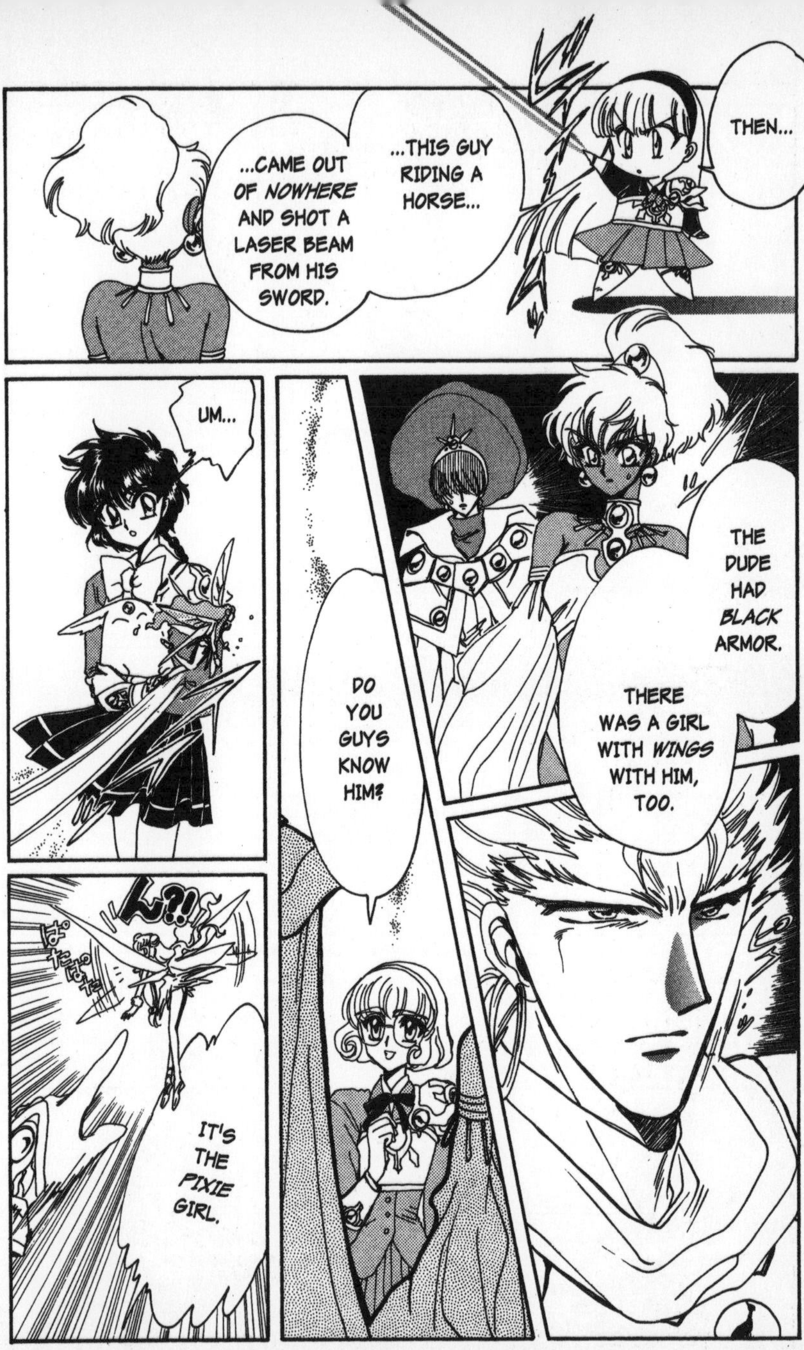
THEN...
...THIS GUY RIDING A HORSE...
...CAME OUT OF NOWHERE AND SHOT A LASER BEAM FROM HIS SWORD.
THE DUDE HAD BLACK ARMOR.
THERE WAS A GIRL WITH WINGS WITH HIM, TOO.
DO YOU GUYS KNOW HIM?
UM...
ん?!
IT'S THE PIXIE GIRL.

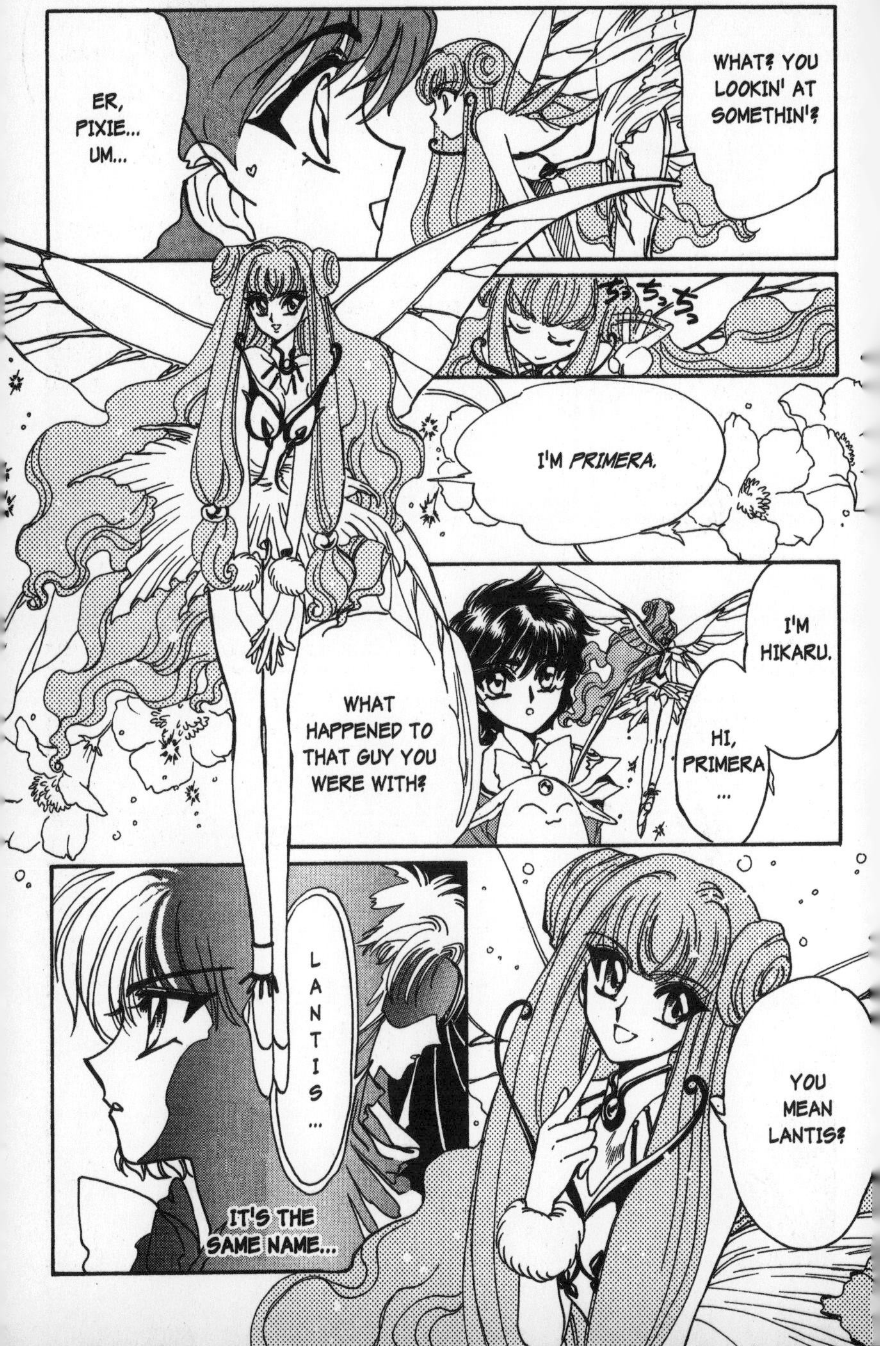
WHAT? YOU LOOKIN' AT SOMETHIN'?
ER, PIXIE... UM...
ちっちっちっ
I'M *PRIMERA.*
I'M HIKARU.
HI, PRIMERA ...
WHAT HAPPENED TO THAT GUY YOU WERE WITH?
YOU MEAN LANTIS?
LANTIS ...
IT'S THE SAME NAME...

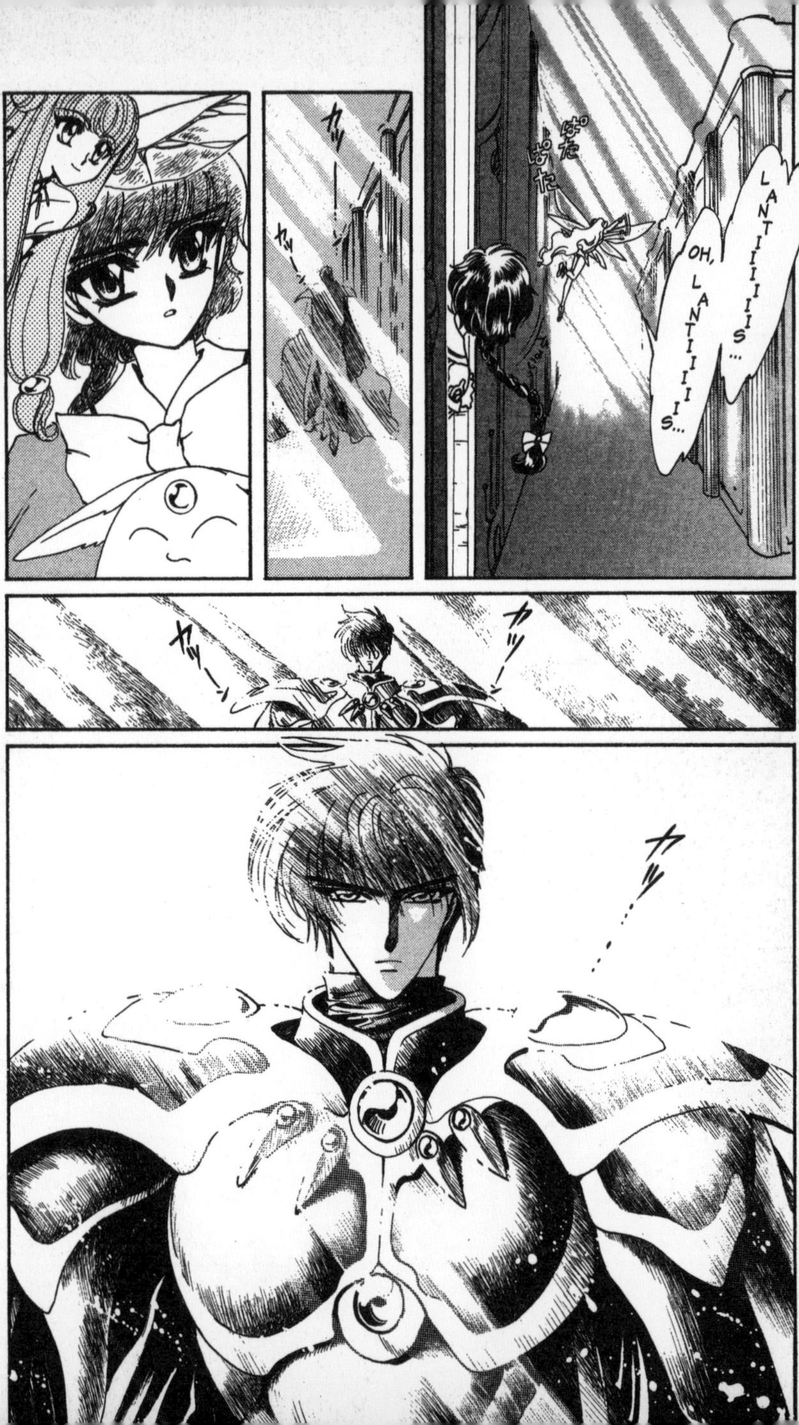
ぱたぱた
LANTIIIIIIS...
OH, LANTIIIIIIS...
カッ
カッ
カッ

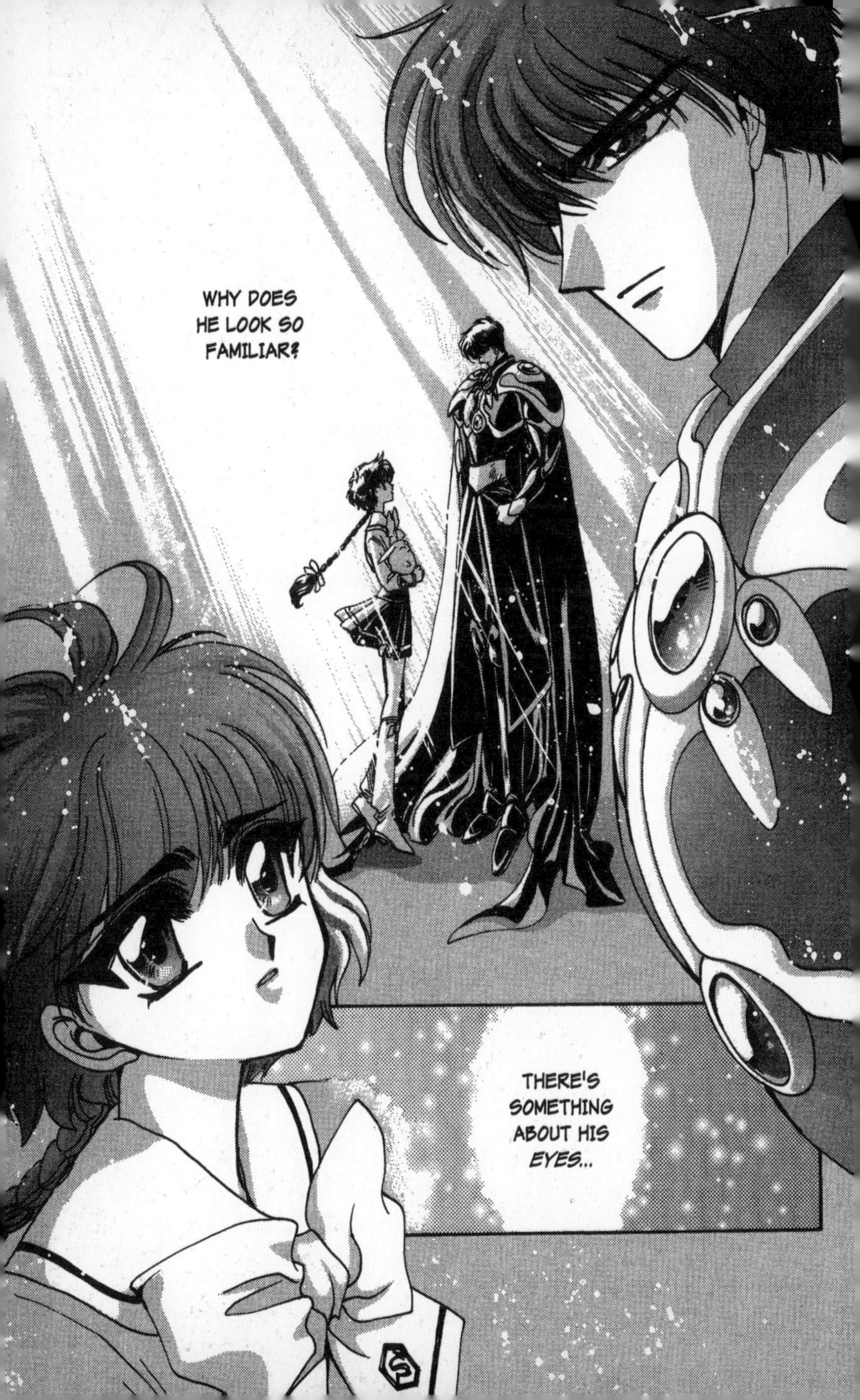
WHY DOES HE LOOK SO FAMILIAR?
THERE'S SOMETHING ABOUT HIS *EYES*...

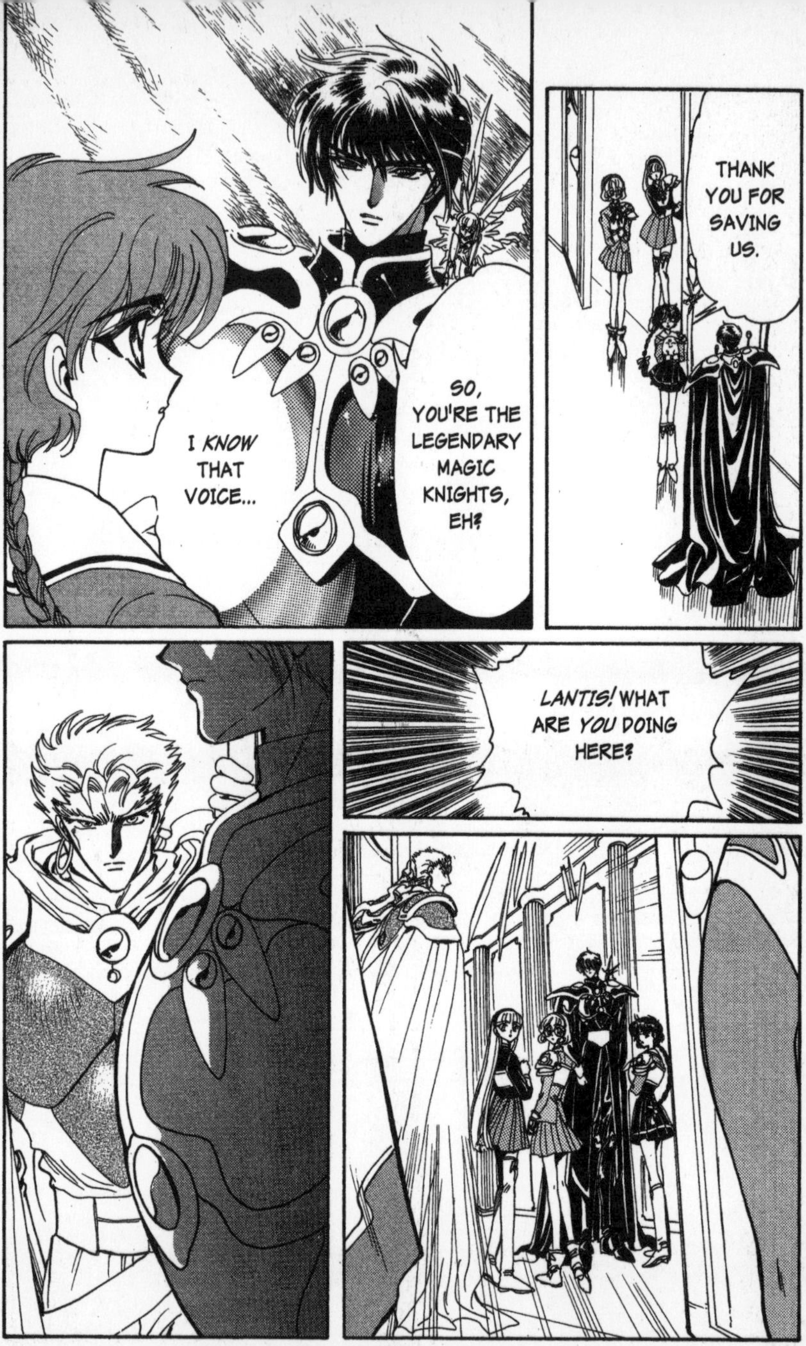
THANK YOU FOR SAVING US.
SO, YOU'RE THE LEGENDARY MAGIC KNIGHTS, EH?
I *KNOW* THAT VOICE...
LANTIS! WHAT ARE *YOU* DOING HERE?

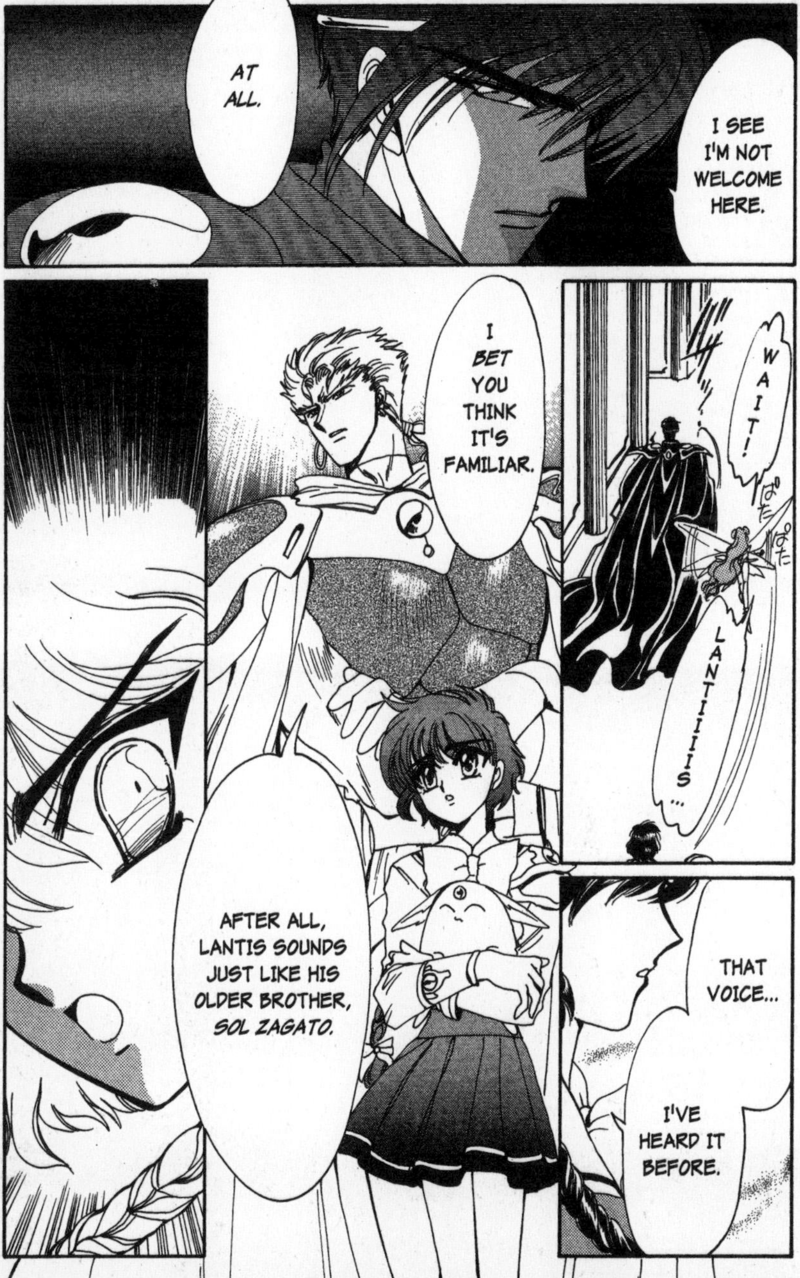
I SEE I'M NOT WELCOME HERE.
AT ALL.
WAIT!
ぱた ぱた
LANTIIIIIS...
THAT VOICE...
I'VE HEARD IT BEFORE.
I BET YOU THINK IT'S FAMILIAR.
AFTER ALL, LANTIS SOUNDS JUST LIKE HIS OLDER BROTHER, SOL ZAGATO.

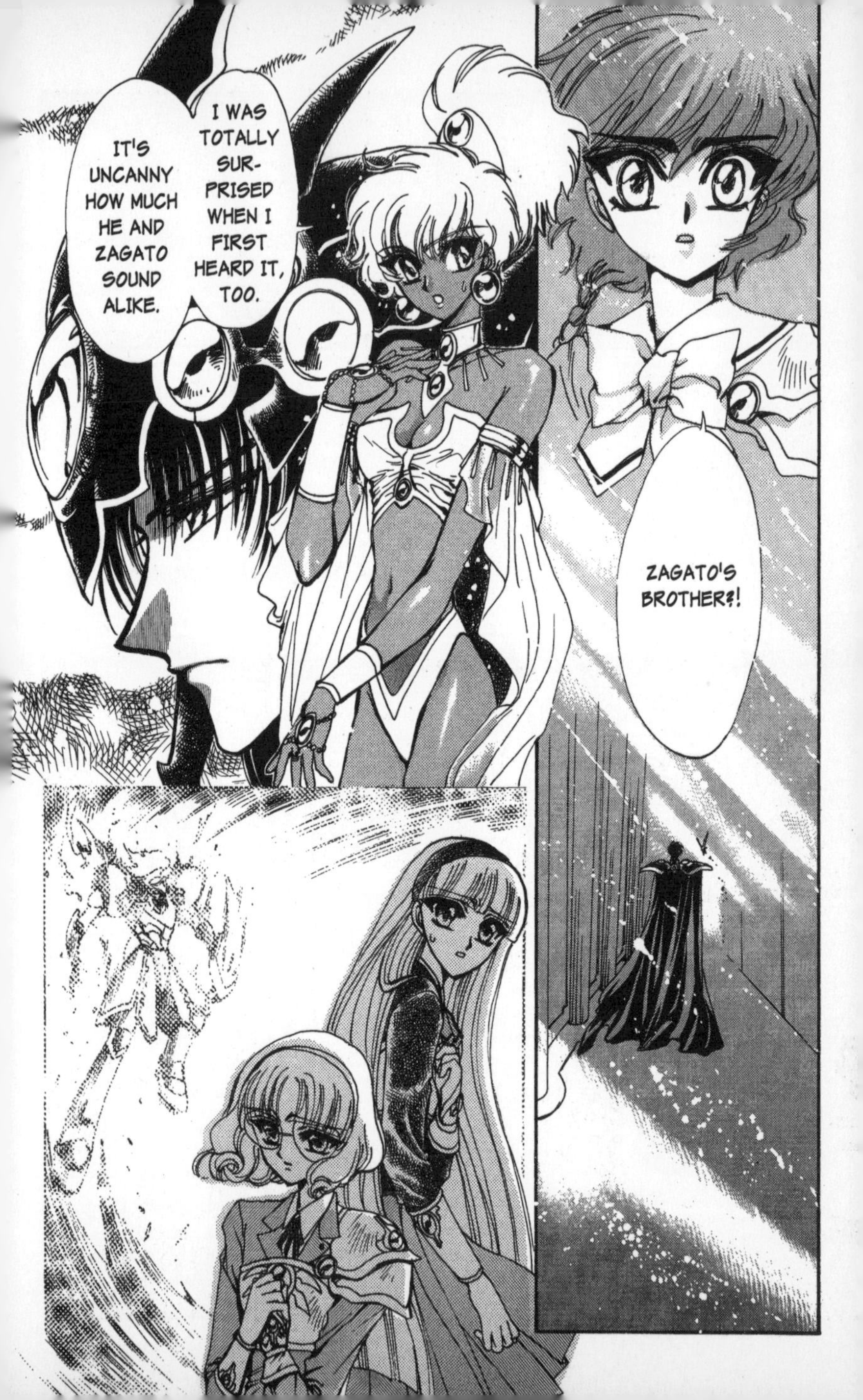
ZAGATO'S BROTHER?!
I WAS TOTALLY SURPRISED WHEN I FIRST HEARD IT, TOO.
IT'S UNCANNY HOW MUCH HE AND ZAGATO SOUND ALIKE.

WELL ...

WHERE WAS HE WHEN WE WERE HERE THE FIRST TIME?

REALLY?

ZAGATO HAD A YOUNGER BROTHER?

I NEVER EVEN HEARD ZAGATO MENTION HAVING A BROTHER.

ME NEITHER.

HE LEFT CEPHIRO? HOW COME?

ONLY HE KNOWS THE REASON.

...LANTIS HAD LEFT THIS COUNTRY LONG BEFORE YOU WERE SUMMONED TO DO BATTLE WITH HIS BROTHER.

AND THEN...

BY THE TIME I CAME TO SERVE PRINCESS EMERAUDE, LANTIS HAD ALREADY DISAPPEARED TO PARTS UNKNOWN.

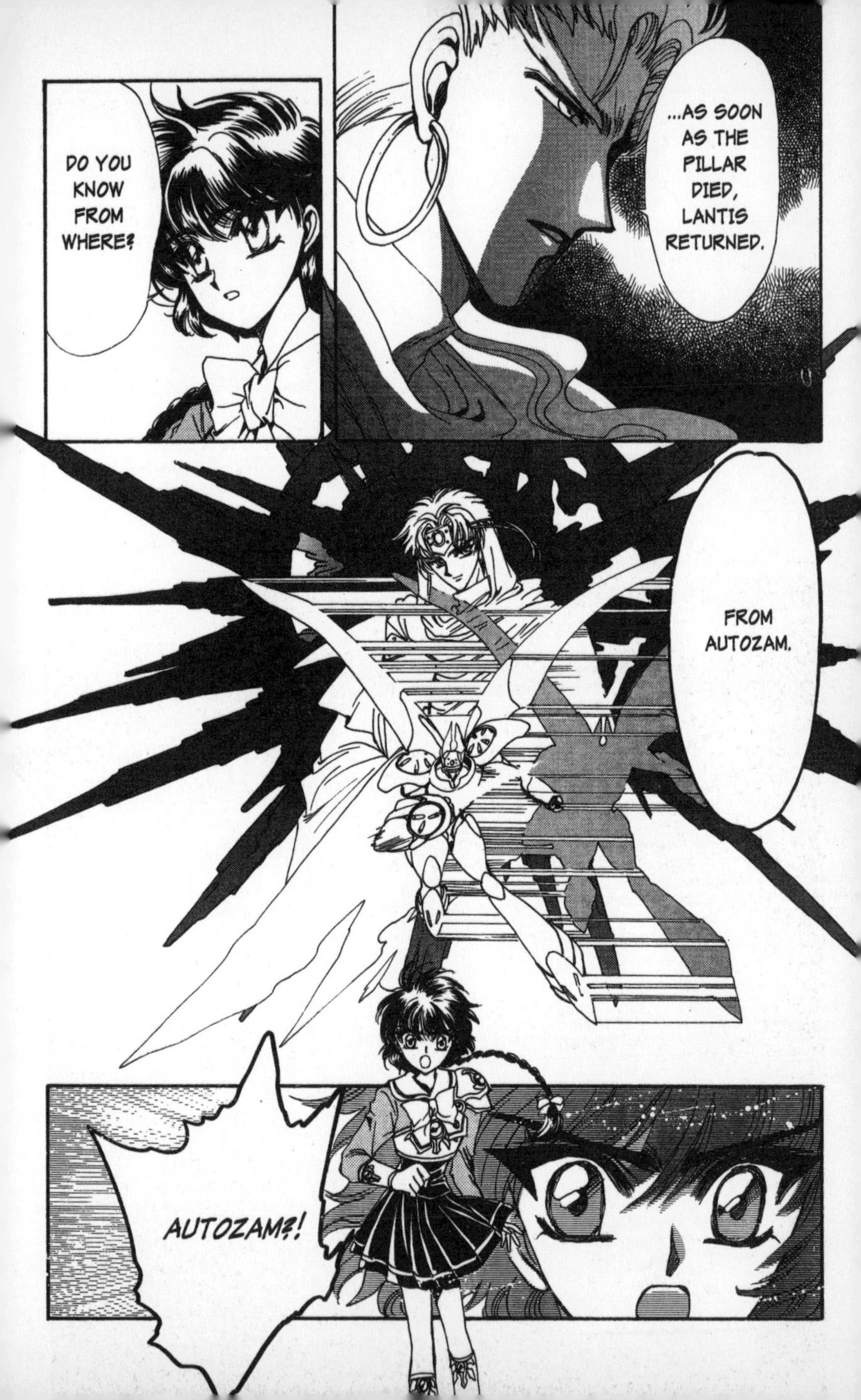
...AS SOON AS THE PILLAR DIED, LANTIS RETURNED.
DO YOU KNOW FROM WHERE?
FROM AUTOZAM.
AUTOZAM?!

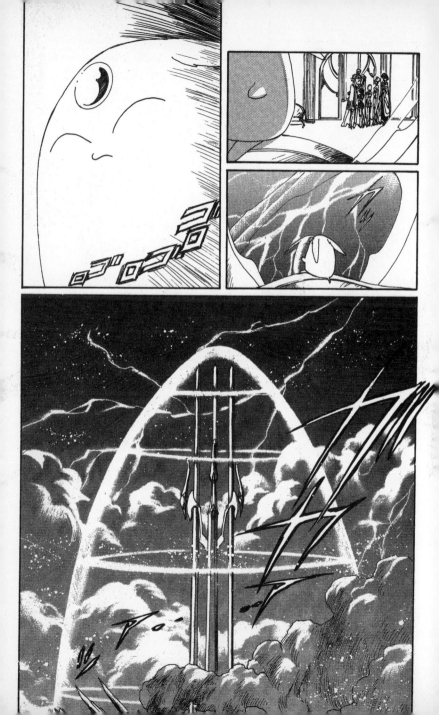

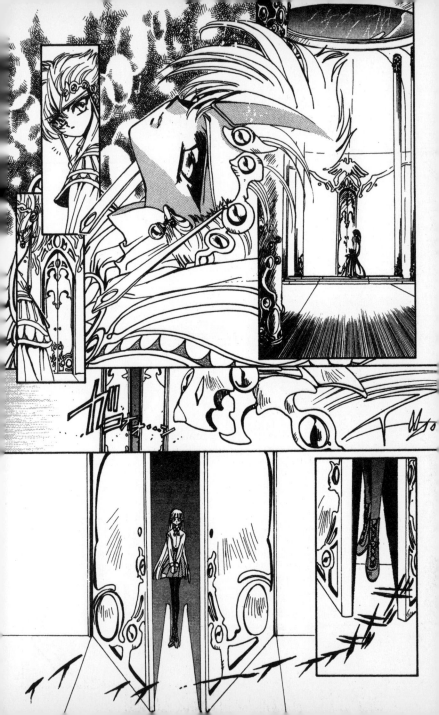

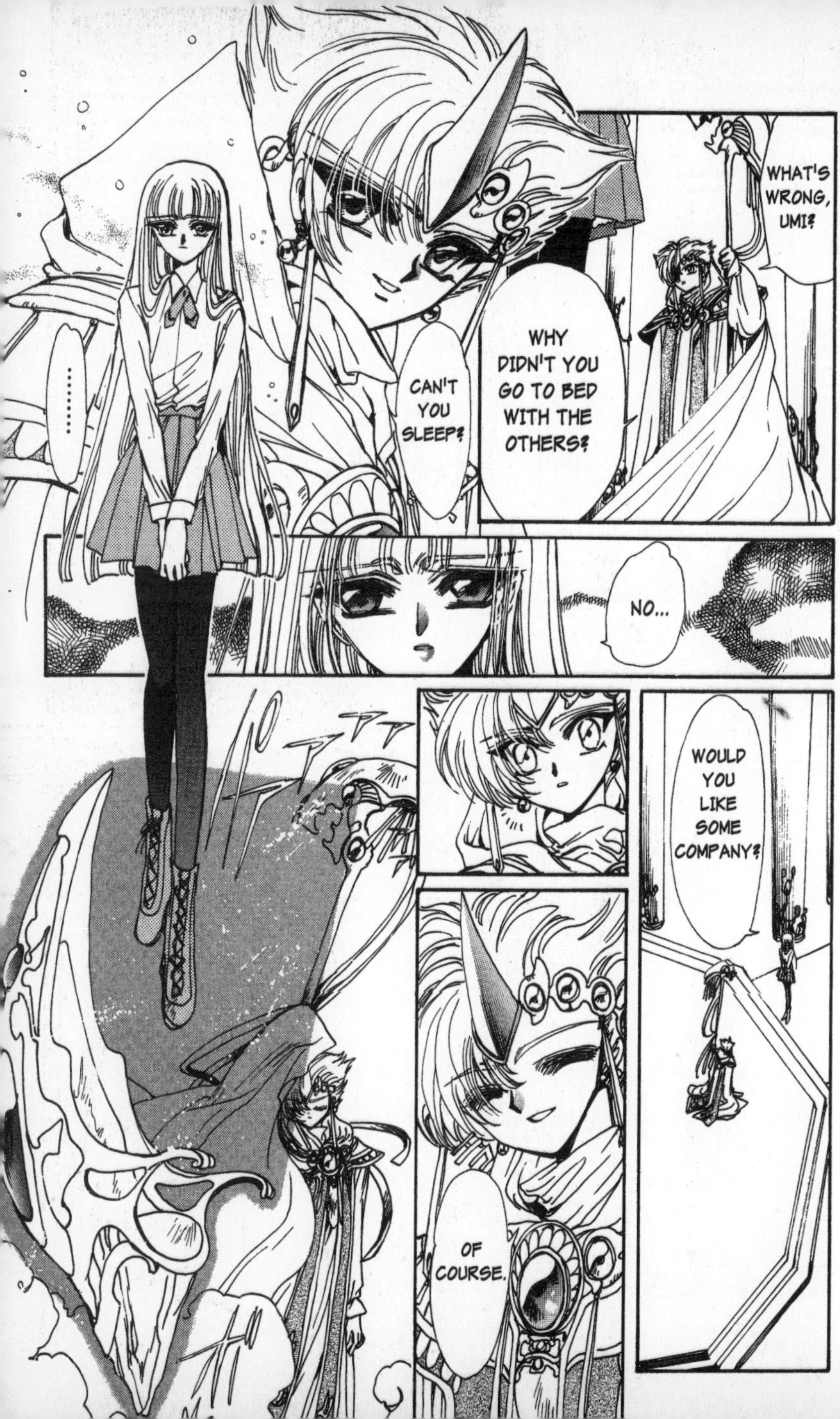
WHAT'S WRONG, UMI?
WHY DIDN'T YOU GO TO BED WITH THE OTHERS?
CAN'T YOU SLEEP?
......
NO...
WOULD YOU LIKE SOME COMPANY?
OF COURSE.

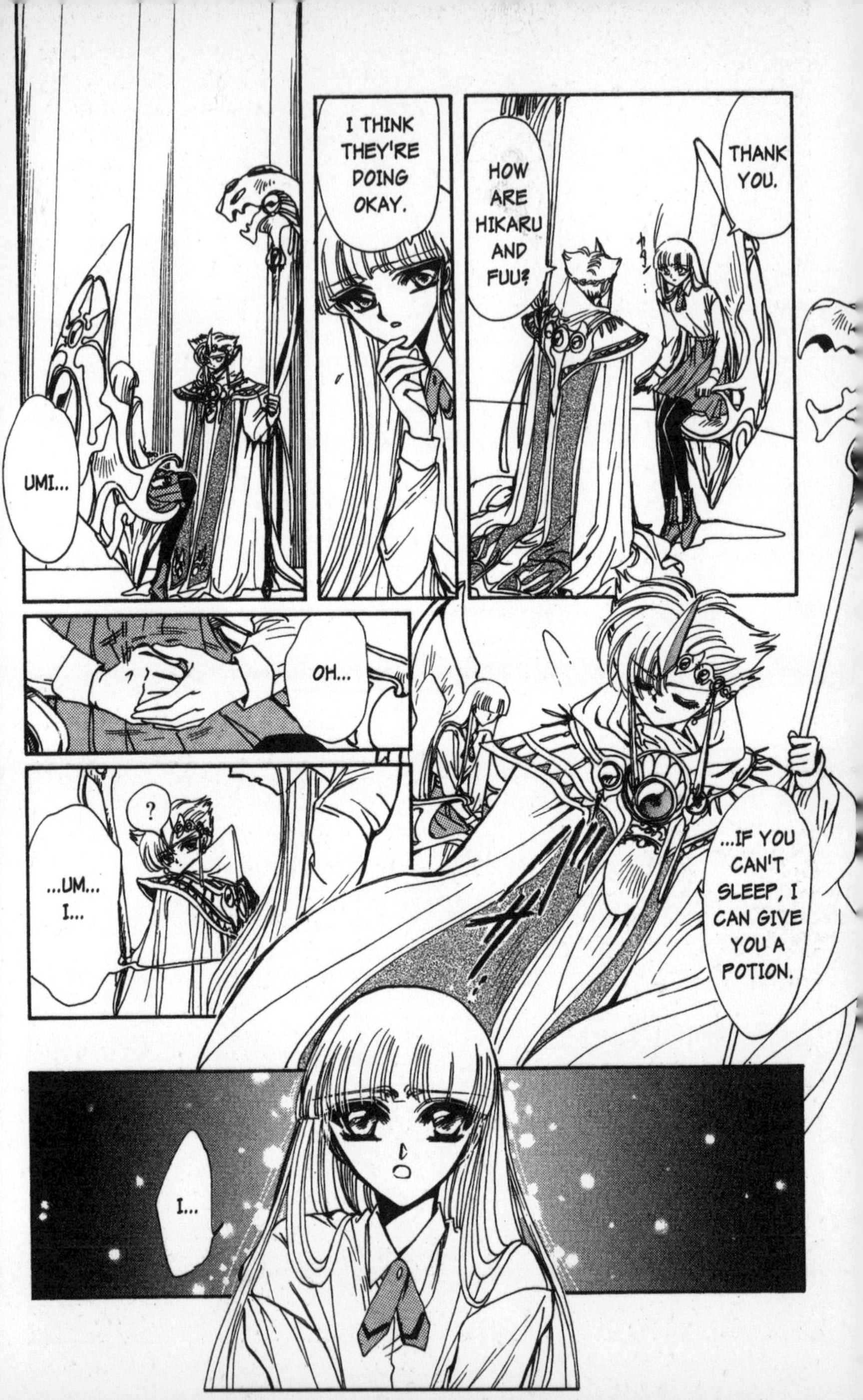
THANK YOU.
HOW ARE HIKARU AND FUU?
I THINK THEY'RE DOING OKAY.
UMI...
...IF YOU CAN'T SLEEP, I CAN GIVE YOU A POTION.
OH...
...UM... I...
I...

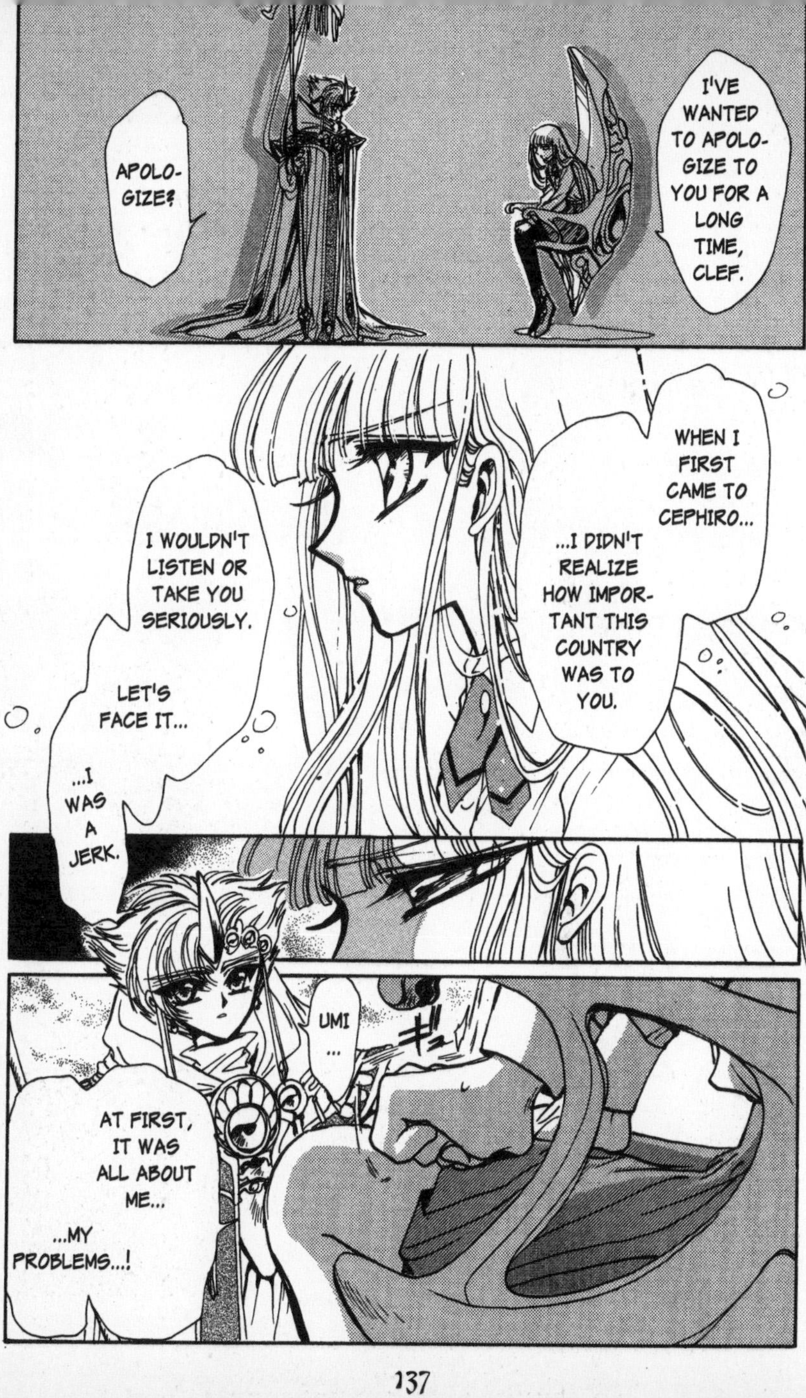
I'VE WANTED TO APOLOGIZE TO YOU FOR A LONG TIME, CLEF.
APOLOGIZE?
WHEN I FIRST CAME TO CEPHIRO...
...I DIDN'T REALIZE HOW IMPORTANT THIS COUNTRY WAS TO YOU.
I WOULDN'T LISTEN OR TAKE YOU SERIOUSLY.
LET'S FACE IT...
...I WAS A JERK.
UMI ...
ギュ
AT FIRST, IT WAS ALL ABOUT ME...
...MY PROBLEMS...!

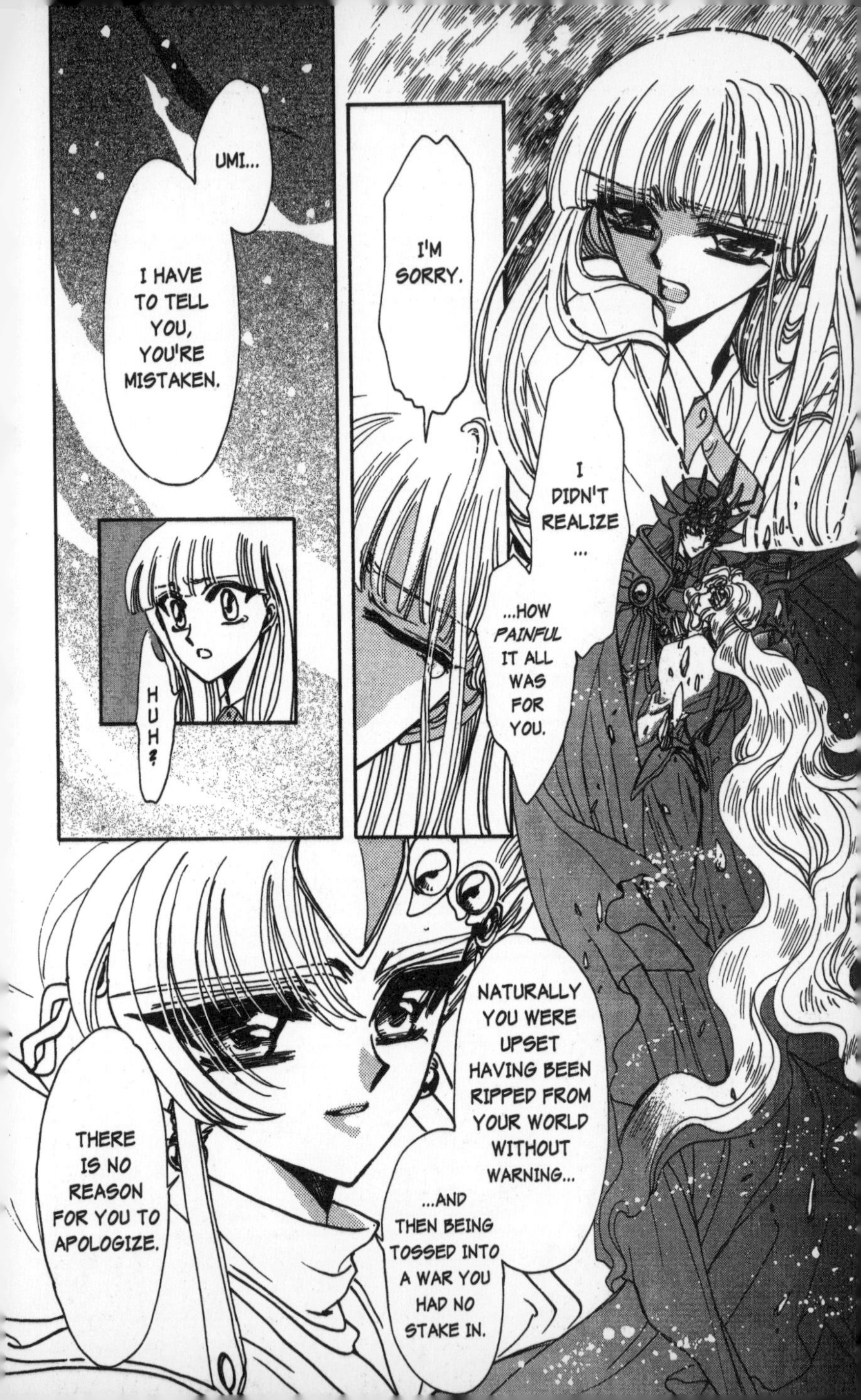
I'M SORRY.
I DIDN'T REALIZE ...
...HOW PAINFUL IT ALL WAS FOR YOU.
UMI...
I HAVE TO TELL YOU, YOU'RE MISTAKEN.
HUH?
NATURALLY YOU WERE UPSET HAVING BEEN RIPPED FROM YOUR WORLD WITHOUT WARNING...
...AND THEN BEING TOSSED INTO A WAR YOU HAD NO STAKE IN.
THERE IS NO REASON FOR YOU TO APOLOGIZE.

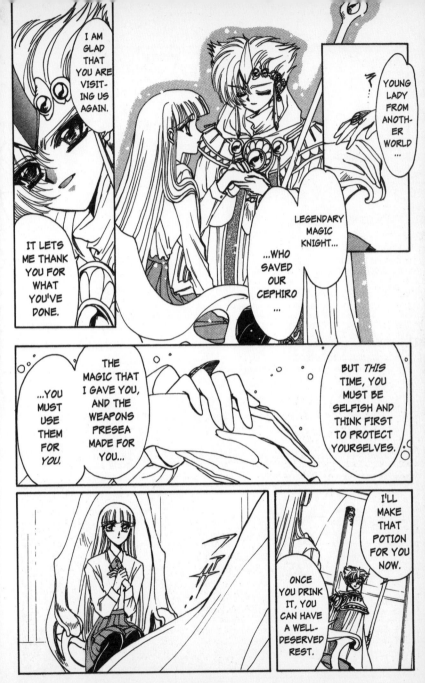

140

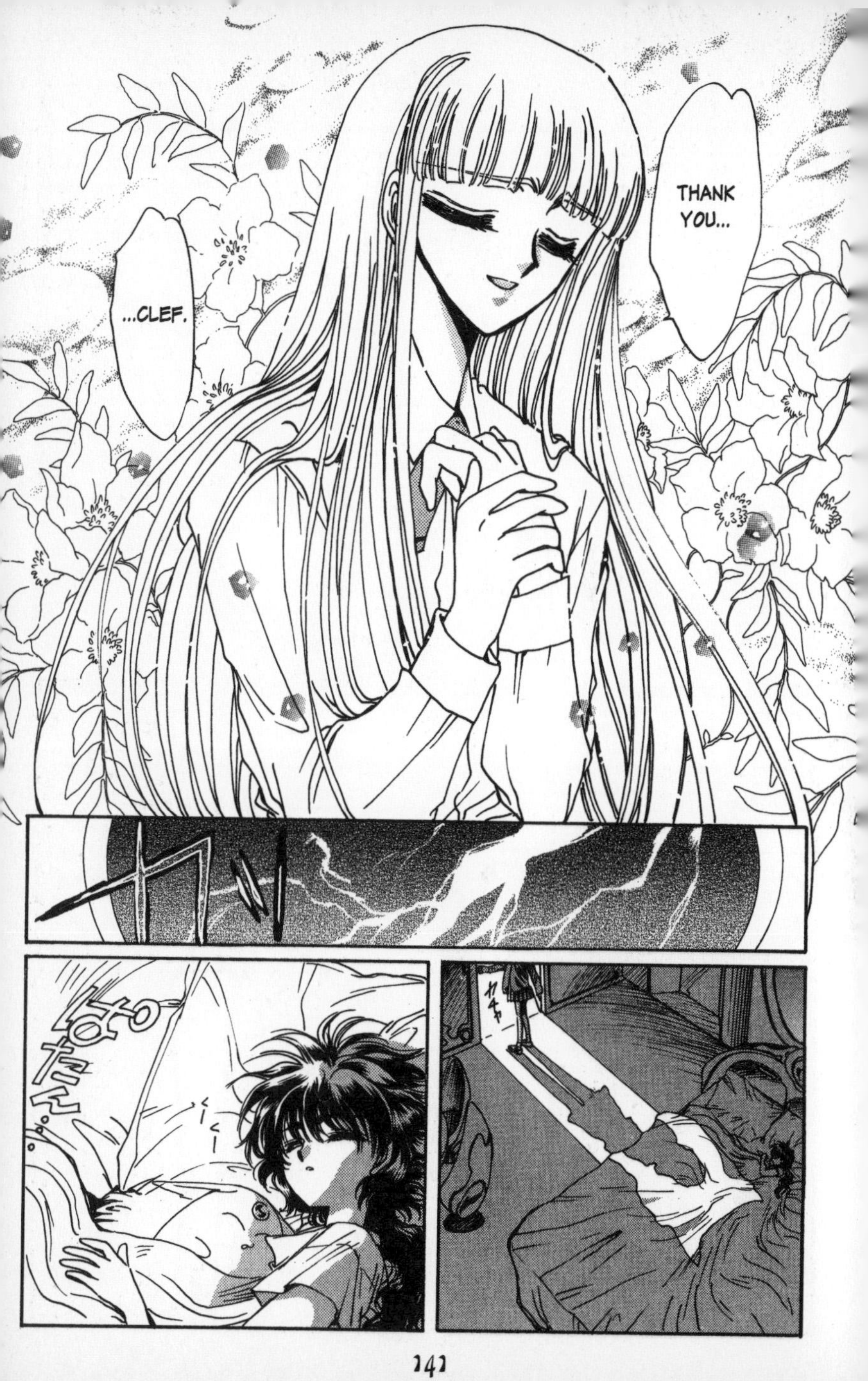
THANK YOU...
...CLEF.

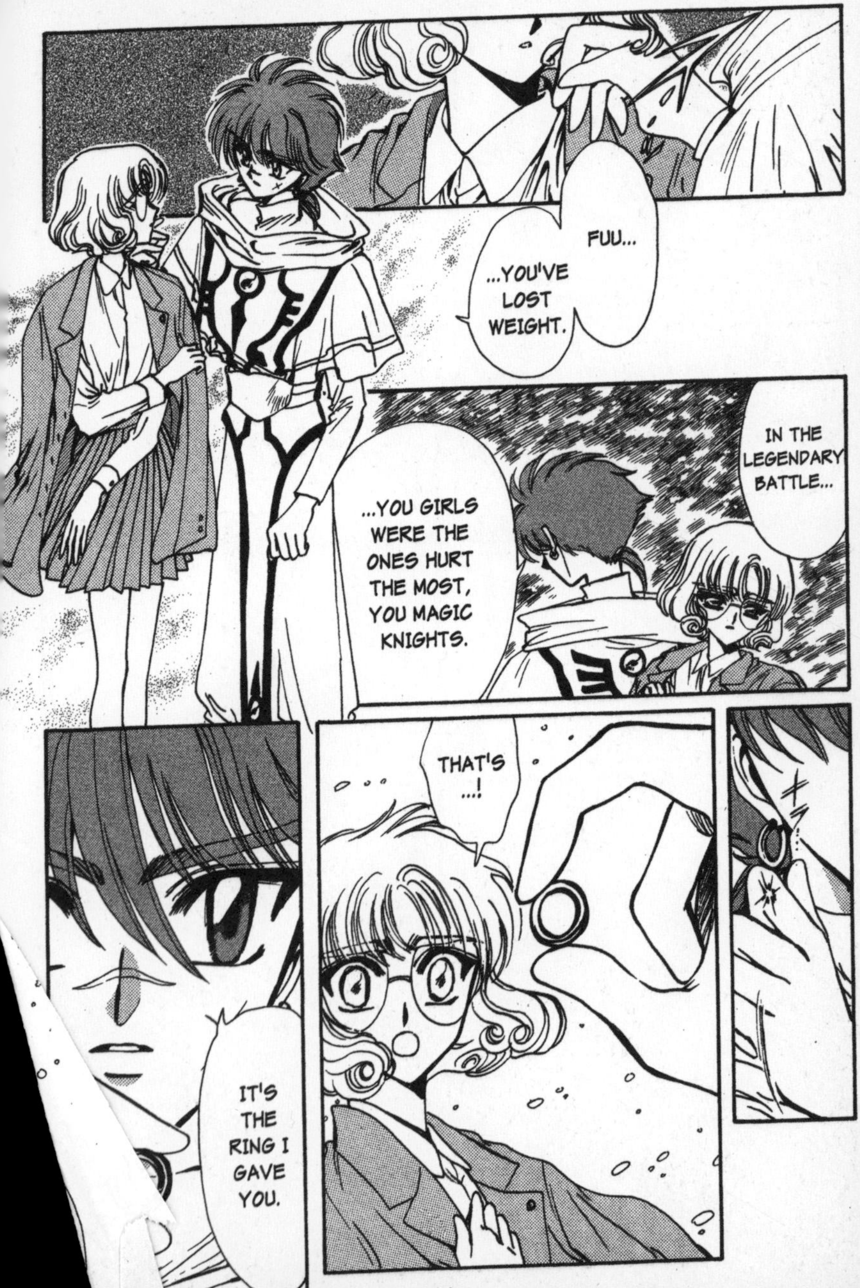
FUU... ...YOU'VE LOST WEIGHT.
IN THE LEGENDARY BATTLE...
...YOU GIRLS WERE THE ONES HURT THE MOST, YOU MAGIC KNIGHTS.
THAT'S ...!
IT'S THE RING I GAVE YOU.

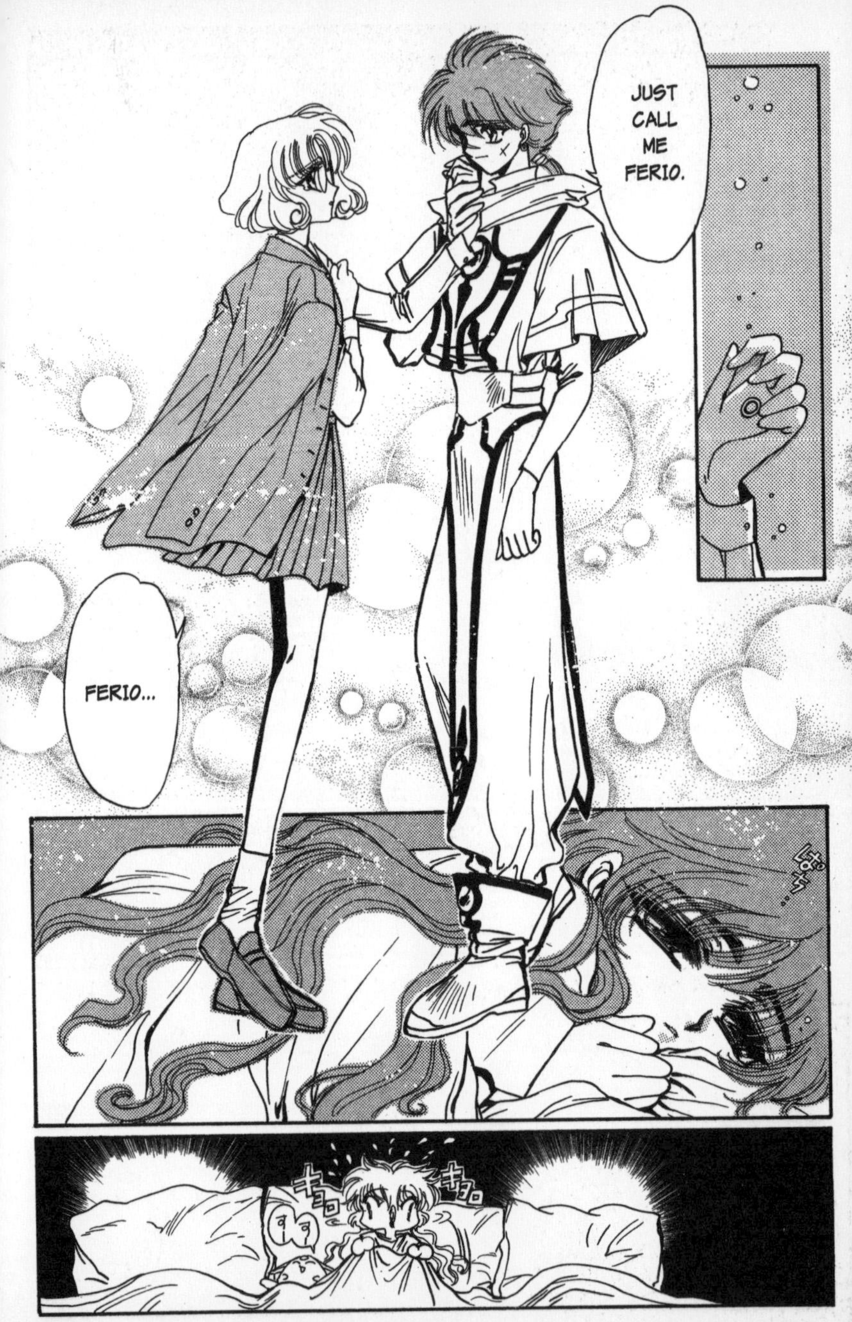
JUST CALL ME FERIO.
FERIO...

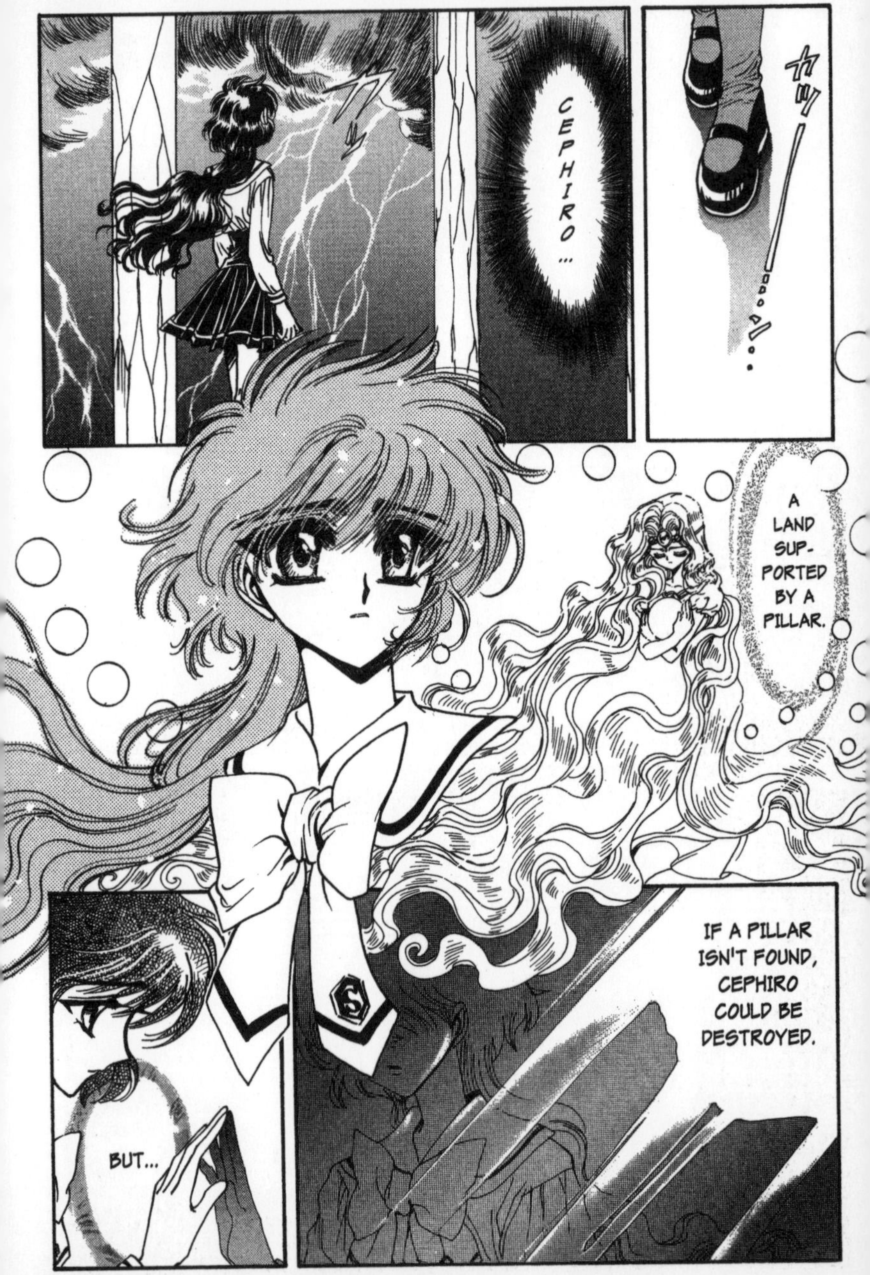
CEPHIRO...
A LAND SUP-PORTED BY A PILLAR.
IF A PILLAR ISN'T FOUND, CEPHIRO COULD BE DESTROYED.
BUT...

...IF A NEW PILLAR IS BORN...

That's why the Pillar alone has a special summoning power.

It's impossible for the Pillar to take her own life.

And no one from Cephiro may harm the Pillar, either.

A power to bring Knights from a world other than Cephiro...in order to eradicate oneself.

...and save Cephiro.

Please... Kill me...

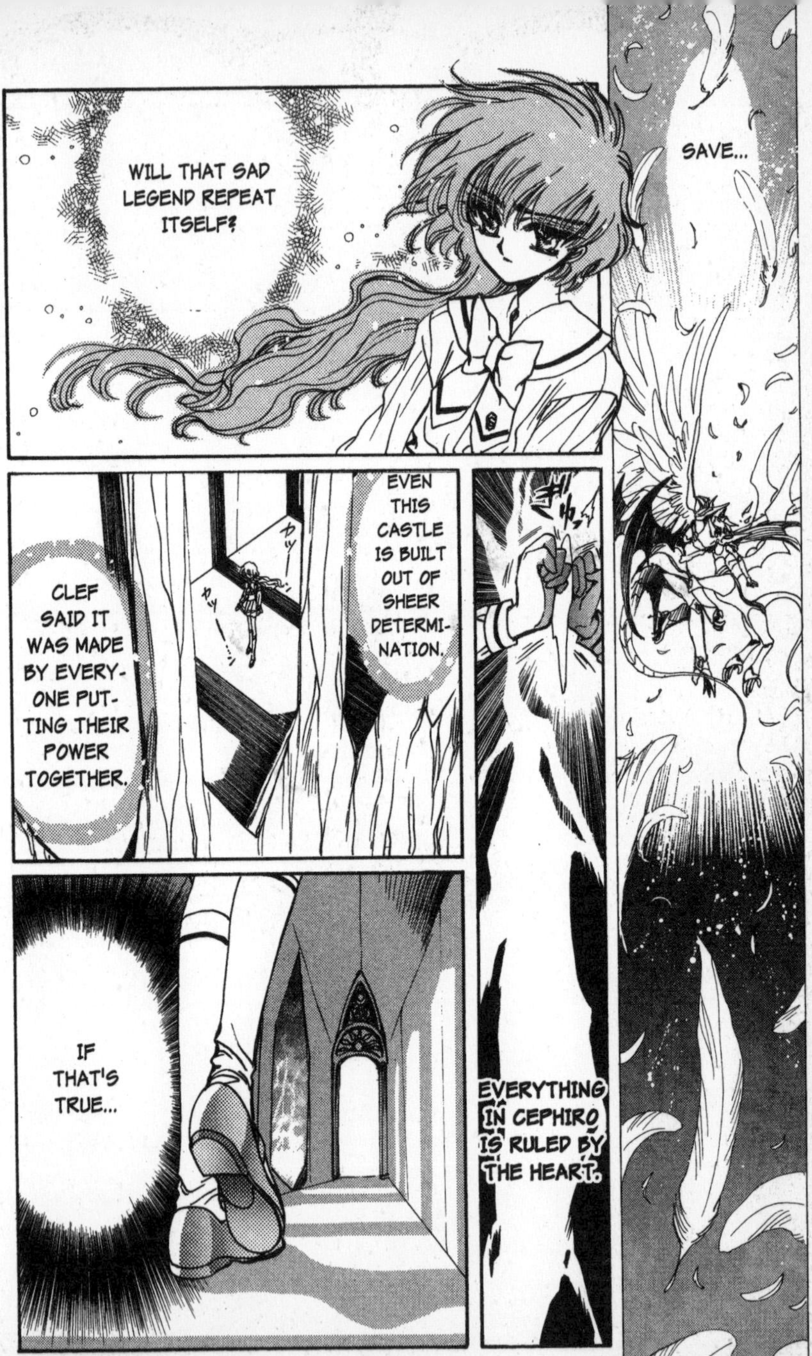
WILL THAT SAD LEGEND REPEAT ITSELF?
SAVE...
CLEF SAID IT WAS MADE BY EVERY-ONE PUT-TING THEIR POWER TOGETHER.
EVEN THIS CASTLE IS BUILT OUT OF SHEER DETERMI-NATION.
IF THAT'S TRUE...
EVERYTHING IN CEPHIRO IS RULED BY THE HEART.

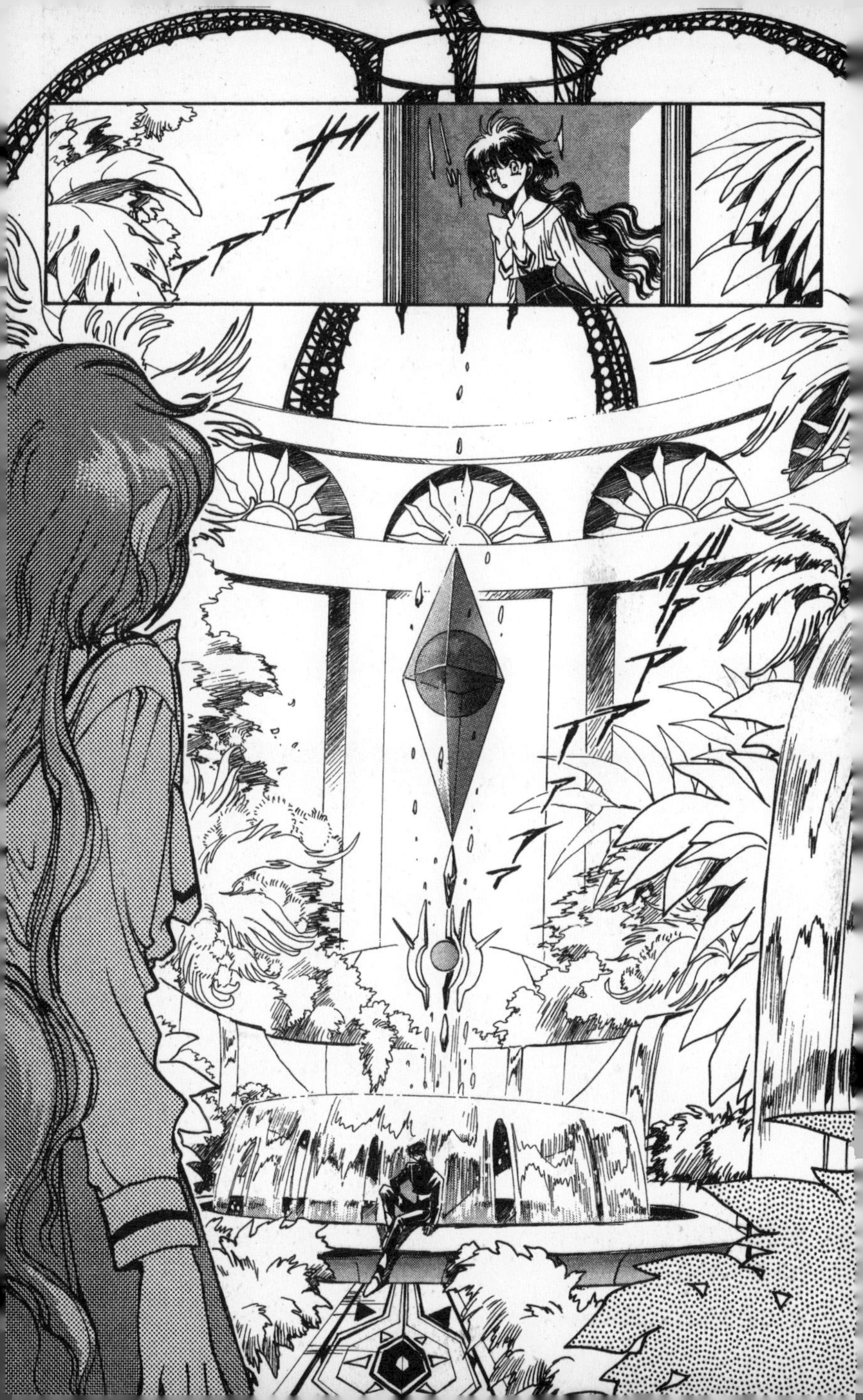
ザァァァァ
ザァァァァァァァ

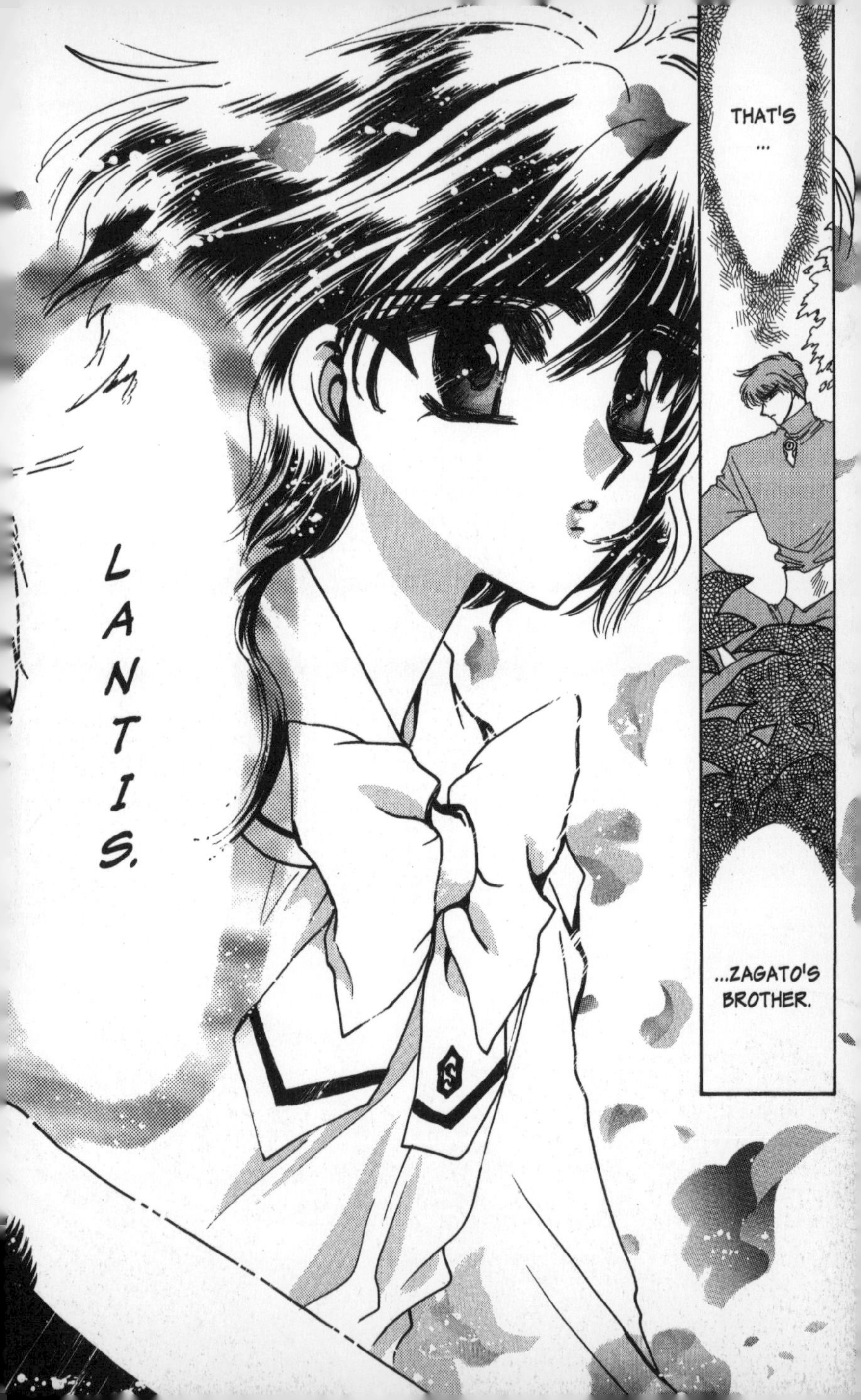
THAT'S ...
...ZAGATO'S BROTHER.
LANTIS.

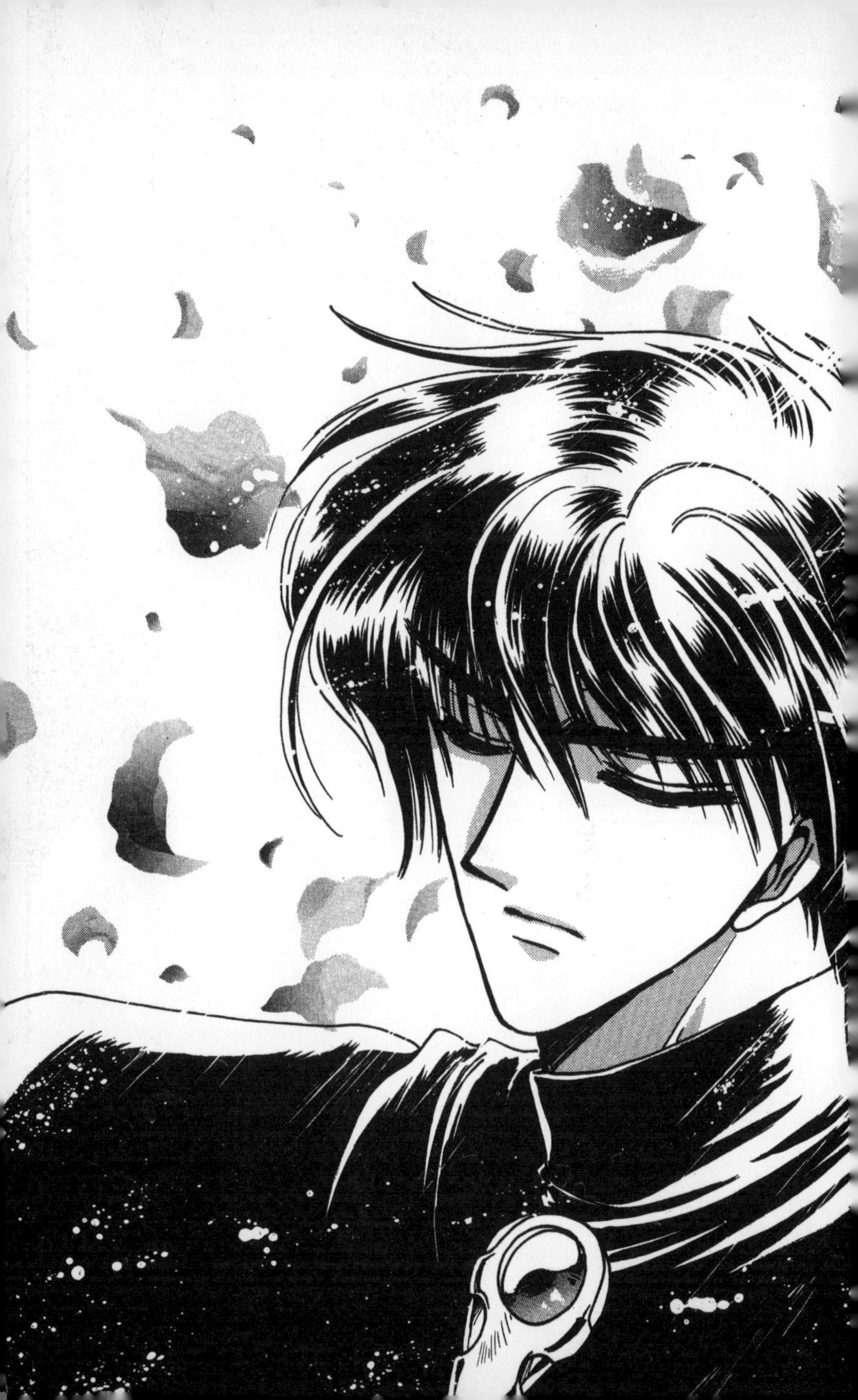

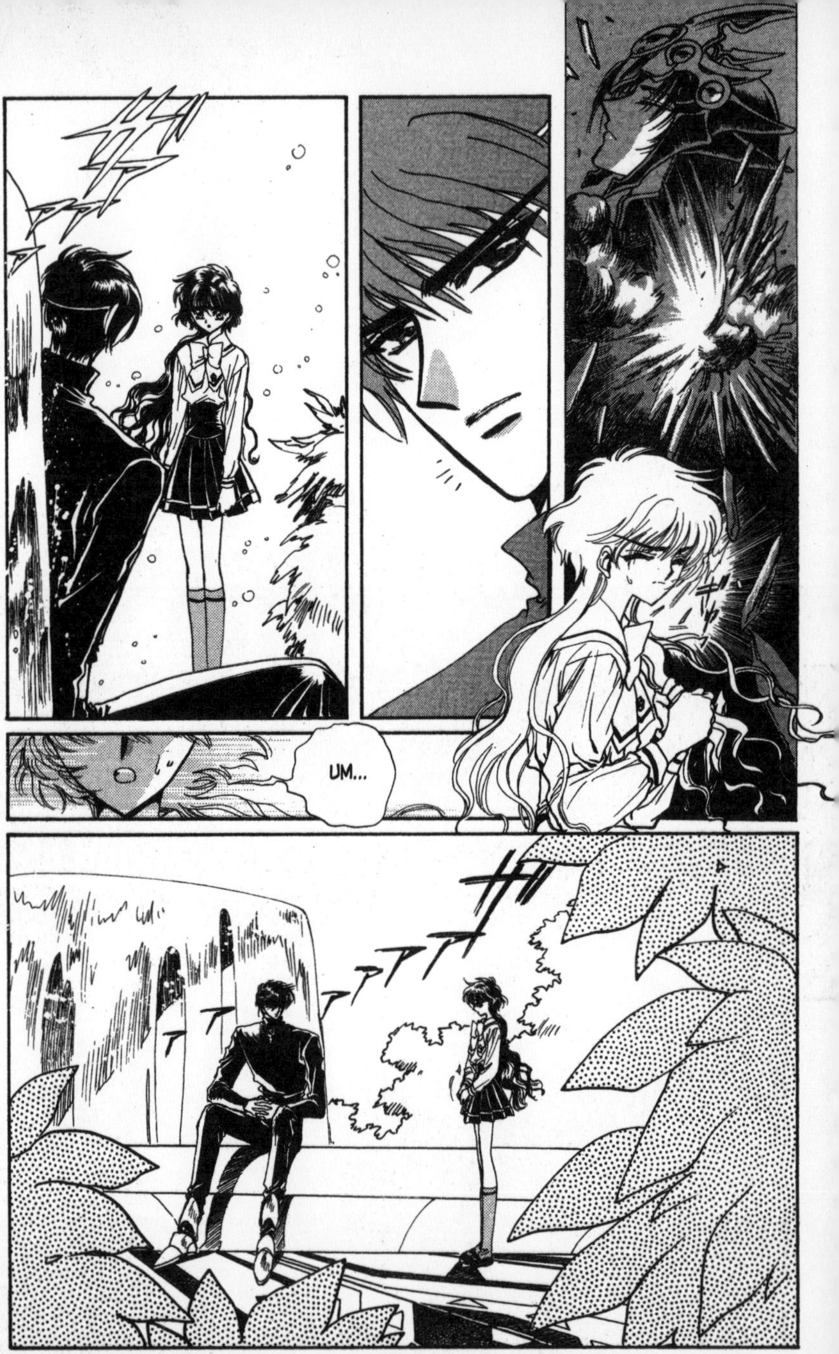
UM...

SO...

...IF YOU HAVE TO BEAT SOMEONE UP, JUST HIT ME!

...I KNOW THEY CRIED WHEN THEY WERE ALONE.

I KNOW IT'S SELFISH OF ME.

I KNOW.

UMI AND FUU WEREN'T THEM-SELVES WHEN WE GOT BACK TO TOKYO.

I WAS FEELING DEPRESSED, AND THEY TRIED TO CHEER ME UP, BUT...

HUH?

I DON'T WANT TO HIT YOU.

158

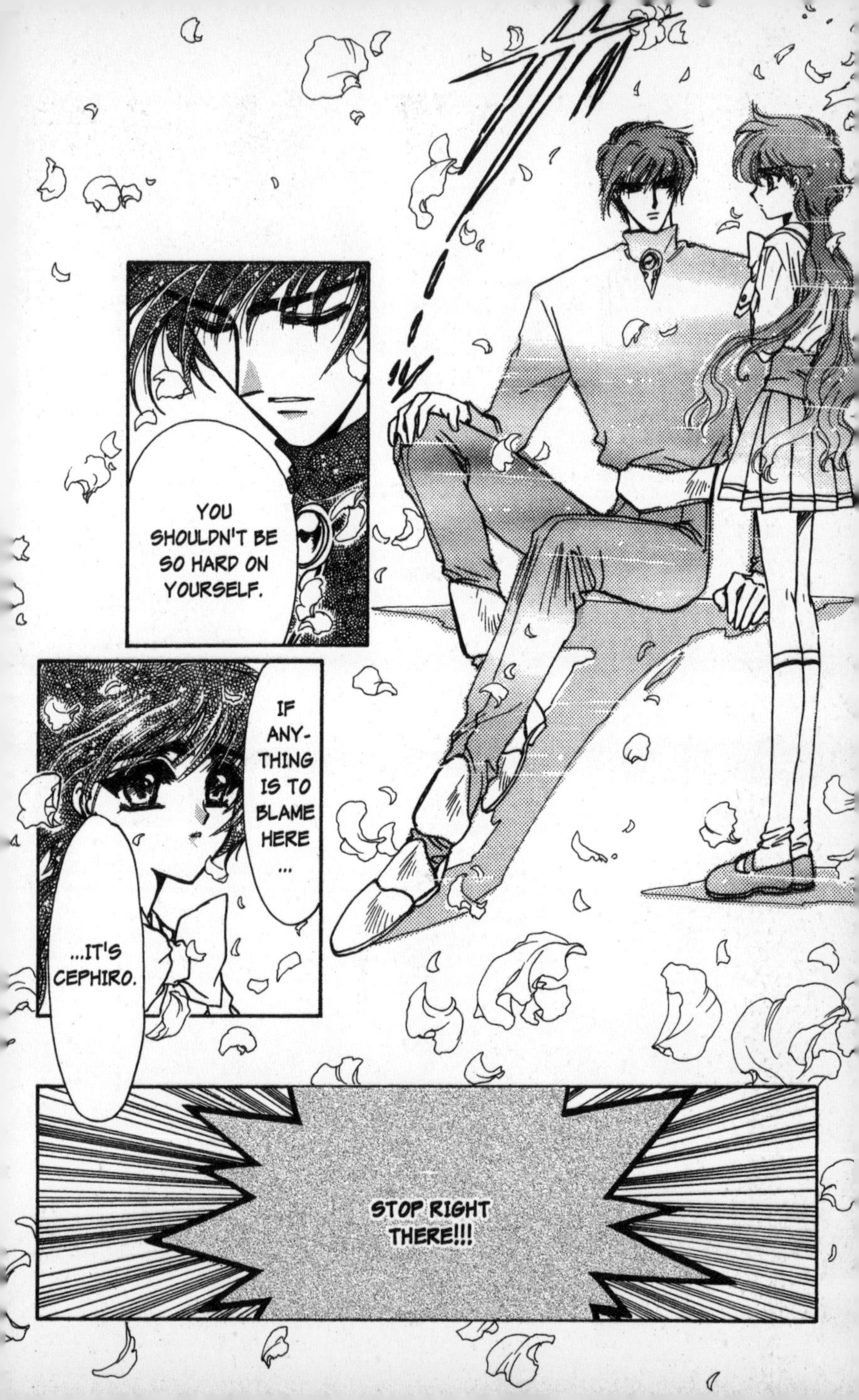
YOU SHOULDN'T BE SO HARD ON YOURSELF.
IF ANYTHING IS TO BLAME HERE ...
...IT'S CEPHIRO.
STOP RIGHT THERE!!!

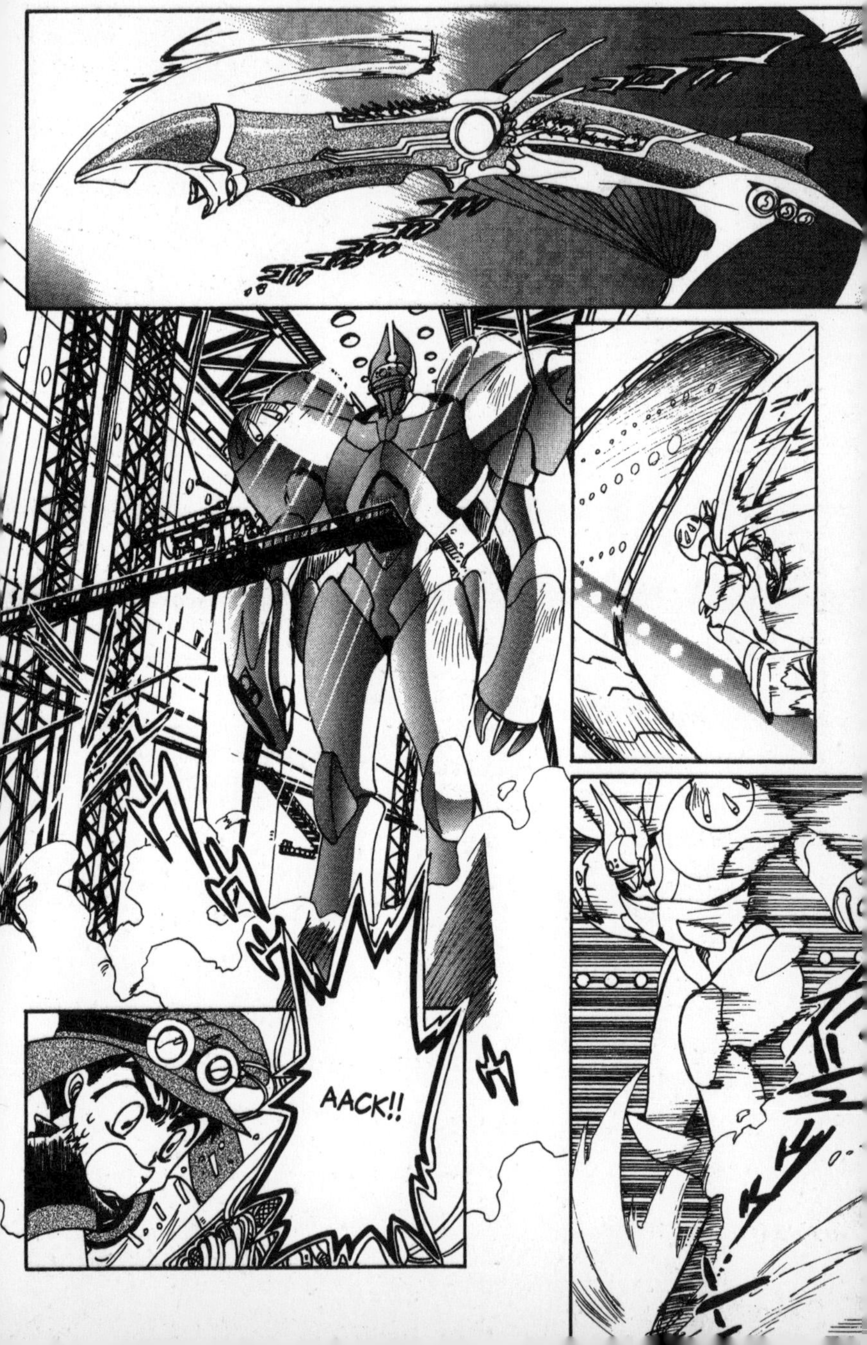
AACK!!

WHUP!

LANTIS
?!

IT
SEEMS
HE DID
GO BACK
TO
CEPHIRO
AFTER
ALL.

YOU USED
TOO MUCH OF
YOUR PSYCHIC
ENERGY...

SO...
TIRED...

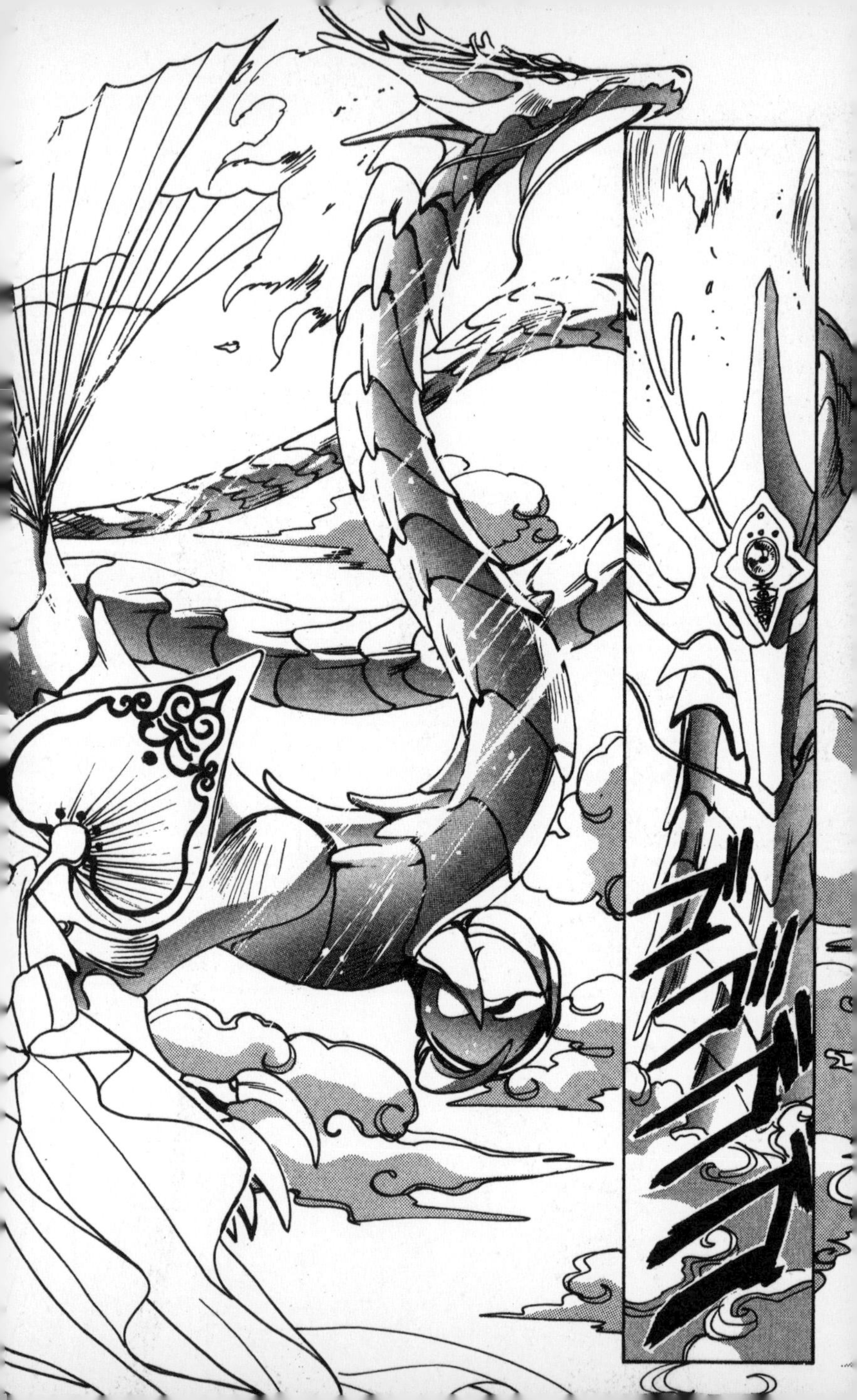

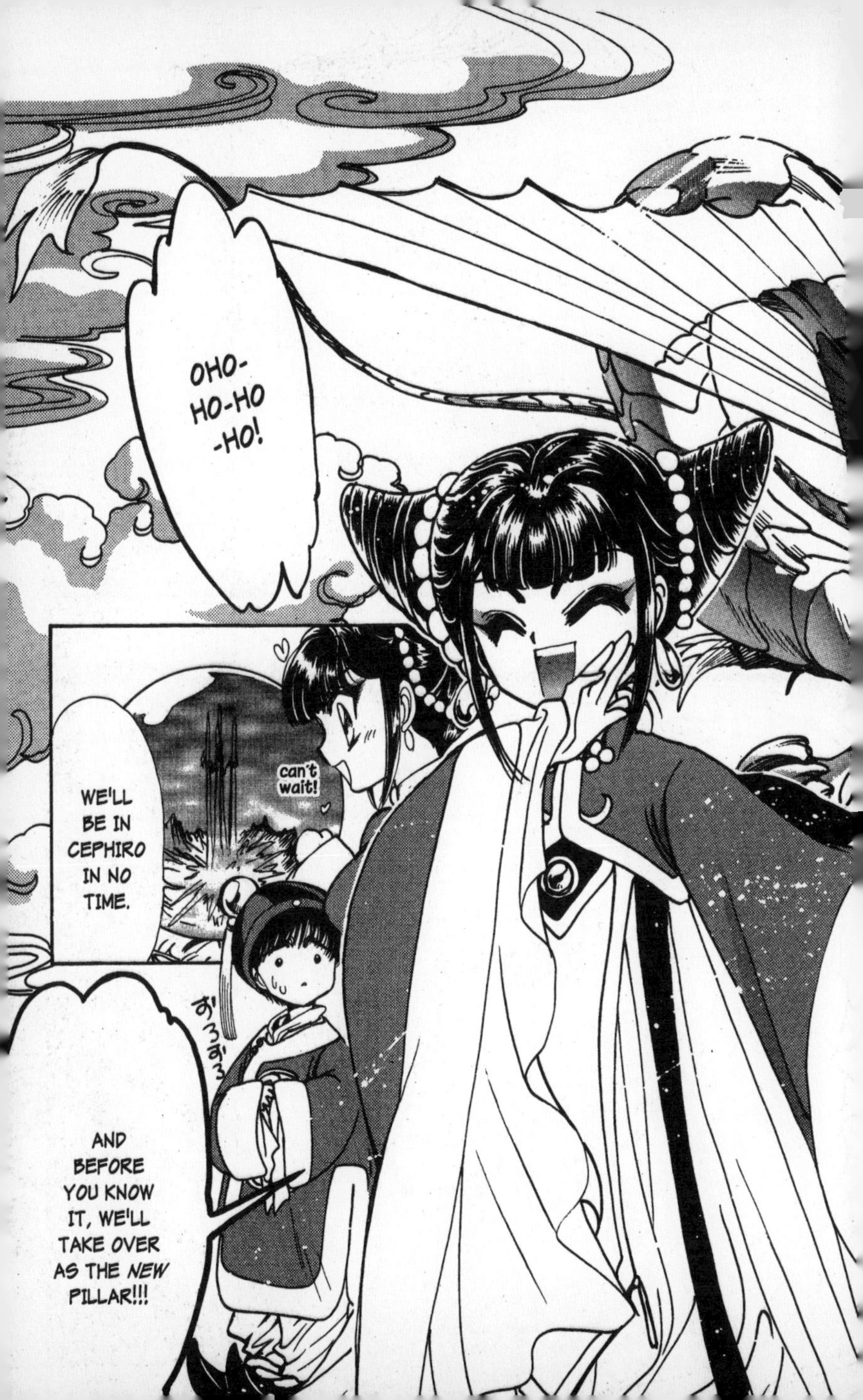
OHO-HO-HO-HO!
can't wait!
WE'LL BE IN CEPHIRO IN NO TIME.
すろすろ
AND BEFORE YOU KNOW IT, WE'LL TAKE OVER AS THE *NEW* PILLAR!!!

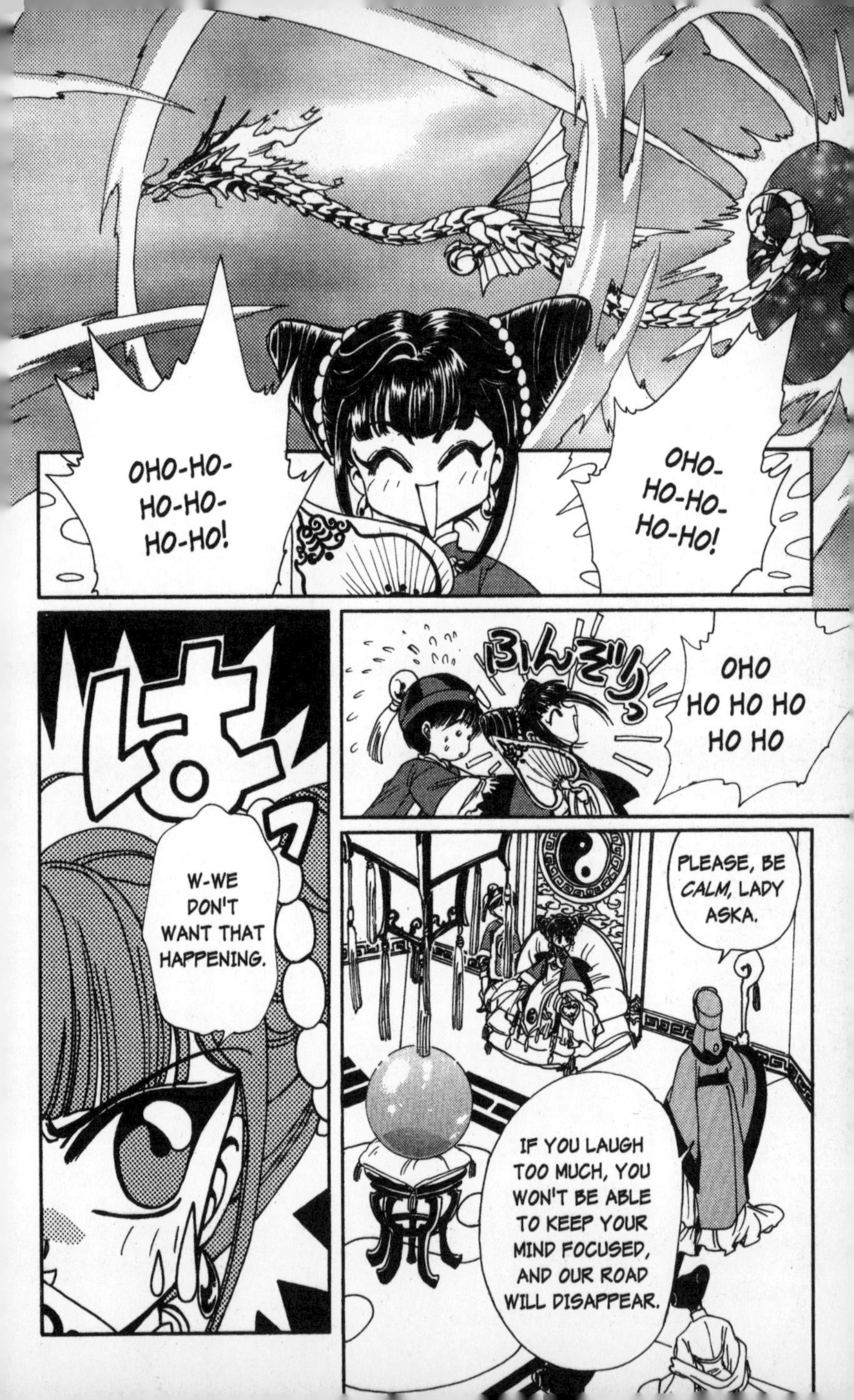
OHO-HO-HO-HO-HO!
OHO-HO-HO-HO-HO-HO!
OHO HO HO HO HO HO
ふんぞりっ
PLEASE, BE CALM, LADY ASKA.
IF YOU LAUGH TOO MUCH, YOU WON'T BE ABLE TO KEEP YOUR MIND FOCUSED, AND OUR ROAD WILL DISAPPEAR.
W-WE DON'T WANT THAT HAPPENING.

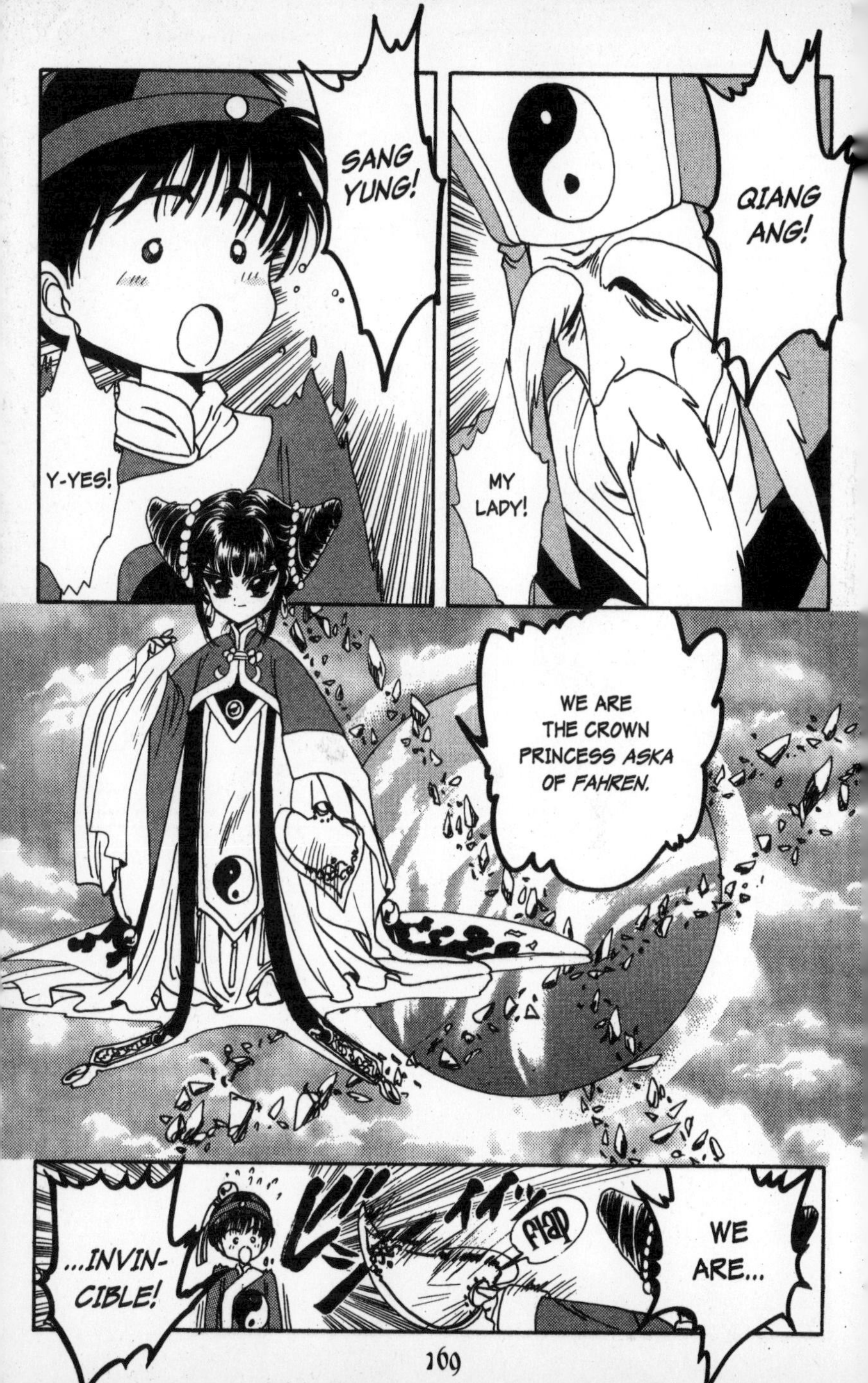
QIANG ANG!
MY LADY!
SANG YUNG!
Y-YES!
WE ARE THE CROWN PRINCESS ASKA OF FAHREN.
WE ARE...
flap
...INVIN-CIBLE!

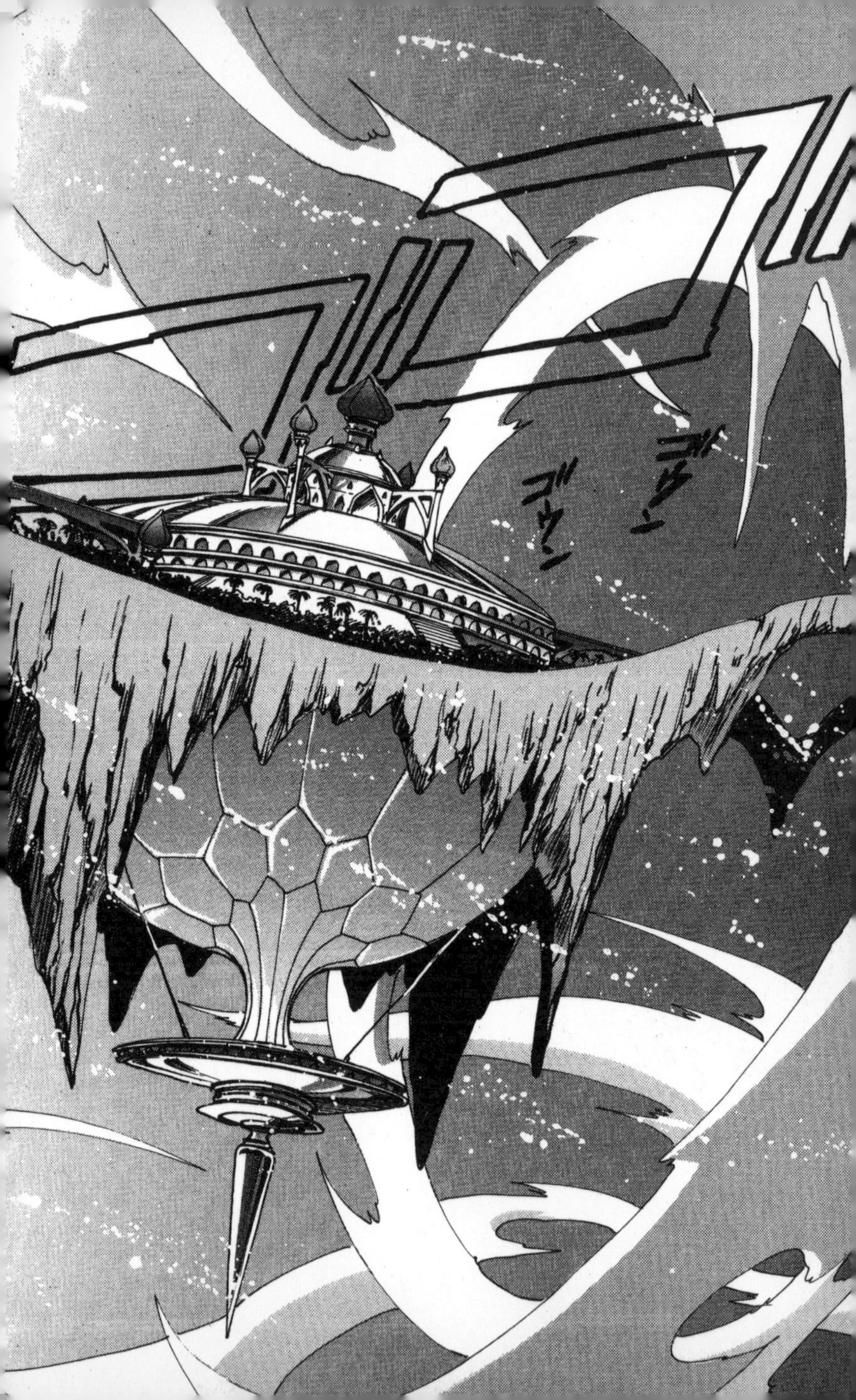

ゴウン
ゴウン

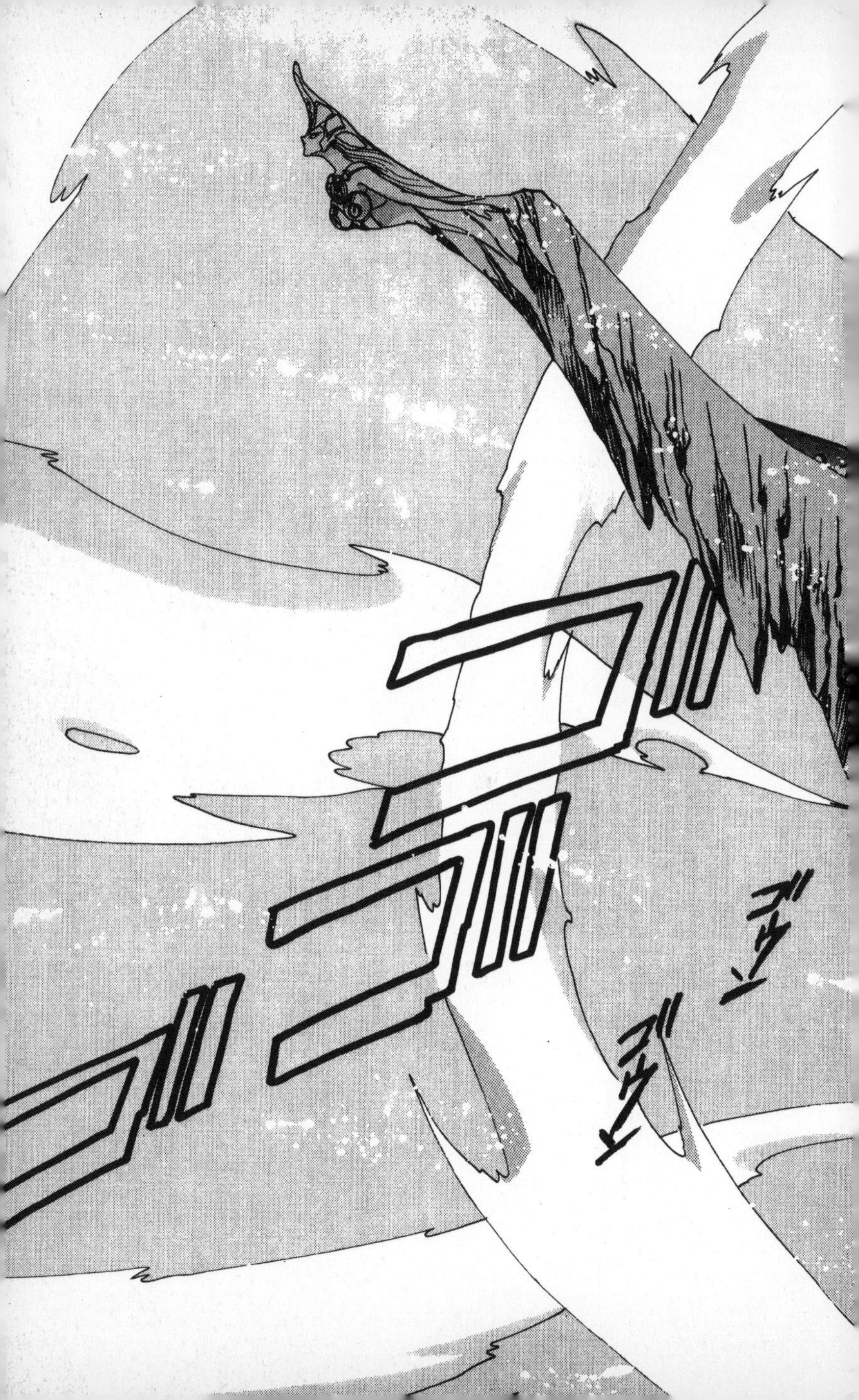
ゴゴゴ
ズゥン
ズゥン

174

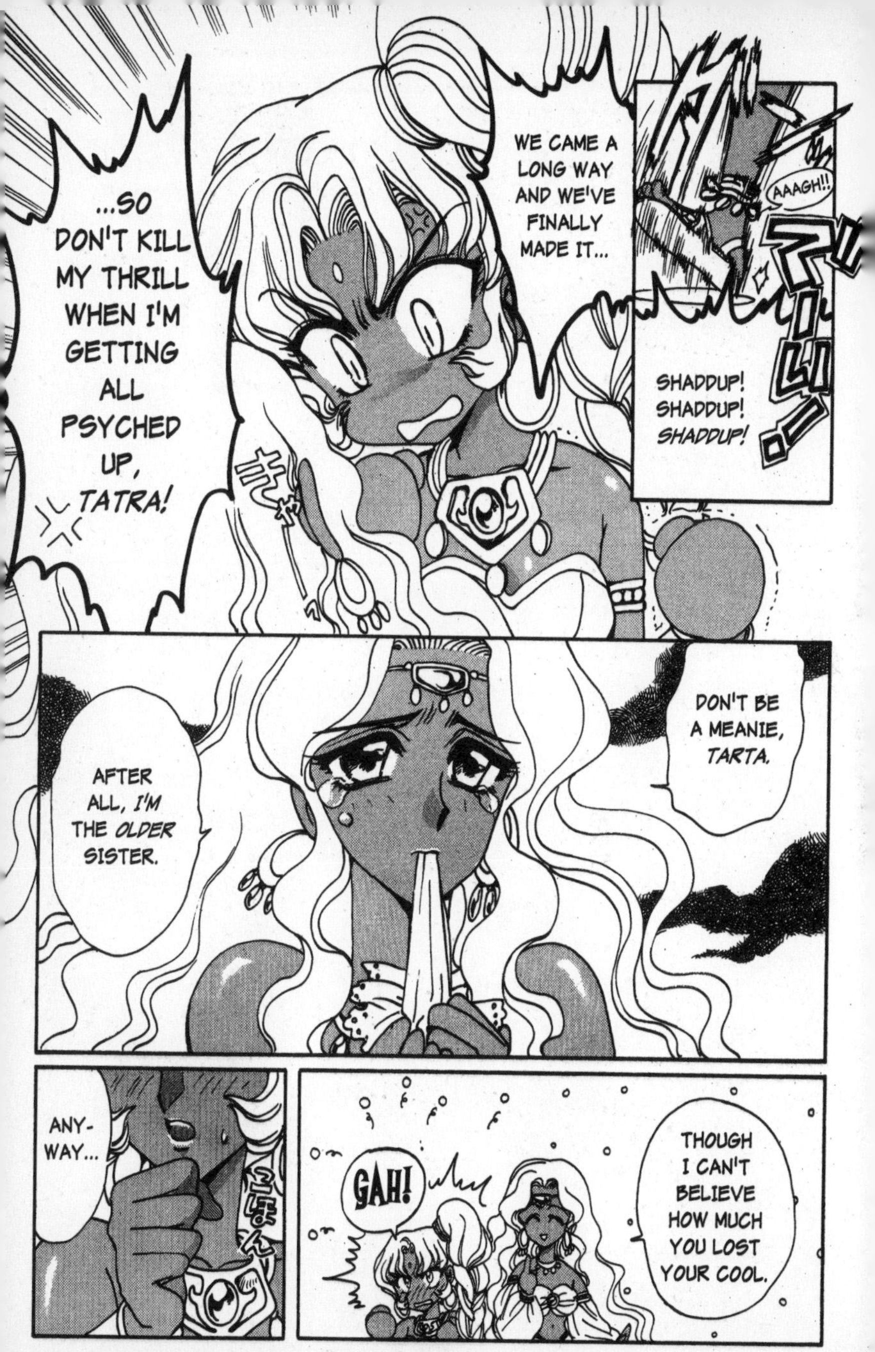
WE CAME A LONG WAY AND WE'VE FINALLY MADE IT...
...SO DON'T KILL MY THRILL WHEN I'M GETTING ALL PSYCHED UP, *TATRA!*
AAAGH!!
SHADDUP! SHADDUP! *SHADDUP!*
DON'T BE A MEANIE, *TARTA.*
AFTER ALL, *I'M* THE *OLDER* SISTER.
THOUGH I CAN'T BELIEVE HOW MUCH YOU LOST YOUR COOL.
GAH!
ANY-WAY...

HOW EXCITING!

AND JUST IN TIME. CHIZETA IS SO SMALL AND CRAMPED.

THAT'S RIGHT. AND WE'RE DOING IT ON A ROAD WE MADE TOGETHER, WITH OUR SISTERLY POWER!

WE HAVE TO TOUCH DOWN ON CEPHIRO AS SOON AS POSSIBLE!

YOU SAID IT!

THIS ROAD IS GOING TO TAKE US THE DISTANCE...

...SO WE CAN BECOME THE PILLAR OF CEPHIRO AND EXPAND OUR TERRITORY.

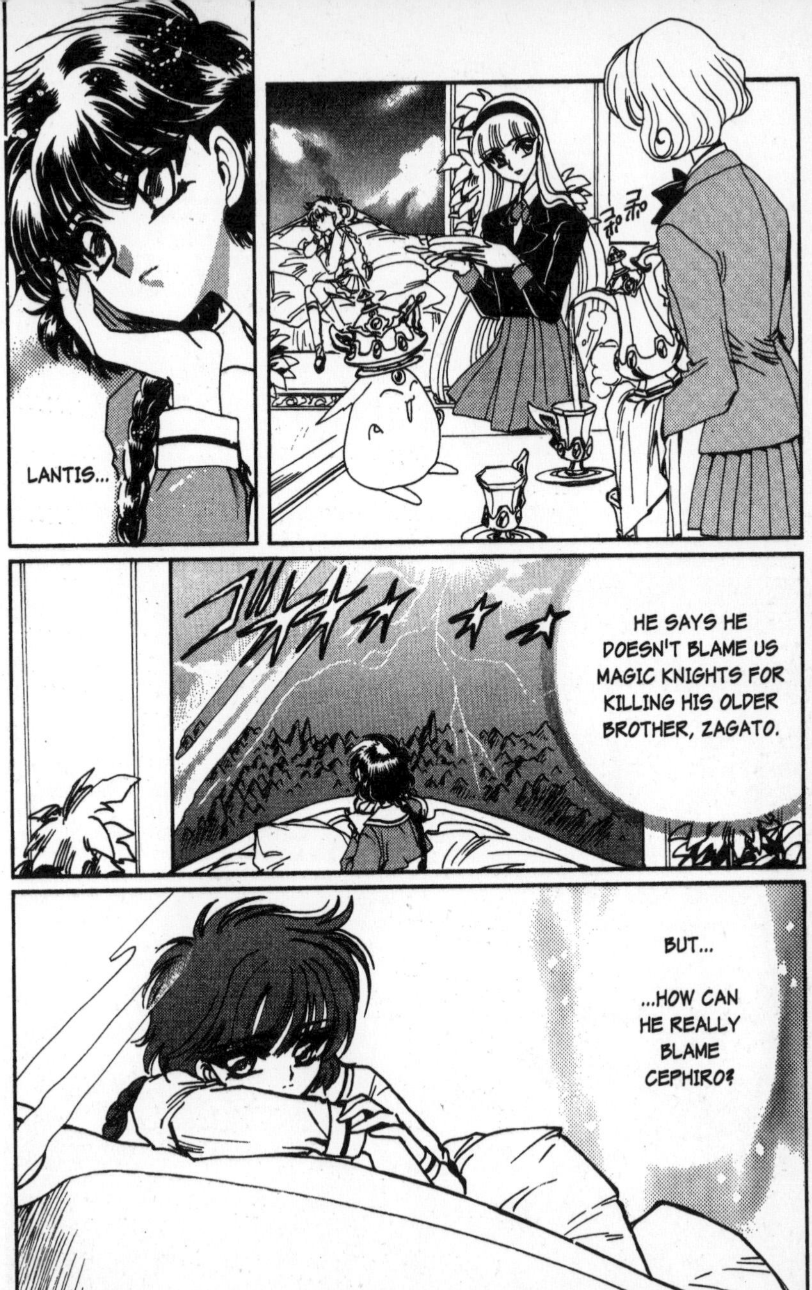
LANTIS...
HE SAYS HE DOESN'T BLAME US MAGIC KNIGHTS FOR KILLING HIS OLDER BROTHER, ZAGATO.
BUT...
...HOW CAN HE REALLY BLAME CEPHIRO?

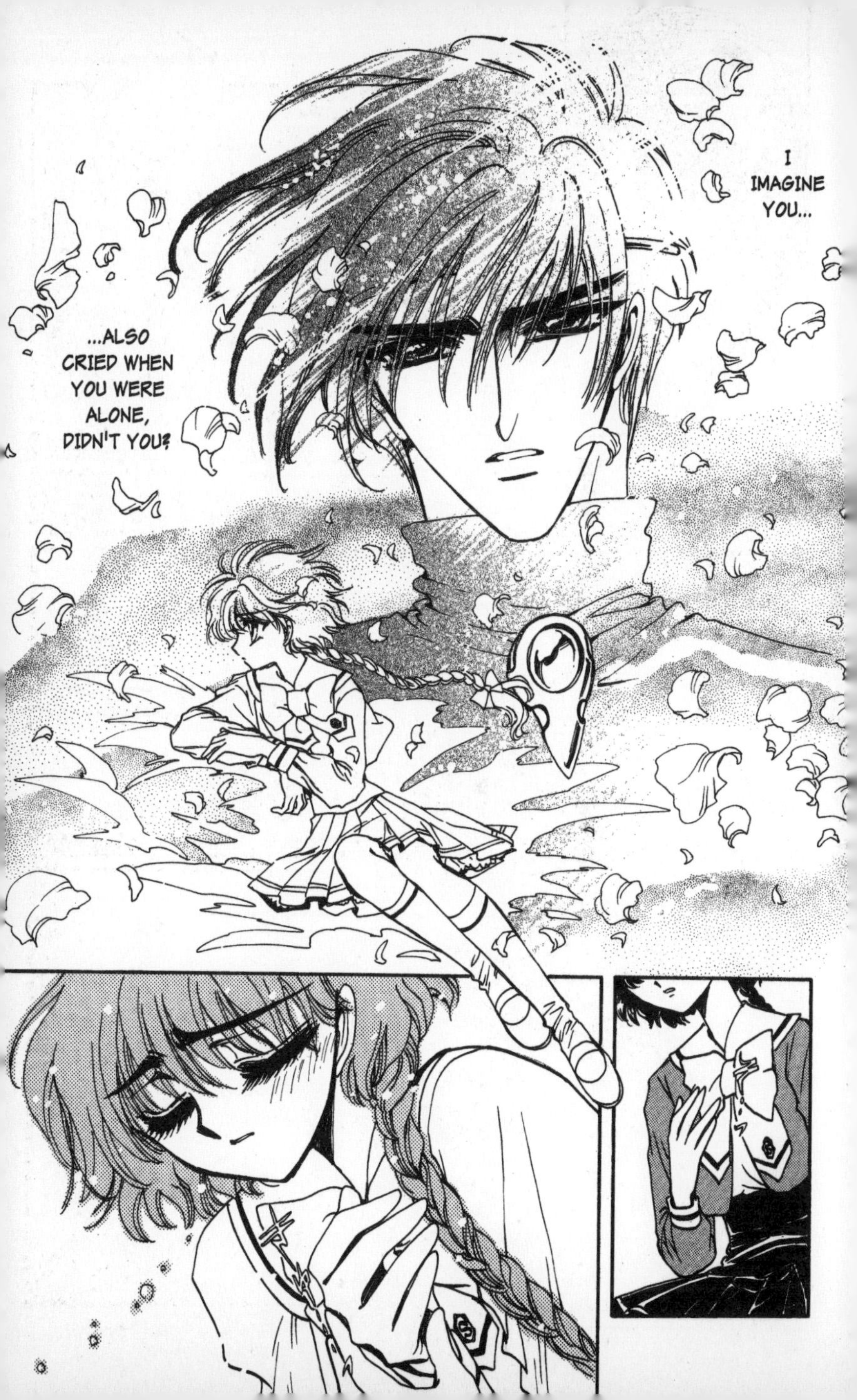
I IMAGINE YOU...
...ALSO CRIED WHEN YOU WERE ALONE, DIDN'T YOU?

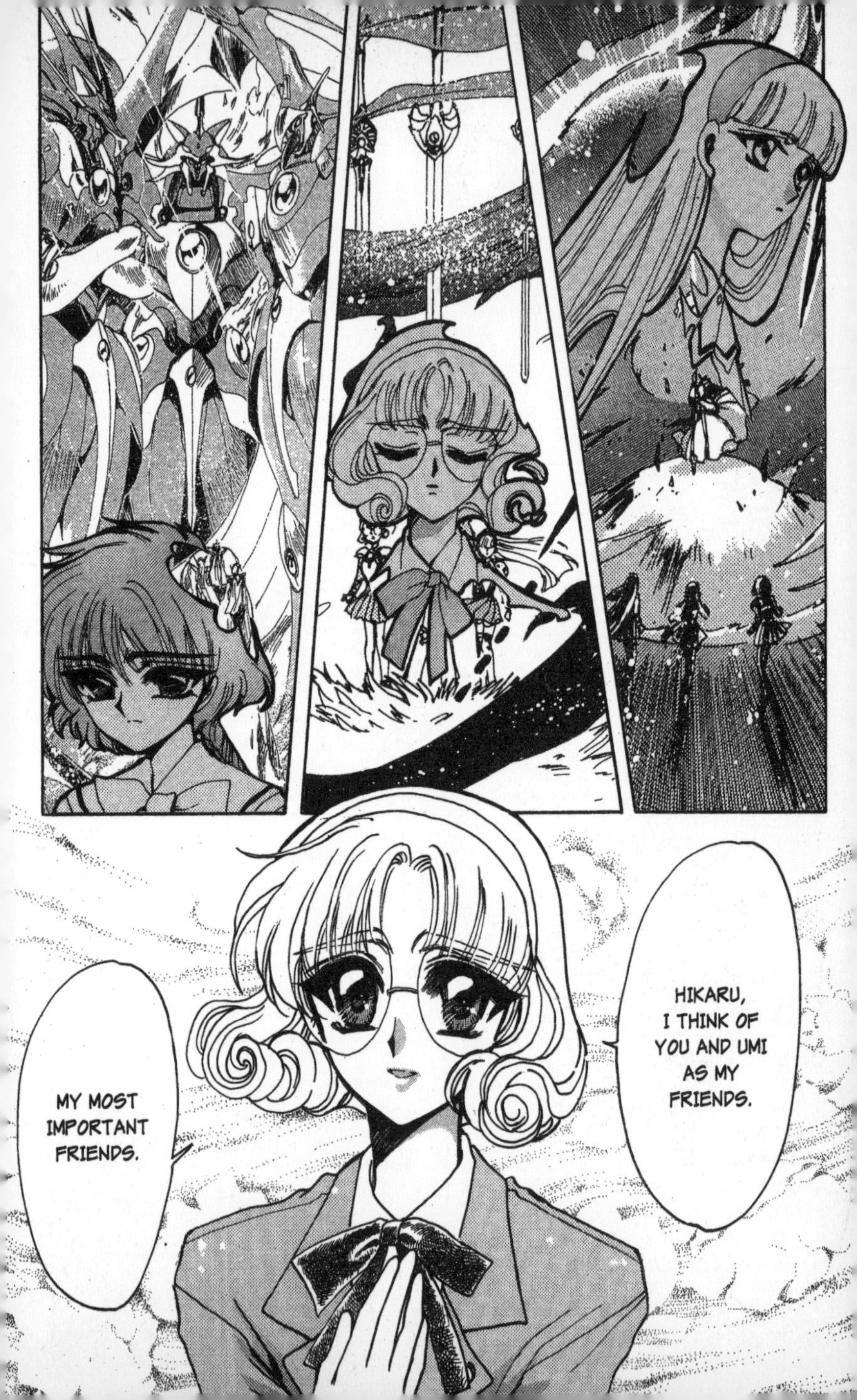
HIKARU, I THINK OF YOU AND UMI AS MY FRIENDS.
MY MOST IMPORTANT FRIENDS.

MY SISTER ONCE TOLD ME...

...IT'S HARD WHEN YOU DON'T HAVE ANYONE WHO UNDERSTANDS YOUR SUFFERING.

I THINK PRETTY SOON THERE IS GOING TO BE A LOT HAPPENING HERE.

...IF YOU'RE NOT ALONE...

BUT...

...IF YOU CAN SHARE YOUR WORRIES AND WORK WITH FRIENDS TO FIND THE SOLUTIONS TO YOUR PROBLEMS...

IT'S LIKE YOU SAID, HIKARU...

...WE'RE AT OUR BEST TOGETHER.

...EVERY-THING WILL BE ALL RIGHT.

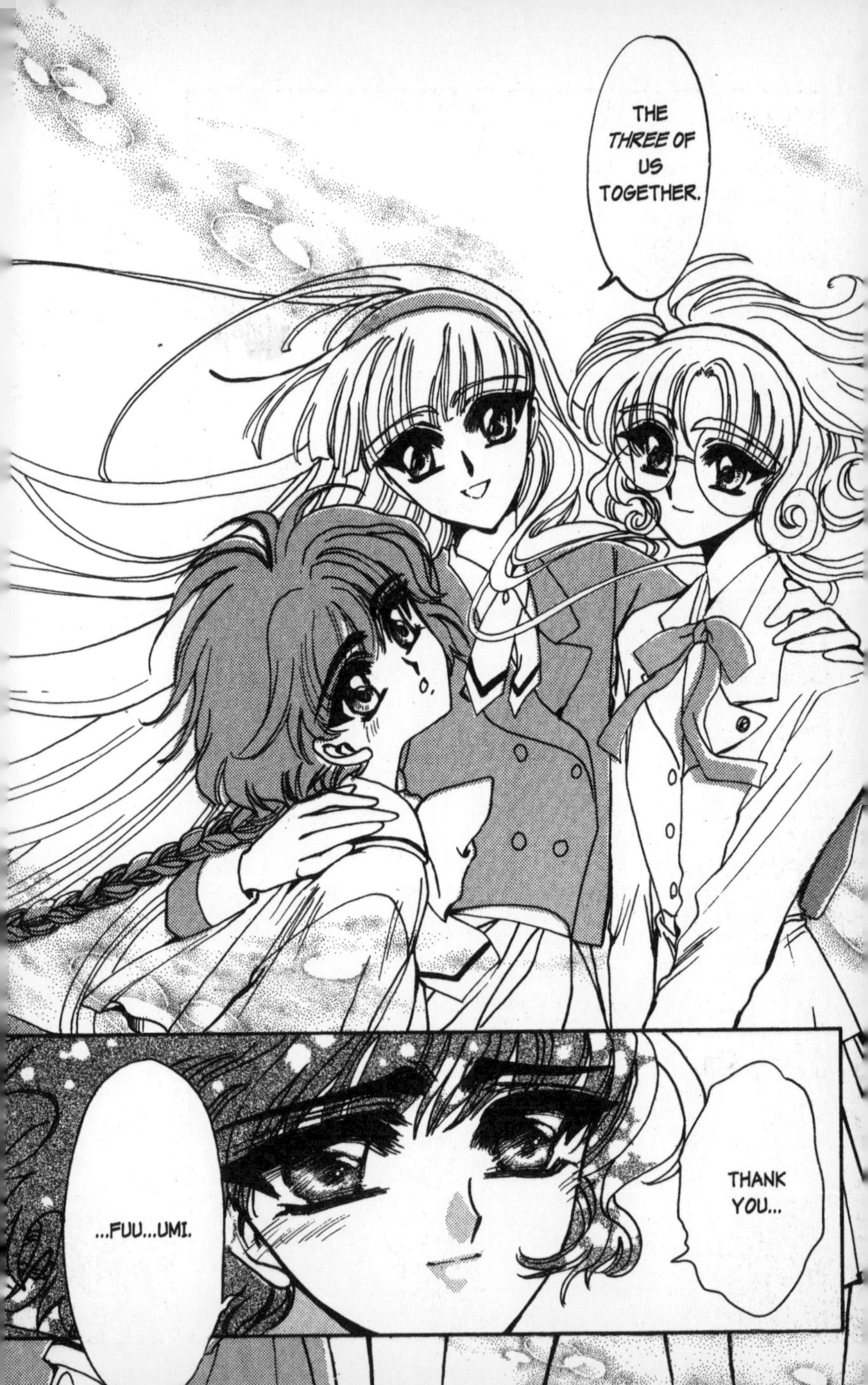
THE *THREE* OF US TOGETHER.
THANK YOU...
...FUU...UMI.

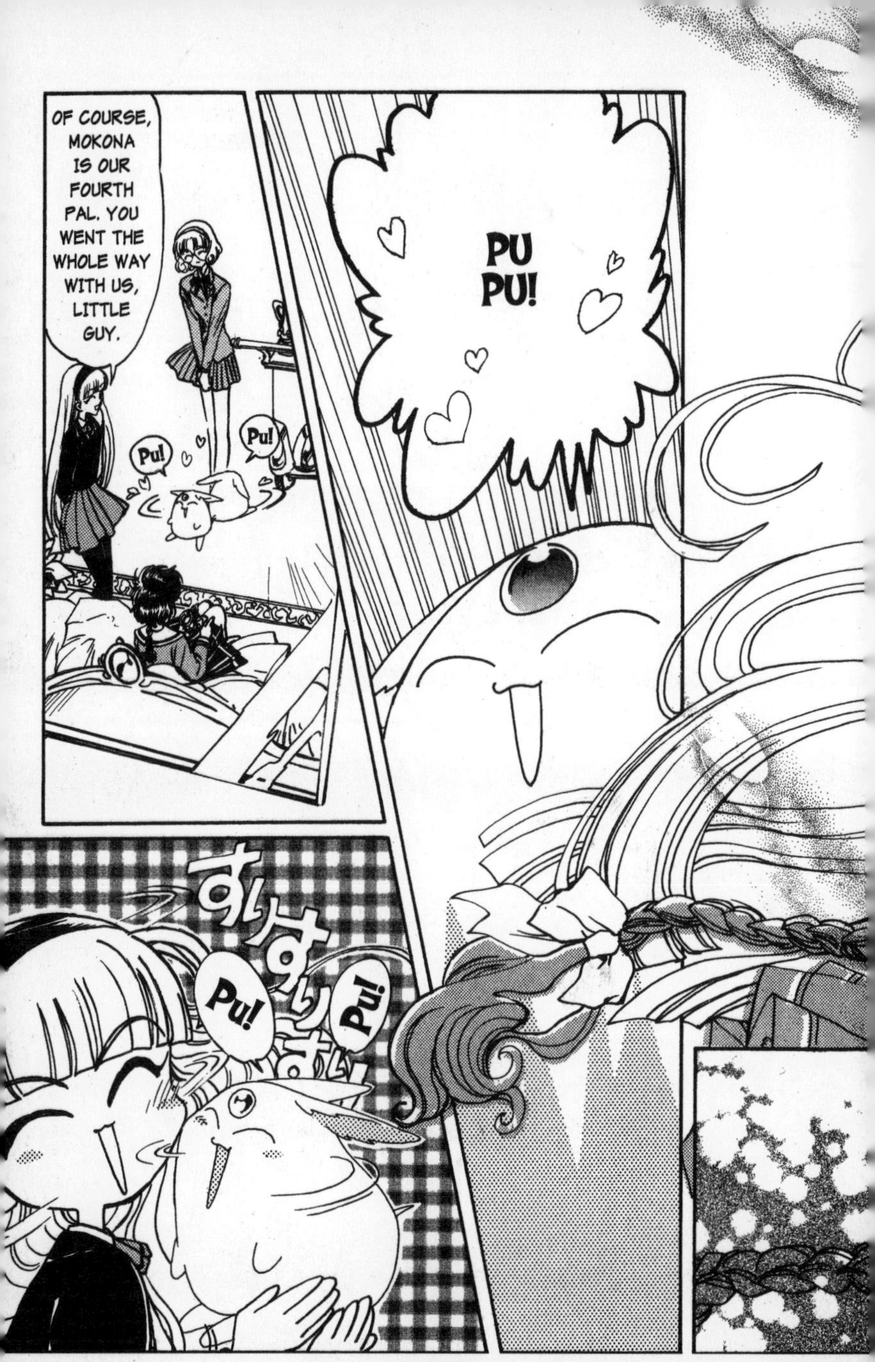
PU PU!
OF COURSE, MOKONA IS OUR FOURTH PAL. YOU WENT THE WHOLE WAY WITH US, LITTLE GUY.
Pu!
Pu!
すいすいすい
Pu!
Pu!

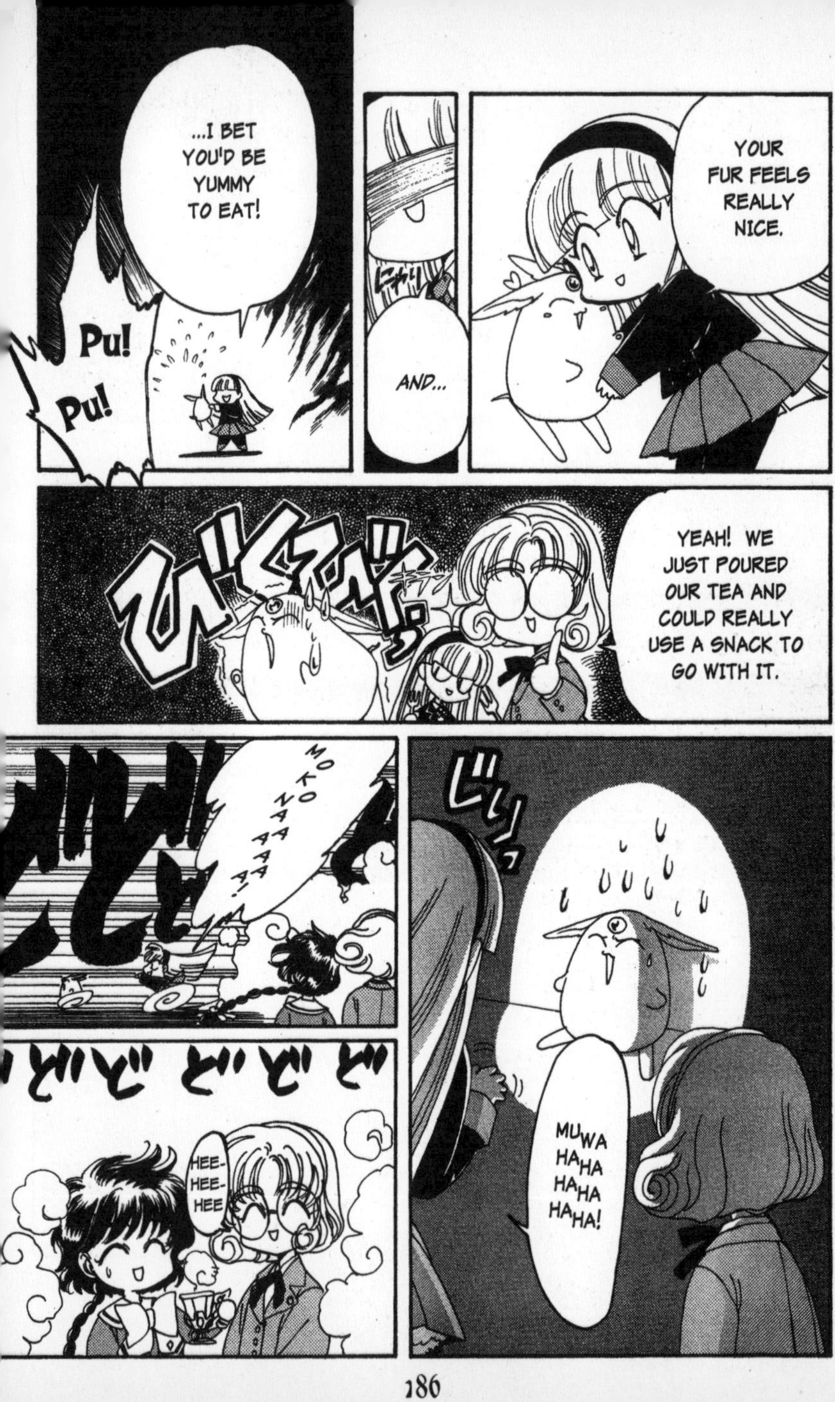
YOUR FUR FEELS REALLY NICE.
AND...
...I BET YOU'D BE YUMMY TO EAT!
Pu!
Pu!
YEAH! WE JUST POURED OUR TEA AND COULD REALLY USE A SNACK TO GO WITH IT.
MUWAHAHAHAHAHAHAHA!
MOKONAAAAAAA!
HEE-HEE-HEE

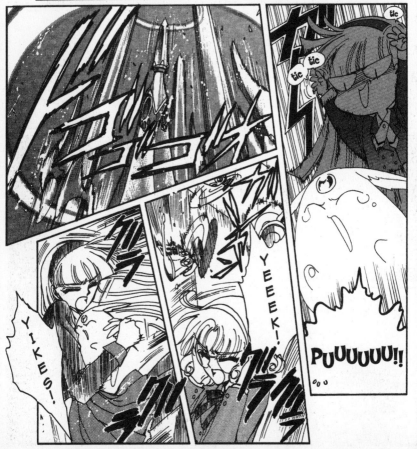

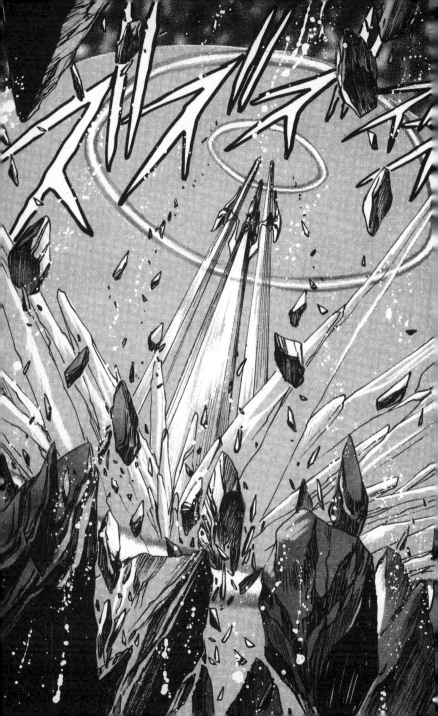

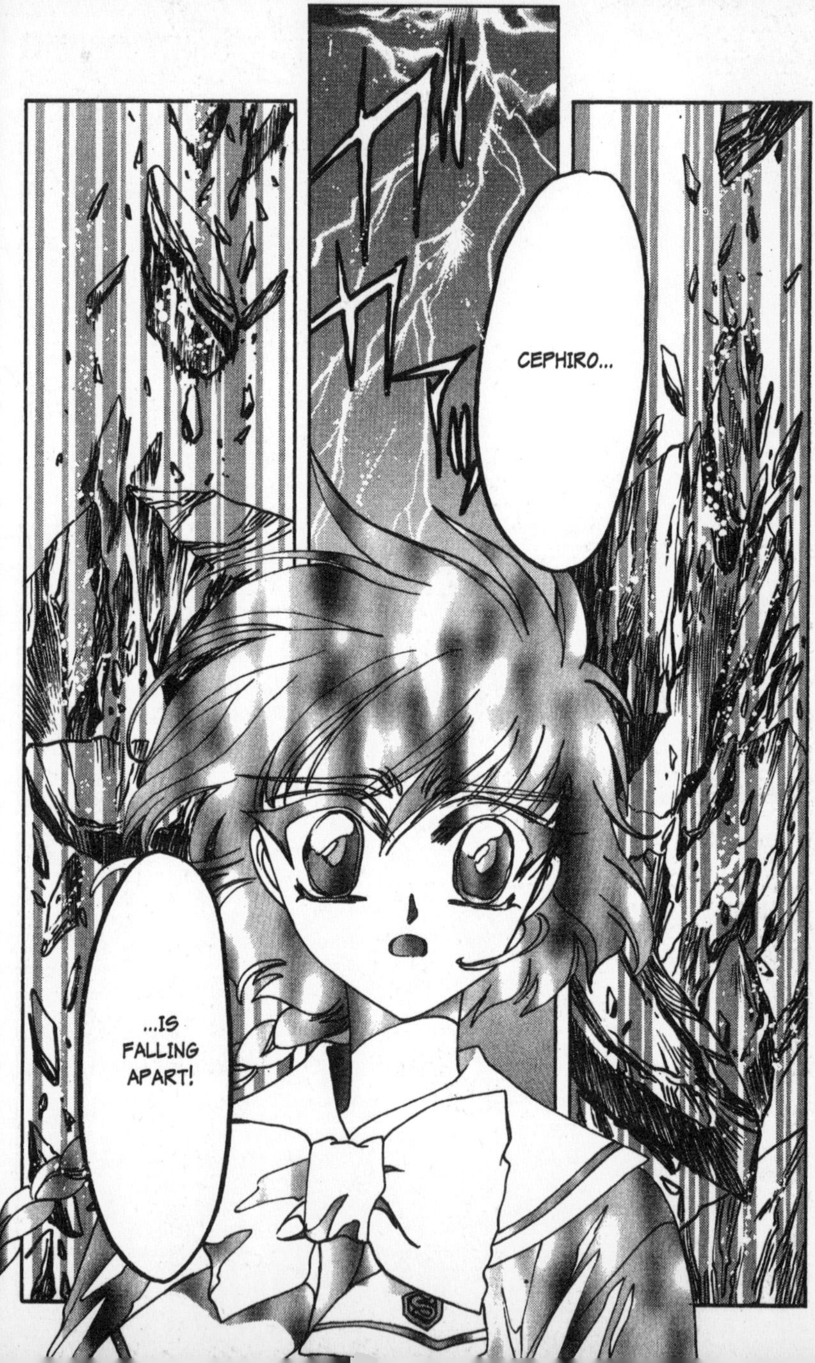
CEPHIRO...
...IS FALLING APART!

192

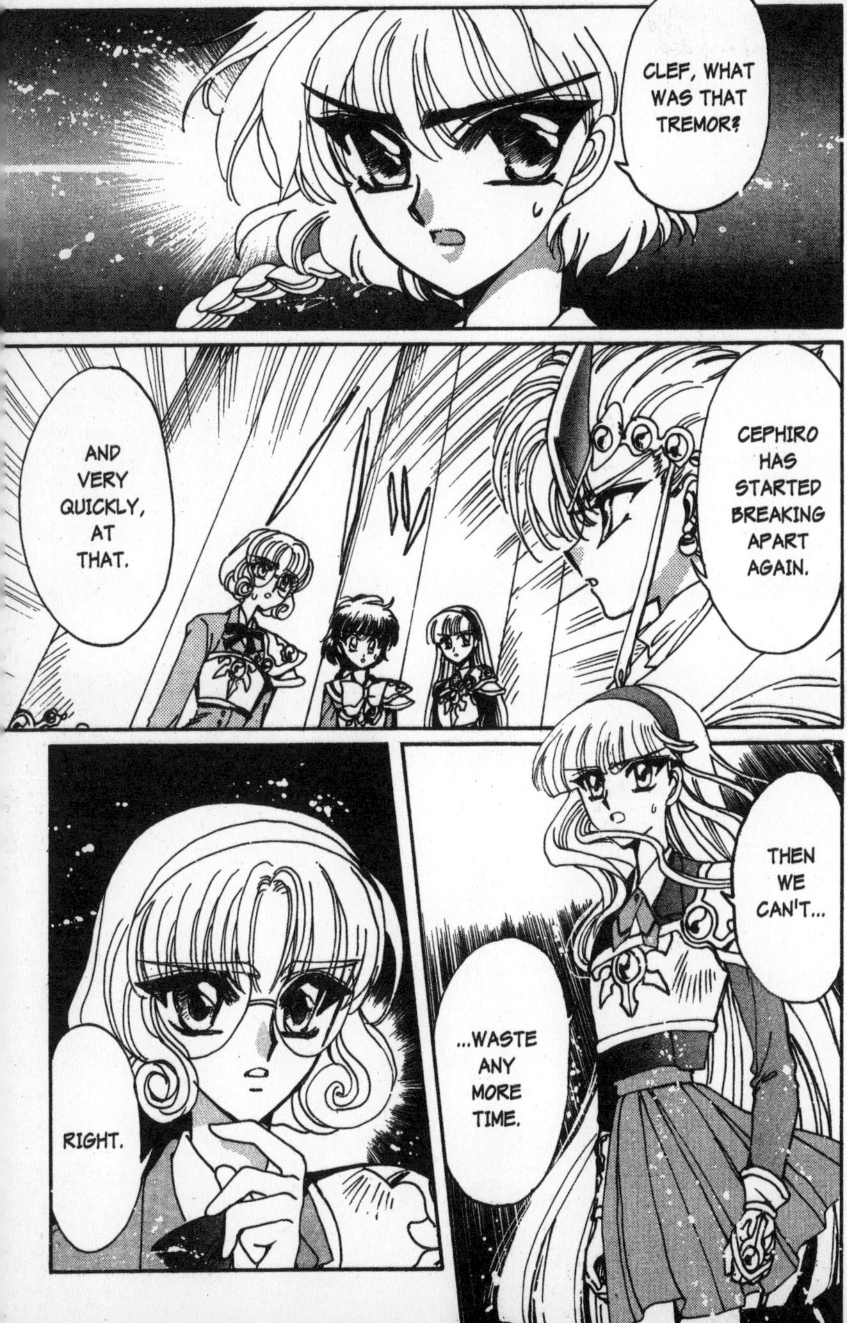
CLEF, WHAT WAS THAT TREMOR?
CEPHIRO HAS STARTED BREAKING APART AGAIN.
AND VERY QUICKLY, AT THAT.
THEN WE CAN'T...
...WASTE ANY MORE TIME.
RIGHT.

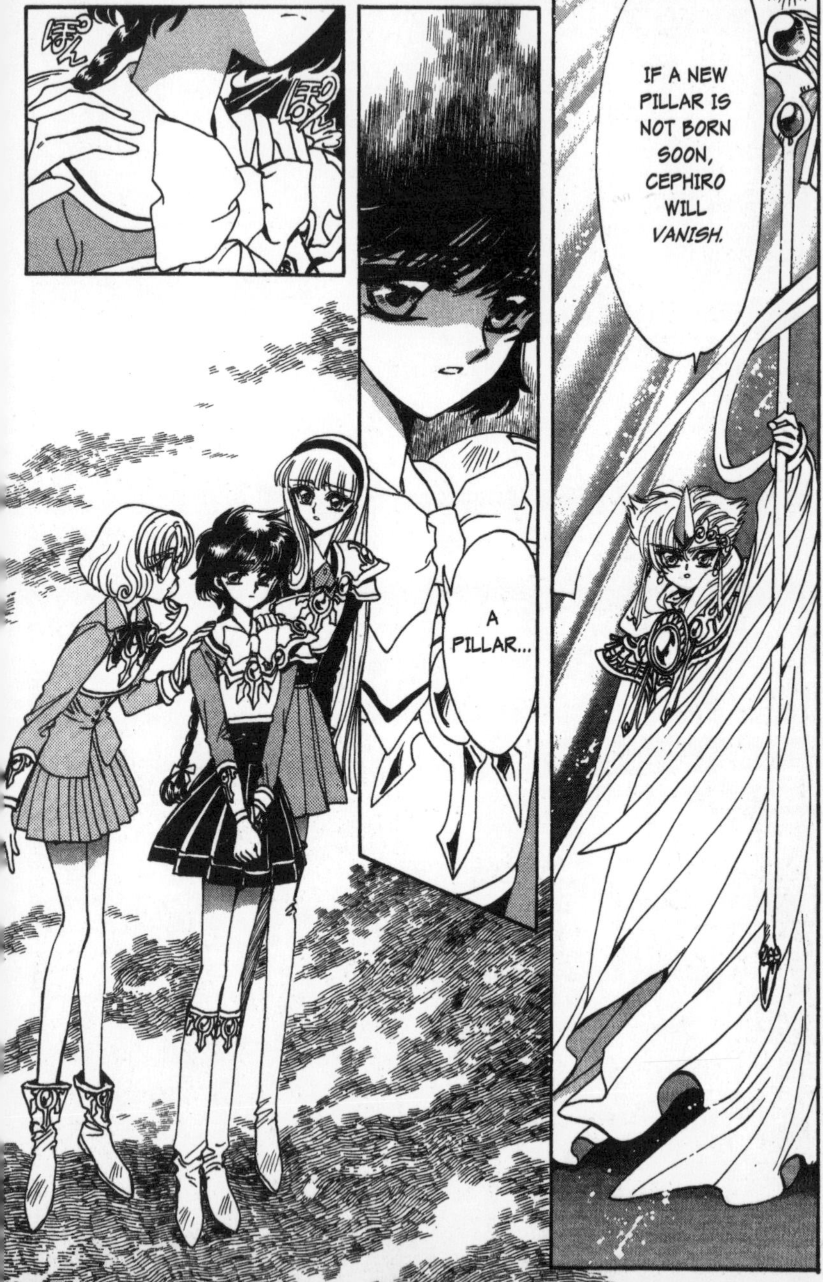
IF A NEW PILLAR IS NOT BORN SOON, CEPHIRO WILL *VANISH.*
A PILLAR...

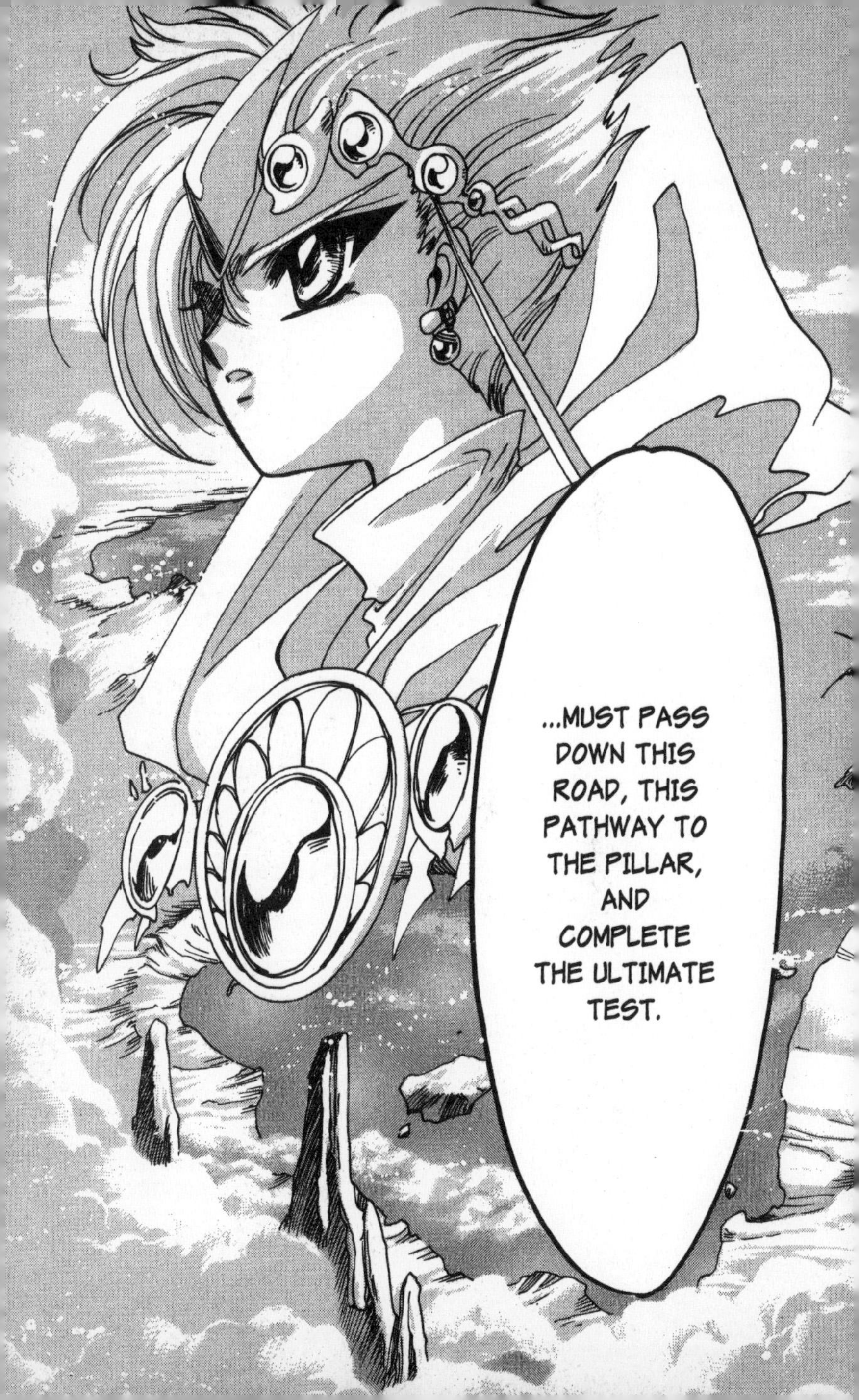
...MUST PASS DOWN THIS ROAD, THIS PATHWAY TO THE PILLAR, AND COMPLETE THE ULTIMATE TEST.

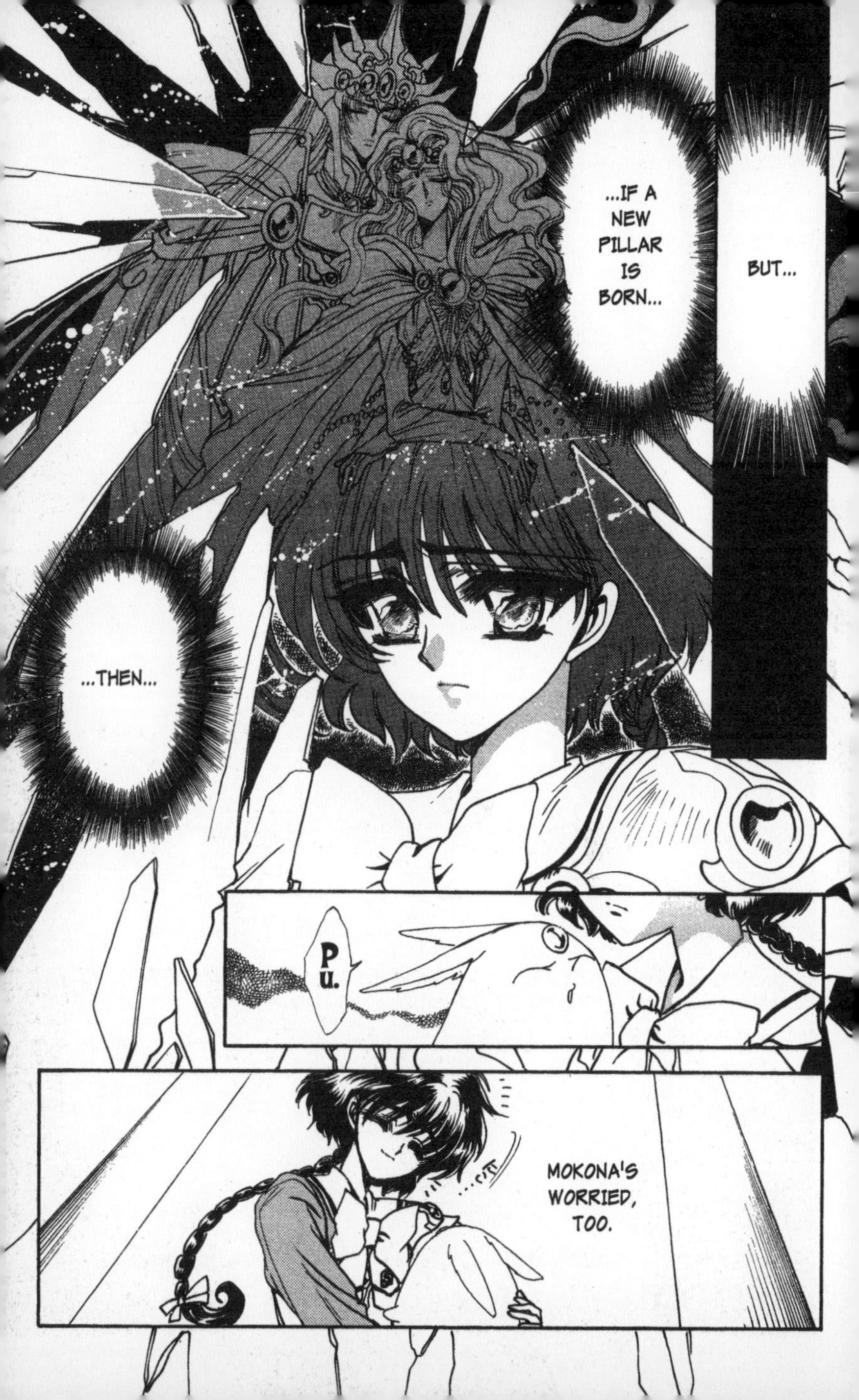
BUT...
...IF A NEW PILLAR IS BORN...
...THEN...
PU.
MOKONA'S WORRIED, TOO.

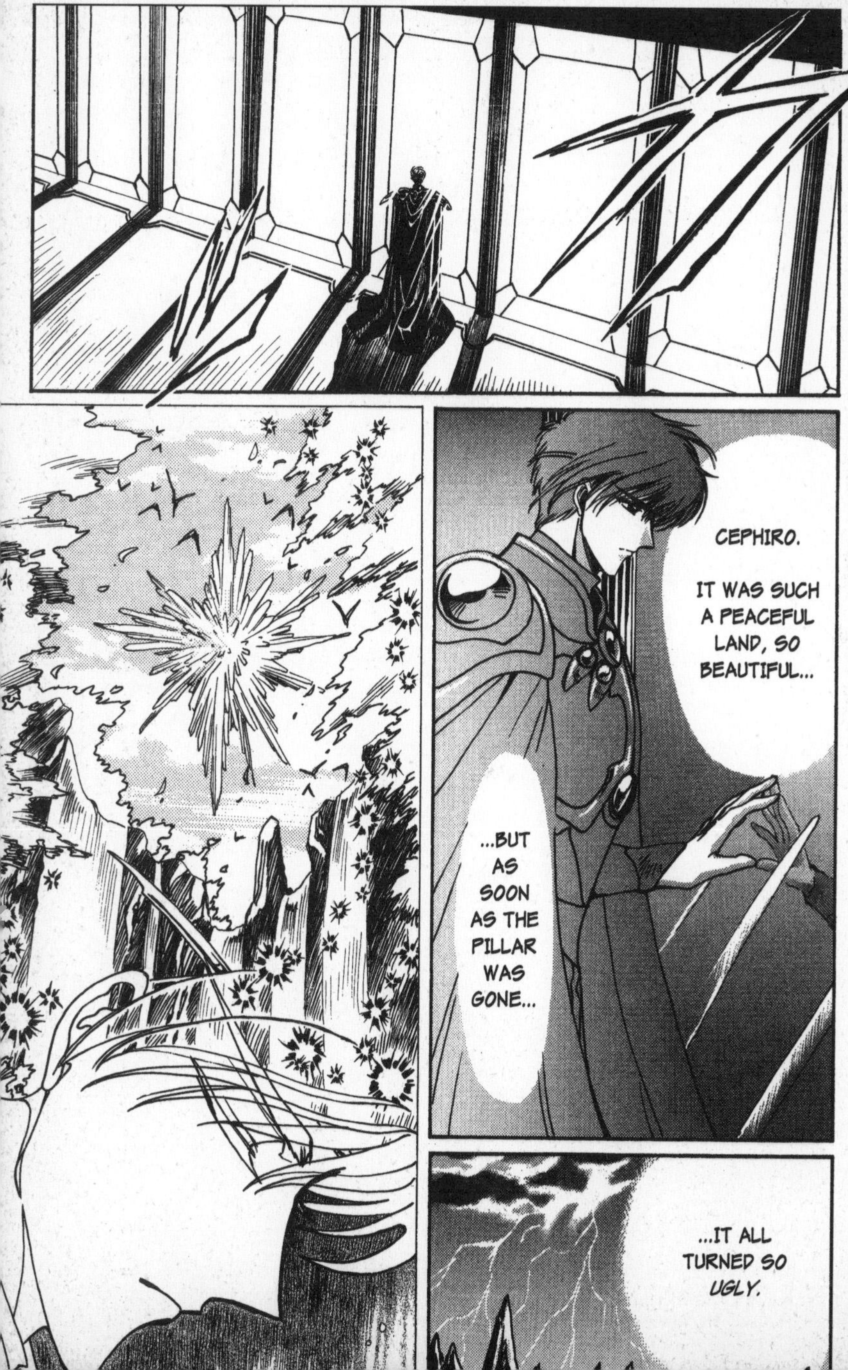
CEPHIRO.
IT WAS SUCH A PEACEFUL LAND, SO BEAUTIFUL...
...BUT AS SOON AS THE PILLAR WAS GONE...
...IT ALL TURNED SO UGLY.

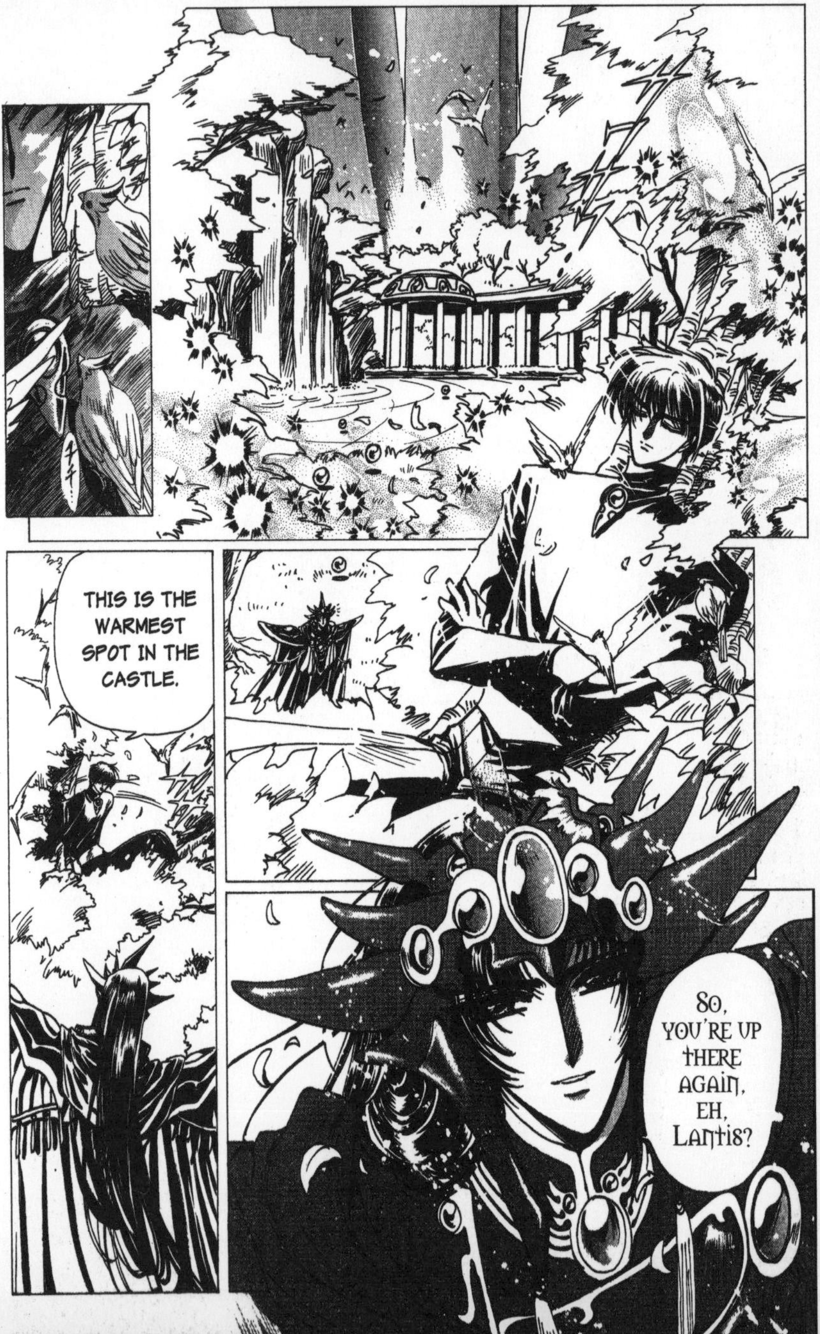
THIS IS THE WARMEST SPOT IN THE CASTLE.
SO, YOU'RE UP THERE AGAIN, EH, LANTIS?

CAIL OR NO CAIL, AS LONG AS PRINCESS EMERAUDE STANDS AS CEPHIRO'S PILLAR...

...THERE ARE NO BATTLES FOR ME TO FIGHT.

...AND THE CAPTAIN OF PRINCESS EMERAUDE'S PRIVATE GUARD, SPEND SO MUCH TIME NAPPING?

HOW CAN THE ONLY CAIL IN CEPHIRO...

THE MONSTER HUNT GETS UNDERWAY AT DUSK.

Lantis...

...WHAT DO YOU THINK OF THE PILLAR?

WHAT'S WRONG, ZAGATO?

IS SOMETHING ON YOUR MIND?

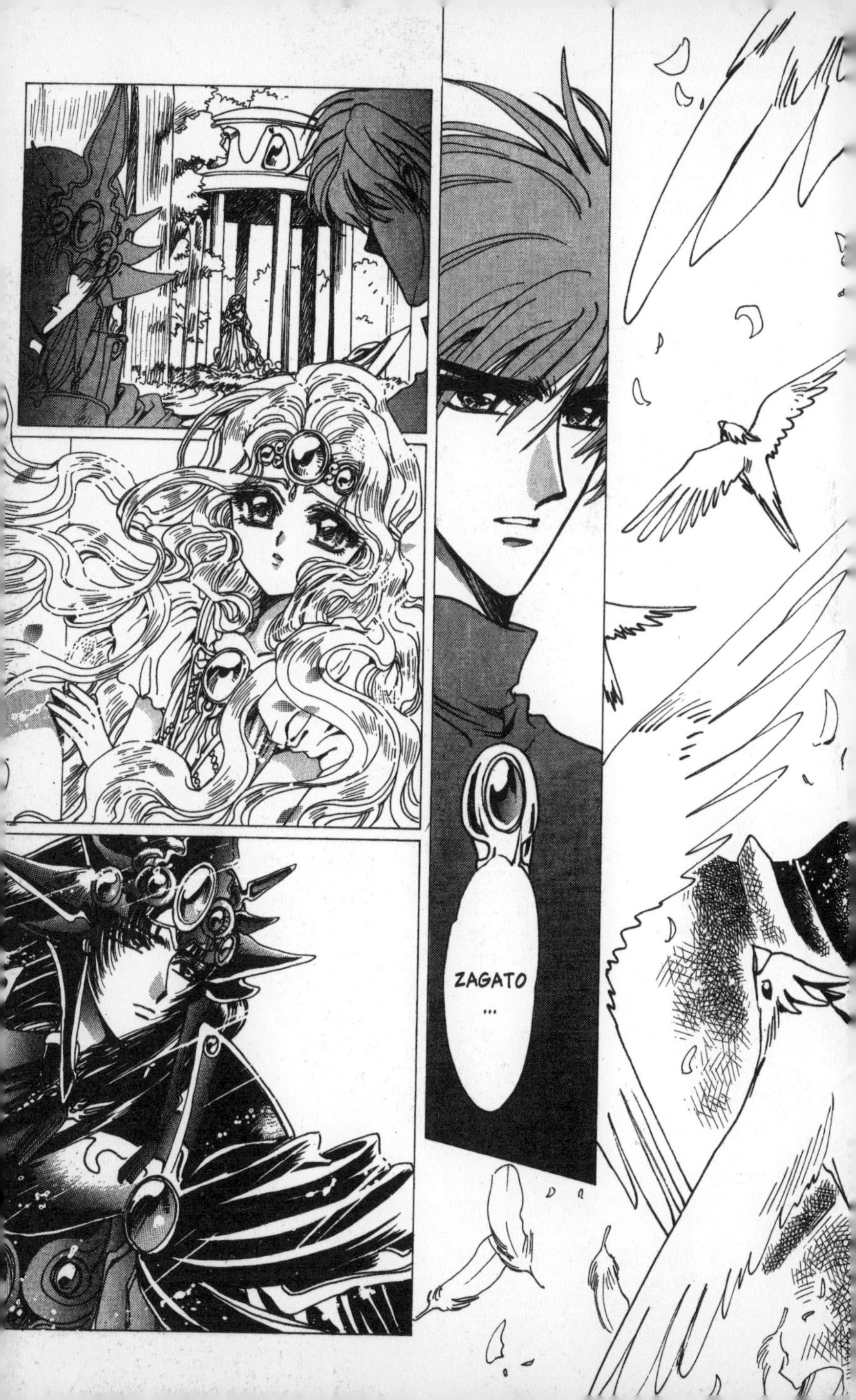
ZAGATO
...

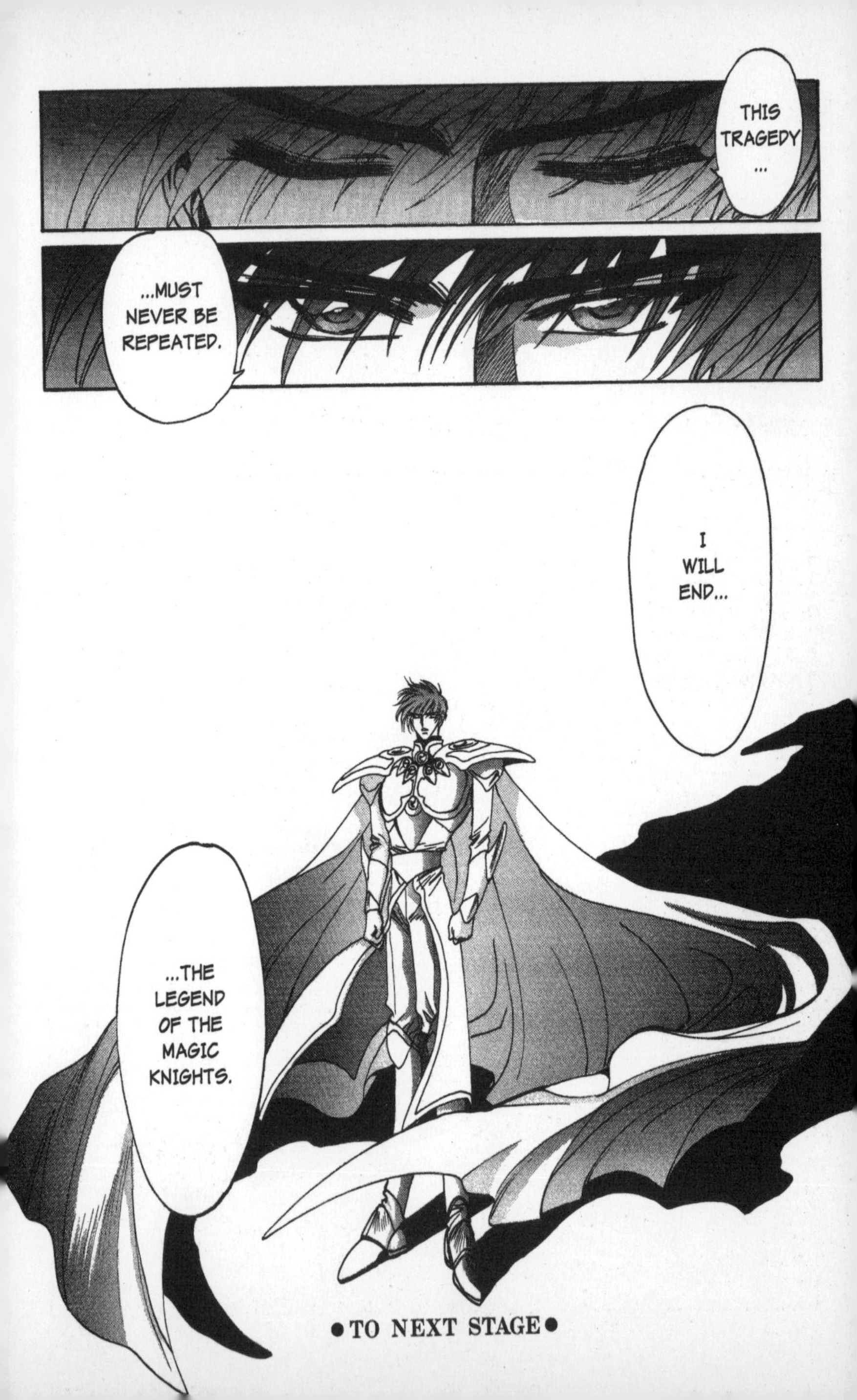
THIS TRAGEDY...
...MUST NEVER BE REPEATED.
I WILL END...
...THE LEGEND OF THE MAGIC KNIGHTS.

•TO NEXT STAGE•

CLAMP TIMES
SPECIAL EDITION

SO, WHAT DID Y'ALL THINK OF RAYEARTH II, VOLUME 1?

HIKARU AND FRIENDS MUST SAVE CEPHIRO AGAIN, BUT THIS TIME THEY DON'T KNOW WHO SUMMONED THEM!

THERE'S AN ANIME FOR THE SECOND SERIES AS WELL!

HAVE YOU SEEN THE RAYEARTH ANIME YET? IT'S AVAILABLE ON DVD AND VHS IN AMERICA, SO YOU HAVE NO EXCUSE!

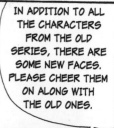

IN ADDITION TO ALL THE CHARACTERS FROM THE OLD SERIES, THERE ARE SOME NEW FACES. PLEASE CHEER THEM ON ALONG WITH THE OLD ONES.

THE EARS CURL OUTWARD.

MEOW

SHE'S AN "AMERICAN CURL" BREED WITH A TABBY COAT AND GOLDEN EYES.

SHE'S JUST A KITTEN NOW-- ABOUT 3 MONTHS OLD.

))

SATSUKI LIKES CATS

KAWAII! SOOO CUTE!

KITTY LIKES TO PLAY SOCCER.

SHE'S A VERY PLAYFUL KITTEN, ALWAYS RUNNING AROUND, EATING, BITING, AND SLEEPING.

COME BACK NEXT VOLUME FOR MORE "TALES OF THE CAT!"

OF COURSE, WE WROTE THIS A LONG TIME AGO. SHE'S ALL GROWN UP NOW.

POUNCE!

SHE JUMPS UP AND KNOCKS THINGS OFF OF OUR DESK.

SHE SECRETLY DRINKS FROM OUR CUPS.

SLURP SLURP

SHE'LL POUNCE ON YOU AND BITE YOU WHEN YOU LEAST EXPECT IT.

OF COURSE, YOU HAVE TO COME BACK TO FIND OUT WHAT HAPPENS TO OUR HEROES!

RAHR!

BUT SHE'S ALWAYS CUTE. (ESPE-CIALLY WHEN SHE'S SLEEPING!)

• TO NEXT STAGE •

Next time in Magic Knight Rayearth 11...

To control Cephiro means to sacrifice oneself to keep it safe. This is a lesson the Magic Knights know only too well, however, the invading countries are not aware of this and continue the assault with greater force. When powerful Djinns, deadly dragons, and menacing mechs attack the peaceful nation, Hikaru, Umi and Fuu don their sacred armor once more to defend the land as Magic Knights!

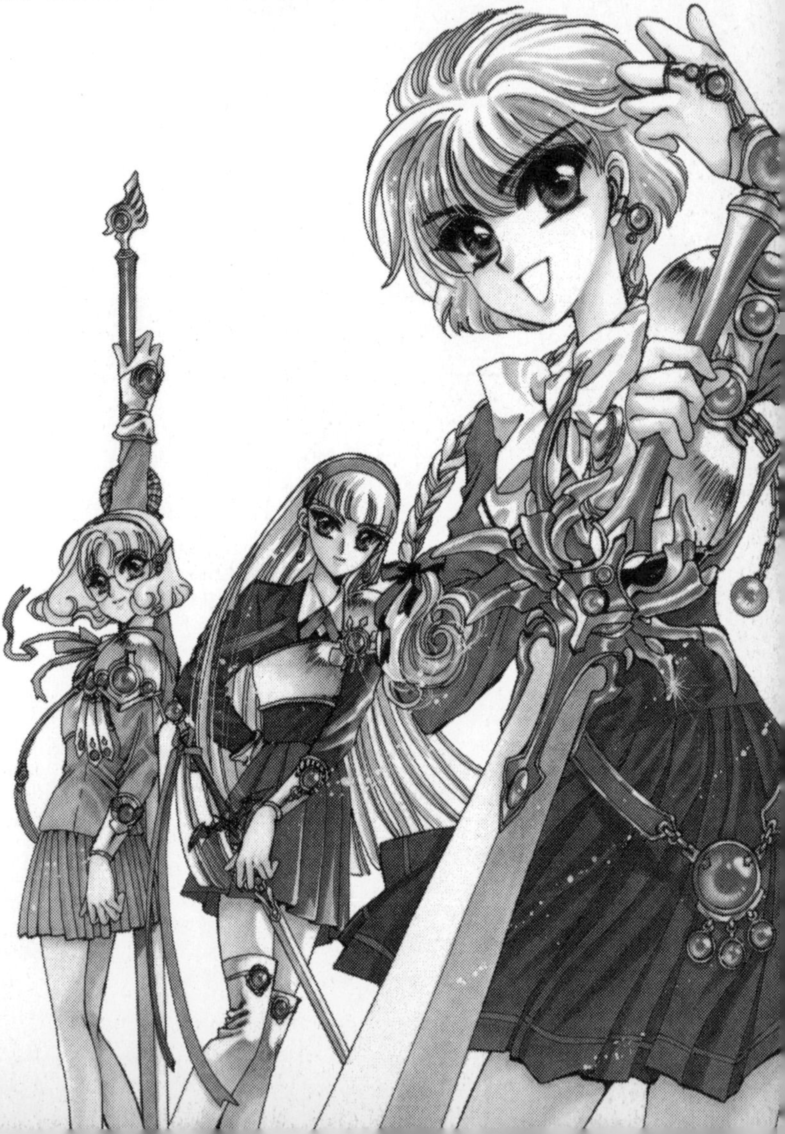

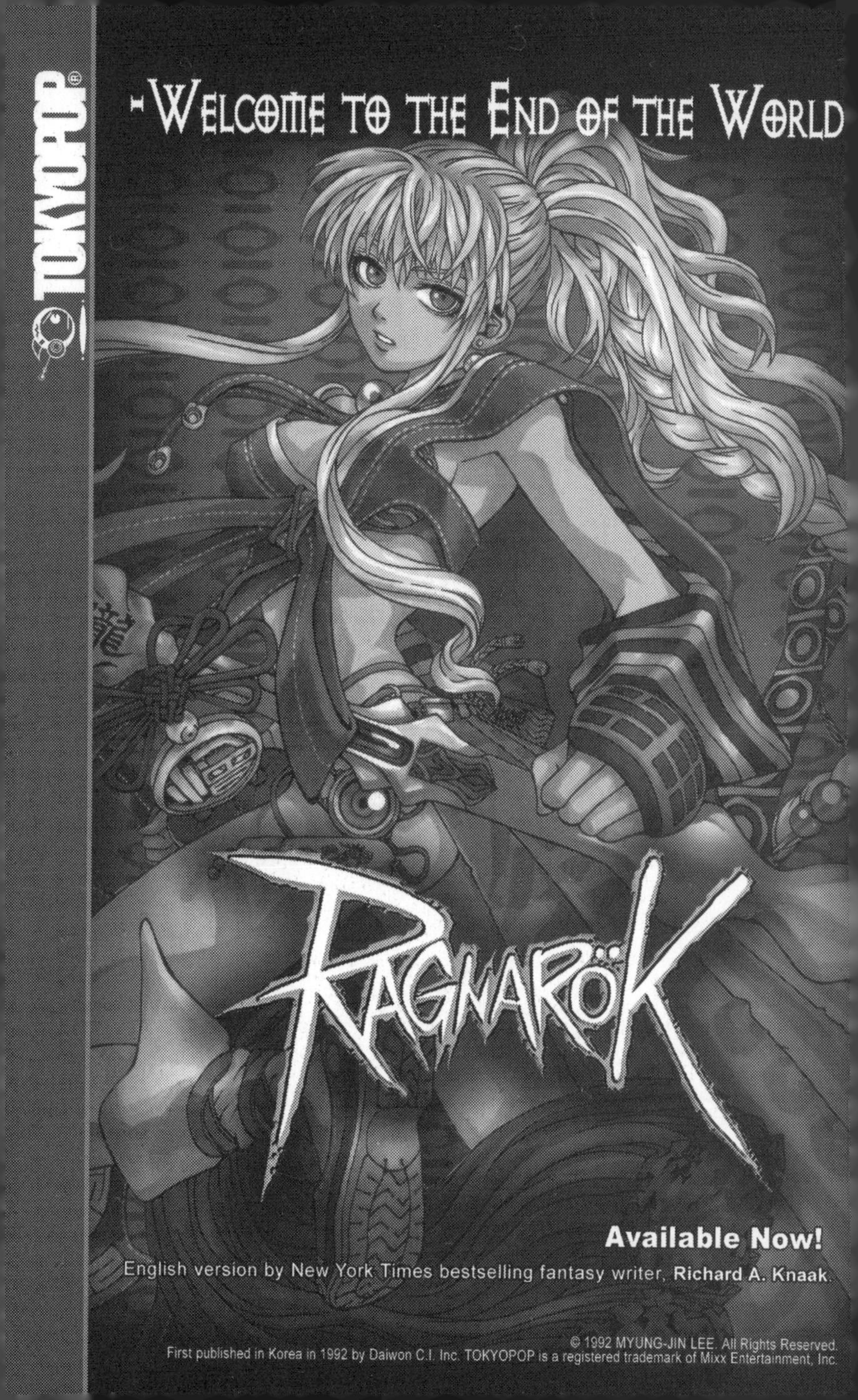

WELCOME TO THE END OF THE WORLD

RAGNARÖK

Available Now!

English version by New York Times bestselling fantasy writer, **Richard A. Knaak**.

TOKYOPOP

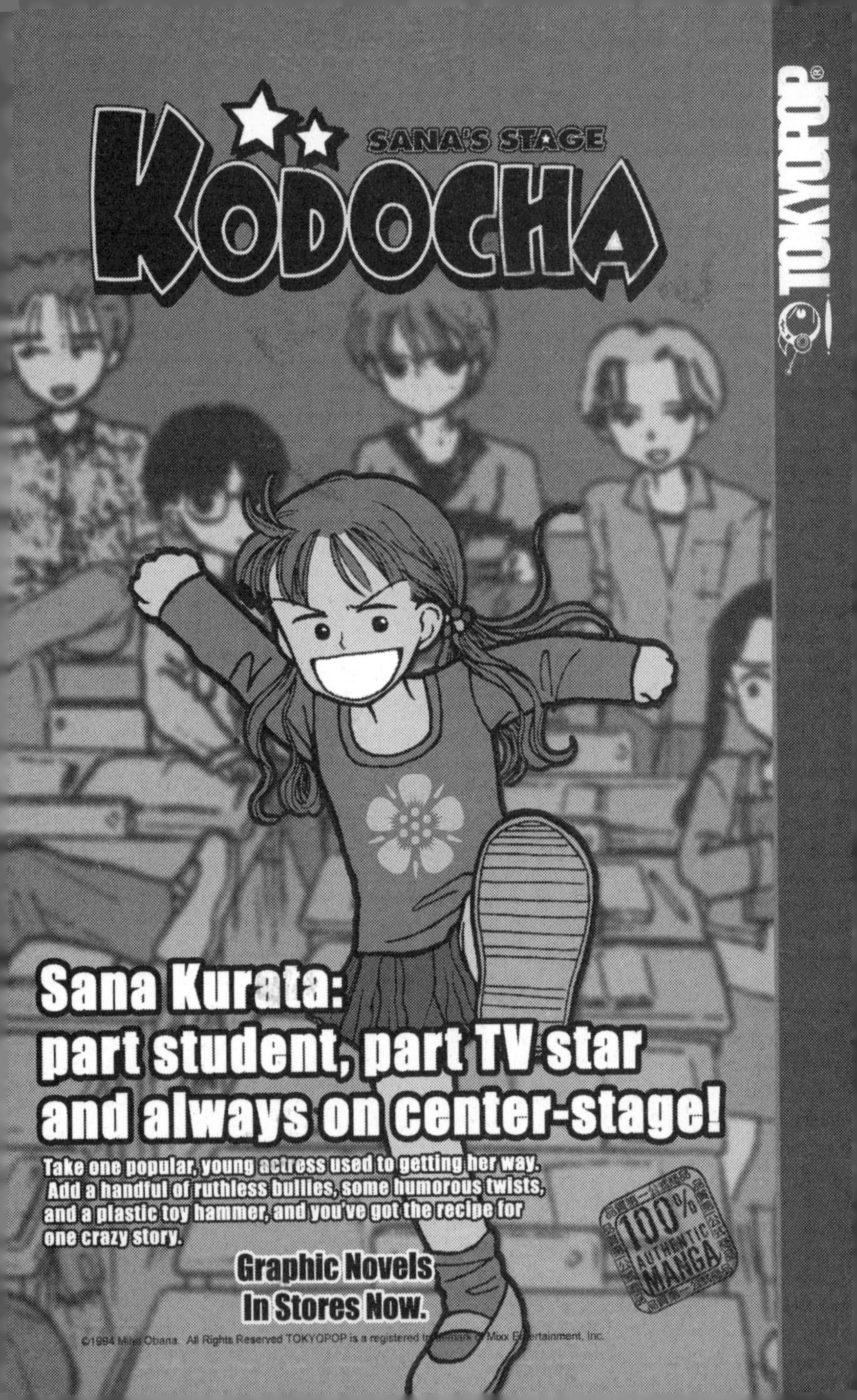
TOKYOPOP
KODOCHA
SANA'S STAGE
Sana Kurata: part student, part TV star and always on center-stage!
Take one popular, young actress used to getting her way. Add a handful of ruthless bullies, some humorous twists, and a plastic toy hammer, and you've got the recipe for one crazy story.
100% AUTHENTIC MANGA
Graphic Novels In Stores Now.
©1994 Miho Obana. All Rights Reserved TOKYOPOP is a registered trademark of Mixx Entertainment, Inc.

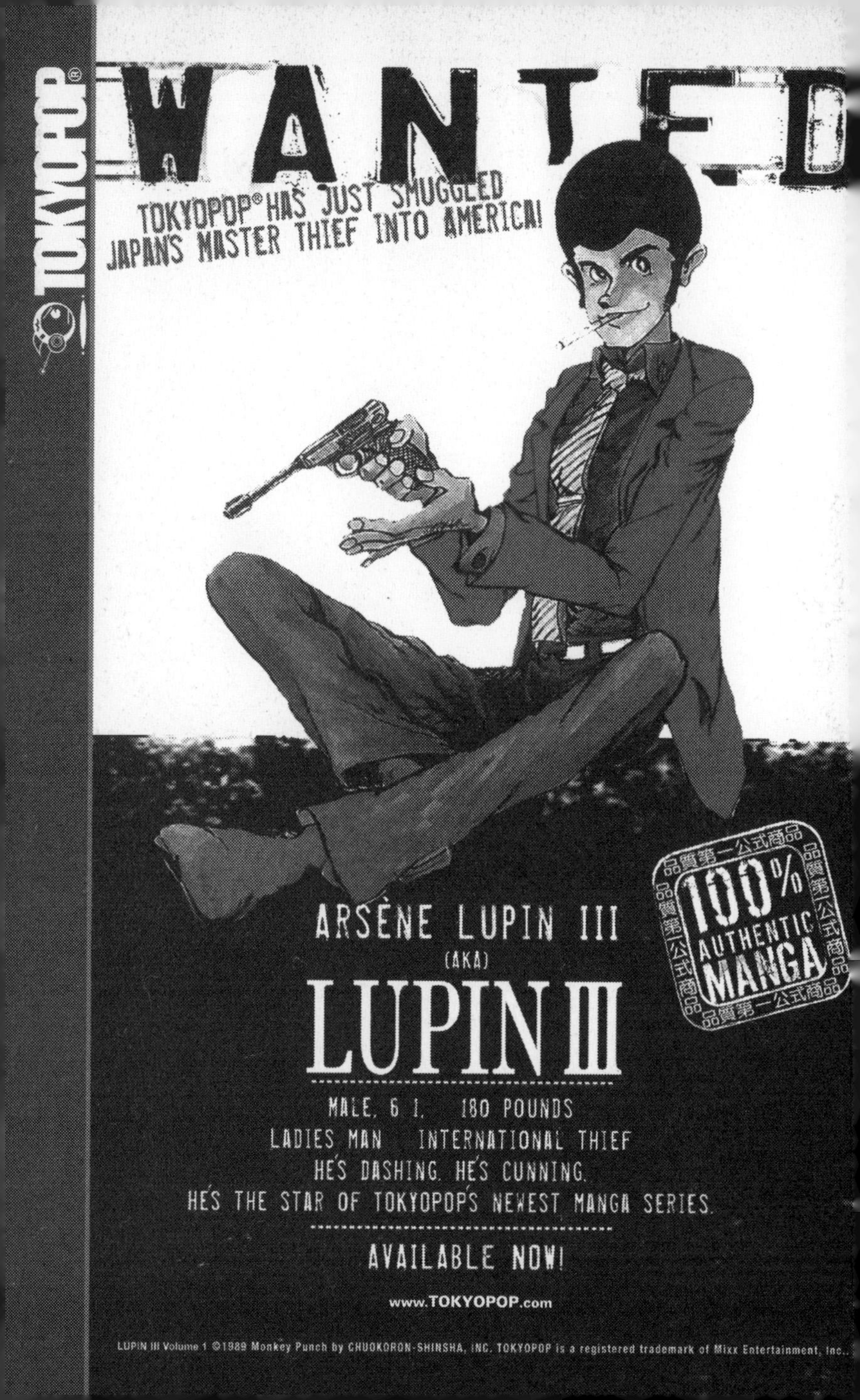
TOKYOPOP®
WANTED
TOKYOPOP® HAS JUST SMUGGLED JAPAN'S MASTER THIEF INTO AMERICA!
100% AUTHENTIC MANGA
ARSÈNE LUPIN III
(AKA)
LUPIN III
MALE, 6'1", 180 POUNDS
LADIES MAN INTERNATIONAL THIEF
HE'S DASHING. HE'S CUNNING.
HE'S THE STAR OF TOKYOPOP'S NEWEST MANGA SERIES.
AVAILABLE NOW!
www.TOKYOPOP.com
LUPIN III Volume 1 ©1989 Monkey Punch by CHUOKORON-SHINSHA, INC. TOKYOPOP is a registered trademark of Mixx Entertainment, Inc.

TOKYOPOP®
INITIAL
頭文字D
INITIALIZE YOUR DREAMS!!
Manga:
Available Now!
Anime:
Coming Soon!
100% AUTHENTIC MANGA
品質第一公式商品
www.TOKYOPOP.com
"Initial D" © Shuichi Shigeno / KODANSHA / anime direction / OB PLANNING. Licensed exclusively
to TOKYOPOP. TOKYOPOP is a registered trademark of Mixx Entertainment, Inc. All rights reserved.

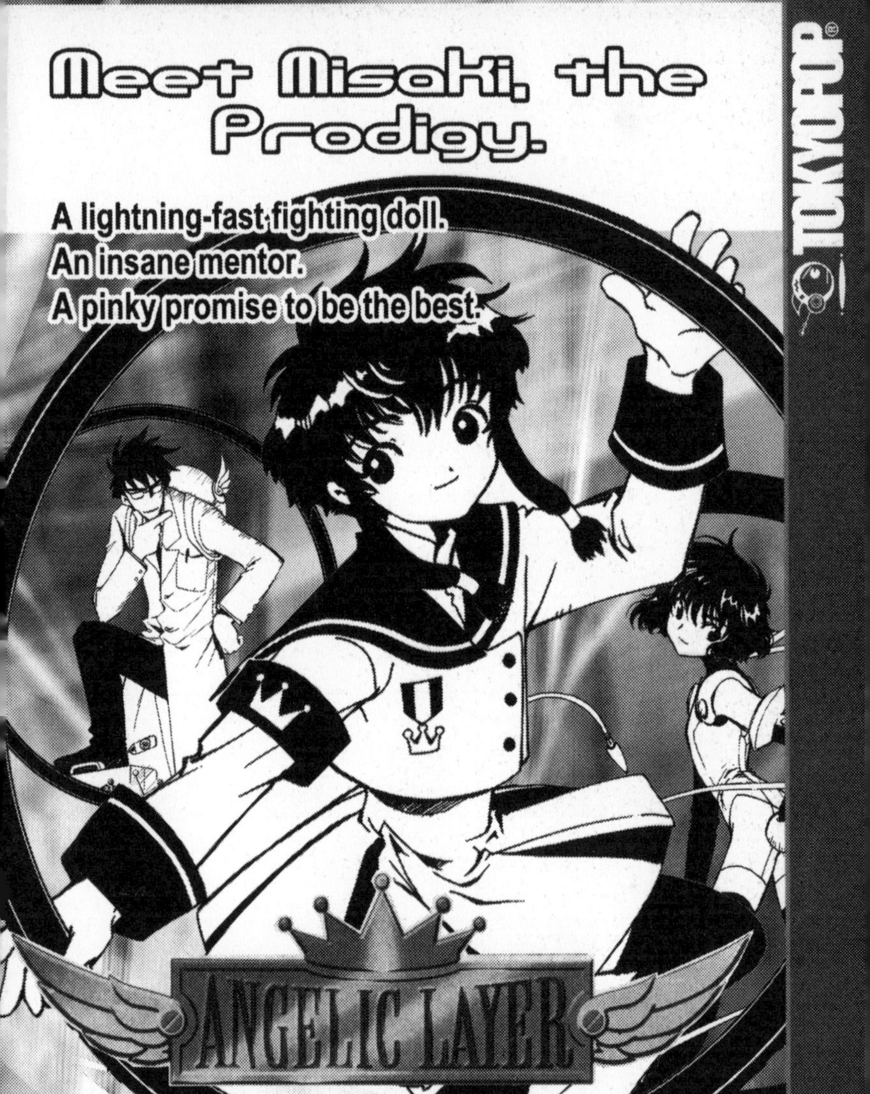
Meet Misaki, the Prodigy.
A lightning-fast fighting doll.
An insane mentor.
A pinky promise to be the best.
ANGELIC LAYER
TOKYOPOP®

TOKYOPOP
GRAB YOUR FAVORITE SHOW AND GO
What's Cine-Manga™?
It's like watching your favorite show come alive in the pages of a book.
Disney's
KiM POSSIBLE
©Disney
Disney's hottest animated series just got a Cine-Manga™ makeover...
Lizzie McGuire • Kim Possible
As seen on Disney Channel and Saturdays on ABC Kids
Look for these TOKYOPOP® books in spring 2003!
© Disney. © Mixx Entertainment, Inc. All rights reserved. TOKYOPOP is a registered trademark of Mixx Entertainment,

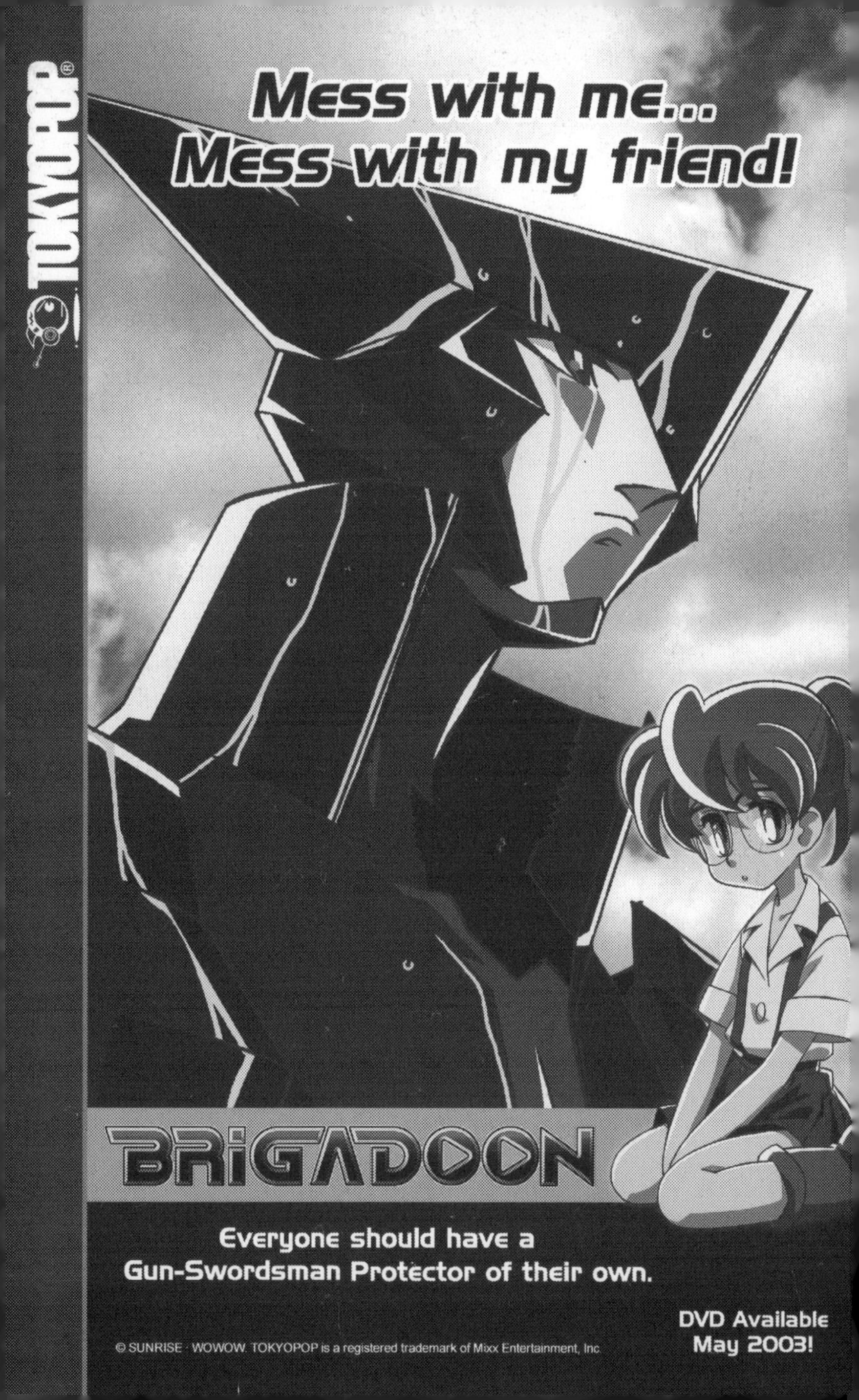
TOKYOPOP
Mess with me...
Mess with my friend!
BRIGADOON
Everyone should have a
Gun-Swordsman Protector of their own.
DVD Available
May 2003!
© SUNRISE · WOWOW. TOKYOPOP is a registered trademark of Mixx Entertainment, Inc.

STOP!

This is the back of the book.
You wouldn't want to spoil a great ending!

This book is printed "manga-style," in the authentic Japanese right-to-left format. Since none of the artwork has been flipped or altered, readers get to experience the story just as the creator intended. You've been asking for it, so TOKYOPOP® delivered: authentic, hot-off-the-press, and far more fun!

DIRECTIONS

If this is your first time reading manga-style, here's a quick guide to help you understand how it works.

It's easy... just start in the top right panel and follow the numbers. Have fun, and look for more 100% authentic manga from TOKYOPOP®!